---

## "THE WORST MISTAKE PARENTS MAKE IN THE HIGH SCHOOL ADMISSION PROCESS IS FAILING TO BE ORGANIZED."

—ADMISSION DIRECTOR,
BAY AREA INDEPENDENT HIGH SCHOOL

Pince-Nez Press's new **High School Admission Workbook** will give you a jump on the admission process.

With pages for parents and for kids to fill out, this workbook elicits educational and co-curricular preferences and priorities, gathers pertinent information needed for applications, and helps schedule test days, shadow dates, and deadlines. The 35-page workbook is unbound and 3-hole punched so you can place it in a binder along with school brochures and applications. It includes:

- lists to prioritize academic and co-curricular interests
- sample applications
- pages to gather reference information
- pages to gather information on past co-curricular and summer activities
- pages for notes on each school
- calendar pages to schedule visits, open houses, deadlines
- and more

Available only from Pince-Nez Press by mail *(not in bookstores)*
$12.95 plus $1.09 tax and $1.96 shipping/handling
To order please send a check for $16.00
(made out to Pince-Nez Press) to:

Pince-Nez Press/HS
1459 18th St.
PMB #175
San Francisco, CA  94107

Or check our website for information on downloading on-line: www.pince-nez.com

# Private High Schools
## of the
# San Francisco Bay Area

### BY
## SUSAN VOGEL

pince-nez press

Cover illustration: Founders Hall, Marin Academy
by Marin Academy student Rashida Lorell

*Private High Schools of the San Francisco Bay Area*

ISBN No.:  0-9648757-9-9
Library of Congress Catalog Card No.:  99-70546
Printed in the United States

Book design:  Mark My Words
Cover design: Peter Pigott

Pince-Nez Press
San Francisco, California
415.267.5978
www.pince-nez.com

# TABLE OF CONTENTS

## SCHOOLS

*=short entries

# Schools by County

## San Francisco

Archbishop Riordan High School
Bridgemont High School
Convent of the Sacred Heart High School
Drew College Preparatory School*
Hebrew Academy of San Francisco*
Immaculate Conception Academy*
The International High School of the French-American International School
Lick-Wilmerding High School
Lycée Français International La Pérouse
Mercy High School
Sacred Heart Cathedral Preparatory
St. Ignatius College Preparatory School
San Francisco University High School
San Francisco Waldorf High School
Stuart Hall High School
The Urban School of San Francisco
Woodside International School

## Marin County

The Branson School (Ross)
Marin Academy (San Rafael)
Marin Catholic High School (Kentfield)
North Bay Marin School (Mill Valley)
San Domenico Upper School (San Anselmo)

## San Mateo County

Crystal Springs Uplands School (Hillsborough)
Menlo School (Atherton)
Mercy High School (Burlingame)
Notre Dame High School (Belmont)
Sacred Heart Preparatory (Atherton)
Junipero Serra High School (San Mateo)
Woodside Priory School (Portola Valley)

## Santa Clara County

Archbishop Mitty High School (San Jose)
Bellarmine College Preparatory (San Jose)
Castilleja School (Palo Alto)
The Harker School (San Jose)
The King's Academy (Sunnyvale)
Notre Dame High School (San Jose)
Pinewood School (Los Altos Hills)
Presentation High School (San Jose)
St. Francis High School (Mountain View)
St. Lawrence Academy (Santa Clara)

## Alameda County

Arrowsmith Academy (Berkeley)
Beacon School (Oakland)
Bishop O'Dowd High School (Oakland)*
The College Preparatory School (Oakland)
The Head-Royce School (Oakland)
Holy Names High School (Oakland)
Maybeck High School (Berkeley)
Moreau Catholic High School (Hayward)
St. Joseph-Notre Dame (Alameda)
St. Mary's College High School (Berkeley)*

## Contra Costa County

The Athenian School (Danville)
Bentley School (Lafayette)
Carondelet High School (Concord)*
De La Salle High School (Concord)*
North Bay Orinda School (Orinda)
Salesian High School (Richmond)
Spraings Academy (Walnut Creek)

# Boarding

The Athenian School (Danville) (coed)
San Domenico Upper School (San Anselmo) (girls)
Woodside Priory School (Portola Valley) (coed school, boys only board)

# All Girls

Carondelet High School (Concord)*
Castilleja School (Palo Alto)
Convent of the Sacred Heart High School (San Francisco)
Holy Names High School (Oakland)
Immaculate Conception Academy (San Francisco)*
Mercy High School-San Francisco
Mercy High School-Burlingame
Notre Dame High School (Belmont)
Notre Dame High School (San Jose)
Presentation High School (San Jose)
San Domenico Upper School (San Anselmo)

# All Boys

Archbishop Riordan High School (San Francisco)
Bellarmine College Preparatory (San Jose)
De La Salle High School (Concord)*
Junipero Serra High School (San Mateo)
Stuart Hall High School (San Francisco)


*=short entries

# INTRODUCTION

Approximately 12% of students across the United States attend private school; in San Francisco that number is closer to 30%. Private high school graduates represent 40% of the students at the country's most selective universities.

Admission to private high schools in the Bay Area is very competitive, with some schools receiving more than eight applications for every opening. The application process is time-consuming and stressful both for parents and applicants. The purpose of this Guide is to help families become aware of their options, to narrow their search to schools that would provide the best academic and social environment for the student, and to make sure that the school is affordable to the family and otherwise meets the family's needs and expectations. Schools do not pay to be included in this Guide—it is not advertising.

The information contained in this Guide is based upon (1) information provided by the schools in response to an eight-page questionnaire sent to the schools; (2) interviews with admission directors and principals; (3) visits to most of the schools (usually a two-hour visit per school including classroom visits); and, in some cases, (4) publicly available information on the schools.

Schools that were not able to provide the extensive information requested by the publication date, or that chose not to, are listed in short entries in the back of this Guide. They are invited to provide full information for future editions.

No one school is best for all students; consequently, no attempt is made to rank or rate schools. Moreover, what families are looking for in a school will vary considerably. Some may be looking for a school that sends a good number of graduates to Ivy League universities; others may be interested in a spiritual environment or a good co-curricular program.

## PRIVATE SCHOOLS

In the lexicon of this Guide, "private schools" means all schools that are not public. Within this very broad category are schools that are set up as non-profit, tax-exempt corporations with boards of trustees ("non-profit" schools), privately owned tax-paying schools ("proprietary" schools), and parochial (church-run) schools.

## "INDEPENDENT" SCHOOLS

Although any school may call itself an "independent school," members of the associations of independent schools, such as the California Association of Independent Schools (CAIS), and the National Association of Independent Schools (NAIS), are non-profit organizations governed by their *own* boards of trustees (as opposed to being governed by a central diocese, a church's board of trustees, or some other off-site power). The NAIS requires that its members be "primarily supported by tuition, charitable contributions, and endowment income rather than by tax or church funds." To be eligible for NAIS membership, schools must be independently governed by a board of trustees, practice nondiscriminatory policies, be accredited by an approved state or regional association, and hold not-for-profit 501(c)(3) status. (For more information, see the NAIS web site at www.NAIS.org and the CAIS web site at www.caisca.org.)

Ideally, a board of trustees will provide oversight of the school's administration. The extent to which this occurs depends on whether the board is closely involved in reviewing and questioning the administration's actions or whether it merely "rubber stamps."

"Independent schools" also distinguish themselves as being college preparatory, offering small class size, and providing individual attention to students. According to the NAIS, its member schools "stress social responsibility and service to the community in their policies and programs and encourage enrollment from all segments of the community." Independent schools may have religious affiliations.

Each independent school is responsible for its own curriculum; most have parent committees that advise the board of trustees and most have parents on their boards. As tax-exempt organizations, they are eligible for grants. Most independent schools expect that parents will make tax-deductible contributions to the school and/or be involved in fundraising activities.

High schools in the Bay Area that are members of the Bay Area Independent High Schools (BAIHS) share admission forms, admissions deadlines, and notification dates. These schools state that they "share a commitment to a rigorous college preparatory curriculum in a supportive atmosphere." The members of the BAIHS included in this Guide are: Arrowsmith Academy, The Athenian School, Beacon High School, Bentley School, The Branson School, Castilleja School, The College Preparatory School, Convent of the Sacred Heart High School, Crystal Springs Uplands School, Drew College Preparatory School, The Harker School, The Head-Royce School, The International High School of the French-American International School, Lick-Wilmerding High School, Marin Academy, Maybeck High School, Menlo School, Sacred Heart Preparatory, San Domenico Upper School, San Francisco University High School, San Francisco Waldorf High School, Stuart Hall High School, The Urban School of San Francisco, and Woodside Priory School.

## PROPRIETARY SCHOOLS

Private "proprietary" schools may be corporations, partnerships, or sole proprietorships. These schools pay taxes like any other business. Donations to them are not tax-deductible though some schools set up foundations to receive contributions. Proprietary schools claim their status allows them to make and implement decisions more quickly and efficiently than non-profit schools since they do not have to seek the authorization or approval of a board of trustees. Moreover, they save administrative time and costs by not having to prepare for and host regular board meetings and educate new board members. (Proprietary schools that are corporations still may be required to have annual shareholder meetings.) Many proprietary schools have parent committees that advise the owners on a broad range of topics.

## Parochial Schools

Finally, this Guide includes numerous schools that have religious affiliations. Few generalities can be made about religious schools except that they all seek to instill moral values. Religious schools range from being very secular in look and feel, with religion being taught in a general and nondogmatic way to students the majority of whom may not be of a particular faith, to being training grounds for missionaries where evangelism is the main goal. Most fall in between. An increasing number of families who are not particularly religious send their children to religious schools for a variety of reasons: family or cultural tradition; appreciation for the concurrent teaching of values alongside academics; and a perception of higher academic standards, higher standards of behavior, and a better peer group.

**CATHOLIC:** Most Bay Area Catholic high schools are not attached to and run by parishes but draw students from the entire diocese or archdiocese (and beyond). Each Catholic secondary school chooses its own curriculum following state guidelines and guidelines published by the archdiocese or diocese. Schools within the same diocese/archdiocese (except for independent Catholic schools which follow the BAIHS schedule) normally share admission deadlines and dates on which they send out acceptance or rejection letters.

The high schools in the Archdiocese of San Francisco are Archbishop Riordan High School, St. Ignatius College Preparatory, Immaculate Conception Academy, Mercy High School-San Francisco, Sacred Heart Cathedral Preparatory High School, Convent of the Sacred Heart High School, Marin Catholic High School, San Domenico Upper School, Junipero Serra High School, Mercy High School-Burlingame, Notre Dame High School-Belmont, Sacred Heart Preparatory, Stuart Hall High School and Woodside Priory. The high schools in the San Jose Diocese are Archbishop Mitty High School, Bellarmine College Preparatory School, Notre Dame High School (San Jose), Presentation High School, St. Lawrence Academy, and St. Francis High School. These schools also share a "Seventh and Eighth Grade School Report" that is given to the applicant's middle school requesting grades and evaluations from the school's principal, counselor, or teacher. (Visit these schools at the Diocese website: www.dsj.org.)

The high schools in the Oakland Diocese are: Bishop O'Dowd High School, Moreau Catholic High School, De La Salle High School, Holy Names High School, St. Joseph-Notre Dame High School, St. Elizabeth High School, St. Mary's College High School, Carondelet High School, and Salesian High School. *(Note that some of these Catholic schools are "independent Catholic schools," i.e., members of the CAIS and NAIS.)*

**CHRISTIAN:** The term "Christian schools" is used in this Guide to refer to schools that call themselves "Christian" schools. Nationwide, nearly as many private school students are enrolled in conservative Christian schools as in non-sectarian schools. These schools account for a large percentage of growth in private schools.

# PUBLIC SCHOOLS

The Bay Area has many excellent public high schools. Information on public schools can be obtained from each school district or from the Department of Education in Sacramento. Numerous web sites provide information on Bay Area public high schools.

A new breed of schools has cropped up—charter schools. These are public schools, not private, though their goal is to operate more like private schools. (Recent efforts have been made, however, to require charter school teachers to join the state teachers' unions.) Families can obtain information on charter schools by calling their local school districts or visiting their web sites.

# COLLEGE PREP OR WHAT?

Most of the schools included in this Guide offer a college preparatory curriculum aimed at fulfilling entrance standards to University of California at Berkeley, one of the top public universities in the nation. (The entrance minimums are discussed below.) Some of the high schools allow students to choose a modified college preparatory curriculum aimed at entrance to California State universities or community colleges, and/or a general non-college prep curriculum.

In their published brochures, many private high schools describe their curriculum as a "rigorous college preparatory curriculum," and appear to be seeking the brightest students with the greatest academic potential. This sort of statement might discourage students who have average test scores or grades from applying. To get a better sense of the breadth of students the school really serves, each school included in this Guide was asked the following question:

*What sort of student do you best serve?*
*(On paper, it can appear that all schools cater to the "best and the brightest" and offer an extremely demanding college prep curriculum. Parents have commented that it seems there's no place for "average" kids. This question is designed to give a sense of the "breadth" of students, in terms of abilities and varied talents/potential, that your school serves).*

Schools were asked if they have an admission cut-off in terms of test scores or grades. They were asked this so that families won't waste their time and money (and get their hopes up) applying to a school that the student has virtually no chance of getting accepted to. To their credit, many schools made it clear what they were looking for: for the most part A's and B's and above-average test scores. Fortunately there are other schools dedicated to helping "average" students reach their potential.

Many schools look beyond grades and test scores for signs of potential in students—often for creativity, curiosity, and ability in sports and other co-curricular activities. Additionally, middle school grades may not really present an accurate picture. High school admission directors know which middle schools give "real" grades and which inflate grades. (Regarding a certain private K-8 school, a high school admission director said facetiously, "There are no 'C' students at that school. Only 'A' and 'B.'" In other words, even the average students appear above-average.) Many schools are looking for a broad range of students with a variety of talents and interests—students who, in the words of many schools, "will contribute to the school community," both academically, and also in sports, arts, and co-curricular activities. Students who have interests and talents in a specific area should seek schools that value these talents and should emphasize these interests in the admission process.

Religious schools are often interested in the potential of the "whole person," rather than in just intellectual potential. A religious school may have a commitment to educating students from varying socioeconomic and ability levels. Moreover, it may accept students who have promise in other areas of importance to its mission, including spiritual and social development.

## ACCREDITATION

"Accreditation" refers to a process offered by various independent agencies to review schools and their programs and deem them as having met certain criteria. Accreditation is optional; schools are not required to be accredited. (Certain exceptions apply for schools receiving public funds.) Public schools have the option of refusing to accept credits from schools that are not accredited.

The main accrediting agency in California is the Accrediting Commission for Schools, which is an arm of the Western Association of Schools and Colleges (ACS/WASC). Accreditation is based in part on the appropriateness of the school's stated goals and objectives for an institution of its type and the degree to which these goals and objectives are being met, as well as the degree to which the school meets WASC criteria.

The accreditation process requires extensive documentation of a school's goals and objectives; "self-studies" in which the school reports on its progress; and a visit to the school by teams of evaluators.

Schools that seek accreditation may apply for candidate or interim status with WASC. All schools are subject to a full review every six years. (The longest term of accreditation given is six years.) If a school has not met all of WASC's criteria, it may receive a shorter term of accreditation requiring additional reports and visits.

If parents have questions about accreditation, they may contact the Accrediting Commission for Schools at (650) 696-1060.

Finally, the Association of Christian Schools International (ACSI) accredits Christian schools, although Christian schools may also apply for WASC accreditation.

Some schools, both non-profit and proprietary, choose not to go through the accreditation process because of the cost and the time involved. In addition, each school must pay the expenses—including airfare, hotel, and meals—for a team of three to four evaluators to study the school for two to three days.

Schools that do not seek accreditation often consider their "stamp of approval" to be satisfied parents and successful college placement, as well as the school's longevity.

## STUDENT BODY

The student body information provided in this guide is intended to give a sense of the students in terms of where they are from geographically, their ethnicity, and family information and middle school background. The middle school information gives families a sense of the sort of school background the high school prefers—some high schools clearly prefer students from an independent school background, others from a parochial school background.

## THE ADMISSION PROCESS

The admission process for Bay Area private high schools officially begins the fall of the student's eighth grade year. Some "prospective parents" (the term used by schools for parents seeking their child's admission to a school) attempt to begin the process when they truly are "prospective" parents—before the child is born. This is discouraged (and seen as rather presumptuous and pathetic) by high schools; one school reported it regularly denies pregnant women's requests for application packets for their fetuses. (A "Prenatal University" was advertised in the East Bay for parents who wish to begin academic study in utero, but their young students are not permitted to apply to high school unless they have reached the eighth grade.) Some high schools invite families of children in grades 6-8 to their open houses, and plenty of parents begin the admission process—at least in terms of attending open houses—during their child's seventh grade year.

Throughout the Bay Area, high school fairs provide students and parents the opportunity to meet with admission directors and obtain information on schools. The dates and locations of the fairs can be obtained from any independent K-8 school or high school. (They are usually held in September in San Francisco and Marin Counties and in October in the East Bay and Contra Costa County and are often not announced to the public. Indeed they may claim to not be open to the public, but no one checks ID at the gate—in fact they can be a mob scene—go early.)

Tours of schools and open houses begin as early as August. Open houses are usually held evenings and weekends and are open to prospective students and their families. Some schools invite both students and parents on the tour—others invite only students. The tour normally involves a visit to classes and an interview of the student and perhaps the parents. Students often "shadow" a current student throughout the day.

Application forms and test scores must be submitted by a certain date. The BAIHS share recommendation forms for applicants' current school principal and math and English teachers. The forms normally ask teachers to evaluate various aspects of the student's academic and personal qualities and rate them on a scale— on the independent school form, from "poor" to "one of the best ever."

Catholic schools within a diocese or archdiocese may choose to use the diocese or archdiocese's standard recommendation form for principals/teachers. For example, in the Diocese of San Jose, Mitty, Presentation, Bellarmine, Saint Francis, Notre Dame (San Jose) and St. Lawrence Academy share a "Seventh and Eight Grade School Report" that asks the principal, teacher, or counselor to report the student's grades (including conduct and effort), and rate the student (excellent, good, fair, poor or don't know) in terms of leadership ability, work/study habits, behavior/conduct, and involvement in activities. Recommendations are sought in terms of how well the person knows the student and to what extent he or she recommends the student personally and academically.

Catholic schools also have the option of using the Diocese clergy recommendation form. Some Catholic schools require it; others tell parents it's optional. There are Catholic high schools that do not use a clergy recommendation form at all—they have a place on the application for the child's baptism date, if applicable. One school's clergy form only seeks verification that the applicant is an active member of the church.

At least one Catholic school that doesn't require the clergy recommendation form says that most applicants submit it anyway. Some forms allow parents to describe the family's spirituality in the event the family is not of any particular faith and does not attend a church. Catholic high schools are becoming increasingly competitive. In some counties, they are unable to accommodate all of the Catholic students graduating from Catholic elementary schools. (One admission director, when asked for advice to students seeking admission to his school, answered, "Be Catholic.") Catholic high schools may turn down a top straight-A non-Catholic student who has scored 90% on an entrance exam for a Catholic student who has scored 70%.

It behooves every family applying to a religious school to provide a clergy recommendation form or a statement describing the family's spirituality. Religious schools will be more accepting of an applicant who is open to spiritual development than one who is not and has no family history of spirituality.

Parents may be asked to write essays, and students often must submit essays. Some schools allow students to prepare their essays at home; others require the student to write the essay at the school, in long-hand. The student portion of the application usually asks students to describe their interests or hobbies, an independent project they have completed in or outside school, to share an important decision they have made, or to discuss a character in a book to whom they relate personally. A typical essay requires students to write about a difficult decision they have made recently when an important value or principle of theirs was challenged.

Some schools seek additional letters of recommendation. Schools that do not request them may accept them nonetheless. But don't "stuff the application." "The thicker the file, the more suspicious we are," said one admission director.

The extent to which the "extra," not-requested letters, artwork, portfolios, even videotapes of the child get reviewed by the admission director depends on the work load (and, judging from the past admission season, most were on over-load, having had a record number of applications). One admission director gave a rule of thumb echoed by others: If you are tempted to send "extras," ask this: Does it demonstrate specific talents or abilities that won't come through in the application packet or process, and are those talents or abilities pertinent to the school's programs? For instance, if the school has a theater program and the child is an aspiring thespian whose talents are captured on a video, the answer would be yes. Otherwise, save the video. ("Send additional recommendations only if they are critical to an understanding of who your child is and if they contain information not addressed elsewhere in the admissions materials," said one ad-mission director.)

Admission directors are dismayed at how competitive the admission process has become and at how much parents and students get wrapped up in it. One said, "We'd prefer that kids actually attend eighth grade."

Most high schools require previous standardized test scores and require appli-cants to take an entrance exam in December or January. Catholic schools admin-ister the STS High School Placement Test (HSPT). Normally it can be taken at any school within the diocese or archdiocese and the results will be sent to the other Catholic schools to which the students is applying within that archdiocese or diocese. It can be sent to other Catholic schools outside the diocese in which it is taken; sometimes this is the responsibility of the applicant to make sure this gets done. (The Archdiocese of San Francisco and the Diocese of San Jose will send the scores. For the Oakland Diocese, double-check with the school.) Many independent schools administer the ISEE (Independent School Entrance Exam) or SSAT (Secondary School Admission Test). Parents who never took a test prep course before applying to graduate school will be either dismayed or happy to learn that bookstores carry prep books to help prepare students for both the HSPT and the ISEE.

Middle school grades must be submitted to the high school. In the event the middle school your child attended did not give grades, the high school will look closely at the teacher evaluations as well as at the child's test scores on standard-ized tests and/or the entrance exam.

Application fees are not refundable (*i.e.,* you do not get your money back if your child is not accepted).

The application process continues through January when many applications are due. Interviews may be held as late as February, and the majority of schools mail acceptance or rejection letters in mid-March. The BAIHS share the same mailing date of approximately March 15; Catholic schools also share a mailing date in mid-March.

Most schools have cut-off dates for admission to the freshman class. At other levels, applications are taken year-round. In San Francisco, most families apply to four or five schools. Some apply to one ("Stupid," said an admission director) and others apply to ten. In the East Bay the typical number is three, and in the Peninsula/South Bay area, three to five.

***Admission Directors' Advice to Parents:*** Start early! The biggest mistake parents make is not being organized: call in time to get shadow slots, get applications in on time. Some schools, by November, have 100 kids on a waiting list to get shadow appointments. Don't bother offering cash, gift baskets, gift certificates to Neiman Marcus, theater tickets, and other goodies. They both reflect badly upon the parents and may guarantee your child will *not* be admitted. The offer of a bribe usually reflects a desperate parent whose child would never be accepted on merit (in other words, the school does not want him or her, gift or no gift). You don't have to attend every open house and every event the school offers—they are for you to find out information on the school, but once you have the information, "Have a life."

***Admission Directors' Advice to Students:*** "Relax. You *will* go to high school. You have to. It's the law." "Relax, be yourself. If you're nervous, don't worry. Everyone is." "If you see something about the school that interests you, bring it up in the interview." "At your first choice school you'll find some of the worst teachers you'll ever have and some of the worst kids you'll ever know. At a school you originally never considered, you'll find some of the best teachers you'll ever have and some of the best kids you'll ever know." (In other words, keep an open mind, explore options.) "Don't only consider the schools your friends are interested in." "Visit every school you apply to. If you are interested in theater, attend a theater performance at the school; if sports, attend a sporting event."

## What to Look for in a High School

Is the **size** of the school right? Large schools offer a larger group of classmates from which to choose friends, and usually more choices of co-curricular activities and sports. A large school may be more appropriate for independent, self-directed student who has already established his or her interests. Small schools often offer more individual attention. They may also offer more opportunities for a student to sample co-curricular activities as a beginner—in large schools, activities may be populated by students who have already reached a level of achievement in the area (such as sports, orchestra, etc.).

Several **new** high schools have started in the last few years. Many, if not all, have grown out of K-8 schools. A new school gives students the opportunity to start new traditions, to help shape the direction of the courses, to perhaps choose the school mascot and colors—in other words, to put their stamp on the school. In a brand new high school, a freshman will be the editor of the newspaper, the lead in the school play and the student body president. For students who want this type of early leadership opportunity, a new school might be the right place.

A new school, however, will not have established sports teams, debate teams, and other activities in which older, experienced students can help the younger ones along and act as role models. Nor will it have a track record of college acceptances.

If the school has grown out of a lower school, parents can seek reassurance from the academic strength of the lower school. If not, they must do an independent evaluation of the school including its financial viability, courses it will offer, graduation requirements, teaching staff, etc.

What is the **class size** and **teaching style**? Some schools have large classes with desks in rows and teachers who lecture. Others have small classes with desks in a U-shape with students initiating discussion. Determine which setting and teaching style is best for your child.

The teacher's daily student load (in a required subject) is also worth evaluating. A teacher who teaches only 60 students a day will likely get to know the students and their work better than one who teaches 120 per day.

Does the school offer the **courses** that are important to you and your child, and is the material what you expect to be taught? High school course offerings are listed in this Guide. Many high schools also provide lists of the textbooks used and the reading required in literature classes. If you expect *The Aeneid*, make sure it's on the list.

Does the school offer **co-curricular activities** that interest your child? Students involved in co-curricular activities do better in school and have more fun. If your child is interested in an activity but has no experience in it, ask the school if beginners can participate.

Eighth grade counselors can be very helpful in recommending high schools that would be a good match for specific students considering their interests, abilities, and learning styles. Parents should take advantage of all such resources that exist at the child's current school.

*Admission Directors' Advice to Students:* "Do you feel that you would fit in at this school? It's important to pay attention to your 'gut reaction' after spending a morning or afternoon at the school. Do you feel that you could excel in that environment? Can you see yourself doing well and enjoying school?" "Try not to let peer pressure influence where you want to go—try to find at least three schools that feel right for you and don't just look at the schools your friends will be going to."

*Admission Directors' Advice to Parents:* One would imagine that by the time their children are in the eighth grade, parents would have a pretty realistic view of their children's abilities and desires. Admission directors report this is not the case. Parents often have unrealistically high expectations of their children, or, nearly as often, they underestimate their children's abilities because they do not understand their developmental stage. Some admission directors recommend parents spend some time observing (and taking notes on) their children, as a stranger might: note their attention span, how they relate to friends and family, whether they prefer to work alone or with others, their degree of independence, and whether they have already developed strong interests or need opportunities to dabble. This effort will pay off when parents are required to submit biographies or write essays about their children for the admissions packet. Admission directors urge parents to set aside their own desires—such as those based upon social status, family expectations, or legacies—and to focus on what is best for their child. Also, says one, "Let your children know that no matter what school they are accepted to, you are proud of them."

## SINGLE SEX OR COED?

In 1994, Myra and David Sadker, researchers at American University, wrote a book entitled *Failing at Fairness: How America's Schools Cheat Girls*. They concluded that in coed classrooms, boys and girls receive very different educations. They observed that boys asked questions or made comments in class eight times more often than girls and that teachers interacted more with boys. Other researchers have observed that teachers expect more from boys and encourage them more—at the expense of girls—and that textbooks underemphasize the importance of women in history, math, and science, or label those who succeed "exceptional." Advocates of all-boys schools say that boys in boys' schools take higher level classes, have a higher degree of concentration, and form stronger friendships with other boys. Single-sex schools also say it's easier to teach sexuality to single sex groups than to mixed groups.

*GIRLS:* Here are several reasons given for choosing a girls' school (borrowed from Immaculate Conception Academy): "(1) You don't have to worry about a bad hair day; (2) You can be yourself; and (3) [You can] walk around with two different shoes—you don't have to look like Miss America (We're talking major relief on this one!)."

*BOYS:* Being with all guys? Here's what the boys say: "You have fewer distractions." "You can be yourself." "You're less self-conscious about your appearance." "You don't have to try to impress girls." The down side? "You don't get experience in relating to girls." Here are ten reasons to consider a boys' school: (borrowed from Archbishop Riordan High School) "1) We specialize in boys; 2) We know what works well for boys; 3) We offer a focused learning environment; 4) We are safe, wholesome, risk-free communities; 5) We balance collaboration and fun with serious academic work; 6) We care about character; 7) We build self-confidence; 8) We foster and value relationships; 9) We provide positive male role models and mentors; 10) We prepare boys for the real world."

# Cost

The high schools included in this Guide charge tuition ranging from $5,000 to more than $16,000 annually. A few years ago, some schools were hesitant to pass the $15,000 mark, but it seems that they've gotten over it: eight schools in this Guide cost more than $16,000 per year. Parents should expect tuition at non-parochial schools to increase every year regardless of the overall state of the economy. (Unfortunately, the schools normally announce their tuition increases in the spring—only a few weeks before the family has to make a deposit for the next year and long after the deadlines for finding a new school have passed.) In addition to tuition, there are activity fees, field trip costs, deposits, textbook costs, and sometimes expected "charitable" contributions. Schools in this Guide were asked to identify all of these so that parents can budget for them.

Most schools ask parents to make one advance payment or two payments—one in the summer before the school year and the other between semesters. Some have monthly payment plans or offer tuition financing through an independent company.

Need-based financial aid is available at most schools; some also offer merit scholarships. Financial aid applications are available with admission applications and are submitted at the same time. The parent receives the financial aid offer (or rejection) with any offer of acceptance. Usually the school will continue the financial aid award for the four years assuming need continues (tax returns and renewal applications are required each year).

Private scholarship funds are increasingly available for students in private schools. Many of these programs are connected with a nationwide private and public voucher movement. (Some of these sources for scholarships funds are listed on the Pince-Nez Press website at www.pince-nez.com) This private voucher movement is essentially a conservative movement lead by business people who believe that free market forces should direct the flow of government dollars into education. They are for the most part extremely critical of the public school system.

## ACADEMIC PROGRAMS

In evaluating a school's academic program, parents and students can look at a number of things: curriculum; graduation requirements; SAT I and II scores; percentage of graduates enrolling in colleges; what colleges graduates attend; number of students in Advanced Placement courses; IB pass rates; education of faculty; courses offered; number of students involved in the National Merit Scholarship Program; and teacher's student load. Good results in some of these categories, of course, may reflect—at least in part—the caliber of the students admitted to the high school, their education to date, and their goals. If a high school admits only students who are the best test-takers and highly motivated to go to top colleges, they will likely produce students who test well and are applying to top colleges.

Schools included in this Guide were asked what percentage of the most recent class's graduates enrolled in colleges and universities, and for the names of the colleges and universities in which the students enrolled. A better measure would be what percentage graduate from college, and from what colleges. Unfortunately most high schools do not track this information. In evaluating these figures, parents should keep in mind that many students begin their college education at a junior college and transfer to a four-year institution. This approach can save families considerable money and can work well for a student who can find smaller classes at a junior college and possibly the opportunity to develop study skills in a less pressured environment.

## CURRICULUM

Most Bay Area private high schools design their curriculum and graduation requirements around the University of California (UC) subject requirements for admissions—the "A-F requirements," though some high schools do not require sufficient study in math, science, and foreign languages to meet these requirements. Be aware that state high school graduation requirements do *not* meet UC or California State University (CSU) admission standards. (The state does not require students to take algebra, geometry, a lab science, or a foreign language.) In fact, only 35% of California public high school students graduate having met the UC and CSU minimum standards for admission. (49% of San Francisco public high school graduates meet the requirements, and 86% of graduates of San Francisco's public alternative Lowell High School.) (Source: schoolwisepress.com—a source for information on public schools)

Under the A-F requirements, students must take 15 units of high school courses in certain subject areas with at least 7 of the 15 units taken in the last two years of high school. The A-F subjects and their requirements are: A. History/Social Science—2 years required; B. English—4 years required (only two semesters of ninth grade English can be used); C. Mathematics—3 years required, 4 recommended; D. Laboratory Science—2 years required, 3 recommended; E. Language other than English—2 years of the same language required, 3 recommended; F. College preparatory electives—2 years required in the areas of visual and performing arts, history, social science, and language other than English—a third year of the language used for the "E" requirement or 2 years of a different language. In addition, students submit SAT scores and scores on three SAT II tests, in writing, math 1 or 2, English literature, foreign languages, science or social studies. (Information on UC admission criteria and policy can be found at www.ucop.edu/ucophome/pres/fsungrad.html)

Advanced Placement (AP) courses are classes taken by students who have fulfilled the high school curriculum in a course. The College Board, which administers the program, offers 32 AP courses. It is up to the high school which, if any, to offer to its students. (The average public high school offers seven.) Following the AP course, students may take an AP exam; those scoring 3 or above are eligible for college credit. (Most public colleges and universities award credit for exams scoring 3 or above; some private universities also do.) Some students are able to enter college as sophomores or even juniors because of AP credits. The extent to which credit is given varies from college to college. Students at international high schools can also receive extensive college credit through the International Baccalaureate (IB), a rigorous exam recognized worldwide (some California public schools now offer it). AP courses can propel a student's GPA above 4.0.

Thirty-four percent of freshmen enrolled in four-year colleges took AP courses in high school. Last year's typical applicant to UCLA had taken nearly seven AP and honors courses in high school. A lawsuit was filed in July, 1999 by the American Civil Liberties Union seeking to force public high schools whose student bodies are primarily African-American and Latino to offer the same AP courses offered by public high schools with a predominately white student body. The suit alleges that the lack of AP courses deprives students access to the UC system.

# FACULTY

Private school teachers are not required by law to have teaching credentials, though many do. A California teaching credential requires a bachelor degree, one year of specialized teacher training, student teaching, a passing score on the CBEST exam and a criminal background check. (California public schools require credentials for teachers though thousands of teachers in California are teaching on "emergency credentials" which, because of a teacher shortage, allow people to teach who have not yet obtained a credential.) The CBEST exam is criticized for being too easy (some say it tests to 6th grade level) and for being culturally biased.

Some people feel that no teacher should be able to teach without a credential; others feel that people with a high level of expertise in a particular field do not necessarily need a credential to have the skills to teach. Private schools are allowed to make their own decisions in this regard—to hire a Ph.D in biology to teach biology absent a credential, or to require all teachers hold credentials.

Among the Catholic schools, the San Francisco Archdiocese requires that all teachers have bachelor's degrees, but they need not have a current teaching credential to be considered for hiring. The individual schools may set that policy if they wish. In a survey performed two years ago, approximately 1/3 of teachers in the Archdiocese had master's degrees and approximately 2/3 had current California teaching credentials. An additional number of teachers had out-of-state credentials from states with which California has reciprocity.

Private schools also set their own policies in the area of teacher continuing education. Few will dispute that teachers who are current in their fields make better teachers. Teachers stay current through teacher in-service days (those days when there is no school), participating in professional activities such as conferences, and, sometimes, sabbaticals.

Teachers in Catholic schools have salary incentives that reward in-service training, though no minimum hours are required. (Religion teachers, however, must be separately certified and participate in 40 hours of in-service every four years.)

State laws have become stricter in recent years with regard to criminal background checks of employees of public and private schools. (This, following the 1997 on-campus murder of a public high school student allegedly by a school employee. Bay Area newspapers have reported two arrests in the past few years of employees at Bay Area private schools for alleged sexual crimes.) In the past, a private school was required to submit the fingerprints of a new unlicensed employee (credentialed teachers have background checks as part of the credentialing process) to the Department of Justice for a background check, but could do it upon hiring the person. The criminal check could take months to complete. Now, the person *seeking* employment must obtain the background check and produce it to the school as a condition of employment. Since 1997, private schools may not hire an unlicensed person until he or she has produced a background clearance; nor may private schools any longer "emplo[y] a person who has been convicted of a violent or serious felony." (Education Code Section 44237 et seq.)

## STANDARDIZED TESTS

A great deal of controversy surrounds the significance of standardized testing. Critics say standardized testing assesses test-taking skills rather than knowledge. Some say the tests are biased.

The Preliminary Scholarship Assessment Test/National Merit Scholarship Qualifying Test (PSAT/NMSQT) is taken in the fall of 11th grade by 1.8 million high school students across the country both as an SAT practice test and to determine semi-finalists in the National Merit Scholarship Program. The test is administered by the Educational Testing Service for the College Board. The PSAT is graded on a scale of 20-80. A combined score of 130 or more is needed for a shot at winning a National Merit Scholarship; a score of approximately 120 will bring a "Commendation," a sort of honorable mention.

The Scholastic Assessment Test (SAT, formerly "Scholastic Aptitude Test") is the most common test taken by high school seniors seeking college admission. The SAT is a three-hour multiple choice test published by the Educational Testing Service under the sponsorship of the College Board. It breaks scores into verbal and math components, each graded from 200 to 800. The mean scores nationally in 1989-99 were 505 for verbal and 512 for math (combined 1017). (California public school students scored 497 on verbal and 516 in math with San Francisco public school students scoring 456 in verbal and 512 in math, and students at San Francisco's highly academic Lowell High School scoring 576 in verbal and 620 in math.) (Source: schoolwisepress.com) Each year only a few students nationwide receive a score of 800 in either area. Recent mean scores for entering freshmen at several colleges and universities are:

| | | |
|---|---|---|
| UC Berkeley | Verbal: 580-710 | Math: 620-730 |
| California State University-Hayward | Verbal: 460 | Math: 470 (combined 800) |
| California Polytechnic State University (San Luis Obispo) | Verbal: 568 | Math: 591 (combined 1124) |
| Duke | Verbal: 690 | Math: 700 (combined 1390) |
| Pepperdine University | Verbal: 620 | Math: 620 |
| Menlo College | Verbal: 470 | Math: 490 (combined 960) |
| San Jose State | Verbal: 300-440 | Math: 390-550 (nonrecentered) |
| Santa Clara University | Verbal: 630-540 | Math: 650-550 (recentered) |

*(Source: www.collegeview.com)*

Note that "recentering" refers to the upward adjustment of the scores of SAT exams taken on or after April 1, 1995. The College Board explains this as follows: "Recentering established the average SAT [I] verbal and math scores near the midpoint of the 200-800 scale."

The SAT II is the new name for the College Board Achievement Test, a test designed to assess mastery of single subjects: Writing (in English), Literature (in English), Spanish, French, German, Modern Hebrew, Latin, Italian, Japanese, Chinese, American History and Social Studies, World History, Mathematics Level I, Mathematics Level IIC, Biology, Chemistry, and Physics. As with the SAT, these are graded from 200 to 800. SAT II scores may be used by colleges for entrance, to direct a student's course of study in college, or to determine whether a student is exempt from taking certain college courses. Some colleges and universities, including the University of California, require applicants to submit both SAT or ACT scores *and* SAT II test scores. (SAT II scores were not requested of the schools in this Guide though some schools provided them.)

High school grade point average (GPA) has always been an important factor in college admission. Evaluation of GPAs has become more difficult because of grade inflation, the practice of weighting GPAs, and the different grading practices in different high schools. Weighting of GPAs refers to a practice of giving more weight in calculating a GPA to grades achieved in specific classes such as AP classes. (Thus, an A in a regular class would result in a 4.0 grade point for the class, whereas an A in an AP class would result in a 5.0 grade point.) Some schools also weight GPAs for a student's taking a certain number of academic courses. (Schools in this Guide were asked if their mean GPA was weighted and if so, how.)

Averages, in general, do not reflect the whole picture. The majority of students in a class may have high SAT scores but a few students who do not test well may "pull down" those scores. Also, the SAT mean might not reflect the entire class since non-college-bound students may skip taking it. (Some schools eliminate ESL students from their mean SAT scores and GPAs.) Therefore, parents should consider average SATs and GPAs along with other information but should also recognize their limitations. (For more information on the SAT and SAT II, see www.collegeboard.org)

## LEARNING DIFFERENCES/DISABILITIES

By the time a child is applying to high school, learning disabilities most likely will have been diagnosed. Thus, parents will be faced with choosing a school that can accommodate the child's learning disability or learning difference. The ability of schools to do this will vary. Every school in this book was asked what special programs or resources it has for students with learning disabilities or differences. Some have special programs that require separate applications. Some schools set aside a certain number of places in each freshmen class for students with learning disabilities and give them additional study labs and assistance. Other schools have no programs or resources but may refer students to outside tutors.

A good source for information for parents seeking to learn more about learning disabilities is the Schwab Foundation for Learning (formerly the Parents' Educational Resource Center) in San Mateo, (650) 655-2410. (www.schwablearning.org)

## UNIFORMS/DRESS CODE

Uniforms have increased in popularity in the past five years, especially in the public sector. Advocates say uniforms help students focus on learning rather than clothes, reduce expensive clothes competition, deter gang issues, and increase school pride and identity. "Dress does affect behavior," says a principal at a boys' school with a uniform policy that allows a wide range of choices but is strictly enforced. Opponents see uniform policies as totalitarian and interfering with students' rights of expression.

Most schools requiring uniforms have a wide range of "wardrobe options." Uniforms today often consist of khaki pants and shorts, polo shirts, corduroys, gabardine slacks, and sweatshirts. Amazingly, the result can range from preppy to deep grunge depending on other aspects of the school's policy, including hairstyles and color, shoes, jewelry, etc. (Black lipstick can dramatically transform an otherwise conservative look.) It is interesting to note that even in private schools without uniforms or dress codes, students tend to "self-uniform," typically wearing jeans and t-shirts or sweatshirts.

Besides dress, schools often restrict other personal ornamentation. Many private schools (but not all) prohibit unnatural hair colors, spikes, and eyebrow, nose, and tongue piercings. (Yet even denied the opportunity to wear "belly shirts" and below-the-rear pants, and even precluded from carving Adidas or Nike logos into the skull, students find a way of expressing their personalities through their appearance. This will be obvious when you visit the schools.)

## STUDENT CONDUCT AND HEALTH

Parents ask, "Are there drugs at that school?" Parents have to assume that every high school student in the nation can acquire drugs if desired. No school can guarantee that its students will never be exposed to drugs and alcohol. Parents do have the ability to evaluate any program the school has to prevent these types of problems and to learn how schools handle these issues when they arise.

All schools must abide by the laws prohibiting illegal drug, tobacco and alcohol possession, use, and distribution by minors. Thus, schools' standard codes of conduct prohibit such activities on campus as well as at school-sponsored events. In this Guide, schools were asked about any additional relevant aspects of their rules of conduct, and more importantly, how they handle students' violation of these rules. One school may immediately expel a student who brings alcohol onto campus; another school may send the students and parents to a counseling program. (Schools that have a "zero tolerance policy" are serious about this—kids sometimes are expelled immediately and unceremoniously with no second chance.) Schools were also asked if they provide education on drug and alcohol use and AIDS awareness. Most do; in some schools, it is part of the religion curriculum. A few provide none, leaving it to families.

A school that responds with hesitation when parents ask how they handle these issues should be looked upon with suspicion. All high schools should be prepared to deal with such issues as drug, alcohol, and tobacco use; sexual activity; harassment based on sex, sexual orientation, race, ethnicity, or religion; and other issues that arise in our society.

## FUNDRAISING AND PARENT PARTICIPATION

All schools would like parents to participate in their fundraising efforts. Indeed, for schools to get certain grants, they must show a high level of parent participation. Often the school cares more about the percentage of participation than the amount of the individual donations. Many schools allow parents to make monthly payments towards their pledge.

Schools often require parents to give a certain amount of their time to the school by participating in fundraising activities, annual school clean-ups, or driving on field trips.

# What Is Your Child Doing After School?

You won't know. At least in most schools. The majority of high schools have an open campus after dismissal time and do not account for students' whereabouts after dismissal. Most private high schools have plenty of after-school activities to keep interested students busy—all on the honor system. Parents who work full-time simply hope their 13-year-old 9th grader will use his or her freedom wisely.

# Editor's Notes

1. "N/P" for "Not provided" indicates that the school gave no direct response to the question asked. If the school provided alternative or explanatory information, such information is included, usually in quotation.

2. Schools appear in this Guide at the Editor's discretion. Schools that would like to be considered for future editions may contact Pince-Nez Press at (415) 267-5978.

3. Information regarding the schools' standing with federal, state, or city/county agencies, allegations of misconduct, lawsuits, and other such information is beyond the scope of this Guide.

4. Financial aid information relates to financial aid provided by or through the school, not aid from other sources.

5. Much of the information in this Guide reflects a compilation and condensation of the information provided by the schools. Quotes indicate that the verbatim response of the school is used. All information provided by the schools is subject to editing.

6. While all efforts have been made to ensure the accuracy of information in this Guide, schools' data change regularly; thus, families should rely on the schools' most up-to-date information for the facts upon which they base their decision.

# Abbreviations & Shortcuts

| | |
|---|---|
| ACSI: | Association of Christian Schools International |
| BAIHS: | Bay Area Independent High Schools |
| C: | College |
| CAIS: | California Association of Independent Schools |
| CC: | Community College |
| f/t: | full-time |
| G: | grade |
| HS: | high school |
| IB: | International Baccalaureate |
| ISEE: | Independent School Entrance Exam |
| JC: | Junior College |
| JV: | Junior Varsity |
| K-8: | Kindergarten through eighth grade |
| N/A: | Not available |
| N/P: | Not provided |
| NAIS: | National Association of Independent Schools |
| PSAT: | Preliminary Scholarship Assessment Test |
| SAT: | Scholastic Assessment Test |
| SSAT: | Secondary School Admission Test |
| SF: | San Francisco |
| HSPT: | High School Placement Test |
| U: | University |
| V: | Varsity |
| WASC: | Western Association of Schools and Colleges |
| WCEA: | Western Catholic Educational Association |

**COLLEGES AND UNIVERSITIES:**

University of California (UC) campuses: Berkeley, Davis, Irvine, Los Angeles (UCLA), Riverside, San Diego, Santa Barbara, Santa Cruz

California State University (CSU) campuses: Chico, Fresno, Fullerton, Hayward, Humboldt, Maritime Academy (Vallejo), Monterey Bay, Sacramento, San Francisco, San Jose, Sonoma, Stanislaus, California State Polytechnic University-San Luis Obispo (Cal Poly-SLO), California State Polytechnic University-Pomona (Cal Poly-Pomona)

Others: New York University (NYU), Massachusetts Institute of Technology (MIT), Rhode Island School of Design (RISD), Southern Methodist University (SMU), University of the Pacific (UOP), University of San Francisco (USF), University of Southern California (USC), University of Virginia (UVA)

# ARCHBISHOP MITTY HIGH SCHOOL

5000 Mitty Avenue
San Jose, CA 95129

(408) 252-6610 *fax (408) 252-0518*
amhs@aimnet.com
www.mitty.com

Tim Brosnan, Principal
Mrs. Diann Ryan, Principal for Supervision and Admissions, (408) 252-6610

## GENERAL

**Coed** day high school. **Catholic** (% Catholic: N/P). Founded in 1965. (Archbishop Mitty is an independent diocesan high school.) **Nonprofit. Enrollment:** Approximately 1,430. **Average class size:** 27. **Accreditation:** WASC (6-year term: 1996-02). **School year:** 9-month calendar (175 instructional days). **School day:** 8 a.m. to 2:45 p.m. **Location:** Off Lawrence Expressway near Highway 280.

## STUDENT BODY

**Geographical breakdown (counties):** 100% from Santa Clara. **Ethnicity:** 65% Caucasian (non-Latino); 15% Asian or Pacific Islander; 12% Latino; 3% African-American; 3% other; and 2% Native American. **Foreign students (I-20 status):** None. **Single parent/two f/t working parent families:** N/P. **Middle schools:** N/P.

## ADMISSION

**Applications due:** Mid-February (call for date). **Application fee:** $55. **Application process:** October through February, 8th graders are invited to spend a morning at Archbishop Mitty from 7:45 to 11 a.m., Mondays, Tuesdays, Thursdays, and Fridays. Visits should be scheduled early because spaces are limited. An open house for families is held in November. The San Jose Diocesan Entrance Exam is given at the school in January. **No. of applications:** 1360+ applications for 380 places. **Admission cut-off:** N/P. **Preferences:** Catholics. **"We are looking for":** N/P. **What sort of student do you best serve?** N/P.

# Costs

**Latest tuition:** $5,970 payable in 10 monthly payments. **Sibling discount:** None. **Tuition increases:** N/P. **Other costs:** Registration fee of $400; textbooks. **Financial aid:** "Available. Call for information." **Percentage of students receiving financial aid/average grant award/no. of full/half tuition grants:** N/P.

# School's Mission Statement/Goals

"Archbishop Mitty High School is a Catholic coeducational, college preparatory school of the Diocese of San Jose. The school embraces the Catholic educational mission of developing community, teaching the message of the Gospels, and promoting service and justice. Through its rigorous academic program, Archbishop Mitty seeks to prepare its students for college and for responsible leadership in the global society of the 21st century. At the same time, the school works diligently with parents to foster the development of each student. Recognizing that each individual is created in the image and likeness of God, the school celebrates and affirms its diverse cultural community and encourages students to respond to their world with competence, insight, understanding, courage, and compassion based on a tradition of faith and moral values."

# Academic Program

**Courses offered (H=Honors, AP=Advanced Placement, (H)=Honors option, (AP)=AP option): Visual and Performing Arts:** Asian Art History, 20th Century Art, Western Art History, Art I, Art II, 2/3 Dimensional Art, Multicultural Arts, Design Art I, Design Art II, Concert Band, Jazz Band, Choir, Concert Choir, String Ensemble, Piano Lab, Acting, Drama/Performance, Stagecraft, Music Theory AP; **English:** English I, English II Accelerated, Writing Workshop, World Literature, English II H, American Literature, English III H, British Literature, Contemporary Authors, Dramatic Literature, Multicultural Literature, Poetry and Prose, Shakespeare, Speech, 20th Century Literature, Writing for College, English IV AP; **Modern Languages:** French 1-4, French H 2 & 3, French 4 AP, Spanish 1-4, Spanish H 2 & 3, Spanish 1A/1B, Spanish 1C/2A, Spanish 2B/2C, Spanish 4 AP; **Math:** Algebra I, Algebra I Accelerated, Geometry (H), Algebra II, Algebra II/Trigonometry, Trigonometry, Analytic Geometry, Statistics (AP), Calculus, Calculus ABAP, Calculus BCAP; **P.E.:** PE 9, Body Shaping, Intermediate Swimming, Softball/Basketball, Team Sports, Volleyball/Badminton, Volleyball/Tennis, Water Polo, Weight Training; **Religious Studies:** Personal Growth, Judeo-Christian Origins, Personal and Social Ethics, Religion 11/Cultural Language and Justice, Bio-Ethics, Comparative Religions, Love and Marriage, Social Justice, Spirituality; **Science:** Integrated Science, Biology (H), Chemistry (H), Biology AP, Physics (AP), Geological Science, Marine Biology; **Social Studies:** World Cultures, World History (H), US History (AP), American Government (AP),

Anthropology, Economics, Psychology, Sociology, Voices of America; **Technology:** Computer Technology and Applications 1 & 2, Desktop Publishing, Multimedia Explorations; **Other:** Student Government, Journalism (yearbook), Writing for Purpose (Newspaper). **Computer lab/training:** The school has more than 200 computers for student training and use in the technology center, library, math tutorial center, counseling center, and student activities office. Students are required to take a semester of technology their freshman year. **Grading:** Letter grades A-F. **Graduation requirements:** 230 units including .5 year visual and performing arts, 4 years English, 2 years modern language, 3 years math, 1 year P.E., 3.5 years religious studies, 2.5 years science, 3.5 years social studies, .5 year computer technology and applications in freshman year. 100 hours of community service. **Average nightly homework:** N/P. **Faculty:** 84 faculty members (N/P re gender, degrees). **Faculty ethnicity:** N/P. **Faculty selection/training:** N/P. **Teacher/student ratio:** 1:17. **Teacher's daily student load in required academic subject:** N/P. **AP courses/exams:** "In 1998, students took 263 AP exams; 83% of exams resulted in scores of 3 or above." (N/P re # subjects, takers, % in AP classes) **Senior class profiles (mean):** N/P. **GPA:** N/P. **National Merit Scholarship Program:** In 1999, the school had 10 finalists and 14 commended students. **College enrollment:** 77% of last year's graduating class enrolled in 4-year colleges, 22% in 2-year colleges. (N/P re colleges. "For 1999 college report, send for school profile.")

## OTHER INDICATORS THE SCHOOL IS ACCOMPLISHING ITS GOALS

N/P.

## CAMPUS/CAMPUS LIFE

**Campus description:** 25 acre campus. **Library**: Open to students from 7:30 a.m. to 4:30 p.m. (N/P sq.ft., # volumes, etc.) **Open/closed campus:** N/P. **Classroom space per student:** N/P. **Lunches:** N/P. **Bus service:** N/P. **Uniform/dress code:** N/P. **Co-curricular activities/clubs:** More than 40 clubs, including African American Student Union, Adventure Camping, Amnesty International, Anglers Club, Intercultural Association, Backpacking Club, Biking Club, California Scholarship Federation, Christian Service Committee, Close-up Club to Washington, D.C., Daily Announcement Club, Film Club, New York Trip, Photography Club, Drama Club, Dance Club, Emmaus Groups, Environmental Club, French Club, Immersion Trips, Intramural, Irish Club, Italian Club, Latin American Student Union, Liturgical Music Group, Math Club, Monarch Service Club, Monarchs in England, newspaper, National Honor Society, Native American Club, Peer Counseling, Performing Arts (Band, Choir, Fall Play, Jazz Band, Jazz Choir, Pep Band, Spring Musical), Perspectives Club (travel and arts), Poetry Club, Reaching Out Program, Retreats, Science Fiction Club, Community Council, Dance Team, LIFE/Emmaus (Campus Ministry Leadership), Spanish Club, Student

Government, SADD, Television Show Production, Yearbook. **Foreign exchange program:** N/P. **Opportunities for community service:** The community service program is administered through each student's religious studies class with students performing a minimum of 25 hours per year. Students have many options including serving food to the homeless at Martha's Kitchen and Loaves & Fishes, visiting the elderly with the Independent Aging Program of Santa Clara County, distributing toys and food to the needy during the Christmas season, working in the Santa Clara Valley Medical Center and other hospitals, visiting foreign countries to volunteer in the Los Niños and Amigos Programs, working with the physically and developmentally disabled at Camp Costanoan, and participating in the Walk for AIDS. **Typical freshman schedule:** 2 semesters each: English I, mathematics, modern language, religious studies; 1 semester each: world cultures, P.E., arts elective, integrated science, and computer technology & applications.

## STUDENT SUPPORT SERVICES

**Counselor/student ratio (not including college counselors):** 1:286. **Counseling:** The school has five counselors all of whom have graduate degrees in counseling psychology. At the beginning of freshman year, each student is assigned an individual counselor for personal counseling and academic and college guidance counseling. The school holds workshops to assist in PSAT and SAT preparation, and assists with college applications. The school also has science and math tutorial centers where students can receive help with areas of difficulty and can make up work missed due to absence. **Learning differences/disabilities:** N/P. **Career apprenticeship programs:** The school sponsors a Corporate Internship Program each summer which assists students in obtaining paid internships with partner Silicon Valley companies.

## STUDENT CONDUCT AND HEALTH

**Code of conduct:** N/P. **How school handles drugs/alcohol usage:** N/P. **Drug/alcohol abuse prevention/AIDS awareness program:** N/P.

## SUMMER PROGRAMS

The school has an academic summer school and numerous sports camps.

## PARENT INVOLVEMENT

**Parent participation:** Voluntary participation through the Archbishop Mitty Parents Association. **Parent/teacher communication:** N/P. **Parent education:** N/P. **Donations:** N/P.

## SPORTS

The school has 51 teams competing in 22 sports. Boys compete in football, cross-country, water polo, basketball, soccer, wrestling, track, baseball, badminton, golf, tennis, swimming, and volleyball. Girls compete in tennis, cross-country, field hockey, water polo, volleyball, basketball, soccer, track, softball, golf, swimming, badminton and competitive dance. Girls compete as members of the Blossom Valley Athletic League. Boys are part of the West Catholic Athletic League.

## OTHER

Students have the opportunity, through the school's immersion program, to do volunteer work in intense one- to two-week sessions. The program is designed "to deepen students' faith, foster an understanding of different cultures, and involve students in partnerships with people in low-income situations to assist them with their development." Current immersion trips include Tijuana, Mexico (Los Niños), Oaxaca, Mexico (Maryknoll), Arizona (Fort Apache), El Salvador (Guarjila), and Appalachia (Glenmary Missions).

## WHAT SETS SCHOOL APART FROM OTHERS

N/P.

## HOW PARENTS/STUDENTS CHARACTERIZE SCHOOL

**Student response(s):** "I really appreciated the open and relaxed environment at Mitty where I was able to interact freely with people of all cultures and backgrounds in a comfortable and honest setting."—Kimathi Blackwood, now a Rice University student

"Because of knowledgeable teachers, challenging classes, and advanced technological resources, Mitty has prepared me to pursue my interests in biological and computational sciences."—Benny Chih, now a Carnegie Mellon student

"The family atmosphere at Mitty helped me to learn about myself, challenge myself to accomplish all that I could, and have fun doing it!"—Kerri Walsh, now a Stanford University student

"Through religious studies courses and campus ministry activities at Mitty, I was able to strengthen my faith by reflecting on what I believed in, by sharing it with others, and by putting it into action."—Megan Greig, now a Seattle Pacific student

# ARCHBISHOP RIORDAN HIGH SCHOOL

175 Phelan Avenue
San Francisco, CA 94112

(415) 586-8200 *fax (415) 587-1310*
riordan.pvt.k12.ca.us

Father Timothy M. Kenney, S.M., Principal
Ms. Linda Nastari, Assistant Principal
Scott Donegan, Admissions Director

## GENERAL

**Boys'** day high school. **Catholic** (Archdiocesan)(74% Catholic; 14% Christian; 12% non-Christian). Founded in 1949, administered by the Marianist Fathers. **Enrollment:** Approximately 700. **Average class size:** 26. **Accreditation:** WASC (6-year term: 1996-02). **School year:** Approximately August 20-May 30 (180 instructional days). **School day:** Approximately 7:45 a.m. to 2:50 p.m. **Location:** Off Ocean Avenue near Highway 280 (southwestern part of the City); across the street from City College. Accessible by BART (Balboa Station), MUNI Metro, and five MUNI bus lines.

## STUDENT BODY

**Geographical breakdown (counties):** Approximately 97% from San Francisco; 1% from San Mateo; 1% from Alameda. **Ethnicity:** 27% Latino; 24% Filipino; 21% Caucasian (non-Latino); 12% Asian; 12% African-American; 4% other. **Foreign students (I-20 status):** 1%. **Single parent families:** 25.1%. **Two f/t working parent families:** 67%. **Middle schools:** 9% of the most recent entering freshman class came from 9 public middle schools; 7% from 6 private, non-parochial schools; 84% from 29 parochial schools.

## ADMISSION

**Applications due:** Approximately December 10 (call for date). **Application fee:** $50 for freshman, $75 for late applications and transfer students, and $100 for international students. **Application process:** Tours of the school for parents and students are given throughout the year. Open houses are held on a Sunday in October and in November. During fall semester, interested students may spend a half day at the school "shadowing" a current student. Applications are due in early December, and the STS High School Placement Examination is administered in January. Decisions are mailed out mid-March. **No. of applications:** 400

applications were received for 200 places in prior year's class. Six new students were admitted to G10, 3 to G11. **Admission cut-off:** "We seek to provide a Catholic education for all levels of society and academic abilities." **Preferences:** None. **"We are looking for** well rounded young men who will get involved and contribute to our school community." **What sort of student do you best serve?** "We do well with boys. Specializing in single gender education, we acknowledge that the emotional maturation of boys is often slower than that of girls. Our curriculum focuses on boys and provides them many different opportunities. Therefore, the young man who is an average student in grammar school or middle school comes to ARHS, finds our environment conducive to learning, and is able to strive for his full potential. Archbishop Riordan High School is a Catholic school of 700 students that engages young men in the process of educating the 'whole person,' promoting individual growth and development in the intellectual, spiritual, social, and physical aspects of life."

# COSTS

**Latest tuition:** $6,750 payable annually, quarterly, or in 10 monthly payments. **Sibling discount:** $500. **Tuition increases:** Approximately 5% annually. **Other costs:** $450 registration fee, $125 book rental fee; uniforms cost approximately $250 for entering freshmen. **Financial aid:** Families may apply for need-based financial aid. In addition, a limited number of academic and service scholarships are awarded to incoming freshman based upon outstanding academic achievement, leadership, and service to school and community in amounts ranging from $500 to $2,000. They are not renewable. **Percentage of students receiving financial aid:** 329 families applied for financial aid last year; of these, 150 received aid totaling $200,000. **Average grant:** Approximately $1,000. **No. of full-tuition grants:** None—the largest award was $1,750. **Grants of half-tuition or more:** None. (Note: Families earning over $55,000 normally do not qualify for financial aid.)

# SCHOOL'S MISSION STATEMENT/GOALS

"Archbishop Riordan High School, an Archdiocesan Catholic school in the Marianist tradition, develops the character of young men and instills gospel values in an environment of academic excellence that reflects the culture of the San Francisco Bay Area.

"The school engages young men in education of the 'whole person,' promoting individual growth and development in the intellectual, spiritual, social, and physical aspects of life. [The school] is a Christian Community of faculty, students, parents, and alumni, who by example, instruction, and concern, mutually support and assist one another to develop Christian values of love of God, love of oneself, and love of others.

"[The school's goals are] 1) to develop in our students a strong character based on an active Christian life of prayer, study, celebration, and service; 2) to provide our students with a broad body of knowledge and the critical-thinking skills to become lifelong learners; 3) to assist our students in developing confidence through athletic competition and to extol the virtues of physical exercise, competition, and good sportsmanship; 4) to encourage student interests in a wide variety of activities in order to prepare our young men to be lifelong participants in their communities; 5) to provide the guidance and discipline necessary for our students to better know themselves."

## ACADEMIC PROGRAM

"Archbishop Riordan utilizes an 'intensive block' schedule commonly known as the 4x4 schedule. The school year is split into two terms ... and students take four courses per term. Each class lasts 80 minutes, thus providing sufficient time for students and teachers to delve more deeply and actively into topics and activities. ... The innovative schedule allows students to take 8 courses per year rather than 6, as is the norm in traditional school schedules. Therefore, over 4 years, students take 8 more classes than students in schools with traditional schedules." The curriculum is designed to fulfill the UC and Cal State university systems' entrance requirements 'with ample room to spare to sample the expanded elective opportunities ....'" Eleven AP courses are offered to juniors and seniors. **Courses offered (AP=Advanced Placement, H=Honors, (AP)=AP option, (H)=Honors option, \*= must qualify to take): Computers:** Computer Applications 1 & 2, Desktop Publishing, Computer Programming; **English:** Intro to Composition Writing, Intro to Literature (H\*), World Literature (H\*), AP English Language/Comp, American Literature, Senior Composition/Lit, Film and Literature, Shakespeare, Journalism; **Math:** Algebra I (H\*), Algebra Ia-b, Plane Algebra, Modern Geometry (H\*), Algebra II, Advanced Algebra (H), Plane Geometry, Modern Geometry, Math Analysis, Trigonometry/Statistics, Calculus BC; **P.E.:** P.E. 9-12; **Religious Studies:** Christian Character and Faith, American Catholic Experience, Scriptures and Sacraments, Life Issues, Christian Lifestyles; **Science:** Physical Science, Ecology, Biology H\*, Chemistry (AP), Earth Science, Anatomy-Physiology, Physics (AP); **Foreign Language:** Spanish I-III, Spanish I-II (Native Speaker), French I-III, AP Spanish Language; **Social Science:** Geography & World History I (H\*), World History II, 1450-present (AP\*), AP European History\*, Economics, World Government, AP US Government & Politics\*; **Visual & Performing Arts:** Intro to Theater Arts, Intro to Video Production, Beginning Band, Intro to Drama, Intermediate Band I-II, Forensics (Speech & Debate), Art I, Concert Band, AP Music Theory\*, 20th Century American Music, Jazz Band, Advanced Video Production, Student Leadership (officeholders); **Resource Specialist Program:** RSP 9-10. **Computer lab/training:** The school has two computer labs—one for the required freshman Computer Applications class with 17 Mac LCIIIs and Mac 580s, and another for Computer Applications 2 and Desktop Publishing, with 47 PowerMacs (5200CD). In addition, the library has 10 computers with Internet access. The computer labs are open all day for student use. **Grading:** Letter grades. Conduct grades ("satisfactory," "warning," and "unacceptable conduct") are also given for each class and homeroom. **Graduation requirements:** 4 years English, 3.5 years religious studies, 3 years mathematics, 3 years social science, 2 years foreign language (French or Spanish), 1 year fine arts or performing arts, 1 semester P.E., 1 semester Computer Applications, 4 years college preparatory electives, 100 hours community service. **Average nightly homework:** 2-3 hours per day. **Faculty:** Of the 53 faculty members, 45 are male, 8 female; 48 are lay faculty, and 5 are Marianist Priests or Brothers. 22 faculty members hold bachelor's degrees as their highest degree; 25 hold master's degrees; and 2 hold doctorates. (1/4 of the faculty are alumni.) **Faculty ethnicity:** 96% Caucasian (non-Latino); 2% Latino; 2% Asian. **Faculty selection/training:** Faculty members are selected "through a rigorous screening process which includes a series of interviews, reference checks, and teaching demonstrations before the school's students. The administration places the highest priority on applicants who possess graduate teaching credentials or master's degrees and who have classroom teaching experience. The faculty continuously refines its knowledge of educational research through scheduled in-service days—featuring outside speakers as well as presentations by faculty members themselves. In addition, teachers and administrators regularly attend professional seminars to continue their education in graduate programs. The school awards grants to its teachers to further their formal education." **Teacher/student ratio:** 1:26. **Teacher's daily student load in required academic subject:** 143. **AP courses/exams:** 15% of students are currently taking AP courses. In 1997, 60 students took 117 AP exams in 7 subjects. 60% received scores of 3 or above. Seniors may participate in the XL program (Accelerated Program for High School Students) and take advanced course work at City College (across the street from the school). Classes may be integrated directly into the day program, and students may opt to receive either high school or college credit. **Senior class profile (mean):** SAT Math 478, SAT Verbal 471. **GPA:** N/P. **National Merit Scholarship Program:** N/P. **College enrollment:** 99% of the graduates of the class of 1999 (157 students) enrolled in colleges and universities (45% in public 4-year colleges; 35% in community colleges; 17% in private 4-year colleges, 2% in technical schools, and 1% in a US military academy). Acceptances include: US campuses (Berkeley, Davis, Irvine, Los Angeles, Riverside, San Diego, Santa Barbara, Santa Cruz), CSU campuses (Cal Poly-Pomona, Cal Poly-SLO, Chico, Fresno, Fullerton, Hayward, Humboldt, Long Beach, Sacramento, San Diego, San Francisco, San Jose, Sonoma), community colleges (San Mateo, City C of San Francisco, Skyline, Chabot, Cuesta, Canada, Los Medanos, Diablo Valley), USF, Santa Clara, St. Mary's, Dominican, Gonzaga, Fordham, Chaminade U, U of San Diego, Clark U, Hampton, Tuskegee U, Menlo C, Bethune-Cookman C (FL), Academy of Art C, Morehouse, U of Puget Sound, Franklin Pierce C (NH), Occidental, American, USC, Northeastern, Northwestern, US Air Force Academy, U of Colorado-Boulder, Florida A & M, Boston U, U of Oregon, Southern Oregon State, Purdue, Sierra Academy of Aeronautics, Embry Riddle.

# OTHER INDICATORS THE SCHOOL IS ACCOMPLISHING ITS GOALS

N/P.

# CAMPUS/CAMPUS LIFE

**Campus description:** Since its founding in 1949, the school has occupied a 400,000 sq. ft. campus in the southwestern part of the City. The building has two classroom wings, a full-size gymnasium, a 1,200-seat theater, a courtyard, a large cafeteria, 41 classrooms, a library, science and computer labs, a locker room, weight room and wrestling room, and a chapel. The school's immediate plans include upgrading the science labs with computers. The grounds include a full-size football field, track, and a baseball diamond. **Library:** Open 7:30 a.m. to 5 p.m., the library has an on-line catalog, 14,000 print volumes, 80 periodical subscriptions, study space for 80 students, and 10 computers with Internet access. **Open/closed campus:** Closed. **Classroom space per student:** N/P. (Classrooms are traditional, with students seated at individual desks facing the front of the classroom.) **Lunches:** The cafeteria is open from 7 a.m. to 1:15 p.m., and provides a hot breakfast and lunch daily for approximately $3/day for breakfast and $4 for lunch. **Bus service:** City bus and BART service only. **Uniform/dress code:** Students choose from black or khaki slacks or shorts, four colors of polo shirts (long or short sleeved), black or white turtlenecks, and school athletic shirts, sweaters, and school sweatshirts. Students may wear casual, dress, or athletic shoes. On dress days, students wear a white dress shirt, tie, white V-neck sweater, khaki slacks, and dress shoes. No hats, dyed hair, pony-tail/braids, or visible tattoos are allowed. Students may wear one stud or post earring. (Note: male teachers are required to teach in dress shirt and tie.) **Co-curricular activities/clubs:** (some in conjunction with the local girls' Catholic schools) African American Student Union, Arab Student Coalition, Art Club, Asian Student Coalition, Block Club, Bowling Club, California Scholarship Federation, Campus Ministry Club, Yell Leaders, Chess Club, Choral Group, Close-Up Program (trip to Washington, D.C.), Computer and Games Club, Crusader Brothers, Crusader Newspaper, Drama, Dance Committee, Euro Club, Philippine American Coalition, Interact, Jazz Band, *Lance* (Yearbook), Lancers Service Club, Literary Magazine, Math Club, Model Club, National Honor Society, Photography Club, Pep Band, Science Club, Ski Activities, Speech & Debate, Stage Crew, Student Government. **Foreign exchange program:** None. **Opportunities for community service:** "Hundreds." **Typical freshman schedule:** Freshmen, in conjunction with their counselors, select from three courses of study: College Prep, Honor, and General College Prep. A typical College Prep course of study is as follows, with 35-45 minute classes: (H=Honors option) English Usage/Introduction to Writing (H), Algebra 1-2 (H), home room (15 minutes), "Munch" morning break (10 minutes), Science (H), Religious Studies, lunch (45 minutes), Fine Arts Survey, Health/P.E., Computer Applications, Band, Video Production, foreign language (H).

# STUDENT SUPPORT SERVICES

**Counselor/student ratio (not including college counselors):** 1:150. **Counseling:** Each grade has a counselor who engages in academic and personal counseling. The school has a peer counseling program to assist students in the lower division with conflict resolution and to provide peer support programs. **College and career counseling** is provided through the four years and includes assemblies, individual counseling, and evening programs (including presentations to parents to discuss college financial aid). The school has a full-time college counselor. **Learning differences/disabilities:** The school has a Resource Specialist Program with 69 students currently enrolled. The Resource Specialist works with classroom teachers to help the teachers understand the student's special need and make the necessary accommodations to maximize the success of each student. To qualify, students must have current psycho-educational assessments and/or an IEP (Individual Educational Plan). Students in the program include "individuals with specific learning exceptionalities, Attention Deficit Disorders and English as a Second Language Needs." Lower division students in the program have an additional class period and meet daily with a Resource Specialist; upper division students meet individually with a Resource Specialist three times a week, depending on need. Students receive specific individual instruction in a variety of areas, study groups, assistance in arranging for extra time for exams, opportunities to study in groups, and other services. The purpose of the program is to "provide students with Learning Exceptionalities additional support in the mainstream ... to help each student achieve [his] maximum potential in each class, while developing the necessary compensation and coping skills to succeed independently." **Career apprenticeship programs:** N/P.

# STUDENT CONDUCT AND HEALTH

**Code of conduct:** The school has behavior rules relating to classroom conduct, insubordination and disrespect, alteration or falsification of documents, inappropriate language, smoking (not allowed on or within 1/4 mile of campus), trespassing, vandalism and graffiti, "hazing," theft, fighting, weapons, gang-related activity, harassment, and drugs and alcohol. **How school handles drugs/alcohol usage:** Students found using, selling, possessing, soliciting, or under the influence of alcohol, illegal narcotics, or controlled substances at any time are liable for dismissal. Students caught selling, providing, or transmitting alcohol or drugs will be expelled. Students who seek help with a substance abuse problem will be referred confidentially to the Guidance Department for assessment, which may lead to professional counseling and drug-testing. **Drug/alcohol abuse prevention/AIDS awareness program:** The required P.E./Health curriculum begins in 9th grade with instruction that includes human sexuality, drug and alcohol abuse education, and sexually transmitted diseases. This instruction continues in the elective P.E. courses for G11-12.

# Summer Programs

The school offers an academic summer session at a cost of $235 per session.

# Parent Involvement

**Parent participation:** Parents are required to attend three evening parent meetings during the year and are invited to join or attend meetings of the Parent Board and the Parent Guild. Three mandatory parent meetings are held during the year. **Parent/teacher communication:** Each semester consists of two quarters. The school mails parents report cards quarterly. Only semester grades appear on the students' transcripts. Teachers send academic deficiency reports mid-quarter for students whose average is less than a "C". Parent teacher conferences are held at the end of the first and third grading periods. **Parent education:** "[In its fifth year], the school's Parent Support Services (PSS) program is a specially-designed program for the parents and guardians of the students…. The PSS program consists of a variety of experiences including: Freshman Parents Cluster meetings; two nationally-acclaimed video-based series on the parenting of teens; various college and career evenings for parents and sons; occasional book-based series on teen and parent issues; special needs groups (such as single parents, Spanish-speaking parents, parents of African-American students, PAAC parents, parents of divorce, families with grief and loss issues, etc.); an interdepartmental Father-Son day for upper classmen; and special presentations (such as study skills and teen health and risk issues). These activities are generally held during weekday evenings unless otherwise specified. Parents and guardians are free to give their suggestions and concerns to the coordinator of the PSS program so that other topics and experiences may be developed." **Donations:** "Each family is required to actively participate in school-wide fundraisers." Every October each student is expected to raise $160 through a Walkathon.

# Sports

The school has nine sports and 24 teams including football, basketball, baseball, wrestling, track, cross-country, golf and tennis. Half the student body participates in team sports, competing in the WCAL. Intramural sports are played during the lunch period.

# Other

The school has a musical instrument program and school band with approximately 50% of students taking instrument lessons. (Students may fulfill their 1 year fine/performing arts requirement by studying a band instrument as a part of the school curriculum.) Ninety percent of the students are beginners at musical instruments. Students who continue with study may try out for the school's Marching Band, Concert Band, Jazz Band, or Wind Ensemble.

## What Sets School Apart From Others

"Archbishop Riordan is the only all-boys high school in San Francisco. It blends the traditional strengths of a structured, supportive Catholic education with research-supported innovations in curriculum, teaching methodology, and assessment. Its expansive Advanced Placement offerings and its Research Specialist Program serve the specialized needs of all its students. The Marianist emphasis on developing academic, spiritual, social, and athletic excellence—manifested in its excellent Music and Drama programs as well as its athletic teams—forms the foundation for success in college and post-secondary careers. Archbishop Riordan proudly offers its resources to all young men of the San Francisco Bay Area who seek an education rooted in Christian values."

## How Parents/Students Characterize School

**Parent response(s):** "I believe that Riordan fosters the academic, social, and spiritual development of young men in a family environment. The faculty and staff know all of the students. Students are not lost in the shuffle. The campus provides activities, athletics and support services from 7 a.m. until sometimes 10 p.m. The campus is often open and busy seven days a week. The staff are dedicated and involved and the students benefit from the extra support. It is a safe environment that parents can feel a part of."

# Arrowsmith Academy

2300 Bancroft Way
Berkeley, CA 94704

(510) 540-0440 *fax (510) 540-0541*
arrwsmth@sirius.com

William Fletcher, Director
Brigitte Bastrenta, Director of Admission/Development, (510) 540-0612 x304

## General

**Coed** day high school. **Nonsectarian.** Founded in 1979. **Nonprofit. Enrollment:** Approximately 100. **Average class size:** 12. **Accreditation:** WASC (6-year term: 1995-01). **School year:** N/P. **School day:** 8:30 a.m. to 3:25 p.m.

**Location:** Located across from the UC Berkeley campus, the school is several blocks from the Berkeley BART station and is accessible by many bus lines.

# Student Body

**Geographical breakdown (counties):** 2% from San Francisco; 69% from Alameda; 28% from Contra Costa; 1% from other counties. **Ethnicity:** 7% Asian; 21% African-American; 64% Caucasian (non-Latino); 7% Latino; 1% Native American. **Foreign students (I-20 status):** 5%. **Single parent families:** 16%. **Two f/t working parent families:** 43%. **Middle schools:** N/P.

# Admission

**Applications due:** March (call for date). **Application fee:** $40. **Application process:** No entrance exams or testing. Application requires references from most recent school and middle school transcripts. **No. of applications:** 30 applications were received for 25 places in prior year's class. Seven new students were admitted to G10, 7 to G11 and 4 to G12. **Admission cut-off:** "No GPA or test score cut-off. We read report cards and recommendations from teachers." **Preferences:** Siblings. **"We are looking for** creative, dedicated students who enjoy being part of a small supporting community." **What sort of student do you best serve?** "Students whose learning styles are not mainstream often flourish at Arrowsmith, though we do not admit students with serious behavior problems or those working significantly below grade level."

# Costs

**Latest tuition:** $9,650 if paid in full before start of school, $9,880 if paid in 2 installments, $10,150 if paid monthly. (Tuition is 15% higher for ESL/foreign students.) **Sibling discount:** None. **Tuition increases:** 3% annually. **Other costs:** None. **Financial aid:** Need-based. **Percentage of students receiving financial aid:** 30%. **Average grant:** $5,083. **No. of full-tuition grants:** 2. **Grants of half-tuition or more:** 50%.

# School's Mission Statement/Goals

"Arrowsmith Academy is a multicultural college preparatory school committed to the individual success of each student. Small, interactive classes celebrate our diversity of learning styles, cultural backgrounds, and personal goals. Supportive personal relationships encourage students to participate as responsible, confident citizens in an increasingly complex world."

# ACADEMIC PROGRAM

The curriculum is college preparatory, following the guidelines set by the state of California and the UC system. "Courses are taught in a seminar style, with an emphasis on interactive discussion and meaningful projects. Critical thinking and expression, problem solving, and communication skills are developed through challenging oral and written assignments." **Courses offered (AP=Advanced Placement, H=Honors, (AP)=AP option, (H)=Honors option): English:** English A-D, American Literature, Autobiography, The Short Story, World Literature (H), Shakespeare, Creative Writing, Journalism, ESL, Advanced ESL; **Math:** Pre-Algebra, Algebra I, Geometry, Algebra II, Pre-Calculus, Calculus; **Science:** General Physical Science, Biology, Earth Science, Chemistry, Physics; **Social Science:** American History, Diversity Studies, World Civilization, US History, Government, Economics; **Foreign Languages:** AP French (on demand), Japanese 1-3, Spanish 1-4, AP Spanish (on demand); **Art:** Drama, A Capella, Dance, The Mural, Self Portrait, Intro to Art, Mixed Media, Advanced Mixed Media, Art and Literature, Content in Art, Portfolio, Printmaking, Drawing, Drawing from Life, Black and White into Color; **P.E.; Other:** Computer Literacy, Conflict Management, Health and Sexuality, Study Skills, Web Page Design. **Computer lab/training:** The school recommends students take one semester of computer classes. (N/P re lab) **Grading:** Letter grades. **Graduation requirements:** (UC admission requirements). **Average nightly homework:** 1-2 hours. **Faculty:** 6 male, 11 female. 9 hold bachelor's degrees as highest degree; 7 hold master's degrees; and 1 holds a doctorate. **Faculty ethnicity:** 61% Caucasian (non-Latino); 19% African-American; 12% Asian; 4% Latino; 1% Filipino; 1% Native American; 2% other. **Faculty selection/training:** N/P. **Teacher/student ratio:** 1:7. **Teacher's daily student load in required academic subject:** 50 students per day. **AP courses/exams:** N/P. **Senior class profile (mean):** SAT Math 557, SAT Verbal 602. **GPA:** 3.06. **National Merit Scholarship Program:** One student in the most recent senior class was commended. **College enrollment:** 70% of last year's graduating class enrolled in 4-year colleges, 20% in 2-year colleges. (Each year several students return to their country of origin to apply to college.) Acceptances include: Santa Rosa CC, CSU-Los Angeles, Santa Barbara CC, UC Santa Cruz, U of Oregon, UC Santa Barbara, Academy of Art, San Francisco Arts International, Art Institute International, SCU-Chico, CSU-Sonoma, St. Mary's, C of Marin, UC Davis, C of the Redwoods, U of Colorado-Boulder, Franklin & Marshall, Lehigh U, Lafayette C (PA), Pitzer, Northwestern, UCLA, UC San Diego, Marymount C, CSU-Fresno, Kettering U (MI).

## OTHER INDICATORS THE SCHOOL IS ACCOMPLISHING ITS GOALS

"We have accepted students who were having difficulties enjoying school in large public schools, and have turned them into highly motivated students who, after two, three, or four years at Arrowsmith went on to the four-year colleges of their choices."

## CAMPUS/CAMPUS LIFE

**Campus description:** Urban campus near the UC Berkeley campus. **Library:** Students have access to UC Berkeley's main library and other UC libraries. **Open/closed campus:** Open at lunch only. **Classroom space per student:** N/P. **Lunches:** Students bring lunches or eat off-campus. **Bus service:** Public transportation only. **Uniforms/dress code:** None. **Co-curricular activities/clubs:** Male and female basketball teams; literary magazine (received "excellent" rating by National Council of English Teachers), A Capella, Dance, Drama. **Foreign exchange program:** The school plans to offer an exchange program with a school in Tokyo. **Opportunities for community service:** Students are placed with agencies in which they have career or personal interests. They have included: *The Daily Californian*, The Humane Society, Lawrence Hall of Science, Woolly Mammoth, child care providers, Amnesty International, Cody's Bookstore, A la Costa School, Institute of Human Origins, St. Mark's Church, Diesel Bookstore, and the Pacific Film Archive. **Typical freshman schedule:** English, Algebra I, World Civilization, P.E., foreign language, and 2 electives.

## STUDENT SUPPORT SERVICES

**Counselor/student ratio (not including college counselors):** 1:50. **Counseling:** Counseling services are available on campus for behavior issues. For serious issues, the family is referred to an outside therapist. The school provides academic, college, and career counseling as well. **Learning differences/disabilities:** "Part-time learning specialist; tutoring." **Career apprenticeship programs:** None.

## STUDENT CONDUCT AND HEALTH

**Code of conduct:** School rules apply during school hours. If rules are broken during non-school hours, the school has a conference with the parents and will recommend counseling. **How school handles drugs/alcohol usage:** "Zero tolerance" for possession, use, or influence during school hours. Penalty: expulsion. No tobacco smoking on campus nor near the campus on the street. Penalty: detention, possible suspension. **Drug/alcohol abuse prevention/AIDS awareness programs:** These issues are addressed in special assemblies and in a year-long required health class.

# SUMMER PROGRAMS

The school has a summer school program. Contact the school for information.

# PARENT INVOLVEMENT

**Parent participation:** Parents are encouraged but not required to be involved in curriculum, development, and fundraising events. **Parent/teacher communication:** Report cards are sent every six weeks with comments for each subject. Any time homework is not returned complete, a note is sent home to the parents. Parent-teacher conferences are held two times a year and any time on request. Parents or the school may request weekly report cards. **Parent education:** Informational evenings with presenters on issues such as "Parenting Teenagers," "Teenagers and Drugs," and "Learning Disabilities and Resources." **Donations:** Parents are asked to make donations to the school annual fund and are strongly encouraged to participate in fundraising events.

# SPORTS

Basketball for boys and girls, soccer for boys.

# OTHER

"Arrowsmith Academy allows each student to reach his/her full potential in each subject taught. It is committed to the success of *each student.*"

# WHAT SETS SCHOOL APART FROM OTHERS

"Emphasis on critical thinking and creativity—multicultural in the curriculum (not just in the diversity of the student body)."

# HOW PARENTS/STUDENTS CHARACTERIZE SCHOOL

**Parent response(s):** "Parents are generally very supportive—they like the fact that their children are treated as individuals with potential instead of groups by grade levels."
**Student response(s):** "Students who graduate are thankful for the sense of responsibility they acquired at Arrowsmith—they also feel confident entering college."

# THE ATHENIAN SCHOOL

2100 Mt. Diablo Scenic Boulevard
Danville, CA 94526

(925) 837-5375 *fax (925) 855-9342*

Eleanor Dase, Head of School
Christopher Beeson, Director of Admission

## GENERAL

**Coed** day and boarding high school (with day-only middle school). **Nonsectarian.** Founded in 1965. **Nonprofit,** member, NAIS, CAIS, BAIHS. **Enrollment:** 383 (262 in grades 9-12, 40 boarding students; 121 in grades 6-8). **Average class size:** 15. **Accreditation:** WASC/CAIS (6-year term: 1998-04). **School year:** 9-month calendar (186 instructional days). **School day:** 8:10 a.m. to 3:40 p.m. **Location:** 75-acre campus in Danville, 32 miles east of San Francisco. School buses serve communities from Oakland and Berkeley to Pleasanton and Livermore twice daily.

## STUDENT BODY

**Geographical breakdown (counties):** 54% from Contra Costa; 42% from Alameda; 5% from other Bay Area communities; 10% from out-of-state or outside the US. Of 41 boarding students, 10 are U.S. citizens and 31 are from 11 other countries in Europe, South America, and Asia. **Ethnicity:** 70% Caucasian (non-Latino); 15% Asian; 8% African-American; 5% Latino; 2% Middle Eastern or East Indian. **Foreign students (I-20 status):** 11%. **Single parent/two f/t working parent families:** N/P. **Middle schools:** 52% of the most recent entering freshman class came from 14 public middle schools; 29% from 8 private, non-parochial schools; 19% from 6 parochial schools.

## ADMISSION

**Applications due:** Approximately January 15 (call for date). **Application fee:** $40. **Application process:** Open Houses for parents and students are held each fall and in January. Interested students visit Athenian for a half-day: observing two classes, taking a student-led tour, and meeting students, faculty, and admission staff. The application consists of an information form, parent and student essays, academic transcripts for the past two years, recommendations, and admission test scores. Athenian accepts either the Independent School Entrance Examination (ISEE) or the Secondary School Admission Test (SSAT); the test should be scheduled well ahead of the application due date. **No. of applications:** 187 applications were received for 60 places in the prior class. Of these, 30 places are typically taken by the school's middle school students. Eleven new students were admitted to G10, 10 to G11, and 2 to G12. **Admission cut-off:** "We look for students who demonstrate they are ready for an academic challenge through strong recent grades, essays, recommendations, and test scores." **Preferences:** N/P. **"We are looking for** students with 1) the demonstrated ability to succeed in our challenging, interdisciplinary and international college preparatory program, 2) an enthusiasm for learning, 3) an interest in taking part in a diverse community of students and teachers, and 4) a willingness to contribute their talents and abilities to the Athenian programs and community." **What sort of students do you best serve?** (See above.)

# COSTS

**Latest tuition:** If a family does not qualify for financial assistance, tuition is $14,650 for day students and $25,500 for boarding students. Payment plans allow for 1, 2, or 11 installments. **Sibling discount:** None. **Tuition increases:** Average 3-6%. **Financial aid:** Athenian administers nearly $800,000 in tuition grants to needy families annually, based on demonstrated need. **Percentage of students receiving financial aid:** 20%. **Average grant:** $10,100. **No. of full-tuition grants:** 16. **Grants of half-tuition or more:** 85% (46).

# SCHOOL'S MISSION STATEMENT/GOALS

**Mission:** "The Athenian School prepares students for the rigorous expectations of college and for lives of purpose and personal fulfillment. We offer a challenging academic program with a difference: intellectual inquiry is active, learning is interactive, the disciplines are interrelated, and analysis and creativity thrive simultaneously. The acquisition of knowledge becomes authentic and joyous.

"We cultivate the personal qualities of each student to become an integrated human being with integrity, strong moral character, aesthetic sensitivity, and physical well-being. The Athenian community requires students to face life directly through open communication, while developing their inner strength to exceed their perceived potential and emerge as compassionate, responsible adults.

"We instill an appreciation of the reciprocal relationship between the individual and cultures, society and the natural world. We value the power and beauty of multiculturalism within our diverse community. We embrace principles of democratic governance, stewardship for the environment, respect for human dignity, and service as a way of life.

"By providing an atmosphere of intellectual, artistic, and physical challenge within the warmth of a nurturing community, we develop in our students the confidence and skills required to meet the complexities of their future."

# ACADEMIC PROGRAM

Athenian divides its academic calendar into three terms: fall, winter and spring. Many courses provide year-long study while seminars occupy a single term. Six academic classes meet four times each week. Each class meets in a long period once each week. In addition, the schedule also allows for periodic advisory group meetings, morning meetings, community service periods, physical education courses, and performing arts periods. **Courses offered (AP=Advanced Placement, H=Honors, (AP)=AP option, (H)=Honors option): Humanities: Core Courses:** G9: Humanities I: Literature (world), Humanities I: Cultures (world), Humanities I: Art; G10: American Studies: Literature, and American Studies: US History; **Literature seminars:** (All can be taken for Honors credit.) Writing Workshop, (AP) Contemp. Women Writers, (AP) African American Writers, (AP) Shakespeare, The Sixties, Major British Writers, Psychology, Human Rights, (AP) Moby Dick, (AP) Romanticism, Fiction Writing, (AP) Modern Classics, (AP) Poetry Writing Workshop, Fiction of Capitalism, Intro to Modern Thought, (AP) Fitzgerald-Hemingway, (AP) Post-Colonial Literature, (AP) Literature of India, 19th Century Women's Lit, Plato, (AP) Japanese Literature, Vietnam, Short Story, Human Sexuality. Each year a designated sequence of appropriate literature seminars prepares students for the AP exam in literature; **History seminars:** European History (AP), Post-Stalinist Russia, Dimensions of Democracy/Civitas I, Humanitas, History of the Holocaust, European History II (AP), Ancient History, US Political System/Civitas II, Society and the Environment, Microeconomics, African-American History, Social & Moral Philosophy, Approaches to Enlightenment, World Events, Macroeconomics; **Elective Seminars:** Paleontology, and Speech and Debate; **English as a Second Language:** ESL History and Culture, ESL Literature, Research and Writing, ESL American Studies; **Math:** Algebra I, Geometry, Algebra II, Algebra II with Trigonometry H, Trigonometry, Math Analysis, Math Analysis/Pre-Calculus H, (AP) Calculus AB, and (AP) Calculus BC, Statistics; **Computer Science:** Computer Applications I and Computer Programming II; **Foreign Languages:** Spanish I, Spanish II, Spanish III (H), Spanish IV (H, AP), French I, French II, French III (H), French IV (H, AP); **Sciences:** Conceptual Physics, Physics AP, Chemistry, Advanced Chemistry H, Biology, Advanced Biology H, Geology, Environmental Science; **Fine Arts:** Arts and Society courses: Humanities I: Art (a core course), AP Art History, Arts and Society: Drama, Art of Architecture, Art of the Explorers and Wanderers, Renaissance Art, Social Drama of the 20th Century, The World of Symphony, World Music, Jazz; **Visual Arts:** Ceramics, Drawing, Advanced Drawing, Drawing with Color, Jewelry, Painting, Photography I, Printmaking, Portrait Photography, Sculpture, Set Design and Construction, Stained Glass, AP Studio Art, Weaving, Fiber Art, Mixed Media, Landscape Art; **Music:** Chorus, Instrumental Production Workshop, Jazz Ensemble, Independent Study Seminars; **Drama:** Acting, Theater Production, Rehearsal and Performance, Scene Study; **Dance:** Dance I, Dance II, Advanced Dance; **P.E.:** Fencing, Indoor Soccer, Swimming, Mountain Biking, Rockclimbing, Tennis, Ultimate Frisbee, Volleyball, Weight

Training. **Special Programs:** The Athenian Wilderness Experience, Interim program, Internships, Independent Study, Round Square international exchange, Network of Complimentary Schools exchange, Outdoor Education programs. **Computer lab/training:** The computer lab has 30 computers. (Computers are also available for student use in the library and Courtside Building.) All 9th grade students receive training on computer use as part of the Humanities curriculum; many other courses throughout the curriculum utilize computers. **Grading:** Letter grades and written evaluations for each course. **Graduation requirements:** 4 years English, 3 years history, 3 years foreign language, 3 years laboratory science, 2 1/3 years fine arts, and P.E. or athletic participation during each year of enrollment. In addition students must complete community service each year and the Athenian Wilderness Experience before the beginning of senior year. **Average nightly homework:** N/P. **Faculty:** 45% male, 55% female. 39% of faculty hold bachelor's degrees as highest degree; 61% hold master's degrees; and 10% hold doctorates. **Faculty ethnicity:** 90% Caucasian (non-Latino); 4% Asian; 4% African-American; 2% Latino. **Faculty selection/training:** "The department chairs perform the initial screening. Select candidates may be asked back to teach a class in their discipline. The entire department is invited to interview the candidate. Faculty and students make evaluations." **Teacher/student ratio:** 1:10. **Teacher's daily student load in required academic subject:** N/P. **AP courses/exams:** Approximately 50% of juniors and seniors are currently taking AP courses. In 1998, 32 students took 44 AP examinations in 7 subjects. 81% received scores of 3 or above. **Senior class profile (mean):** SAT Math 605, SAT Verbal 585. **GPA:** 3.23. **National Merit Scholarship Program:** Three finalists, 7 commended in the class of 1998. **College enrollment:** 98% of last year's graduating class enrolled in 4-year colleges, including: MIT, Boston U, Brown, Carnegie-Mellon, Haverford, Emory, Lewis & Clark, Scripps, Smith, UC Berkeley, UCLA, UC Davis, UC Santa Barbara, Johns Hopkins, Tulane, Columbia, Duke, and U of Pennsylvania.

## OTHER INDICATORS THE SCHOOL IS ACCOMPLISHING ITS GOALS

N/P.

## CAMPUS/CAMPUS LIFE

**Campus description:** The school's campus is spread over 75 acres of rolling, oak-covered hills at the base of Mount Diablo. Its academic buildings include 24 classrooms; the Fuller Brawner Science Center with laboratories; Kate and Dyke Brown Hall (student-services offices and assembly, cafeteria, and theater space); three computer laboratories; two small faculty/administrative buildings, two dormitories and a boarding activities center; art and drama studios; and the Fuller Commons building (a student lounge and meeting space). In addition, the campus includes a large gymnasium, competition swimming pool, four athletic fields, tennis courts, 15 faculty residences, and eight buildings housing grades 6-8.

**Library:** 15,000 print volumes; 43 periodical subscriptions and 6 electronic subscriptions; computers with Internet access; on-line catalog; study space for 50-75 students. Open to students 8 a.m. to 4 p.m., and 7 p.m. to 10 p.m. Monday-Wednesday. (N/P sq. ft.) **Open/closed campus:** Open. **Classroom space per student:** 68 sq. ft. **Lunches:** Hot lunches, sandwiches, and salads may be purchased in the cafeteria. **Bus service:** Athenian's bus picks up students from North Berkeley and Oakland to Pleasanton and Livermore. Many of the buses also stop at BART stations. Cost varies. (Transportation costs are considered in financial aid.) **Uniforms/dress code:** Students are to dress in good taste and wear clothes that are clean and in good repair. **Co-curricular activities/clubs:** Activities and organizations include newspaper, Chess Club, International Student Organization, literary magazine, orchestra, Community Action Board, Debate, admission hosts, theater tech. group, Interweave, Multicultural Alliance, Round Square International Exchange and Service, and yearbook. **Foreign exchange program:** Athenian is a member of the Round Square Conference of International Schools, which provides international exchange opportunities at the more than 40 Round Square schools in nine countries on five continents. In addition, Athenian hosts exchange students each year from Round Square schools. **Opportunities for community service:** More than 200 organizations and activities. In G9 students participate in organized events on and off campus. In their junior and senior years, students arrange and complete a project in their individual areas of interest. **Typical freshman schedule:** Humanities I: Literature, Humanities I: Cultures, Humanities I: Fine Arts, mathematics (typically Algebra I, Geometry, or Algebra II), Conceptual Physics, and foreign language (Spanish or French: I, II, or III). Physical education, performing arts, community service, and advisory meeting periods are also part of the 9th grade weekly schedule.

## STUDENT SUPPORT SERVICES

**Counselor/student ratio (not including college counselors):** 1:10. **Counseling:** Academic: Students meet every other week with a faculty member who serves as their academic advisor. That teacher also serves as the primary contact for parents for academic and extracurricular affairs. Counseling: The counseling program includes peer education, advising and support programs for students, staff, and families. College: A full-time college counselor provides individual and group guidance regarding college and university selection, application, and admission. The college counseling program brings college representatives and speakers to campus every year. The College Counseling Office also provides a library of publications, videos, and computer databases for exploring colleges and financial aid. The office also facilitates test preparation programs. **Learning differences/disabilities:** "Teachers can provide some basic accommodations, but we have no special programs or resources." **Career apprenticeship programs:** N/P.

## STUDENT CONDUCT AND HEALTH

**Code of conduct:** In addition to prohibiting illegal activities, the school states, "We hold all members responsible for dealing with each other in a humane and gentle way. We prize the display of responsibility and good taste. Integrity, respect, and trust are treasured standards." **How school handles drugs/alcohol usage:** A student Discipline Committee makes recommendations to the Dean of Students regarding the consequences of rules infractions (which range from community service and privilege reductions to expulsion from the school). **Drug/ alcohol abuse prevention/AIDS awareness program:** Each year, the health program brings speakers and seminars to campus to educate Upper School students about drugs, alcohol, and sexually transmitted diseases, including AIDS. In addition, the sophomore health class addresses each of these issues. The school also offers an optional course on human sexuality through the Humanities Department.

## SUMMER PROGRAMS

Programs include Devil Mountain Summer Camp, Summer School, Athenian Sports Camp, the Summer English Language Program for international students, and programs run by outside groups who use the school's facility. Prices vary.

## PARENT INVOLVEMENT

**Parent participation:** Parents are strongly encouraged to participate in the Athenian Parent Association, which coordinates parents' volunteer and fundraising activities, provides informational and social programs, and serves as a conduit for parent input to the school. Parent volunteering includes work days and organizing events such as the annual auction and Spring Fling. **Parent/teacher communication:** Parents and students receive grades with comments at least 3 times a year; in some cases, midterm grades and comments can increase the reports to 6 times per year. In addition parents receive an annual report from the student's academic advisor. Additional conferences are available. **Parent education:** "The school psychologist provides workshops, seminars, and information coffees for all parents of Athenian students." **Donations:** "Because tuition does not cover the entire expense of educating students at Athenian, parents are strongly encouraged to contribute as they are able."

## SPORTS

Interscholastic sports teams include soccer, volleyball, tennis, cross-country, basketball, baseball, swimming, and wrestling. P.E. classes include martial arts, yoga, weight training, ultimate frisbee, and rock climbing, among others.

# What Sets the School Apart from Others

"The Athenian School's rigorous and stimulating college preparatory curriculum emphasizes inquiry, analytical thinking, effective communication, and interdisciplinary understanding. Several distinctive features further distinguish the school:

- Engaging seminar courses on a wide variety of topics in literature and history;
- Strength in the arts and participatory community government;
- An extraordinary campus supports the school's programs by providing a beautiful and inspiring setting;
- Bus service bringing together students from throughout the East Bay;
- An excellent and well-developed community service program;
- Residential faculty (over 20) and students (nearly 40) make Athenian the Bay Area's only coeducational boarding program. This facet of the school increases the availability of faculty to both day and boarding students and helps foster the strong sense of community, which supports students and faculty alike;
- An extensive wilderness experience;
- Diversity (International and Domestic): The Athenian student body represents a wide variety of communities from the Bay Area, the United States, and around the world which come together in an educational environment which places greatest emphasis upon education and mutual respect among its members;
- Innovative interim experiences;
- A vital international exchange program: As the only American member of the prestigious Round Square Conference of International Schools, Athenian fosters international understanding and a commitment to diversity."

# How Parents/Students Characterize School

**Parent response(s):** "Athenian students have a right to be proud: over 80% are admitted to their first choice college. Graduates attend a variety of institutions from MIT, Harvard, the University of Pennsylvania and Dartmouth, to Stanford, University of Chicago, Pomona, all UC campuses."

"The most outstanding element of the college preparatory school is its personnel. Their character, love of teaching, and involvement with the students is of a quality rarely seen in education."

"Athenian is about relationships: between areas of study; between teachers and students; between students and the world."

**Student response(s):** "At Athenian I learned how to use my mind to the fullest; I was well ahead of my peers in college."

"I learned not just to read textbooks but to take in the material, process it, and apply it to everyday life."

"Athenian helped me learn to be comfortable with adults; I find it easier to approach my professors than other students do."

"Here everyone has a sense of multicultural community."

"Athenian is a journey through yourself that leads you to discover what is important and valuable."

# BEACON HIGH SCHOOL

2101 Livingston Street
Oakland, CA 94606

(510) 436-4466 *fax (510) 437-2313*
www.beaconschools.org
admissions@beaconschools.org

Thelma Farley, Director of Education
Alexandra Baroni, Director of Admissions

## GENERAL

**Coed** day high school. **Nonsectarian.** Founded in 1990 (lower school, preK-8, founded in 1982). **Nonprofit. Enrollment:** 48. **Average class size:** 15 (no class larger than 20). **Accreditation:** None (the school has not sought accreditation). **School year:** Mid-Sept. to mid-July (approx. 210 instructional days). **School day:** 8:15 a.m. to 2:45 p.m. **Location:** Just south of Jack London Square on the Oakland waterfront. Off the 16th or 23rd Street exit from Highway 880; within walking or biking distance of the Fruitvale BART station.

## STUDENT BODY

**Geographical breakdown (counties):** 86% from Alameda; 14% from Contra Costa. **Ethnicity:** 80% Caucasian (non-Latino); 8% African-American; 8% Latino; 4% Asian. **Foreign students (I-20 status):** 0. **Middle schools:** 1/3 of the latest freshman class came from the school's middle school; 1/3 from public middle schools; 1/3 from private non-parochial schools. (N/P # schools)

## ADMISSION

**Applications due:** Accepted year-round for admission in September, January and April. For fall admission, call for exact date. **Application fee:** $50. **Application process:** The school holds Student-Parent Information Nights once each trimester throughout the year. Interested students are strongly recommended to schedule a Visitor Day on campus. The application includes a student statement, parent/guardian questionnaire, student questionnaire, reference letter from a non-teacher or non-family member who knows the student well, and the standard BAIHS recommendation forms. The Director of Education meets with each applicant to assess his or her skills. **No. of applications:** N/P. One new student was admitted to G10, 2 to G11, 2 to G12. **Preferences:** None. **Admission cut-off:** None. **"We are looking for** students who want to succeed in a non-traditional school. This means hard working, clear-thinking, imaginative and creative students representing multiple intelligences." **What sort of student do you best serve?** "A range of students who reflect a microcosm of the real world."

## Costs

**Latest tuition:** $10,200 (payable in 1, 3, or monthly payments; 5% discount if paid in full by August 1). **Sibling discount:** 5%. **Tuition increases:** Approximately 6% annually. **Other costs:** $350 for fees, $150 for books. **Percentage of students receiving financial aid:** 15%. **Average grant:** N/P. **No. of full-tuition grants:** None. **Grants of half-tuition or more:** N/P.

## School's Mission Statement/Goals

"Every student develops in a unique way; intellectually, socially and physically. Every student has an individual learning style. Beacon School educates the whole person through a developmentally-responsive, arts-enriched curriculum, designed to make every student a self-confident life-long learner."

## Academic Program

"Beacon's curriculum is adolescent-responsive maximizing each student's success because learning is made relevant to the unique perspective of the adolescent learner and tailored to each individual's learning style and rate of progress. The curriculum is organized around four major components: Core Skills (Numerary, Literacy, Cultural Knowledge, and Science), Integrated Studies, Experiential Studies and an Advisory Guidance System. ... Class placement is based on individual learning needs rather than on age or ability. There is no tracking. Cultural and learning-style differences and varying ability levels are accommodated. Classroom arrangements are informal and designed to facilitate interaction and allow for both independent and collaborative learning. ... Much of the workload is self-paced, where students can see continuous progress as they work through mastery-linked units of instruction. Assessment is individualized ... and based on the student's personal knowledge and skill mastery, not on comparison with others. The result is a feeling of empowerment, an enjoyment of learning and an absence of much of the angst and alienation that is usually part of the high school experience." The school operates on trimesters and utilizes block scheduling—students take three courses each trimester with courses meeting daily for 145 minutes. **Courses offered:** N/P. "By design, AP courses are not offered. Honors options are available in every course. Students may opt for the challenge group." **Special programs:** Students can get credit for experiential learning (independent study projects) including experimental living and working settings. **Computer lab/ training:** 18 computers (Pentium PCs, and PowerMacs) partially networked (3 with Internet access); full-time technology teacher. The technology department has received awards, including an Emmy for CD-ROMs students produced. All students must take a technology course. **Grading:** A-C. If students do not achieve 80% achievement in a class (a "C"), they receive a "No Grade" and are required to repeat the course. **Graduation requirements:** Designed to exceed the UC admission requirements. 4+ years English; 4+ years math, 4 years science including 2 lab science; 2-3 years foreign language; 4 years fine arts. **Average nightly homework (Mon-Th):** G9: 1 hour; G10-12: 2 hours. **Faculty:** Of the 6 full time and 7 part-time faculty members, 60% are male, 40% female. **Faculty ethnicity:** 55% Caucasian (non-Latino); 33% African-American. **Faculty selection/training:** All faculty members hold master's degrees. "Teaching credentials, in-services at school and continuing education." **Teacher/student ratio:** 1:10. **Teacher's daily student load in required academic subject:** 36. **AP courses/ exams:** None. **Senior class profile (mean):** SAT Math 560, SAT Verbal 580. **GPA:** 3.0. **National Merit Scholarship Program:** Two National Merit Scholarship recipients and 2 finalists in the past 4 years. **College enrollment:** 85% of last year's graduating class enrolled in 4-year colleges, 2% in 2-year colleges, including: Lewis & Clark, Sarah Lawrence, Oberlin, Linfield C, Evergreen State, CSU-Sonoma, CSU-Monterey Bay, U of Puget Sound, So. Oregon U, CSU-Humboldt, U of Oregon, and Boston U.

## OTHER INDICATORS THE SCHOOL IS ACCOMPLISHING ITS GOALS

"Beacon is a new school. Most other indicators at this time are anecdotal, *i.e.*, parent and student satisfaction ratings, retention, and attendance."

## CAMPUS/CAMPUS LIFE

**Campus description:** The school is in a converted warehouse in the Oakland Industrial Arts area. Completely renovated in 1991, the building houses the school's preschool and elementary school upstairs and the high school on the main floor. The high school has 7 classrooms, a computer lab, dance studio, two art studios, a library/student lounge, and a science lab. **Library:** "The library is open to classes and independent students at teacher discretion throughout the day." (N/P re sq. ft., # volumes, etc.) **Open/closed campus:** Open campus. **Classroom space per student:** 1,000 sq.ft. **Lunches:** Students bring lunches or eat at local delis within walking distance of campus. **Bus service:** Public only. **Uniforms/dress code:** None. **Co-curricular activities/clubs:** Clubs form around student interests year-to-year. Currently they include the Drama Club and Japanese Club. The school holds yearly camping trips/retreats for all students and staff. **Foreign exchange program:** None. **Opportunities for community service:** "Daily." **Typical freshman schedule:** "3 periods of approximately 145 minutes each."

## Student Support Services

**Counselor-student ratio (not including college counselor):** 1:15. **Counseling:** At the beginning of their freshman year, students are assigned an advisor. They meet in advisory groups of 15 students (same gender) for 45 minutes each week throughout their four years at the school to discuss academic and personal issues. The school's Program Coordinators act as college counselors. **Learning disabilities/differences:** "The school has the flexibility to accept students with a range of learning styles but not students with severe learning disabilities. 10-15% of the student body have learning disabilities." **Career apprenticeship programs:** The school assists students in finding internships on an individual basis.

## Student Conduct and Health

**Code of conduct:** Standard. **How school handles drug/alcohol usage:** Zero tolerance. For the first offense, the student's parent/guardian must attend a meeting on campus and obtain a drug evaluation by an outside specialist. If the evaluation concludes the student needs treatment, continued enrollment will be dependent on the student's successful completion of the program. Failure to meet the goals of the treatment, including sobriety, will result in immediate dismissal from the school. Designated smoking area off campus. **Drug/alcohol abuse prevention/AIDS awareness programs:** N/P.

## Summer Programs

None, as the school year runs on an extended year schedule of Sept.-July 1.

## Parent Involvement

**Parent participation:** Not required but solicited based on program needs. **Parent/teacher communication:** "Frequently and as needed." **Parent education:** "Regular phone contacts, conflict resolution sessions, written reports sent home four times each trimester.." **Donations:** N/P.

## SPORTS

All students are invited to participate in sports, including competitive sports, without the requirement of try-outs. Students compete in cross-country, basketball, volleyball, and track & field. The school is a member of the California Interscholastic Federation. The Nuba Dance Company rehearses in the school's dance studio—its founder is on the school's faculty.

## WHAT SETS SCHOOL APART FROM OTHERS

"Beacon is a small school that celebrates students' individual learning styles. The extended year and block scheduling allow in-depth learning. An integrated curriculum ensures that each class incorporates art and technology. Students have a lot of opportunities for individual expression. The school's technology program has been highly recognized. Beacon technology students are the only high schools students to win an Emmy—they were honored by NATAS Northern California Chapter at their 1996 Emmy Ceremony for work done to create an innovative CD-ROM. Beacon students also received a Silver Award in the International Invision Awards Competition sponsored by New Media Magazine for work on another CD-ROM. Beacon technology opportunities are supplemented through collaborative arrangement with Silicon Valley firms, including Silicon Graphics and Sun Microsystems."

## HOW PARENTS/STUDENTS CHARACTERIZE SCHOOL

**Parent response(s):** "It's the only extended-year high school in the country. Double-length class periods give kids sufficient time to explore subjects in depth. Student-teacher interaction is frequent. Individualism is encouraged. ... Beacon develops the whole child, not just the part that scores high on standardized tests (although Beacon students do score high on tests). ... Beacon is not for everyone. For example, those wanting to become high school football stars would not be satisfied. We wanted our son to start his high school career as a member of a positive, inspiring, intimate learning community, and at Beacon High, we found it."

**Student response(s):** "What are Beacon's strengths? Creative learning, feel[ing] physically and mentally safe ... classes based on student ideas and discussion."

"Beacon High treats students as individuals. Teachers care about you and how you're doing. They know it's not easy being a teenager and they help you along by tailoring your assignments to your particular style and pace."

"My old school building was like a giant cage. Beacon is really laid back and that's the good thing."

# BELLARMINE COLLEGE PREPARATORY

850 Elm Street
San Jose, CA 95126

(408) 294-9224 *fax (408) 294-1894*
www.bcp.org

Mark Pierotti, Principal
Bill Chambers, Director of Admission

## GENERAL

**Boys'** day high school. **Catholic** (Jesuit) (68% Catholic). Founded in 1851 at Santa Clara University. **Nonprofit. Enrollment:** Approximately 1,350. **Average class size:** 26. **Accreditation:** WASC (6-year term: 1996-02). **School year:** 9-month calendar (N/P re instructional days). **School day:** 8:30 a.m. to 2:15 p.m. **Location:** Near downtown San Jose. The College Park CalTrain station is on campus; the Light Rail stops nearby. Close to Highways 880, 280, and 101.

## STUDENT BODY

**Geographical breakdown (counties):** Approximately 75% from Santa Clara; 15% from San Mateo; 5% from Alameda; 5% from Santa Cruz. **Ethnicity:** Approx. 56% Caucasian (non-Latino); 11% Latino; 8.5% Filipino; 5% African-American; 5% Chinese; 2% Japanese; 1.5% Vietnamese; 1% Korean; 1% American Indian; other non-White 8%. **Foreign students (I-20 status):** N/P. **Single parent/two f/t working parent families:** N/P. **Middle schools:** Of the most recent entering freshman class, 50% came from 40 parochial schools; 10% from private, non-parochial schools. (N/P re rest)

## ADMISSION

**Applications due:** Approximately February 10 (call for date) for 9th grade applicants, May 1 for other grades. Decisions are mailed in late March for 9th grade, early June for other grades. **Application fee:** $55. **Application process:** In December, Bellarmine hosts an open house for seventh and eighth grade students and families. Eighth graders may make an appointment to shadow a current student for a day. Entrance exams are given in January and may be sent to all Diocese schools. The school shares teacher recommendation forms with other Diocese high schools. A clergy recommendation is not required. **No. of applications:** 1,030 applications were received for 360 places in prior year's class. Ten new students were admitted to G10, 4 to G11, and 2 to G12. **Admission cut-**

**off:** "Median test score and GPA of applicants: 82% nationally, 3.5 GPA." **Preferences:** Catholics. **"We are looking for** grades, test scores, recommendations, results of Diocese entrance exam, active involvement in parish, and ability to maintain academic excellence while demonstrating a high level of involvement in extracurricular activities." **What sort of student do you best serve?** "We serve the college-bound student who wishes to become involved in a variety of co-curricular activities, while also experiencing the benefits of Jesuit education. There is a family atmosphere here, and we hope that students will seek to give something back to the school."

## Costs

**Latest tuition:** $6,165 payable in 10 monthly payments. **Sibling discount:** None. **Tuition increases:** 5% annually. **Other costs:** Books. **Financial aid:** Financial aid is need-based and includes a work-grant component. ($1,000 grant requires student to work 33 hours, $2,000 grant, 66 hours.) **Percentage of students receiving financial aid:** 17%. **Average grant:** $2,500. **Grants of half-tuition or more:** 42%.

## School's Mission Statement/Goals

"Bellarmine College Preparatory is a community of men and women gathered together by God for the purpose of educating the student to seek justice and truth throughout his life. We are a Catholic school in the tradition of St. Ignatius of Loyola, the Founder of the Society of Jesus. As such, our entire school program is dedicated to forming 'men for others'—persons whose lives will be dedicated to bringing all their God-given talents to fullness and to live according to the pattern of service inaugurated by Jesus Christ."

## Academic Program

**Courses offered (H=Honors, AP=Advanced Placement, (H)=Honors option, (AP)=AP option): English:** English 1, English 2 (H), American Literature 1 & 2, Holocaust Literature, Modern Literature, Modern American Authors, Mythology of Wilderness 1 & 2, Creative Writing, English 4 H, Science Fiction, British Literature 1 & 2, The Short Story, Faulkner Seminar, Survey of Dramatic Literature, Shakespeare 1 & 2, Poetry and Prayer 1 & 2, Literature of the Counterculture, Creative Writing 2—Writing for Publication, Modern Gothic Literature, African-American Literature, Literature of Northern California, Literature of Latin America, Screen Writing, Literature of Media; **Social Science:** Global Studies, World History, US History (AP), US History Seminar H, Intro to Psychology, Psychology H, American Government, International Relations, Contemporary Eastern Europe, Conflict in the Modern World, Economics, California and the Southwest, The African-American Experience, Intro to Asian Studies; **Math:** Algebra 1 & 1 Accelerated, Geometry (H), Algebra 2 (H), Transition to College Math, Trigonometry, Pre-Calculus & Honors, Integrated Pre-Calculus/Physics H, Calculus, AP Calculus AB & BC, Probability and Statistics, Computer Science (AP), Business Computing; **Foreign Language:** Mandarin Chinese 1, 2, 3 (H), 4 (H), French 1, 2, 3, 4 (AP), Spanish 1, 2, 3 (H), 4 (AP), Latin 1, 2, 3, AP 4; **Science:** General Science, Biology (H, AP), Chemistry (H, AP), Integrated Physics/Pre-Calculus H, Physics H, Anatomy and Physiology, Geology, Environmental Science AP; **Religious Studies:** Intro to Catholic Christianity, Hebrew Scriptures, Christian Scriptures, Christian Morality, Social Justice/College Guidance, Comparative Religion, Prayer and Meditation, Marriage and Family, Contemporary Issues in Christianity, Liturgy Workshop, Confirmation, God's Planet: A Theology of Nature, Philosophy for the Believing Person, Ministry; **Fine Arts:** Fine Arts 1 & 2, Drawing, Ceramics 1 & 2, Art History, Mixed Media Sculpture, Music Appreciation 1 & 2, Acting, Concert Band, Jazz Improvisation for Vocal and Instrumental Music, Chorus, Landscape; **P.E.:** Physical Education 1, Advanced Physical Education. **Computer lab/training:** The school has IBMs and Macs; school computers are networked. (N/P re training) **Grading:** N/P. **Graduation requirements:** N/P. **Average nightly homework:** G9: 1.5 hours; G10-12: 2 hours. **Faculty:** 75% male, 25% female. 35% of faculty hold bachelor's degrees as highest degree; 60% hold master's degrees; and 5% hold doctorates. Twelve Jesuits are on the faculty. **Faculty ethnicity:** 91% Caucasian (non-Latino); 4% Latino; 3% Asian; 2% African-American. **Faculty selection/training:** "Faculty are selected from a large, highly competitive pool of applicants. Teachers are awarded enrichment grants during the summer. Teachers participate in in-services during the year." **Teacher/student ratio:** 1:17. **Teacher's daily student load in required academic subject:** "5 classes." **AP courses/exams:** In 1997, students took 325 AP examinations. 90% received scores of 3 or above. (N/P re # subjects, takers, % in AP courses) **Senior class profile (mean):** SAT Math 623, SAT Verbal 611. **GPA:** N/P. **National Merit Scholarship Program:** 20 National Merit Finalists. **College enrollment:** 93.5% of last year's graduating class enrolled in 4-year colleges or universities, 6% in 2-year colleges including: UC Berkeley (23), UC Davis (10), UC Irvine (5), UCLA (16), UC Santa Barbara (9), UC Riverside (5), UC San Diego (11), UC Santa Cruz (9), Cal Poly SLO (13), CSU-Chico (7), CSU-Humboldt (3), CSU-Sacramento (1), CSU-San Diego (11), CSU-San Francisco (3), CSU-San Jose (18), CSU-Stanislaus (1), C of the Holy Cross, Fordham, Georgetown (4), Gonzaga (3), Loyola Marymount (13), Santa Clara (39), Seattle U (2), USF, US Air Force Academy (2), US Air Force Academy Prep, US Military Academy West Point, US Naval Academy, US Naval Academy Prep, Northwestern Academy Prep, community colleges (27), Azusa Pacific U, California C of Arts and Crafts, California Lutheran U (2), Menlo C, Pomona, St. Mary's, Stanford (6), Thomas Aquinas C, U of San Diego, UOP (2), USC (11), Westmont C, Boston U (2), Brandeis, Brown, Clark Atlanta, Colorado State-Fort Collins, Columbia (3), Duke, Florida A&M, Harvard (2), Howard, Lewis & Clark, Morehouse (2), NYU, Northern Arizona, Northwestern, Rensselaer Polytechnic, St. Mary's (MD), Salve Regina U, Tulane, U of Arizona (4), U of Colorado-Boulder, U of Miami, U of Nevada-Reno, U of Oregon, U of Portland, U of Washington, Wesleyan, Whitman, and Yale.

## OTHER INDICATORS THE SCHOOL IS ACCOMPLISHING ITS GOALS

N/P.

## CAMPUS/CAMPUS LIFE

**Campus description:** The campus consists of 19 acres in a residential area of San Jose near The Alameda (an historic avenue). It includes classrooms and administration buildings; a Science Center; a 225-seat theater; Jesuit residence; new 40-meter pool; soccer, baseball, and football fields; and an all-weather track. A new chapel was completed in 1999. **Library**: 37,000 print volumes; 35 computers; open to students from 8 a.m. to 4 p.m. (N/P re study space, subscriptions, etc.) **Open/closed campus:** Closed. **Classroom space per student:** N/P. **Lunches:** "Available on campus." **Bus service:** None. **Uniform/dress code:** Dress code. **Co-curricular activities/clubs: Faith:** Agape/Campus Unity, Campus Ministry, Christian Life Community, Laudate Deum Fellowship; **Service-Oriented Clubs:** Block B Club, Community Service Core Group, Environmental Action Society, Immersion Program, Service Club; **Scholastic:** Bellarmine Tutorial Society, California Scholarship Federation, Chess Club, Computer Programming Club, Dead Language Society/Latin, French Club, Library Club, Literary Seminar, Mac Users Group, Math Club, National Forensic League, Science Fiction Club, Strategic Games Club; **Leadership:** Amnesty International, Democrats Club, Republican Club, Student Government/ASB, Yell Leaders; **Ethnic Clubs:** African-American Student Union, Asian Society, Filipino Student Association, Indian Student Coalition, Irish Club, Italian Brotherhood, Jewish Life Community, La Raza Unida, Vietnamese Brotherhood; **Arts:** Anime/Japanimation Club, Band: Pep/Concert/Jazz, Cardinal Newspaper, Choir, Club Mud/Ceramics/Arts, Film Watchers Association, Music & Music Appreciation, Photography Club, Highlander Poetry Club, Sanguine Humours/Improv, Theatre Arts, Theatre Tech Crew; **Athletics/Hobbies:** Auto Club, Billiards Club, Bowling Club, Fishing Club, Golf Club, Ice Hockey Club, Intramurals, International Soccer Club, Magicians Club, Mountain Bike Club, Ski Club, Student Athletic Trainers, Triathalon Club, Ultimate Frisbee Club. **Foreign exchange program:** None. **Opportunities for community service:** 100 hours required; opportunities include immersion trips to Mexico, El Salvador, Uruguay. **Typical freshman schedule:** 6 periods of 50-minute classes, with 5 classes per day: English I, math, foreign language, 1 semester social studies, 1 semester fine arts, religious studies, science.

## Student Support Services

Counselor/student ratio (not including college counselors): 1:130. **Counseling:** The school offers personal and academic counseling and has three full-time college and career counselors. **Learning disabilities/differences:** "A part-time counselor focuses specifically on working with students who have learning differences." **Career apprenticeship programs:** None.

## Student Conduct and Health

**Code of conduct:** Standard. **How school handles drugs/alcohol usage:** "Varies." **Drug/alcohol abuse prevention/AIDS awareness program:** Included in curriculum.

## Summer Programs

N/P.

## Parent Involvement

**Parent participation:** N/P. **Parent/teacher communication:** "Mentoring, parent-teacher conferences." **Parent education:** "Regular programs throughout the year focusing on drug and alcohol education, human sexuality, and parenting generally are provided by the school's counseling department." **Donations:** N/P.

## Sports

Boys compete through the WCAL in football, baseball, water polo, swimming, tennis, golf, track, cross-country, basketball, soccer, volleyball, and wrestling.

## What Sets School Apart From Others

"College prep environment on a Catholic, Jesuit campus. We emphasize educating the whole person: mind, heart, spirit, body, imagination."

## How Parents/Students Characterize School

N/P.

*Illustration by Bentley student Sabina Paradi*

# BENTLEY SCHOOL

1000 Upper Happy Valley Road
Lafayette, CA 94549

(925) 283-2101 *fax (925)299-0469*
bheim@bentlaf.org

Robert A. Munro, Head of School
Pat Finlayson, Director of Admissions, (510) 843-2512
William H. Heim, III, Director of Upper School

## GENERAL

**Coed** day high school. (The school's K-8 campus is located at 1 Hiller Drive in Oakland.) **Nonsectarian.** The K-8 school was founded in 1920. The high school, begun in 1998 with grades 9-10, will be adding grade 11 in 1999-00 and 12 in 2000-01. **Nonprofit,** member CAIS, NAIS. **Enrollment:** Currently 80. The school has capacity for entering freshmen classes of 80 students. **Average class size:** 10. **Accreditation:** "Candidate for accreditation; approved by the Schools Commission of the WASC (Western Association of Schools and Colleges, Accrediting Commission for Schools, 533 Airport Blvd., Suite 200, Burlingame, CA 94101/Phone (650) 696-1060)." **School year:** 10-month calendar (approx.

175 instructional days). **School day:** 8 a.m. to 3:15 p.m. **Location:** Just off Highway 24 in Lafayette, a suburb 5 miles east of Oakland, 10 miles east of San Francisco. Shuttles pick up students at the Rockridge BART station and other locations.

## STUDENT BODY

**Geographical breakdown (counties):** 50% from Alameda County; 50% from Contra Costa. **Ethnicity:** 64% Caucasian (non-Latino); 32% Asian; 4% African-American. **Foreign students (I-20 status):** 0. **Single parent/two f/t working parent families:** N/P. **Middle schools:** 33% of the latest freshman class came from the school's own lower school; 33% from public middle schools; 33% from private non-parochial schools. (N/P re # schools)

## ADMISSION

**Applications due:** Late January (call for exact date). **Application fee:** $40. **Application process:** The school hosts open houses from November through January. Applicants are interviewed by a member of the Admissions Committee and submit transcripts, past test scores, and teacher recommendations. Applicants must write an essay and take the ISEE. Decisions are mailed mid-March. **No. of applications:** 94 applications were received for 45 places in the first freshman class. 10 new students were admitted to G 10. **Admission cut-off:** None. **Preferences:** None. **"We are looking for** individuals who want to challenge themselves to constantly extend their limits." **What sort of student do you best serve?** "Students with average to high abilities who are serious about improving themselves both academically and as individuals."

## COSTS

**Latest tuition:** $13,780. **Sibling discount:** None. **Tuition increases:** Approximately 5% annually. **Other costs:** $300-$500. **Percentage of students receiving financial aid:** 16%. **Average grant:** $7,500. **No. of full tuition grants:** 0. **Grants of half-tuition or more:** 55%.

## SCHOOL'S MISSION STATEMENT/GOALS

"Statement of Purpose: Bentley School is a coeducational day school providing a quality education for children with high potential who come from families who are supportive of our goals. We serve the various communities of the East Bay and strive to reflect in our population the diverse socio-economic and multicultural composition of these communities.

"Our primary goal is to teach fundamental skills and develop understanding in the traditional academic areas of English, mathematics, the sciences and social studies. Balance in the curriculum is maintained by providing courses in art, music, drama, physical education and foreign languages. Students are encouraged to use the computer as an important tool in the learning and research process. We focus on the development of thinking and reasoning skills to lead to age appropriate analysis and synthesis. Study habits are developed which help students transition from a relatively directed to an independent learning environment. The school maintains a low student-teacher ratio and provides a broad and challenging curriculum across all grade levels.

"In addition to providing a stimulating academic program, students' social skills and values are enhanced in a climate of mutual trust and friendship. Students are expected to meet obligations; to honor promises; to fulfill responsibilities; to understand and respect the rights, uniqueness and individuality of others; and to think about what is 'right' and 'wrong.' The Bentley experience is nurturing, promotes self-improvement and encourages a spirit of caring and respect for people and our environment."

## ACADEMIC PROGRAM

"Bentley's mission is to prepare students for success in the ever-shrinking global community of the 21st century. Inherent in this mission is the school's commitment to a rigorous, traditional college preparatory curriculum. During the first two years in the upper school, all students generally take a predetermined set of core courses. Those courses are designed to prepare students for the more demanding junior and senior years when students have the opportunity to undertake advanced placement work in a variety of areas. Seniors may pursue course work at a local university. Students graduate with a regular college preparatory diploma, or with an honors or high honors diploma." **Courses offered (AP=Advanced Placement, H=Honors, (AP)=AP option, (H)=Honors option): English:** American Literature, British Literature, Public Speaking, Classical Literature, World Literature, AP Literature & Composition, AP Language and Composition, Creative Writing, African American Literature, Shakespeare, Poetry; **Math:** Algebra I, Geometry, Algebra II (H), Pre-Calculus (H), AP Calculus (AB & BC), Descriptive Statistics, Applied Statistics; **History:** Modern European History, US History (AP), 20th Century World History, Ancient & Medieval History, AP European History, Theory of Knowledge, Asian Studies, American Foreign Policy (1945-present), AP Comparative Government, AP Economics; **Computer Science:** Computer Literacy I-II, Advanced Computer Literacy, AP Computer Science; **Science:** Biology (AP), Chemistry (AP), Physics (AP), (B or C) Conceptual Physics, Marine Biology, Environmental Science; **Social Science:** Introduction to Psychology, Leadership; **Foreign Language:** Spanish and French through AP Spanish and French Language, AP Spanish and French Literature, Latin I through AP Latin; **Art/Performing Arts:** Introduction to Visual Art, Art II, Art History, Drawing and Painting, AP Art History, AP Music Theory, Acting, Introduction to Theater Arts, Introduction to Musical Arts, Chorus, Music Theory, Jazz Ensemble, Chamber Music Ensemble, Ceramics, Sculpture. **Spe-**

**cial programs:** A Mini-Semester Week, held each winter, allows students to take courses outside the traditional curriculum. Examples: "Life with Picasso," "A History of 20th Century Sport," "Greek Comedy Central," and "Web Page Design." **Computer lab/training:** The school has two computer labs with PCs. (N/P re #) **Grading:** A-F. **Graduation requirements:** 22 credits and a GPA of 2.0 minimum, including 4.5 years English (public speaking, American and British literature required), 4 years history (US and 20th Century World History required), 3 years science (chemistry, biology, and physics required), 3 years language, 2 years art, 6 seasons physical activity, 60 hours community service, senior essay, and computer literacy. **Average nightly homework (Mon-Th):** G9-10: 30-40 min. per class; G11-12: 40-50 min. per class. **Faculty:** Of the 10 full-time faculty members, 50% are male, 50% female. 50% hold master's degrees, 25% hold doctoral degrees. **Faculty ethnicity:** 88% Caucasian (non-Latino); 12% Latino. **Faculty selection/training:** "Faculty is selected based upon experience (primarily in independent schools), educational preparation (degree must be held in subject area taught), ability to contribute to extra-curricular program, and ability to fulfill responsibilities as an advisor to 7-9 students. The school has in-services, continuing education and summer workshops for teachers." **Teacher/student ratio:** 1:7. **Teacher's daily student load in required academic subject:** 45. **AP courses and exams:** (Not applicable since the school at press time had only 9th and 10th graders.) **Senior class profile (mean):** N/A. **National Merit Scholarship Program:** N/A. **College enrollment:** N/A.

## OTHER INDICATORS THE SCHOOL IS ACCOMPLISHING ITS GOALS

"In its first year, the Upper School division received recognition from students and parents for its strong academic program, diverse extra-curricular activities, and exemplary advisee program. The school is further recognized for its solid sense of caring and community."

## CAMPUS/CAMPUS LIFE

**Campus description:** The campus is located in the community of Lafayette on a 12-acre campus abutting the north side of Highway 24. The campus has four new buildings which house classrooms, science labs, an art studio, library, computer lab, and offices. A fifth building is dedicated to music. The outdoor area includes a soccer field and basketball facilities. Tennis courts are anticipated during the 1999-2000 year. The school has landscaped grounds with a central courtyard that provides informal seating for socializing and study. **Library:** 2,000 sq. ft.; 4,000 print volumes; 30 periodical subscriptions; 16 computers (all with Internet access); 8 CD-ROMs; on-line catalog; study space for 36 students. Open to students from 7:30 a.m. to 5 p.m.; full-time librarian. **Closed campus. Classroom space per student:** 30 sq.ft. **Lunches:** Hot lunches are available daily. **Bus service:** Private van service from Rockridge BART station and other locations.

**Uniforms/dress code:** "The dress code requires that clothing be whole, clean and appropriate for the classroom. Students are permitted to wear jeans." **Co-curricular activities/clubs:** Sports, drama, music, literary magazine, yearbook, and student council. **Foreign exchange program:** None at this time. **Opportunities for community service:** 60 hours required for graduation. Students fulfill this requirement by working with the Community Service Coordinator to identify appropriate projects. **Typical freshman schedule:** 7 periods of approximately 50 minutes each. A typical day could include Classical Literature, Ancient & Medieval History, Geometry, Physics, foreign language and a class in theater, art, and/or music.

## STUDENT SUPPORT SERVICES

**Counselor/student ratio:** 1:8. **Counseling:** Each student is assigned a faculty advisor who acts as a personal counselor as well as an academic advisor. Teachers engage in tutoring as do peer tutors. The school has a full-time college counselor. **Learning disabilities/differences:** No special programs. **Career apprenticeship programs:** None.

## STUDENT CONDUCT AND HEALTH

**Code of conduct:** Standard. **How school handles drug/alcohol usage:** "Zero tolerance." **Drug/alcohol abuse prevention/AIDS awareness programs:** N/P.

## SUMMER PROGRAMS

Yes. (Contact school.)

## PARENT INVOLVEMENT

**Parent participation:** Parents are invited to participate in a Parents' Advisory Council. **Parent/teacher communication:** N/P. **Parent education:** N/P. **Donations:** Families are requested to contribute to the school's Annual Giving Fund.

## SPORTS

Students participate in the Bay Counties League. Currently the school offers girls' tennis, basketball, soccer, crew, volleyball, and cross-country. Boys' sports include tennis, basketball, soccer, crew, baseball, and cross-country.

## Other

"All entering students participate in a retreat just prior to the beginning of classes in September. The retreat provides the opportunity for students to discuss high school, socialize, meet teachers, and participate in outdoor activities, including river rafting, a ropes course, swimming, and hiking."

## What Sets School Apart From Others

1) Traditional, core-centered/focused approach to the academic curriculum.
2) Strong emphasis on the development of the students' nonacademic talents.
3) Strong emphasis on the importance of integrity (student "directed" Honor Code) and a sense of community.

## How Parents/Students Characterize School

N/P.

# The Branson School

P.O. Box 887
Ross, CA 94957

(415) 454-3612 *fax (415) 454-4669*
www.branson.org

Richard P. Fitzgerald, Headmaster
Bridget N. Anderson, Director of Admissions

## General

**Coed** day high school. **Nonsectarian.** Founded as the San Rafael Girls' School in 1916. **Nonprofit**, member CAIS, NAIS, BAIHS. **Enrollment: 320. Average class size:** 14. **Accreditation:** WASC/CAIS (6-year term: 1999-05). **School year:** N/P. **School day:** 8 a.m. to 3 p.m., M, W, Th; 2:10 p.m. dismissal Tuesday, and 2:20 p.m. Friday. **Location:** The Branson School is located in the town of Ross, 15 miles north of San Francisco.

## Student Body

**Geographical breakdown (most recent entering class):** 9% from San Francisco; 5% from East Bay; 7.5% from Novato area; remainder from Marin. **Eth-**

**nic breakdown (most recent entering class):** 88% Caucasian (non-Latino); 6% African-American; 5% Asian; 1% Latino. **Foreign students (I-20 status):** N/P. **Single parent/two f/t working parent families:** N/P. **Middle schools:** "Branson accepted students last year from 22 feeder schools in Marin, San Francisco, Contra Costa, Alameda, and Sonoma Counties and from Brazil." (N/P re #, type schools)

## Admission

**Applications due:** Approximately January 20 (call for date). **Application fee:** $100. **Application process:** Inquiries should be made when the student is in the 8th grade. The school hosts open houses in October and December. Interested students should schedule a tour and interview in the fall of their 8th grade year. Students must take the SSAT. Notifications are mailed mid-March. **No. of applications:** 450+ applications were received for 80 places in prior year's class. Six new students were admitted to G10, 4 to G11. **Admission cut-off:** "We look for students who are academically motivated, have a strong academic history, and who truly want to be part of and can contribute to our community." **Preferences:** N/P. **"We are looking for** students who are highly academically motivated, who can benefit from the Branson School program and can contribute to the community, who can be successful in academic and extracurricular activities, and who have a serious desire to attend the school." **What sort of student do you best serve?** "Students who are passionate about learning; solid academic students who are bright and ready for a rigorous academic program; students who have pursued outside interests (*i.e.*, sports, fine arts, community service, etc.)."

## Costs

**Latest tuition:** $15,500 payable in a $1,000 deposit in March, and payment of $10,625 in June and $3,825 in January. **Sibling discount:** None. **Tuition increases:** Approximately 7% annually. **Other costs:** $1,000 for books, dues, cultural and social events. Additional charges for private music lessons and special outdoor trips. **Financial aid:** Need-based financial aid is available. Nearly $500,000 in scholarship funds were awarded to 49 students for 1998-99. **Percentage of students receiving financial aid:** 15%. **Average grant:** $11,500. **No. of full-tuition grants:** N/P. **Grants of half-tuition or more:** 81%.

## School's Mission Statement/Goals

School philosophy: "The Branson School dedicates itself to the full development of the individual student in preparation for the challenges of higher education and life. We promote enduring habits of intellectual curiosity, appreciation for the arts and physical fitness, and respect for the self and others. We emphasize integrity, honesty, and the development of moral and ethical principles as a framework for responsible behavior at Branson and beyond. The Branson program is dedicated to the development of students' intellect and creativity. We acknowledge that students have different capacities and learn in different ways. Students develop their own strengths as learners and emphasis is placed on each student achieving his or her potential. We foster habits of inquiry, independent thinking, and imagination through a rich and rigorous curriculum. In creating music, dance, theater, and visual arts, Branson students experience spontaneity and self-discovery. We encourage physical fitness, team spirit, and sportsmanship through a strong physical education and sports program. Extracurricular activities and community service teach students to exercise leadership and to work cooperatively toward shared goals. We value and celebrate fairness, generosity, compassion, and courtesy. The essence of Branson is a deep respect for every individual, regardless of cultural, racial, and philosophical differences. Service to causes greater than self is a natural outgrowth of this respect for the individual. We recognize that the accomplishment of our goals requires a partnership of students, faculty, and parents; we work hard at nurturing this cooperative effort. Our intent is that students leave Branson strong in character, well-prepared for other education, determined to develop fully their own gifts, and ready to share those gifts generously with the wider community."

# ACADEMIC PROGRAM

**Courses offered (AP=Advanced Placement, H=Honors; (AP)=AP option, (H)= Honors option): Technology:** Introduction to Technology, Advanced Technology, Electronic Publishing, Web Page Design, Multimedia Content Creation, Computer Programming; **English:** English I-II, British Literature I-III Honors, Dramatic Literature I: Shakespeare, Dramatic Literature II: Modern, Dramatic Literature III: Contemporary, American Literature I-III H, 20th Century Fiction I-III, World Literature I-III H, European Literature, Fundamentals of English, Modern Poetry, Modern Poetry: the American Experience, Writing Workshop, Watching Film Like Reading Literature, AP Workshop; **Arts:** Chorus, Chamber Singers, Junior Combo, Senior Combo, Big Band, Orchestra/Advanced Chamber Ensemble, private instruction, Dance II-IV, Dance Performance, Boys' Dance, Advanced Acting, AP Art History, Drawing and Painting I-III, Ceramics I-III, Photography I-III, History of Photography, Painting I-III, Modern Design, A World of Art History, Folk Art of Many Cultures, Fundamentals of Music, Music Theory I-II, Synthesizer/Multi-track I-III, History of Jazz, Romantic Movement in Music, Music of the 20th Century, Music of the 18th Century, Acting I-III, History of Modern Dance, Strong Women, Strong Men, Theater of the Avant Garde, Art of Comedy, Sharing the Arena: Theater and Politics; **Languages:** French I-II, French III H, French IV AP Culture and Composition, AP French Literature, 20th-Century French Literature, German I-II, German III H, AP German IV, AP German H, German V H, Japanese I-II, Japanese III H, Latin I-II, Latin III H, Spanish I-II, Spanish III H, Spanish IV AP Culture and

Composition, AP Hispanic Literature; **History:** Roots of Civilization, US History and Civics H, AP Modern European History, AP American Government and Politics, AP Comparative Government, Punji Stake: Vietnam I-II, African-American History, Comparative Religions, Europe Between the Wars, History of Philosophy, History of Japan, History of South Africa, History of Russia, Golden Ages, History of Latin America, Post WWII US History through 1960s; **Math:** Algebra I, Algebra I/Geometry, Geometry, Geometry/Algebra II, Algebra II, Computer Programming, Pre-Calculus (H), AP Statistics, AP Calculus AB, AP Calculus BC; **Other:** Independent Study, Freshman Seminar, Psychology Seminar, The World of Business; **P.E.:** P.E. 9, Recreational Sports, Interscholastic Sports, Dance, Alternate Activity Program (other sports); **Science:** Environmental Science, Biology, Chemistry (H, AP), Physics (H, AP), Advanced Astrophysics, AP Biology, Human Biology, Conceptual Physical Science, Marine Biology. **Computer lab/training:** The school has a computer lab with 20 Mac computers. All freshmen take two trimesters of Introduction to Technology. **Grading:** A-F. Teachers write progress reports twice a year, or more often for students experiencing difficulty. **Graduation requirements:** 4 years English, 3 years math, 2 years lab science, 3 years of one foreign language, 2 years history, 2 years fine arts, (3 years history and science and 4 years math and foreign language recommended); community service. Each student must be enrolled in at least 4 academic solids each trimester. The school recommends that sophomores and junior carry a minimum of 5. **Average nightly homework:** G9: 1.5 hours; G10: 2.5 hours; G11-12: 2.5 to 3-4. **Faculty:** Of the 37 full-time and 5 part-time faculty members, 22 are women, 20 are men. 19 hold bachelor's degrees as highest degree; 16 hold master's degrees; and 2 hold doctorates. **Faculty ethnicity:** "22% of the Branson teachers are 'teachers of color.'" **Faculty selection/training:** "Candidates come to this school from a variety of sources: application on file, personal recommendations, placement agencies, referrals, job fairs, advertising. The Department Head begins the process with a telephone interview. Promising candidates visit the campus, preferably teach a class and are interviewed by faculty and administrators. Our professional development budget is growing. Our Head has taken a strong position encouraging progressive growth." **Teacher/student ratio:** 1:8. **Teacher's daily student load in required academic subject:** N/P. **AP courses/exams:** 83% of seniors took AP courses. (N/P re AP exam scores) **Senior class profile (mean):** SAT Math median score 626, SAT Verbal median score 604. (N/P re mean scores) (Mean SAT II scores were 606 in writing and 614 in math.) **GPA:** N/P. **National Merit Scholarship Program:** Ten students in the class of 1997-98 were National Merit Scholars; all ten were named semi-finalists; two were awarded National Merit Scholarships. **College enrollment:** 100% of the class of 1999 enrolled in 4-year universities including Barnard, Bates, Boston U, Brown, Carnegie-Mellon, Claremont McKenna, Colby, Dominican (San Rafael), Emory, Duke, George Washington, Georgetown, Harvard, Haverford, Kenyon, Loyola Marymount, Middlebury, Mt. Holyoke, NYU, Pepperdine, Princeton, Santa Clara, Scripps, Stanford, Tufts, Tulane, UCLA, UC Santa Barbara, UC Davis, UC Berkeley, UC San Diego, UC Santa Cruz, U of Colorado-Boulder, U of Denver, UOP, U of Arizona, U of Pennsylvania, U of Portland, USC, U of Utah, Vanderbilt, Wellesley, Wesleyan, Wheaton, Williams, and Yale.

## OTHER INDICATORS THE SCHOOL IS ACCOMPLISHING ITS GOALS
N/P.

## CAMPUS/CAMPUS LIFE

**Campus description:** The school is located on the site of a former estate and dairy farm in Ross, a small, residential town in a wooded area 15 miles north of San Francisco. The 17-acre campus, nearly hidden by oak trees and foliage, includes twelve buildings, a new gymnasium complex, a playing field, pool, art gallery, tennis courts, and an auditorium and theater. The campus has the feel of a small village with tile-roofed, cottage-style buildings clustered around common areas where students gather and study. **Library**: N/P. **Open/closed campus:** N/P. **Classroom space per student:** N/P. **Lunches:** N/P. **Bus service:** N/P. **Uniforms/dress code:** None. **Co-curricular activities/clubs:** N/P. **Foreign exchange program:** N/P. **Opportunities for community service:** N/P. **Typical freshman schedule:** Introduction to Western Tradition and British Literature, Roots of Civilization, Algebra I or Algebra/Geometry, Environmental Science or Biology Honors, foreign language (French, Spanish, Latin, German or Japanese), Fine Arts, Introduction to Technology, P.E.

## STUDENT SUPPORT SERVICES

**Counselor/student ratio (not including college counselors):** 1:320. **Counseling:** A full-time licensed therapist is available to counsel students. College counseling begins the sophomore year with advisee groups preparing to take the PSAT and SAT II; in junior year, students take the PSAT in October, and meet with the college counselor in advisee groups and individually. College representatives visit the school in the fall and families attend informational meetings and meet with the college counselor. Seniors meet with college representatives, and take the SATs; families and/or students meet the counselor to prepare applications. **Learning differences/disabilities:** "The Allen Rand Center was established by a Branson family to serve as an on-campus resource for students. Staffed by a trained learning specialist, the Rand Center is a quiet study area, a place for small group study sessions, and one-on-one tutorials and extended time testing." **Career apprenticeship programs:** "Though the school does not get involved personally to find the students summer work, the College Counselor is active in suggesting summer programs for our students. A summer activities bulletin board keeps current announcements and brochures advertising summer opportunities."

## STUDENT CONDUCT AND HEALTH

**Code of conduct:** A judicial counsel of students and faculty members suggests effective disciplinary measures to the Headmaster. The Senate, composed of class officers and elected faculty, decides issues of improper conduct, including rule-breaking. **How school handles drugs/alcohol usage:** "Advisory Committee for Drugs and Alcohol (ACODA)." **Drug/alcohol abuse prevention/AIDS awareness programs:** N/P.

## SUMMER PROGRAMS

The school has a six-week summer session for students entering G6-12. Classes, camps, and workshops are offered including computer, driver's ed, SAT prep, art, languages, and science. Tutoring is available in almost all school disciplines. Recent offerings include Technology Camp, Softball Pitching Clinic, Jewelry Making, and Marin Shakespeare Young Company. **Cost:** Approximately $495 per course (or $585 for credit). (Discount for additional courses.)

## PARENT INVOLVEMENT

**Parent participation:** N/P. **Parent/teacher communication:** "Progress reports two times a year, conversations with Dean and teachers." **Parent education:** "Each class Dean and grade level mentors invite parents to an evening coffee at the beginning of the school year. Plans for the year, as well as issues specific to the grade level are discussed. Throughout the year, the Parents' Association invites both faculty, administration and speakers from the community to present information on topics of interest to the school." **Donations:** "Annual fundraisers, etc."

## SPORTS

More than 85% of the student body participates in one or more sport. The school has more than 25 interscholastic teams in 14 sports including: for boys and girls, soccer, tennis, volleyball, cross-country, swimming, badminton, and basketball; for girls, softball; and for boys, lacrosse. Also offered are fencing, crew, horseback riding, martial arts, aerobics, and golf. The girls' soccer team scored #1 in the nation in 1996.

## WHAT SETS SCHOOL APART FROM OTHERS

N/P.

## HOW PARENTS/STUDENTS CHARACTERIZE SCHOOL

N/P.

# BRIDGEMONT HIGH SCHOOL

777 Brotherhood Way
San Francisco, CA 94132

(415) 333-7600 *fax (415) 333-7603*

Dr. Wilbur F. Martin, Administrator
Kimberly Brackett, Director of Admissions, (415) 582-0142

## GENERAL

**Coed** day high school and junior high. **Independent Christian.** Founded in 1974. **Nonprofit,** member BAIHS. **Enrollment:** Approximately 100. **Average class size:** 15. **Accreditation:** WASC/ACSI (6-year term: 1996-02). **School year:** N/P. **School day:** 8:20 a.m. to 3:10 p.m. **Location:** The school is located 1/4 mile west of 19th Avenue on Brotherhood Way, near Park Merced and San Francisco State University.

## STUDENT BODY

**Geographical breakdown:** 68% from San Francisco; 26% from Northern Peninsula; 6% from East Bay. **Ethnicity:** 35% Caucasian (non-Latino); 22% Asian; 20% Latino; 20% African-American; 3% other. **Foreign students (I-20 status):** 10%. **Single parent families:** 30%. **Two f/t working parent families:** 60%. **Middle schools:** 50% of the most recent entering freshman class came from public middle schools and 50% from private, non-parochial schools. (N/P re schools) A good number of students come from Fellowship Academy (San Francisco), West Portal Lutheran School (San Francisco), Church of the Highlands (San Bruno), and Hilldale School (Daly City).

## ADMISSION

**Applications due:** Rolling admission. **Application fee:** $40 ($100 for foreign I-20 status application). **Application process:** The school requires a completed application, past years' transcripts, most recent standardized tests (TOEFL may be required for foreign students), and current recommendations from a principal or counselor, math teacher and English teacher. **No. of applications:** 43 applications were received for 30 places in prior year's class. Of these, 9 places were taken by the school's middle school students. Three new students were admitted to G10, 1 to G11 and 1 to G12. **Admission cut-off:** "For admission, students must have a GPA of 2.0 or higher and average to above-average standardized test scores." **Preferences:** Siblings. **"We are looking for** college-bound students seeking to develop their skills in leadership and communication through a rigorous program of academics and extracurricular activities." **What sort of student do you best serve?** N/P.

# Costs

**Latest tuition:** $5,559 ($3,774 for jr. high) payable annually, semi-annually, or monthly. **Sibling discount:** 10%. **Tuition increases:** 10%-15% annually (though there was no increase in the past year). **Other costs:** Registration and fees are $1,100 for senior high, $950 for junior high (includes a 1-week field studies program). **Financial aid:** Financial aid is based on a combination of demonstrated financial need and academic GPA (2.5 minimum is required). **Percentage of students receiving financial aid:** 20%. **Average grant:** $1,000. **No. of full-tuition grants:** 1. **Grants of half-tuition or more:** 5%.

# School's Mission Statement/Goals

"Bridgemont provides a college preparatory high school curriculum and an academic middle school that is committed to Christ-centered, biblically-based education focused on the development of the whole person."

# Academic Program

"The curricular and extracurricular programs and activities of Bridgemont are designed to prepare students for their academic and career pursuits. The school is committed to the provision of this program in the framework and atmosphere of Christian love, discipline, and ethics, built on the foundation of Biblical truth.

"The Bridgemont student is provided with a required and elective program that meets the State of California graduation requirements as well as the entry requirements of the California State University and University of California systems. The school is committed to cultivating and developing the God-given talents and abilities of each student so that each might have the opportunity to know and to serve God as a responsible, productive citizen." **Courses offered (AP=Advanced Placement, H=Honors; (AP)=AP option, (H)=Honors option):** English 1-4, English Literature, American Literature, World Literature, AP English Literature, US History, Government and Economics, AP Economics, World Studies 1-4, Algebra 1-4, Geometry 1-2, Biology 1-2, Spanish 1-4, French 1-6, Bible Survey 1-4, Study Skills, Field Studies, Yearbook/Photography, Pre-Calculus 1-2, Calculus 1-2, Earth Science 1-2, Chemistry 1-2, Chemistry in the Community, AP Environmental Science, Physics 1-2, Art 1-6, Wood Art, Drama, Sports P.E., Health, Keyboarding/Introduction to Computers, Computer Programming, Cooking, Library, Office or Teacher's Aide. **Computer lab/training:** N/P. **Grading:** N/P. **Graduation requirements:** 4 years English, 3 years history, 3 years math, 3 years science, 2 years foreign language, 1 year fine arts, 4 years P.E., 4 years Bible. **Average nightly homework:** 2 hours. **Faculty:** 60% male, 40% female. 80% hold bachelor's degrees as highest degree; 15% hold master's degrees; 5% hold doctorates. **Faculty ethnicity:** 90% Caucasian (non-Latino); 10% Asian. **Faculty selection/training:** Teachers must have a California credential or must have a BA degree (minimum) and be actively working toward a credential. (N/P re training) **Teacher/student ratio:** 1:7. **Teacher's daily student load in required academic subject:** N/P. **AP courses/exams:** The school has just begun offering AP courses. **Senior class profile (mean):** SAT Math 483, SAT Verbal 473. **GPA:** 3.12. **National Merit Scholarship Program:** N/P. **College enrollment:** 70% of last year's graduating class enrolled in 4-year colleges, 20% in 2-year colleges, including: USF, CSU-SF, UC Berkeley, Cal Poly, Notre Dame, SF City C, and C of San Mateo.

# OTHER INDICATORS THE SCHOOL IS ACCOMPLISHING ITS GOALS

N/P.

# CAMPUS/CAMPUS LIFE

**Campus description:** In January, 1999, the school relocated to Brotherhood Way, a street in the Park Merced area of San Francisco lined with several churches and schools. The school leases two wings of a one-story building attached to the Church of Christ and has access to its chapel. The school's space includes 11 classrooms, offices, a library, and a large cafeteria/multipurpose room. It utilizes nearby public and private parks and gyms for its athletic program. Current plans include installing portables to house an expanded library, classrooms, and science labs. **Library:** 8,000 print volumes; 2 computers; 13 periodical subscriptions; Internet access forthcoming. Study space for 30. Open to students 7:30 a.m. to 4 p.m. Part-time librarian. (N/P re sq. ft.) **Open/closed campus:** Closed. **Classroom space per student:** N/P. **Lunches:** A Student Council-run concession stand is open daily during breaks and lunch period. **Bus service:** Public bus access. **Uniform/dress code:** Dress code. **Co-curricular activities/clubs:** Activities include Student Council, Field Studies, Drama Club, Art Club, Choir, Athletics, City Escape, and Annual Boat Races. **Foreign exchange program:** None. **Opportunities for community service:** Bible classes have community service opportunities throughout the year. Other ministry opportunities include chapel offering projects and a junior high ministry team that reaches out to inner-city children with drama, music, puppet teams and multi-media presentations. **Typical freshman schedule:** English 1-2, Algebra 1-2 or Geometry 1-2, World Studies 1-2, Study Skills, P.E./Health, Bible and electives.

## STUDENT SUPPORT SERVICES

**Counselor/student ratio (not including college counselors):** 1:75. **Counseling:** The school provides academic, college, and career counseling. An after-school tutor is available free of charge two days per week. All teachers remain on campus until 4 p.m. and are available to students. **Learning differences/disabilities:** "No special programs or resources although the small class size and availability of teachers for one hour after school enables students with minor learning differences/disabilities to succeed." **Career apprenticeship programs:** "The college and career counselor posts job opportunities on a student bulletin board. Personal recommendations are also given."

## STUDENT CONDUCT AND HEALTH

**Code of conduct:** Standard. **How school handles drugs/alcohol usage:** Immediate expulsion. **Drug/alcohol abuse prevention/AIDS awareness program:** Included in health curriculum.

## SUMMER PROGRAMS

None.

## PARENT INVOLVEMENT

**Parent participation:** Parents are required to give twenty volunteer hours per year or $300. The school has an active Parent-Teacher Association. **Parent/teacher communication:** Teachers communicate grade deficiencies through regular progress reports and phone calls. Mid-term parent-teacher conferences are strongly encouraged. **Parent education:** Parents are invited to a college planning seminar. **Donations:** Encouraged but not required.

## SPORTS

Junior high through varsity sports (boys' and girls'), include basketball, soccer, and volleyball. (CYO league championships last year in boys' volleyball and junior high girls' basketball.)

## WHAT SETS SCHOOL APART FROM OTHERS

"The school's small size allows all students to participate in sports and extracurricular activities such as school plays and student government. Its small class size ensures individual attention. It is one of only 29 schools in California that has a dual ACSI/WASC accreditation."

## How Parents/Students Characterize School

"Family atmosphere."

# Castilleja School

1310 Bryant Street
Palo Alto, CA 94301

(650) 328-3160 *fax (650) 326-8036*
www.castilleja.org
info@castilleja.org

Joan Lonergan, Head of School
Jill Lee, Director of Admission and Financial Aid

## General

Girls' day high school and middle school. **Nonsectarian.** Founded in 1907. **Nonprofit**, member CAIS, NAIS, BAIHS. **Enrollment**: 385. **Average class size:** 15 for middle school, 14 for high school. **Accreditation**: WASC/CAIS (6-year term: 1997-03). **School year**: 9-month calendar. (N/P re # instructional days) **Location:** Castilleja is located in Palo Alto, near Stanford University. It has a van service to and from the Palo Alto University Avenue CalTrain station. Car pool lists are made available to the parent body. Some parents have contracted a van service in certain residential areas, although the school does not take responsibility for the service.

## Student Body

**Geographical breakdown (counties):** Majority from San Mateo and Santa Clara; 4% from East Bay; 1% from San Francisco. **Ethnicity:** Approximately 68% Caucasian (non-Latino); 23% Asian-American (including Indo-American); 5% African-American; 3% Latino. **Percentage foreign students (I-20 status):** 1%. **Single parent families:** 3%. **Two f/t working parent families:** 60%. **Middle schools:** 56% of the most recent entering freshman class came from Castilleja's middle school; of new freshmen, 56% were from public middle schools, 27% from private, non-parochial schools, and 15% from parochial schools. (N/P re # schools)

# ADMISSION

**Applications due:** Call for date, generally January. **Application fee:** $50. **Application process:** Student and parent questionnaires, teacher recommendations, standardized testing, transcripts, on-campus interviews. Details are provided in the admission packet. **No. of applications:** "Four applications were received for every opening in prior year's class." Castilleja does not admit new students to G12. **Admission cut-off:** "We do not have an absolute cut-off. Typically admitted students have earned primarily A's and B's." **Preferences:** "We value the relationships we have developed with current families, and, to that end, siblings are given special consideration in the admission process. As with all applicants, the sibling candidate must be a strong student and good citizen in order to gain admission to Castilleja." **"We are looking for** self-motivated, enthusiastic learners who will both contribute to and benefit from our community." **What sort of students do you best serve?** "Castilleja students are curious, motivated students who possess a sincere eagerness to learn and an understanding of the advantages of a single-sex educational environment."

# COSTS

**Latest tuition:** $15,200 payable in two installments, generally, although a 10-month payment plan is available. **Sibling discount:** None. **Tuition increases:** 5-7% annually. **Other costs:** $300-500; $200 for uniforms. **Financial aid:** Tuition assistance is offered based upon need and does not negatively affect the admission decision. **Percentage of students receiving financial aid:** 13%. **Average grant:** $8,500. **No. of full-tuition grants:** "It is the school's philosophy that every family contributes something, although the amount encompasses a broad range." **Grants of half-tuition or more:** 61%.

# SCHOOL'S MISSION STATEMENT/GOALS

"Castilleja School educates young women by fostering their intellectual, physical, creative, and emotional growth through an exemplary college preparatory experience within a diverse and supportive community. By blending tradition with thoughtful innovation, the curriculum encourages both individual achievement and collaborative learning. Castilleja's comprehensive program promotes the development of character, compassion, curiosity, and the capacity for effective leadership."

# STATEMENT OF PHILOSOPHY:

"Castilleja's philosophy is shaped by both tradition and current research that affirm the academic and personal advantages of girls' schools. We demonstrate this conviction in the conscious attention we pay to the needs, issues, pedagogies, and opportunities particular to girls. While our emphasis is on the development of the intellect, Castilleja is committed to the education of the whole person: heart, body, and spirit as well as mind.

"Castilleja is committed to excellence. We believe in small classes led by dedicated teachers who exhibit strong academic preparation, enthusiasm for teaching and learning, and concern for each student. We value a curriculum that blends traditional teaching with thoughtful innovation, and we applaud both individual achievement and successful collaboration. We expect students to master information, use technology effectively, and develop the critical thinking skills that support lifelong learning. Castilleja recognizes the importance of parents who are involved with their daughters' education and encourages them to work in partnership with the school.

"Castilleja fosters leadership in the classroom and through a wide assortment of extracurricular offerings, including team sports, clubs, community service projects, student government, dramatic and musical performance, peer tutoring and counseling, art and science exhibits, teaching assistantships, and exchange programs. We recognize each student's individuality and help her excel in her unique interests.

"Castilleja expects its students to participate as citizens of a small school and a larger world. We promote, through experience and example, the development of self-confidence and concern for others, and the capacity for responsible risk-taking and ethical decision-making. Conscience, Courtesy, Character, Courage, and Charity—Castilleja's Five C's which date back to the school's founding headmistress—still resonate, reminding students that personal values must accompany academic achievement. Castilleja prepares its graduates to succeed at the most competitive colleges in the nation and to pursue lives committed to personal fulfillment, social responsibility, and leadership."

## ACADEMIC PROGRAM

"Castilleja's academic program is college preparatory in nature, designed to be intrinsically enjoyable and to help students make informed choices about their future roles in society. The school's pedagogical approaches and course offerings are informed by research findings which focus on the distinctive ways in which girls learn.

"The educational program combines the tradition of academic excellence with educational innovation, strong individual achievement with an emphasis on team-building, a knowledge of Western culture within a global awareness, and the development of self-confidence with compassion for other human beings."

**Courses offered (AP=Advanced Placement, H=Honors, (AP)=AP option, (H)=Honors option): English:** English I-II, English III H, AP English electives: African-American Literature, American Literature Before 1900, Autobiography, The Character of Nature, Coming of Age, Contemporary Global Literature, Creative Writing, Ethnic Voices, Friends and Lovers, The Heroine, Literature of Social Reflection, Modern European Literature, Prose and Poetry, Rebellion,

Shakespeare, Tragic Mode, 20th Century American Literature; **Fine and Performing Arts:** Advanced Theater Arts, Art History I and II, Ceramics, Chorus, Computer Art and Illustration, Design, Drama, Drawing and Painting, Intro to the Arts, Mixed Media, Music History, Music Theory, Public Speaking, Take Five, Advanced Art, Advanced Ceramics, Advanced Drawing and Painting, AP Portfolio Preparation, H Chorus; **Modern and Classical Languages:** French I-IV, Seminaire Avance, Japanese I-V, Latin I-IV, Spanish I-IV, Advanced Spanish Seminar, AP French V & VI, AP Latin V, and AP Spanish V and VI; **History and Social Studies:** African Studies, The American Political System, Civil Liberties, Cultures and Civilizations, East Asian Studies, Economics, The Individual and Society, International Relations, Intro to Philosophy, Intro to Psychology, Modern American Society, Russian History, US History (AP), AP Macroeconomics, AP European History Seminar, Contemporary American Culture; **Math:** Algebra I (H), Algebra II, Geometry and Algebra with Transformations (H), Data, Models & Predictions (H), Pre-Calculus, Mathematical Analysis of Change (H), Calculus, Statistics and Data Analysis, AP Calculus AB, AP Calculus BC, Computer Science; **Science:** Biology, (H, AP), Chemistry (H, AP), Physics (H), Marine Biology; Human Physiology, Ecology & Environmental Issues, Biotechnology & Bioethics; **P.E.:** P.E. 9 & 10, Self Defense, Lifetime Fitness. **Computer lab/training:** The school's newly remodeled Arrillaga Family Campus has 3 computer labs, including a high-performance Graphics Lab with 3 Sun Sparcstations and 8 Silicon Graphics Indys, as well as Multimedia and training labs with 38 Macintoshes and PowerPCs. The network includes a fiber optic backbone and high-end Cisco systems switches which allow 200 to 400 mbs of backbone speed between buildings. The school uses a high speed DSL line to connect its 300 node network to the Internet. The school has 2 Apple computer labs, a Unix based multimedia lab, a library study lab and a drop-in study lab. The school uses both AppleShare and Novell servers to support its users. **Grading**: A-F on a quarter system. 1st and 3rd quarter grades are accompanied by detailed and personalized comment cards. **Graduation requirements**: 4 years English, 3 years math, 2 years lab science, 3 years of one foreign language, 3 years history, 1 year fine/performing arts, 2 years P.E., 1 year electives, 60 hours community service, Human Development I and II. **Average nightly homework:** Approximately 3 hours. **Faculty:** Of the 42 full-time and 14 part-time faculty members, 9 are male, 45 are female; 82% hold advanced degrees. **Faculty ethnicity:** 85% Caucasian (non-Latino); 7% Asian (including Filipino); 6% Latino; 2% African-American (9% of are from international backgrounds). **Faculty selection/training:** "Once it is determined that an opening will occur, the appropriate faculty and administrators review the needs of the school including future curricular developments, educational background and teaching experience of the candidate. Prospective faculty members are solicited through national search organizations and other school contacts. The interview process involves teaching a sample lesson, campus tour, observing a class, and interviewing with the Academic Dean, Head of School, and the Department Head. All faculty undergo formal reviews on a regular basis. Castilleja encourages professional growth by making available funding for national conferences, advanced courses, summer stipends, and the like. The school also sponsors bi-annual in-service days which consist of a nationally regarded educational expert working with all faculty for a day or attending several seminars at the California Association of Independent Schools conference." **Teacher/ student ratio:** 1:8. **Teacher's daily student load in required academic subject:** 52-66 (depending on the academic department). **AP courses/exams:** 50% of students are currently taking AP courses. In 1998-99, 91 students took 185 AP examinations in 15 subjects. 93% received scores of 3 or above. **Senior class profile (mean):** SAT Math 672, SAT Verbal 663. (Middle 50% range 650-690 Verbal, 660-700 Math.) **GPA:** "First 5th 4.24-3.95, Second 5th 3.94-3.72, Third 5th 3.69-3.38, Fourth 5th 3.35-2.97, Fifth 5th 2.94-2.28." **National Merit Scholarship Program:** Of 54 students in the Class of 1999, 10 were semifinalists, 12 commended. **College enrollment:** 99% percent of last year's graduating class enrolled in 4-year universities including Dartmouth, Gonzaga, UC Davis, UC Berkeley, UC San Diego, UCLA, UVA, SMU, Hampton, Stanford, Regis, Williams, Vanderbilt, Trinity, CSU-Long Beach, UOP, Pitzer, Yale, St. Andrew's, U of Michigan, Claremont-McKenna, Wesleyan, Brandeis, St. Mary's, Whitmar, Whittier, SCU-San Jose, Georgetown, MIT, Bowdoin, Colgate, Santa Clara, and Cornell.

## OTHER INDICATORS THE SCHOOL IS ACCOMPLISHING ITS GOALS

"Our commitment to providing opportunities for students to do their best work and be their best selves manifests itself not only through our course offerings but also in this environment of small classes and close teacher-student relations. Ours is a real community, where teachers come to know their students as individuals both in the classroom and out. It is an atmosphere that fosters respect for learning and encourages challenges, where students know they will find the support and resources they need for both academic and extracurricular risk-taking."

## CAMPUS/CAMPUS LIFE

**Campus description:** The school is housed in a circa 1910 building and four buildings surrounding a spacious circular courtyard. The campus includes a swimming pool, gymnasium, and an athletic field. A former residence hall has been renovated and now houses a student center, library, dining facilities, foreign language classrooms, and a state-of-the-art language lab, senior lounge, multimedia and training labs, faculty center, and offices. The campus also includes two art studios and a gallery, a dance studio, and a theater. Construction completed in the summer of 1997 includes complete renovation of the science wing and the creation of new middle school facilities (which includes six classrooms, a student lounge, meeting rooms, and middle school offices). **Library:** The Espinosa Library/Media Center includes a 12,000 volume automated library, electronic databases and Internet access from 20 workstations. (N/P re sq. ft., # seats) **Open/**

**closed campus:** Closed except for senior privileges. **Classroom space per student:** N/P. **Lunches:** A full lunch and snack program is mandatory and was developed with a nutritionist. **Bus service:** Van service to and from the Palo Alto University Avenue CalTrain station. Cost: $450. Some parents have contracted a van service to take students from certain residential areas to school. **Uniform/ dress code:** White or navy blue collared shirts (polo shirts, for example), or red Castilleja sweatshirt with uniform light blue skirt or navy blue pants (no jeans or sweat pant material); uniform shorts. Dress white uniform for traditional or formal occasions. **Co-curricular activities/clubs:** More than 30 clubs, including *Mochuelo* (literary magazine), *Counterpoint* (newspaper), and *Paintbrush* (yearbook), Asian Culture Club, Current Affairs, Art Club, Flute Choir, Clarinet Club, String Club, A Capella Singers, Drama Club. **Foreign exchange programs:** The school has organized exchanges with the Junshin School in Tokyo and is working on expanding such opportunities. The school sponsors trips to various countries for short-term study and also brings international students to school for their junior year through ASSIST. **Opportunities for community service:** Ecumenical Hunger Club, Palo Alto Nursing Home Club, Beechwood Tutoring Club, overseas programs including Amigos de las Americas and Los Niños. Opportunities are printed each September in a community service handbook and distributed to all students. **Typical freshman schedule:** Most students will take English, biology, history, math, foreign language, (human development and physical education for one semester). Some students take a fine arts class as well as or instead of one of the core academic classes mentioned above. Classes meet for an average of four periods a week for 45-75 minutes each time.

# Student Support Services

**Counselor/student ratio (not including college counselors):** 1:96. (1 full-time licensed counselor, 1 counseling intern, and the Dean of Students.) **Counseling:** The school has a part-time licensed clinical social worker available to students for group and individual sessions. All students meet weekly with a faculty advisor in groups of 8-10 students. Advisors monitor the social and academic progress of their advisees, explain school policies, discuss community issues, assist in course selection, serve as a resource, and provide support. Freshmen have an 11th grade peer advisor who co-facilitates the group. Every grade participates in annual retreats focusing on themes and skills which foster growth and group strength.

Castilleja offers an academic counseling program to assist students in the planning of their academic programs—the goal of the entire process being to ensure that the student has a course load that will best meet her needs and the school's demands. Castilleja offers peer tutoring to assist students in academic need as well as to provide leadership opportunities for the student body. Castilleja has a full-time college counselor who maintains a close relationship with each student beginning in her junior year. The Castilleja Internship Program brings a Career Speaker Series to campus and facilitates internships with agencies and businesses within the area such as SGI and Lucille Packard Children's Hospital.

**Learning differences/disabilities:** "We have no formal program, although we do make accommodations for students who need extra time on exams and standardized tests." **Career apprenticeship programs:** "Castilleja supports student efforts to find summer jobs in several ways. We set up and manage a summer internship program available to sophomores, juniors, and seniors. The program offers 15 to 20 seven-week internships in professional fields such as medicine, technology, small business, journalism, and politics. Students must complete an application and interviewing process to participate in the program. We also offer a workshop on finding summer jobs and internships, and provide reference material for students doing a job search *(i.e.,* books on internships, sample resumes for high school students, interviewing tips, *etc.*). Job and internship openings are posted on a school job board. We also host career speaker events throughout the year."

# Student Conduct and Health

**Code of conduct:** Students who commit serious infractions risk "severe consequences, including the possibility of suspension or expulsion." Serious infractions include, in addition to illegal activities, dishonesty of any kind, behavior that causes significant physical or emotional harm to others in the school community *(e.g.,* harassment), and "behavior at or away from school that seriously violates the school's philosophy or negatively reflects upon the character of the school." Most disciplinary offenses are heard by a Student-Faculty Judicial Council made up of five students and three faculty. **How school handles drug/alcohol usage:** "If a student is concerned about her own drug or alcohol use, or the drug or alcohol use of a peer, the response will not be punitive. Students may seek help from either the Counselor or the Dean of Students. At a minimum, any student who commits a serious infraction will be out on a one-year probation." **Drug/ alcohol abuse prevention/AIDS awareness program:** These issues are addressed within the Human Development Department as part of the broader concept of health and wellness. The department's goal is to offer courses which contribute to the development of emotional literacy and resiliency in Castilleja students. Resources are also available through the school counselor.

# Summer Program

Castilleja has a summer camp program for girls completing grades 1-6. It also joins four other independent schools on the Peninsula in providing a full-scholarship Summer Bridge program for girls completing grade 6-8 in East Palo Alto and Redwood City public schools.

# PARENT INVOLVEMENT

**Parent participation:** "Castilleja parents make many contributions to the life of the school through annual and capital fundraising events and through various volunteer opportunities. The school encourages all parents to become involved and values the high percentage of parents who volunteer their time and financial support." **Parent/teacher communication:** The school sends grades on a quarterly basis. First and third quarter grades are accompanied by comment cards for every student from every teacher. These narratives are the essential means of evaluating students. Progress reports are used to inform parents of dramatic shifts in a student's academic performance. Faculty advisors are also an important contact person for parents. **Parent education:** "In the upper school, Castilleja has a series of parent seminars sponsored by the Human Development Department that focus on adolescent issues, including healthy communication, decision making, and boundaries; sexuality and body image; drugs and alcohol; and negotiating transitions into high school and college. In addition, we have hosted special speakers on adolescent girls such as Mary Pipher, author of *Reviving Ophelia*." **Donations:** (See above.)

# SPORTS

Sixty-three percent of students participate in competitive sports through the Private School Athletic League, the Girls' Private School League, and the Peninsula Athletic League. Sports include volleyball, swimming, tennis, cross-country, basketball, soccer, track and field, water polo, softball, and badminton.

# WHAT SETS SCHOOL APART FROM OTHERS

"Academic excellence and a focus on leadership development both in and out of the classroom are all within the context of an all-girls educational environment, an essential distinction from other schools in Northern California."

# HOW PARENTS/STUDENT CHARACTERIZE SCHOOL

**Parent response(s):** "We realize that it is no small undertaking to evaluate the progress of many students; the faculty does so with obvious care and a concern for the wholeness of the student. This just confirms our belief that education at Castilleja extends beyond the dynamism of the classroom into those many other formal and informal opportunities when students interact with faculty and staff members. The girls are very fortunate, and we, as parents, remain grateful."
**Student response(s):** "It is a friendly environment where students are able to express their thoughts and feelings freely without having to worry about whether they are right or wrong. Castilleja creates a strong base for our future. We are free to our own opinions, and the teachers enforce our creativity to make us individu-

als in society. The equality found in this school is far superior to the ones that I know, and the simple fact that we are all different but one at the same time creates trust between everyone. The trust and friendship between all of the students and the teachers creates a great work environment and it makes you feel welcome. You are never an outsider at Castilleja. I feel Castilleja is unique in the fact that we are all able to share our ideas no matter how different they are, and that we are free to be ourselves, and not what others make us to be." "The teachers are amazing; they aren't only your teachers, they are your friends."
"To me, Castilleja is a school where your classmates are always there to lend an ear and help you with your problems. It is a school where the teachers are always ready to give you extra help if you need it, and truly care that you do well. It is a school that challenges the students to achieve their best and put their best effort into all tasks. It is a school where individuality is encouraged and accepted. That is how I characterize Castilleja."

# THE COLLEGE PREPARATORY SCHOOL

6100 Broadway
Oakland, CA 94618

(510) 652-0111 *fax (510) 652-7467*
Lucia_heldt@CPS.pvt.k12.ca.us

Janet Schwarz, Head of School
Lucia Heldt, Director of Admissions, (510) 652-4364

## GENERAL

**Coed** day high school. **Nonsectarian.** Founded in 1960. **Nonprofit**, member CAIS, NAIS, BAIHS. **Enrollment:** 327. **Average class size:** 14. **Accreditation:** WASC/CAIS (6-year term: 1996-02). **School year:** 9.5-month calendar (156 instructional days). **School day:** 8 a.m. to 3:15 p.m. **Location:** The school is located at the Berkeley/Oakland border near Lake Temescal. It is accessible from the Rockridge BART station and by AC transit.

## STUDENT BODY

**Geographical breakdown (counties):** 73% from Alameda; 17% from Contra Costa; 10% from other counties. **Ethnicity:** 67% Caucasian (non-Latino); 13% Asian-American; 7% African-American; 6% Latino; 7% other. **Foreign students (I-20 status):** 0. **Single/two f/t working parent families:** N/P. **Middle schools:** The latest entering freshman class came from 26 schools: 23% from public middle schools; 72% from private, non-parochial schools; 5% from parochial schools. (N/P # schools)

## ADMISSION

**Applications due**: Initial forms are due early December; all forms, mid-January (call for exact dates). **Application fee:** $50. **Application process:** Interested families should contact the admissions director in the fall of the student's 8th grade year. Admission is based upon grades, teacher recommendations (English and math or science), and the results of an entrance examination. Applicant interviews begin in October. Three November open houses are held for students and parents. Each applicant is interviewed by a member of the Admissions Committee beginning in October. Student classroom visits are optional. Entrance exams are given at the school in January, and acceptances are sent mid-March. **No. of applications:** 340 applications were received for 83 places in most recent freshman class. Four new students were admitted to G10, 2 to G11, 1 to G12. **Admission cut-off:** None. **Preferences:** "Faculty children and students of color are encouraged to apply." **"We are looking for** bright, energetic, and motivated young people, willing to give to the school community, who are potential candidates for four-year colleges or universities. The school's *raison d'etre* is to provide this highly selective group of students with a program that will stimulate their intellectual curiosity and growth. Special attention is paid to each student's willingness to share and contribute to the lives of others." **What sort of student do you best serve?** "Academically talented students of promising character. We do not have a GPA cutoff. We look closely at what the student can contribute to the school and in what area(s) the student can excel, whether it be academics, art, debate, or other areas."

## COSTS

**Latest tuition:** $14,750 payable in 3 payments. **Sibling discount:** No. **Tuition increases:** Approximately 5% annually. **Other costs:** Approximately $500 for books, art supplies, class retreats, etc. **Financial aid:** Need-based financial aid and loans are available. **Percentage of students receiving financial aid:** 17% receive grants totaling $488,200. **Average grant:** $8,718. **No. of full-tuition grants:** 0. **Grants of half-tuition or more:** 75% of awards range from 50%-90% of tuition.

## SCHOOL'S MISSION STATEMENT/GOALS

"Our purpose is to prepare our students for productive ethical lives in college and beyond through a challenging and stimulating education in an atmosphere of consideration, trust, and mutual responsibility."

# ACADEMIC PROGRAM

The curriculum is designed to meet the following goals: "to develop powers of clear expression in writing and speech both in English and in at least one foreign language; to impart a sense of historical and cultural perspective; to ensure a solid understanding of science and mathematics; to encourage development of the aesthetic sense through careful integration of the arts into the curriculum; and to fulfill the school's belief in the necessity of physical education for all students." **Courses offered (AP=Advanced Placement, H=Honors, (AP)=AP option, (H)=Honors option): Arts:** Drawing and Design, Advanced Art: 2-dimensional Studio, Advanced Art: 3-dimensional Studio, Beginning and Advanced Photography, Acting, Performance Class, Chorus, Advanced Vocal Ensemble, Jazz Choir, Beginning Instruments, Jazz Workshop, Orchestra, Chamber Music, Jazz Band, AP Music Theory, Beginning Dance, Intermediate Dance, Advanced Dance; **English:** English I-II, Satire, Modern Poetry, American Lit. I, Latin American Fiction of the 20th Century, The Age of Revolution, Creative Writing: Poetry, Modern Fiction, The Essay, Shakespeare, Strange Journeys (Dante, Eliot, *etc.*), Writers of Color, Falling from Grace; **History:** World Civilizations, Western Civilization, US History, Presidential Elections, Immigrant Experience, The History of Modern Africa, Comparative Revolutions, Philosophy; **Foreign Languages:** French I-III, France Today, The Adolescent Experience as Portrayed in Literature from France and Francophone Africa, Beginning German (I/II Accelerated), Intermediate German (II/III Accelerated), German III-IV, Japanese I-III, Latin I-V, Spanish I-III, Advanced Spanish Language, Literature and Culture, Spanish Short Stories and Poetry, Magic Realism (Latin American); **Math:** Mathematics I-IV (CPS integrated math curriculum), Mathematics V: AP Calculus, AP Statistics; **P.E.**; **Science:** Integrated Laboratory Science I-III, AP Biology, AP Chemistry, Physics, Marine Biology, Natural History of California, History of Science, Biochemistry, Issues in Science; **Other offerings:** Forensics, Psychology, Independent Study, Publications and Multimedia, Freshman Foundations, Intraterm (week-long internships, community service projects or mini-courses in the Spring on and off campus, which have included Animation, Gospel Singing, Cycling, and Chinese Art, geological tours of California, and building homes in Mexico), Retreat Program (see "Other," below). **Computer lab/training:** The school has 2 computer labs, each with 11 PowerMacs; the Student Commons has 3 Pentium PCs; PowerMacs with appropriate software are in the Art, Spanish, and Statistics classrooms and there are 8 Pentium laptops in the science building. The campus is completely networked. Computer literacy is part of the required Freshman Foundations course. The school has a full-time technology director and a full-time technology integrator. **Grading**: A-F letter grades and teacher evaluations 4 times a year. **Graduation requirements:** 4 years English, 3 years history, completion of level III math, completion of level III foreign language, 3 years science, four semesters fine arts, 3 years P.E. **Average nightly homework:** G9-10: 30-40 min. per class; G11-12: 40-50 min. per class. **Faculty:** Of the 54 faculty members, 45% are male, 55% female; 35% hold bachelor's degrees as highest degree;

50% hold master's degrees; and 15% hold doctorates. **Faculty ethnicity:** 75% Caucasian (non-Latino); 11% African-American; 7% Hispanic/Latino; 7% Asian. **Faculty selection/training:** "Faculty are selected for thorough knowledge of their subjects and strong teaching skills. Prospective teachers are required to make a related presentation and they have interviews with several members of the administration and faculty. The school has a generous professional development fund that both encourages and permits continuing education." **Teacher/student ratio:** 1:8. **Teacher's student load in required academic subject:** Approximately 60. **AP courses/exams:** 37% of the most recent year's class took AP courses. In 1997-98, 122 students took 228 AP exams in 16 subjects. 97% scored 3 or above. (Note that the percentage of students taking AP courses does not reflect the students taking the school's regular English and history courses that prepare students for the AP exams.) **Senior class profile (mean):** SAT Math 699, SAT Verbal 695. **GPA:** 3.3 (academic courses only). **National Merit Scholarship Program:** 60% of the students in the class of 1999 were either semi-finalists (22 students) or commended (23 students). **College enrollment:** 100% of last year's graduating class enrolled in 4-year colleges, including: Cornell (3), Dartmouth, Deep Springs, Emerson, Emory, Georgetown (2), Harvard, Haverford, CSU-Humboldt, Julliard, MIT (2), Mt. Holyoke, NYU (3, + 1 in 2000), Northwestern, Pomona, Smith, Stanford (5, + 1 from Class of '98), Tufts (4), US Naval Academy, UC Berkeley (9), UC Davis (3), UCLA (5), UC San Diego, UC Santa Barbara (6), UC Santa Cruz (7), U of Colorado, U of Penn, Vassar, Wellesley (2), and Yale (2). (One student deferred enrollment to 2000.)

## OTHER INDICATORS THE SCHOOL IS ACCOMPLISHING ITS GOALS

"Alumni have continued to follow the school's motto: *Mens Conscia Recti,* 'a mind aware of what is right.' CPS graduates have excelled not only academically (as attested to by their college placement, their enrollment in graduate programs, and their involvement in teaching, research, medicine, law, and business) but also in contributing to their communities: as environmentalists, political activists, and community volunteers, as artists, writers, musicians, and actors. They have served in the Peace Corps and in other volunteer capacities around the world."

## CAMPUS/CAMPUS LIFE

**Campus description:** The campus consists of 14 buildings in a wooded area abutting the Oakland Hills. Two rows of wood shingle-sided buildings face each other on either side of a wooded canyon; classrooms and offices open onto the common walkways and courtyards between the buildings. Several classrooms have round tables for a discussion format. A native plant garden and landscaped walkways provide students with outdoor spaces for socializing, studying, and engaging in informal activities such as games of chess. An amphitheater is tucked away on the hillside. A new science building opened in September, 1998; renovation and expansion of the library was completed in April 1999; and a history lecture hall and math department conference room will be completed during the 1999-2000 school year. **Library**: 3,000 square feet; study space for 54 students plus additional seating areas; 60 periodical subscriptions, plus 5 dailies; 10,000 print volumes; private study room and reference/teaching room (both multimedia equipped), 6 Pentium computers with Internet access and plans to add 30 more; on-line catalog. **Open/closed campus:** Open. **Classroom space per student:** N/P. **Lunches:** None served on campus. **Bus service:** Public transportation to Rockridge BART; free shuttle service from BART to campus. **Uniforms/dress code:** "Common sense and good taste." **Co-curricular activities/clubs:** Activities include Math Club, Pride-in-Diversity Club, Backpacking Club, school publications, and the school's nationally ranked debate team. **Foreign exchange program:** None. **Opportunities for community service:** Shelters, soup kitchens, tutoring at Oakland schools, CPS Partners Program (see Summer Programs, below), Christmas in April, Habitat for Humanity (house building in Mexico), Adopt-a-Family, Oxfam (an international relief program). **Typical freshman schedule:** English I, Math I or II, Science I, foreign language (French, Spanish, Latin, Japanese, or German), World Civilizations, arts (visual, dance, drama, music) or Debate, P.E.

## STUDENT SUPPORT SERVICES

**Counselor/student ratio (not including college counselors):** 1:328. **Counseling:** The school has a full-time counselor whose assistance ranges from study skills to short-term crisis counseling. She provides drug, alcohol, AIDS, etc. education for G9-10; participates in retreats for all classes; and helps the Dean of Students coordinate the advisor program (selected seniors act as advisors to small groups of in-coming freshmen). Each student, in addition, has an academic advisor. The school has a full-time college counselor. **Learning differences/disabilities:** "The school does not test students but, when needed, recommends outside sources for assessment and then makes suitable accommodations on an individual basis in line with professional recommendations." **Career apprenticeship programs:** "No formal programs. Informal information and advice are available from counselors."

## STUDENT CONDUCT/HEALTH

**Code of conduct:** In addition to standard rules, "the school reserves the right to discipline students who, by their conduct, damage the reputation of the school." Smoking is not allowed on campus or within 300 feet of the nearest school boundary. **How school handles drugs/alcohol usage**: "Sale or distribution of illegal drugs or alcohol on campus or at a school event will result in immediate expulsion, and possession, using, or being under the influence of illegal drugs or alcohol on campus or at a school event will lead to immediate suspension with the possibility of expulsion; a second violation will result in immediate expulsion."

**Drug/alcohol abuse prevention/AIDS awareness programs:** These issues are discussed in Freshman and Sophomore Foundations, required courses which introduce students to issues faced by adolescents, including stress, peer pressure, relationships with parents, drugs and alcohol, and sexuality, and which help students develop decision-making skills.

## SUMMER PROGRAMS

The school offers a tuition-free "Partners Program" during the summer for economically disadvantaged students who are bright, able, and motivated for an academic high school experience. CPS students serve as teaching assistants.

## PARENT INVOLVEMENT

**Parent participation:** Parents voluntarily serve the school through the Parents Association as well as by gardening on campus, judging debates, participating in open houses, etc. No required hours. **Parent/teacher communication:** Report cards four times a year, conferences with advisors, teachers, and the assistant head as well. **Parent education:** "Informational and/or support events are organized by the school and by the Parents' Association as needed in response to issues as they arise." **Donations:** Parents are solicited for the Annual Fund, House Tour, and capital drives.

## SPORTS

Students compete in the Bay Counties League in coed cross-country and swimming; girls' volleyball, tennis, basketball, and soccer; boys' soccer, basketball, volleyball, tennis, and baseball. The school also has a track club.

## OTHER

Each grade level attends a yearly retreat designed to achieve particular goals of the school. The 9th grade retreat focuses on integrating new 9th graders into the school; the 10th grade retreat deals with issues surrounding adolescence; the 11th grade retreat is intended to encourage leadership among students; and the senior retreat is about the transition from high school to college.

## WHAT SETS SCHOOL APART FROM OTHERS

"A small, close community of students, teachers, and staff, CPS is enriched by everyone's energy and commitment. Small classes place a premium on participation and intellectual engagement, and an active program of team sports, debate, and arts performances—in dance, drama, visual arts, and music—keeps everyone both involved and appreciative."

## How Parents/Students Characterize School

**Parent response(s):** A former CPS parent remarked, "The accomplishment of CPS is an extraordinary warmth among its students. Adolescence is usually not marked by its tolerance but the students of CPS cherish diversity. ... As a group, they lend moral and affectionate support to each of their number. There is a palpable embracing of the individual by the student body. ... As a consequence each child at CPS realizes his talents about as close to the fullest as is humanly conceivable."

**Student response(s):** "I love this school. I love this school because I'm only seventeen years old and I have learned already to be a man—who is depended on and respected. I've learned to trust and be trusted, to share my feelings, my thoughts, my opinions. I've learned to love people in different ways. I love this place because I came in cynical and vain, and I'm leaving with a sense of hope and with a feeling of peace."— Amit Chadha, '97

# Convent of the Sacred Heart High School

2222 Broadway
San Francisco, CA 94115

(415) 563-2900 *fax (415) 292-3183*
www.sacred.sf.ca.us

Douglas H. Grant, Head of School
Anne Spyropoulos, High School Admissions Coordinator,
spyropoulos@sacred.sf.ca.us

## General

**Girls'** day high school. **Independent Catholic** (49% Catholic). Founded in 1887. **Nonprofit**, member CAIS, NAIS, BAIHS. **Enrollment:** Approximately 198. **Average class size:** 14. **Accreditation:** WASC/CAIS (6-year term: 1999-05), Sacred Heart Network. **School year:** 9-month calendar (180 instructional days). **School day:** 8:15 a.m. to 3:15 p.m. **Location:** Located in Pacific Heights, Convent of the Sacred Heart High School is accessible by the 1, 22, 24, 41, and 45 MUNI bus lines.

## STUDENT BODY

**Geographical breakdown (counties):** 78% from San Francisco; 14% from Marin; 2% from San Mateo; 5% from Alameda; 1% from Contra Costa. **Ethnicity:** 62% Caucasian (non-Latino); 26% Asian; 6% Latina; 5% African-American; 1% other. **Foreign students (I-20 status):** 1%. **Single parent/two f/t working parent families:** N/P. **Middle schools:** 37% of the most recent entering freshman class came from Convent of the Sacred Heart Elementary School; 12% from public middle schools; 22% from private, non-parochial schools; 29% from parochial schools. (N/P re # schools)

## ADMISSION

**Applications due:** Approximately January 8 (call for date). **Application fee:** $75. **Application process:** Tours are conducted September through February. In November, applicants and their families may attend an open house and have the opportunity to see classes in session. **No. of applications:** "Five applications for every available spot." One new student was admitted to G11. **Admission cutoff:** None. **Preferences:** Siblings and legacies. **"We are looking for** young women who want to be engaged in their education, and are willing to take on a strong academic program and leadership roles within the school community." **What sort of student do you best serve?** (See statement under "Other indicators that the school is accomplishing its goals.")

## COSTS

**Latest tuition:** $14,250 payable in 1 or 2 payments or through a 10-month payment plan. **Sibling discount:** None. **Tuition increases:** Approximately 6.74% annually. **Other costs:** Approximately $300-600 for books, $200 for uniforms. **Percentage of students receiving financial aid:** 40%. **Average grant:** $6,320. **No. of full/half-tuition grants:** N/P.

## SCHOOL'S MISSION STATEMENT/GOALS

Philosophy: "The schools of the Sacred Heart in the United States, members of a world-wide network, offer an education that is marked by a distinctive spirit. Sacred Heart schools are committed to the individual student's total development: spiritual, intellectual, emotional, and physical. Sacred Heart schools emphasize serious study, social responsibility, and growth in faith. Sacred Heart schools commit themselves to educate to: a personal and active faith in God; a deep respect for intellectual values; a social awareness which impels to action; the building of a community as a Christian value; and personal growth in an atmosphere of wise freedom."

# ACADEMIC PROGRAM

"Every student is enrolled in a challenging and enriching academic program. The program emphasizes serious study and teaches to each student's total spiritual, intellectual, emotional and physical development. The administration, faculty, and student body are committed to intellectual honesty and leadership development. Students are treated seriously as scholars and leaders. Each student is required to take a minimum of six courses for credit each semester. Every student graduates with a program which satisfies the University of California course requirements for admission." **Courses offered (AP=Advanced Placement, H=Honors, (AP)=AP option, (H)=Honors option):** Religious Studies I-IV, Philosophy, English I (H), English II (H), American Literature (H), British Literature, English Literature and Composition (AP), Creative Writing, Writers Workshop, Controversial Literature, Contemporary Novel, Journalism, History I-II, US History (AP), American Politics & Policy, Asian Studies, American Government (AP), International Relations, Economics, Environmental Science (AP), Comparative Government and Politics (AP), European History (AP), Psychology (AP), French 1-2, French 3 (H), French 4 (H), French Language (AP), French Literature (AP), Japanese 1-4, Spanish 1-2, Spanish 3 (H), Spanish Language (AP), Spanish Literature (AP), Mandarin I, Advanced Mandarin, Integrated Science, Biology (AP), Chemistry (H, AP), Physics, Physiology, Integrated Mathematics including Algebra/Geometry/Trigonometry I-III (H in II, III), Pre-Calculus, Pre-Calculus with Calculus (H), Calculus, Calculus AB (AP), Statistics, Introduction to Art for Freshmen, Humanities, Art Studio (AP), Art History (AP), Choir, Drama, Notables, Instrumental Music, Independent Study, Ceramics, Photography, Seminar in Art (Drawing, Painting, Printmaking, The Art of Crafts), Open Studio, P.E. I-II, Team Sports, Physical Education (Independent Study—high level outside studies outside school), Computer Studies I-II, Computer Science A (AP), Computer Science AB (AP). **Computer lab/training:** Each student has an e-mail address and has access to over 100 computers on campus, all of which are linked to the Internet. Technology is integrated throughout the curriculum. Students have access to equipment including scanners and digital cameras and are required to take 1 year of computer science. **Grading:** A-F. **Graduation requirements:** 4 years English, 4 years history, 4 years mathematics, 4 years theology, 3 years lab science, 3 years foreign language, 2 years P.E., 1 year fine arts, 1 year computer science, 100 hours community service. (Requirements designed to satisfy UC admission standards.) **Average nightly homework:** 3-3.5 hours. **Faculty:** Of the 33 faculty members, 10 are male, 23 female. 45% of faculty hold bachelor's degrees as their highest degree; 45% hold master's degrees; and 10% hold doctorates. **Faculty ethnicity:** 88% Caucasian (non-Latino); 6% Latino; 6% Asian. **Faculty selection/training:** "We look for teachers who are knowledgeable in their subject area, who have a strong commitment to education, who desire small classes for interactive learning, who want to support students outside of the classroom through athletics, service, or club activities, who will accept and embrace the goals of Sacred Heart education, who understand the benefits of teaching in a single sex environment and who have the desire and ability to engage students in the classroom. Departments take advantage of CSH's full support for professional development by attending conferences and workshops together." **Teacher/student ratio:** 1:6. **Teacher's daily student load in required academic subject:** 70. **AP courses/exams:** All of prior year's seniors took at least one AP course. In May, 1998, 73 students took 137 AP examinations in 15 subjects. 94 exams received scores of 3 or above. (See "Other indicators . . ." section below.) **Senior class profile (mean):** SAT Math 562 (560 median), SAT Verbal 580 (590 median). ("Math: of 48 seniors, 7 had a score of 650 or higher, 19 of 550-640, 16 of 450-540 and 4 of 430 or lower; Verbal: of 48 seniors, 16 had scores of 650 or higher, 23 of 550-640, 5 of 450-540, and 4 of 430 or lower.") **GPA:** 3.20 (six semesters, 46 seniors, academic courses only, no weighting). ("12 students had GPAs of 3.5 and higher; 18 of 3.0-3.49; 12 of 2.5-2.9; and 4 lower than 2.49.") **National Merit Scholarship Program:** One member of the Class of 1999 was a finalist, 1 commended. **College enrollment:** 95% of the Class of 1999 enrolled in 4-year colleges, 5% in 2-year colleges. Acceptances included: USC (10), UC Santa Cruz (9), USF (9), Santa Clara (7), UC Davis (7) UC Santa Barbara (7), U of Colorado-Boulder (6), Boston U (5), St. Mary's (5), SMU (4), CSU-SF (4), UC Riverside (4), UC San Diego (4), UC Irvine (4), Occidental (4), Whittier (4), CSU-Long Beach (4), George Washington (3), NYU (3), American U (3), UOP (3), U of Portland (3), Wheaton (3), Columbia (2), Dickinson (2), Dominican (2), Fordham (2), Holy Names (2), Loyola Marymount (2), Manhattanville C (2), MIT (2), Regis (2), Seattle U (2), U of Oregon (2), U of San Diego (2), U of Washington (2), Wellesley (2), CSU-Los Angeles (2), CSU-San Diego (2), UCLA (2), Amherst, Boston C, Bowdoin, Clark Atlanta, Colorado C, Cornell, De Paul, Drew U, Duke, Evergreen State, Franklin C of Switzerland, Georgetown, Gonzaga, Goucher, Hamilton C, Hampshire C, Hawaii Pacific, Indiana U, Lehigh, Northwestern, Pitzer, Princeton, Sarah Lawrence, Scripps, Skidmore, Spelman, Stanford, Tulane, Union C, U of Denver, U of Miami, U of Puget Sound, U of Utah, Wells C, Whitman, Villanova, Cal Poly-SLO, CSU-Humboldt, CSU-Monterey, and SCU-Stanislaus.

## OTHER INDICATORS THE SCHOOL IS ACCOMPLISHING ITS GOALS

"Due to our small student body and class size, we are able to concentrate on individual students at every level. One of our strongest programs is our AP program, with 17 different class offerings providing an AP opportunity for every student. In the fall of 1997, every senior enrolled in at least one AP class. In the last graduating class, 13 students received AP Scholar Awards, including two receiving the AP National Scholar Award, granted to students who receive an average grade of 4 on eight or more AP exams on full-year courses.

"CSH's reputation as an outstanding program for young women in San Francisco reaches beyond Bay Area communities to the college community as well. Over 70 college representatives come to our campus each fall to speak with students. Our graduates attend some of the most competitive colleges in the United

States and abroad. CSH has been recognized by the US Department of Education as a Blue Ribbon School."

# CAMPUS/CAMPUS LIFE

**Campus description:** The school is housed in the three-story Flood Mansion at the crest of the Pacific Heights neighborhood, overlooking the San Francisco Bay and the Golden Gate Bridge. The building has ground floor meeting rooms, classrooms, and a chapel; second floor student center, computer lab, and classrooms and offices; and a third floor library, art studio, and classrooms. Downstairs is a theater, and cafeteria. The campus also includes a full-size gymnasium and indoor track. **Library:** Open 8 a.m. to 4 p.m. Approximately 6,500 print volumes; on-line catalog; 25 periodical subscriptions; study seating for 35 students. (N/P re sq. ft., computers) **Open/closed campus:** Open for juniors and seniors; sophomores may sign out but must return to campus. **Classroom space per student:** N/P. **Lunches:** Students bring their lunches or eat in the cafeteria; juniors and seniors may eat off campus. **Bus service:** Public only. **Uniforms/ dress code:** Uniforms consist of gray skirt, white shirt, and burgundy sweater. Seniors wear blue sweaters. Beginning second quarter, students may wear khaki pants. No unnatural hair colors or facial piercings. Occasional free dress days. **Co-curricular activities/clubs:** Clubs include Art, Black History Celebration, Close-Up (travel to Washington, D.C.), College Hostess, Network Homelessness Project, Debate, Environmental, Girls' Athletic Association, International Students, Junior Statesmen of America, Newspaper, Outdoors, Publicity, Social, Spirit, Student Admissions, Students Against Drunk Driving (SADD), Yearbook. Activities include Student Council, Clubs Council, Guest Speakers Program, National Honor Society, California Scholarship Federation. **Foreign exchange program:** Students may participate in an exchange program among eighteen Sacred Heart schools in the US. Students live with a host family or board at a Sacred Heart school with boarding facilities. (Sophomores and juniors with a B+ average are eligible to apply.) **Opportunities for community service:** Students fulfill their required 100 hours of community service through a variety of activities relating to the elderly, the environment, the handicapped, the sick, the economically disadvantaged, and the newly immigrated. **Typical freshman schedule:** English I (honors option), Theology I, History I, French, Spanish, Japanese or Mandarin, Integrated Math I (honors option), Integrated Science or Biology, Computer Studies I (1 semester), Introduction to Art (1 semester), and Physical Education I.

# STUDENT SUPPORT SERVICES

**Counselor/student ratio (not including college counselors):** "35 faculty members serve as counselors to the school's 198 students." **Counseling:** The school has a part-time counselor in the office of Student Services and a part-time Community Service Director. The Head of School and Dean of Studies provide academic counseling and advising to students. The **college counseling** office consists of the College Counselor and an Assistant College Counselor. During the freshman year, students take the National Education Development Test. Freshman and sophomores have one group presentation each year by the college counselor and meet individually with the college counselor as well. Sophomores also take the PSAT in the spring. During the junior year, students take the PSAT in the fall, have weekly group meetings and individual sessions with the College Counselor, and take the ACT, SAT I, and SAT II in the spring. Seniors continue to meet with the college counselor both individually and in group sessions, and take the SAT I, and SAT II again in the fall. **Learning differences/disabilities:** No special programs or resources. **Career apprenticeship programs:** Students are kept apprised of various summer programs and opportunities through the monthly newsletter.

## Student Conduct and Health

**Code of conduct:** The Code of Ethics, discussed in the Student Handbook, focuses on respect for others, respect for others' property and school property, respect for education, and school spirit. **How school handles drugs/alcohol usage:** "Drug and alcohol usage or possession will not be tolerated and will result in serious punishment of either expulsion or suspension. This policy is in effect whether a student is on campus, in uniform, or attending a school sponsored function." **Drug/alcohol abuse prevention/AIDS awareness program:** Drug/alcohol abuse prevention is part of the freshman/sophomore community program and is often the subject of guest speakers on campus. These subjects are also discussed in classes. Sexually transmitted diseases are discussed as part of the human sexuality curriculum, which includes topics of body image and self-acceptance, building healthy relationships, and family planning. The program includes guest speakers, lecturers, and in-class discussion.

## Summer Programs

Students participate in a variety of summer programs on their own. CSH also offers trips every summer—last summer CSH students traveled to Europe. Summer activities are published monthly in the school newsletter.

## Parent Involvement

**Parent participation:** Parents are invited to participate through the Parents' Association as Room Parents, and as volunteers for various events and activities. **Parent/teacher communication:** Formal reports are sent to parents four times a year. Other evaluations are given as needed. **Parent education:** Speaker series; evening presentations for parents on admission and financial aid/scholarships. **Donations:** N/P.

## SPORTS

CSH students compete through the Bay Counties Athletic League in volleyball, cross-country, tennis, basketball, swimming, and soccer. LaCrosse has been introduced as a club sport and students may participate in crew.

## WHAT SETS SCHOOL APART FROM OTHERS

"A strong academic program which utilizes San Francisco and all the resources the city has to offer. Leadership opportunities for young women and a values-based education."

## HOW PARENTS/STUDENTS CHARACTERIZE SCHOOL

N/P.

# CRYSTAL SPRINGS UPLANDS SCHOOL

400 Uplands Drive
Hillsborough, California 94010

(650) 342-4175 *fax (650) 342-7611*
www.csus.com

Richard A. Drew, Head of School
Jennifer L. Blake, Director of Admission, admission@csus.com

## GENERAL

**Coed** day high school. **Nonsectarian.** Founded in 1952 by parents. (Girls' school until mid-1970's.) The school has a middle school G6-8. **Nonprofit**, member CAIS, NAIS, BAIHS. **Enrollment:** Approximately 354 in G6-12, 240 in G9-12 (by 1999-2000, the school hopes to have 400 students). **Average class size:** 15. **Accreditation:** WASC/CAIS (6-year term: 1996-2002). **School year:** 9-month calendar (166 instructional days). **School day:** 8:25 a.m. to 3:10 p.m. **Location:** Crystal Springs Uplands School is located on a 10-acre suburban campus in Hillsborough, a community 20 miles south of San Francisco.

## STUDENT BODY

**Geographical breakdown (counties):** 88% from San Mateo; 7% from Santa Clara; 5% from San Francisco. **Ethnicity:** 66% Caucasian (non-Latino); 22%

Asian; 5% Latino; 4% African-American; 3% other. **Foreign students (I-20 status):** N/P. **Single parent families:** 10%. **Two f/t working parent families:** 50%. **Middle schools:** 25% of the most recent entering freshman class came from public middle schools; 23% from private, non-parochial schools; 2% from parochial schools; and 50% from Crystal Springs Uplands School's middle school. (N/P re # schools) "The class of 2004 will have students from Crocker Middle School (Hillsborough), Corte Madera (Portola Valley), Woodside Elementary (Woodside), Nueva School (Hillsborough), Bowditch Middle (Foster City) and Ralston (Belmont)."

# ADMISSION

**Applications due:** Approximately January 20 (call for date). **Application fee:** $60. **Application process:** Applicants should submit Part I of an application form (which includes basic biographical information and a parent's assessment of child), the fee, and a recent photograph. The school will then schedule a school visit. Prior to the visit, the student fills out a form responding to questions about his or her interests and opinions. Teacher and Counselor/Principal recommendations (BAIHS forms) and school transcripts must be submitted as well as recent test scores (SSAT or STS HSPT). The school administers the HSPT for applicants on campus on two dates during the application period. Student visits involve a half-day on campus and include lunch. Family open houses are held on three weekends in October, November and January. Decisions are mailed out in mid-March, the same date as the other members of the BAIHS. **No. of applications:** 150 applications were received for 60 places in prior year's class. Of these, 30 places were taken by the school's middle school students and 30 were given to students entering from other middle schools. No new students were admitted to G10-12, although some years there is room for transfer students. **Admission cut-off:** "Most successful applicants are doing well in their current school (A-B students). There are no cut-offs but students need to be trying their best and exhibiting an enthusiasm for learning." **Preferences:** "We like to see siblings of currents students apply, but they are not always brought into the school." **"We are looking for** students who exhibit an enthusiasm for learning, a willingness to take academic risks, and the energy to contribute positively to the school community. The Admissions Committee looks for high levels of academic achievement as well as talents in other areas such as the arts, athletics, leadership, and service." **What sort of student does the school best serve?** "As a small school, we need a variety of students in each class. Many people think that the only students who thrive here in high school are those who were 'straight A' students in middle school. That simply is not the case. We do look for motivated and engaged students, but we can't have all 'A' students—we would be a boring place. Students who are accepted into our school tend to have passions, for an academic subject, for a sport, for a cause, or for a community. Having a mix of students serves the school well, for students learn as much from one another when they are hanging out as they do inside the classroom."

# Costs

**Latest tuition:** $14,300 payable in 1 advance payment or in 2 installments if tuition insurance is purchased at a cost of approximately $150. A 10-payment plan is also available through Tuition Management Systems (tuition insurance must be purchased). **Sibling discount:** None. **Tuition increases:** Approximately 4% annually. **Other costs:** Consolidated fee of approximately $600; supply/activity deposit. **Financial aid:** Aid is need-based. **Percentage of students receiving financial aid:** Approximately 18%. **Average grant:** $9,700. **No. of full/half-tuition scholarships:** N/P. **Grants of half-tuition or more:** 86%.

# School's Mission/Goals

(Philosophy:) "We believe that students learn best in an environment that promotes learning in diverse ways about a complex world, stimulates intellectual and creative development, nurtures the individual within a community of mutual trust, caring, and respect, [and] balances academic and extracurricular interests and accomplishments. We encourage critical thinking and intellectual risk-taking, responsibility for one's ideas and actions, personal integrity, ethical awareness, and multicultural understanding, individual leadership and cooperative interaction, [and] respect for one's self and for the views of others. We endeavor to equip students with a spirit of inquiry, a respect for human potential, a sense of responsibility for the environment and to the global community, [and] a feeling of joy in lifelong learning."

# Academic Program

"CSU is committed to offering a challenging academic program in a supportive environment. We encourage students to take risks in their thinking, whether that occurs in class discussion or in writing. We hope to graduate students who are fascinated by ideas and who have their own points of view and who are interested in sharing their ideas with others." **Courses offered (AP=Advanced Placement, H=Honors, (AP)=AP option, (H)=Honors option): English:** English I, II, III, IV (H) and second semester electives in G10-12, Creative Writing; **History:** Comparative Cultures, Modern Europe, US History and Government (more than 80% AP), AP European History, AP American Government and Politics, AP Comparative Government and Politics, Psychology, History of Art (H); **Foreign Languages:** French I-III, French III (H), French Language (AP), French Literature (AP), French Culture, Spanish I-III, Spanish III (H), Spanish Literature (AP), Spanish Language (AP); **Math:** Algebra I, Geometry, Algebra II (H), Pre-Calculus, Pre-Calculus/Calculus (H), AB Calculus (AP), BC Calculus (AP), Multivariable Calculus (H, AP), Linear Algebra (H, AP); **Science:** Biology (AP), Chemistry (H), Astronomy, Physics (H, AP), C++ Programming (AP); **Arts:** Art

(H, AP), Ceramics, Photography (H), Digital Photography, Graphic Design, Dance (H), Dance Production, Advanced Dance Performance, Acting I-III, Production and Design, Mixed Chorus, Crystal Chorus, Madrigals, Mann's Men, Vick's Chicks, Instrumental Techniques, Ensembles (Jazz, Wind, String, Brass), Chamber Orchestra, Bell Choir, AP Music Theory. **Computer lab/training:** The school has two computer labs with 35 PowerMacs. 8-10 additional Macs are available to students for word processing. Elective courses and mini-seminars are available in Beginning Skills, Graphic Design, C++ Programming, and Advanced Topics. **Grading:** Letter grades, given at quarters and semesters. **Graduation requirements:** 4 years English, 3 years history, 3 years foreign language, 3 years mathematics, 3 years laboratory science, 2 years fine arts, and 3 years human development seminars. P.E. or athletics are required through junior year. **Average nightly homework:** Depends on AP classes, but in general, G9: 2.5-3 hours; G10-12: 3 hours. **Faculty:** Of the 37 full-time and 10 part-time faculty members, 24 are male, 25 female; 31 hold master's degrees; 6 hold doctorates; and 2 hold JDs. **Faculty ethnicity:** 82% Caucasian (non-Latino); 8% African-American; 8% Asian/Pacific Islander; 2% Latino. **Faculty selection/training:** "Faculty are selected through a search process (search organizations, unsolicited resumes, word-of-mouth). They are interviewed by the relevant department and the administration, and give on-site teaching demonstrations. The decision is made by the Head of School after consultation with the department head. Faculty remains current and qualified with professional development assistance (workshops, school visits, classes) and in-service programs as well as peer assessment." **Teacher/student ratio:** 1:10. **Teacher's daily student load in required academic subject:** 63. **AP courses/exams:** Varies by grade level. Among seniors, 95% take AP courses. In fall, 1998, 46 students took 91 AP exams as juniors in 8 subjects; 96% received scores of 3 or above (39% received scores of 5, 33% scores of 4). One AP scholar with honors; 11 AP scholars. **Senior class profile (mean):** "SAT Verbal middle 50% 710-580, SAT Math middle 50% 720-600." SAT II (mean): WR 664; M637; AH653; FR593; SP659; PH681; BY689; CH608." **GPA:** 3.40 (weighted)(N/P re how weighted). **National Merit Scholarship Program:** 8 semifinalists, 12 commended students, 1 National Hispanic Scholar, and 1 National Achievement Scholar in the most recent class. **College enrollment:** 100% of last year's graduating class enrolled in 4-year colleges including: Reed, Tulane, Carleton, CSU-San Jose, Colgate, U of Chicago, UC Davis (2), NYU (2), UC Santa Cruz (2), UCLA, Harvey Mudd, U of Pennsylvania (2), Brown, Haverford, MIT, Georgetown, Duke, Pepperdine (2), U of Arizona, Brandeis (2), Oakland U, U of Puget Sound, UC Santa Barbara (4), Swarthmore, UC Berkeley (3), Hampshire, Pomona (2), Princeton, U of Vermont, USF, Northwestern, Harvard, U of Michigan, Tufts, Loyola Marymount, Stanford (4), UC San Diego (2), Amherst (deferred for a year to do volunteer work in Honduras), Smith, Boston U, Carnegie Mellon, Columbia, Dartmouth, Pitzer, Parsons/Pratt, Colorado C, and Cornell.

## OTHER INDICATORS THE SCHOOL IS ACCOMPLISHING ITS GOALS

"The vitality in the classroom, the strong interest in learning and the mutual respect of teachers and students are indicators that CSU is a good place for students. Another measure of our success is the high level of community involvement. Parents, siblings, and current students come to the plays, the performances, the games, and other school events in large numbers, supporting one another. Finally, when our graduates go on to college, they are forceful in seeking similar relationships with their professors as they had with their CSU teachers. Graduates recognize the importance of their one-on-one relationships with teachers and coaches."

## CAMPUS/CAMPUS LIFE

**Campus description:** Crystal Springs Uplands School has a ten-acre suburban campus located on the San Francisco Peninsula midway between San Francisco and Palo Alto. The main building is the Crocker mansion, an 85-year-old building now housing the library, administrative offices, and classrooms. Two newer buildings house a 400-seat theater, student center and cafeteria, gym, interactive classrooms, five science laboratories, a computer laboratory, and fine arts facilities. The outdoor campus includes tennis courts and a large field for soccer and other outdoor sports. **Library:** The school's library, in a wing of the Crocker mansion, includes 2 separate study rooms providing study space for 70 students; an on-line catalog; 7 computers with Internet access; 11,250 print volumes; and 36 periodical subscriptions. Open to students 8:15 a.m. to 5 p.m. (N/P re sq. ft.) **Open/closed campus:** Closed. **Classroom space per student:** N/P. Note: Most classrooms are set up with desks in a U-shape. Few classes are lecture-based. **Lunches:** Hot lunches and cold snacks are provided daily; the cost is included in the tuition. **Bus service:** Students from San Francisco to San Jose may take CalTrain to the San Mateo station, where a SamTrans bus meets them and takes them to the school. Late afternoon and evening shuttles are available for students following after-school activities. **Uniform/dress code:** No formal dress code although students are expected to use their discretion. T-shirts advertising alcohol are not allowed but dyed hair and facial piercings are okay. **Co-curricular activities/clubs:** Activities include Crystal Ball (Yearbook), Asian Awareness Club, Students of Color Club, Cardinal Club, Spanish Club, French Club, Math Team, Junior Statesmen of America, newspaper, literary magazines, International Thespian Society, Oxfam/Amnesty International, Rainbow Alliance Club (gay/straight students), Fuzzy Green Environmentalists, Peer Helpers, Key Club (admissions), Outdoors Club, Mountain Biking Club, Star Trek/Sci-Fi Club, Humanities Festival, and Crystal Chorus. **Foreign exchange program:** The school has summer programs in France, Spain, China, and India. Students have spent semesters at other schools in the US and abroad. **Opportunities for community service:** Though not required, students volunteer with a wide variety of charities including working in soup kitchens, elderly homes, homeless shelters, and the American Red Cross. **Typical freshman schedule:** 6 to 8 periods of 45-65 minutes each plus one 80-minute science lab each week; 35 minutes for lunch; and, Tuesday-Thursday, a 40-minute consultation/snack period. Advisory, Biology, French II, Comparative Cultures, English 9, Geometry, P.E./Fitness, study hall.

## STUDENT SUPPORT SERVICES

**Counselor/student ratio (not including college counselors):** 1:350. **Counseling:** Each student has an advisor; in addition, teachers work closely with students. A health counselor is available for personal counseling. Students approach the counselor for help or students are referred to counseling if the school notices changes in the student's behavior or attitude. The **college counselor** is the academic dean of the high school. College counseling begins in earnest during the junior year as students are encouraged to explore colleges spring break or summer before the senior year. During the 1st semester of the senior year, all students take "College Quest," to meet with the college counselor and manage the college application process. **Learning differences/disabilities:** "Students with documented learning disabilities are given accommodations (*i.e.*, extra time, use of laptops for essays tests). Special programs are not available." **Career apprenticeship programs:** "Interested students are encouraged to speak with the development office about possible internships. Sophomores and juniors are also invited to apply for a summer grant to explore an area of interest. Also, all high school students interested in teaching have the opportunity to work as assistant teachers in one of our summer school programs."

## STUDENT CONDUCT AND HEALTH

**Code of conduct:** The school has three major rules: remaining on campus, abstaining from drugs, alcohol, and/or tobacco at school or on campus, and being honest. **How school handles drugs/alcohol usage:** "The customary penalty for use of drugs in connection with school life is immediate expulsion, if a student is 'caught.' However, if we hear a student is struggling with a potential addiction, or we suspect one, we will refer the student to counseling." **Drug/alcohol abuse prevention/AIDS awareness program:** Middle school students learn about sexuality, HIV/AIDS, and related issues in G7 and about tobacco, alcohol, and other drugs and addictions in G8. Ninth graders are presented with topics ranging from depression and suicide to eating disorders, sexuality, and violence. The program for G10-12 includes voluntary smoking cessation groups.

## SUMMER PROGRAMS

For students entering GK-9 the following fall, the school offers a five-week morning and afternoon summer program. Cost: $700 per half-day program.

## PARENT INVOLVEMENT

**Parent participation:** Not required, but welcomed. Parents plan and organize the major school fundraiser and may be asked to sit on school committees or to serve on the Board of Trustees. Other volunteering, including driving students to away games, or being an active member of the CSU Parent Association, is encouraged. **Parent/teacher communication:** Quarter and semester grades are sent home, and twice a year parent(s), the student, and the advisor meet to discuss the student's progress. Teachers or advisors call parents if a student is experiencing academic difficulty. Dean's notices (usually behavior and discipline) and progress reports (mid-quarter academic notices for students having difficulty) are also sent to parents. **Parent education:** "CSU recognizes that adolescence is tough for teenagers and the adults who live with them. The CSU Parent Association offers programs to the entire parent body (*i.e.*, a lecture by Mary Pipher) and to grade level parents where an expert might speak to specific issues (adjusting to high school, driving, social issues)." **Donations:** "CSU Fund supports school programs annually. Over 90% of parents participate each year."

## SPORTS

Middle and high school students participate in interscholastic athletic teams, including coed badminton and golf; girls' cross-country, volleyball, tennis, soccer, basketball, and swimming; and boys' cross-country, volleyball, tennis, soccer, basketball, swimming, and baseball. There is also a boys' in-line hockey club. Normally more than 80% of the students participate in team sports. The school is planning to expand the athletic facilities to include at least two more basketball courts and a large fitness center.

## OTHER

"The school has strong music and theater departments, which include an English Hand Bell Choir and singing and theater groups which perform in the school's 400-seat theater."

# WHAT SETS SCHOOL APART FROM OTHERS

"What sets CSU apart from other good independent schools is the contrast between the way we look and the way we act. We look like a traditional college preparatory school but we act like a small college. Again and again CSU students rave about the relationships they develop with their teachers. We ask a great deal of our students, academically, athletically, and extracurricularly, and students respond well to these challenges and then challenge us! Our students are unafraid to be different and are encouraged to take academic risks. Our students thrive in the world 'after CSU' and we think that is in part because they learn so much from the CSU community during their four to seven years here."

# HOW PARENTS/STUDENTS CHARACTERIZE SCHOOL

**Parent response(s):** "My son and daughter both graduated from CSU and what has amazed me is how central the school has remained in their lives. They credit CSU with teaching them how to write and how to think for themselves; I cannot imagine a better place for them to have gone to school!"

**Student response(s):** "Aside from having played a total of thirteen sports seasons in my past six and a half years at CSU, I've been amazed by the other 349 people that I go to school with. Whether their strength be in math or the sciences, or English and history and language, or just ... everything, every student here is a student first. But we are also musicians, actors and actresses, athletes, computer wizards and student leaders. ...

"Participating in student government has given me the opportunity to experience the amazing support system here. There is a mutual respect between the faculty/administration and the students. All of us students are taught by teachers. That's a given. But what isn't a given is how committed these teachers are to helping us understand and make connections. The commitment to academic excellence isn't just about getting good grades and taking the hardest classes. Teachers here at CSU meet with their students during free periods, study halls, before and after school, and even at lunch, if necessary, to help us out. It's amazing how supportive they are of our activities and interests, even outside the classroom. I see my teachers at games, plays, and other events that we participate in. I have grown during my time at CSU in ways that I never thought possible."

*Illustration by Brian Muramatsu*

# THE HARKER SCHOOL

500 Saratoga Avenue
San Jose, CA 95129

(408) 249-2510 *fax (408) 984-2325*
www.harker.org
rutht@harker.org

Diana Nichols, Head of School
Nan Nielsen, Director of Admissions

## GENERAL

**Coed** day high school (with middle school sharing campus; elementary school on a separate nearby campus). **Nonsectarian.** Founded in 1893 as Manzanita Hall. (The present school was formed in 1972 by the merger of the Palo Alto Academy and the Harker Day School.) The high school was begun in 1998, and will be adding a grade each year. **Nonprofit,** member CAIS. **Enrollment:** Currently 215; expected to reach capacity at 520. **Average class size:** 15. **Accreditation:** WASC/CAIS (expected Spring 2000). **School year:** 9.5-month calendar (approx 175 instructional days). **School day:** Varies; approximately 8:10 a.m. to between 1:40 and 3:06 p.m. **Location:** Just off Highway 280 (Saratoga Ave. exit) in San Jose.

## STUDENT BODY

**Geographical breakdown (counties):** 90% from Santa Clara; 6% from the East Bay; 3.6% from San Mateo. **Ethnicity:** 44% Caucasian (non-Latino); 28% Asian; 23% East Indian; 4% Latino; 1% African-American. **Foreign students (I-20 status):** 0. **Middle schools:** 52 of the latest freshman class came from the school's middle school; 2 came from 2 parochial schools; 28 from 15 public middle schools; 15 from 7 private non-parochial schools. A good number of students come from Challenger, Carden and Cupertino schools.

## ADMISSION

**Applications due:** Mid-January (call for exact date). **Application fee:** $50. **Application process:** Open houses are held in November and early January. Applicants submit an application and schedule an interview. The application includes applicant statements and parent statements. The school uses the BAIHS forms for math and English teacher recommendations. The school also seeks a letter of personal recommendation. Applicants take the ERB CTPIII admission test on two dates in January. SSAT and ISEE scores are also accepted. Decisions are sent mid-March. (Admission forms are available on the school's web site at www.harker.org) **No. of applications:** 229 applications were received for 100 places in the most recent freshman class. Seven new students were admitted to G10. **Preferences:** First priority is given to current middle school students who meet the requirements of all A's and B's and strong ERB test scores. **Admission cut-off:** A's and B's, minimum 70th percentile in reading comprehension and math. **"We are looking for** students who seek a strong academic program with opportunities for sports, drama, debate, music, art and technology." **What sort of student do you best serve?** "Students with a keen interest in learning, a commitment to preparing for a university education, and interest in active participation in an area beyond academics. Sports, debate, drama, music, computers and technology are areas in which our students are involved."

## COSTS

**Latest tuition:** $15,200 (includes daily hot lunch) (payable in one payment August 1, or through payment plans provided by outside agencies). **Sibling discount:** None. **Tuition increases:** N/P. **Other costs:** $350-400 for books. **Financial aid:**

Need-based. **Percentage of students receiving financial aid: 15%. Average grant:** $9,500. **No. of full/half tuition grants:** N/P. **Grants of half-tuition or more:** 70%.

## School's Mission Statement/Goals

"Academic excellence is achieved through the development of intellectual curiosity, personal accountability, and a love of learning. Our comprehensive program and dedicated staff help students discover, develop and enjoy their unique talents. Kindness, respect and integrity are instilled within a safe and nurturing environment. We are a dynamic community that honors individuality, embraces diversity and prepares students to take their place as global citizens."

## Academic Program

The academic year is divided into three trimesters. Classes meet four times a week and include three 42-minute periods and one 75-minute period. **Courses offered/to be offered (AP=Advanced Placement, H=Honors; (AP)=AP option, (H)=Honors option): English:** The Myth and the Journey (H), A Survey of British Literature (H), A Survey of American Literature (H), AP English, Literature into Film, Contemporary American Fiction & Poetry, Literature of the Holocaust, Shakespeare's Tragedies & Comedies, Creative Writing, Satire & Comedy, Madness in Literature, Asian Masterpieces, Great Women Writers, Great Novels; **Mathematics:** Algebra I, Algebra II/Trigonometry (H), Geometry (H), Probability, Statistics (AP), Pre-Calculus (H), Analytic Geometry H, AP Calculus AB, AP Calculus BC, Multivariable Calculus, Linear Algebra, Differential Equations, Math Appreciation, Mathematics of Fractals and Chaos; **History:** World History (The Early Modern World, The World in the 19th Century, The World in the 20th Century), Economics, American History (AP), Intermediate Economics, Africa & The World, Asia: China, Japan, India, The Middle East; **Technology:** Introduction to Computers and Multimedia, Current Topics in Technology, Web Page Design I-II, Programming I-II, AP Computer Science-Beginning, AP Computer Science-Intermediate, AP Computer Science-Advanced, Graphics Programming, General Topics in Computer Science, Desktop Publishing, Multimedia Authoring, Advanced Multimedia Authoring, Programming Computer Graphics, Directed Study in Technology; **Science:** Conceptual Physics, Physics H, Introduction to Chemistry, Chemistry H, Introduction to Biology, Biology H, AP Physics, AP Chemistry, AP Biology, Geology, The Human Genome Project, Astronomy, Evolution, Electronics, Ecology, Human Anatomy & Physiology, Independent Study in Science; **Foreign Language:** First-Third Year Spanish, Spanish II/III H, Adv. Spanish Conversation & Composition, AP Spanish Language, Literature of the Spanish Speaking World, AP Spanish Literature, The Mexican American Experience, Spain's Golden Age, Contemporary Spanish Theater, First-Third Year French, French II/III H, Adv. French Conversation & Composition, AP French Language, Survey of French Literature, AP French Literature, French Short Stories, The Art & Museums of Paris, France Today, First-Fourth Year Japanese, Advanced Japanese Seminar, Independent Study in Japanese, First-Third Year Latin, AP Latin Literature, Advanced Literature in Latin; **Fine Arts:** The Study of Performing Arts, Art Appreciation Through the Study of Visual Arts, Acting, Acting-Advanced Scene Study, Acting for Various Media, Young Director's Workshop, Student Directed Showcase, Shakespeare Dramas, Greek Drama, Musical Theater Workshop, Scriptwriting for Stage and Screen, Advanced Public Speaking, Debate, Beginning Ballet, Intermediate Ballet, Advanced Ballet, Beginning-Advanced Jazz Dance, Beginning-Advanced Modern Dance, Beginning Choreography, Choreography for Performance, Dance Appreciation, Choir, Jazz Choir, Madrigals Group, Music Theory, Music History & Famous Composers, Music Appreciation/World Music, Orchestra, Jazz Ensemble, Advanced String & Woodwind Ensemble, Technical Workshop, Film Appreciation, Design & Composition, Basic Drawing, Advanced Drawing, American Art History, Painting, Ceramics, Sculpture Exploration, Print Making, Stained Glass, Beginning Architecture; **P.E.:** Aerobics, Intramural Basketball, Cheerleading, Beginning Fencing, Fitness, Scuba, Self-Defense, Swimming, Ultimate Frisbee, Recreational Volleyball, Weight lifting for Sports (see sports, below, for competitive teams); **Other:** Introduction to Engineering, Graphic Arts, Advanced Architecture, Video Yearbook, Dance Production, Spanish Civilization, Latin American Civilization, French Civilization, Public Speaking (required), Ethics. **Computer lab/training:** The school has two computer labs, one with PCs the other Macs. (N/P re #) One year of technology is required. **Grading:** Letter grades. **Graduation requirements:** 4 years English, 3 years math (including Geometry and Algebra II), 3 terms fine arts, mastery through the third year of a foreign language, 2 years history, 3 years of a lab science, 1 term of health, public speaking, and ethics, 1 year of technology, and 1 year beyond the basic requirement of a particular subject in the student's area of interest. **Average nightly homework (Mon-Th):** G9: 3 hours. (N/P re other grades) **Faculty:** N/P. **Faculty ethnicity:** 86% Caucasian (non-Latino); 7% Latino; 7% East Indian. **Faculty selection and training:** "Faculty are selected through a rigorous screening program involving interviews and on-site teaching demonstrations. All faculty have either a valid teaching credential or (at a minimum) a master's degree with previous teaching experience. Various on-site workshops are provided throughout the year. Additionally, all faculty are required to attend at least one continuing education workshop/seminar per school year off-site." **Teacher/student ratio:** 1:7. **Teacher's daily student load in required academic subject:** Maximum 75. **AP courses and exams:** (At the time of publication, the school had only a freshman class; one freshman student enrolled in AP Calculus AB.) **Senior class profile (mean):** Not applicable. At the time of publication, the school has not had its first senior class. **College enrollment:** Not applicable.

# Other Indicators the School is Accomplishing its Goals

N/P.

# Campus/Campus Life

**Campus description:** The high school shares a 16-acre campus with the middle school. The campus has seven buildings with lawns and gardens between them. These buildings house middle school classrooms, offices, dance, art, and music studios, a gym, and the high school student lounge ("The Edge"), which serves lunch to high school students daily. The high school building, Dobbins Hall, is a new two-story building with classrooms, science labs, computer labs, and a faculty lounge. The campus's outdoor area includes a pool, tennis courts, playing fields and outdoor basketball courts. The school plans to build a new technology center and student union with additional classrooms, a parking garage, and tennis courts (ground-breaking scheduled for Spring, 2000). Future growth includes a theater, expanded library, and new gymnasium. **Library:** 2,100 sq. ft.; 11,000 print volumes; 55 periodical subscriptions (and subscription to ProQuest Direct Platinum indexed database of more than 5,000 publications); 21 computers (all with Internet access); 10 CD-ROMs, on-line catalog, study space for 50. Open to students from 7:30 a.m. to 5 p.m. Full-time librarian. **Open/closed campus:** Closed. **Classroom space per student:** N/P. **Lunches:** Hot lunches are served daily; cost is included in tuition. **Bus service:** A shuttle picks up students from CalTrain. **Uniforms/dress code:** The dress code prohibits blue jeans (unless worn with coat and tie or, for girls, blazer), sweat pants, or athletic style shorts; no clothing with references to drugs, alcohol, violence or sexually suggestive material; no piercings other than ears; no military-style clothing, no hats; no t-shirts or midriff shirts. (Some special dress days require boys to wear coat and tie and dress slacks, girls to wear dress, skirt, or dressy pant suit.) **Co-curricular activities/clubs:** Art, Astronomy, Chess, Community Service, Computer, Dance, Debate/Speech, Environmental Action, foreign language, literary magazine, math, newspaper, Outdoor Activity, Photography, Spirit, Theater, Tutoring, Video. **Foreign exchange program:** Summer travel only. **Opportunities for community service:** Community service is encouraged but not required. **Typical freshman schedule:** English, math, foreign language, world history, P.E., fine arts, technology.

# Student Support Services

**Counselor-student ratio (not including college counselors):** 1:200. **Counseling:** A full-time counselor does academic tracking and follow-up and is available for support regarding social and emotional issues. A full-time **college counselor**

works with the students beginning freshman year; at capacity, the high school will have 3 full-time college counselors. **Learning disabilities/differences:** "We are not a school for students with significant learning problems. Faculty and administration work with students and families to enhance the learning environment of all students." **Career apprenticeship programs:** "As the school grows we are developing a mentor program and opportunities for summer internships in industry."

## Student Conduct and Health

**Code of conduct:** Standard. **How school handles drug/alcohol usage**: On first alcohol/tobacco violation (on campus/campus event), the student is suspended and required to obtain counseling; on second violation, the student is dismissed. For other controlled substances (on campus) the student is dismissed, for off-campus, the student is required to obtain counseling. **Drug/alcohol abuse prevention/AIDS awareness programs:** N/P.

## Summer Programs

Sports camps and an academic summer school are available.

## Parent Involvement

**Parent participation:** N/P. **Parent/teacher communication:** Parent-teacher conferences are held each fall. Report cards are issued three times per year. In addition, teachers communicate with parents on an as-needed basis by phone and e-mail. All teachers post their assignments on their web site. **Parent education:** Occasional speakers address various issues relating to education, teenagers, college admission, and financing college education. **Donations:** Not required. Parents provide fund raising support through the Annual Giving Campaign and the Capital Campaign. Donations to Annual Giving range from $50 to $14,000.

## Sports

Aerobics, baseball, basketball, cross-country, fencing, field hockey, football, golf, lacrosse, scuba diving, self-defense, soccer, softball, swimming, tennis, track and field, volleyball, wrestling, and weight-lifting.

## What Sets School Apart From Others

"Our small class size and academic rigor exist in an atmosphere where the expectations are for strong individual effort and personal responsibility. The faculty have created a caring and supportive environment with enough structure to provide guidance and enough freedom to support the development of individual accountability and a positive self-image. Incorporation of technology in the curriculum is well-developed and ever-increasing. Clubs, sports, and activities ensure that, for Harker students, school, and life, are more than just books."

## How Parents/Students Characterize School

N/P.

# The Head-Royce School

4315 Lincoln Avenue
Oakland, CA 94602

(510) 531-1300 *fax (510) 530-8329*
www.hrs.pvt.k12.ca.us

Paul D. Chapman, Head of School
Crystal Land, Director of Admissions, cland@hrs.pvt.k12.ca.us

## General

**Coed** day high school with K-5 lower school and G6-8 middle school. **Nonsectarian.** Founded in 1887 as the Anna Head School, a girls' school, it merged with the Josiah Royce School, its "sibling" boys' school, in 1971. **Nonprofit**, member CAIS, NAIS, BAIHS. **Enrollment:** Approximately 300 in the high school. **Average class size:** 15. **Accreditation**: WASC/CAIS (6-year term: 1999-05). **School year:** 10-month calendar (176 instructional days). **School day:** 8:25 a.m. to 3:20 p.m. **Location:** The school is located on a 14-acre campus in a residential neighborhood in the Oakland Hills between Highways 13 and 580. Students can take BART to the Fruitvale station and take the #53 AC Transit bus to campus. Three AC buses provide supplemental transit from Berkeley and Oakland to the campus. A private bus service transports students from Contra Costa County.

# STUDENT BODY

**Geographical breakdown (counties):** 90% from Alameda; 10% from Contra Costa. **Ethnicity:** 68% Caucasian (non-Latino); 10% African-American; 8% Asian; 4% Latino. **Foreign students (I-20 status):** 0. **Single parent/two f/t working parent families:** N/P. **Middle schools:** 32% of the most recent entering freshman class came from 7 public middle schools; 56% from 11 private, non-parochial schools; 12% from 3 parochial schools. A good number of students come from Prospect Sierra (El Cerrito) and 7 Hills (Walnut Creek).

# ADMISSION

**Applications due**: Approximately January 20 (call for date). **Application fee**: $50. **Application process:** Parents should complete an application in early December and schedule their child for the ISEE to be taken in December or January. Prospective students spend a half day on the campus between November and February for class visits and an interview. They also provide a writing sample at the time of the visit. Transcripts and recommendations from current math and English teachers are required as well as a student statement. **No. of applications:** 220 applications were received for 25 places in the prior year's class. (50 slots for the 80-student class were taken by the school's middle school students.) **Admission cut-off:** "Most of our students have a B average or above and score 70% and above on the ISEE." **Preferences:** Siblings; students of color; and children of faculty, alumni, and trustees. **"We are looking for** intellectually curious, academically motivated, community-minded students who will contribute to the school community and profit from small class instruction with talented and engaging faculty." **What sort of student do you best serve?** (Same as above.)

# COST

**Latest tuition:** $14,450 payable in 2 installments. (Other payment plans are available.) **Sibling discount:** None. **Tuition increases:** Approximately 5% annually. **Other costs:** Books ($400-500), activity fee ($150), P.E. uniforms, calculators, supplies, and transportation. **Financial aid**: Need-based financial aid is available (no merit scholarships). **Percentage of students receiving financial aid:** 13% of K-12 students. **Average grant:** $10,000 for high school students. **No. of full-tuition grants:** 0. **No. of half-tuition grants:** "Awards vary from 10-90% of tuition costs." **Grants of half-tuition or more:** 50%.

# SCHOOL'S MISSION STATEMENT/GOALS

"The mission of Head-Royce is to inspire in our students a lifelong love of learning and exuberance for academic excellence, to promote understanding of and respect for the diversity that makes our society strong, and to encourage constructive and responsible citizenship. ... The school nurtures the development of the whole child through a program that seeks: to develop intellectual abilities such as scholarship and disciplined critical thinking; to foster in each student integrity, ethical behavior, self-esteem, compassion, and a sense of humor; to nurture aesthetic abilities such as creativity, imagination, musical and visual talent; to promote leadership and social responsibility, an appreciation of individual and cultural differences, and a respect for the opinions of others; and to encourage joyful, healthy living and physical fitness. All members of the Head-Royce community—students, alumni, faculty, staff, administrators, parents, and trustees—are dedicated to a balanced educational environment within which each student can thrive."

## ACADEMIC PROGRAM

**Courses offered (AP=Advanced Placement, H=Honors, (AP)=AP option, (H)=Honors option): Computer Science:** Keyboarding and Word Processing, AP Computer Science, Advanced Program Design Seminar; **English**: English 9: Composition and Literature, English 10: Composition and American Literature, English 11: Western Classical Literature, English 12: Contemporary Women's Literature, Creative Writing, Japanese Literature and Culture, Latin American Literature, Literature and Film, Literature of the American West, Modern Drama and Playwriting, Science Fiction, Shakespeare, or Southern Writers. Electives include: Expository Writing, Speech and Debate I, Speech and Debate II, Public Speaking; **Arts:** Intro to 2-dimensional Art/Advanced 2-dimensional Art, AP Art Studio, Intro to Film and Video/Advanced Film and Video, Graphic Design, Drama I, Drama II, Intro to Theater, Intro to 3-dimensional Art/Advanced 3-dimensional Art, Photography/Advanced Photography, Photojournalism, Head-Royce Symphony, Head-Royce Orchestra, Jazz Band, The Head-Royce Chorus, Colla Voce (vocal ensemble), AP Music Theory; **Foreign Languages:** French I-IV, Advanced French Seminar, AP French Language, AP French Literature, Latin I-V, AP Latin: Vergil, Spanish I-V, Advanced Spanish Seminar, AP Spanish Language, AP Spanish Literature; **History:** History 9: History of the Emerging World, History 10: US History, AP US History Seminar, History 11: Western Culture and Civilization, AP European History Seminar, History 12: AP Art History, Introduction to Economics, Intro to Political Philosophy and Ethics, Intro to Psychology, Issues in Latin America, The Legacy of Vietnam, Understanding the Middle East, The US from 1945 to 1975, Comparative World Religions; **Math:** Algebra B, Algebra I-II, Algebra II H, Geometry, Geometry H, Pre-Calculus, Pre-Calculus H, Calculus, AP Calculus; **Science:** Conceptual Physics, Chemistry, Biology (AP), AP Physics, Science 12: Astronomy, Genetics and Biotechnology, Ecology and Natural History of the Bay Area, Electronics, Biotechnology: Applications and Ethics, Marine Biology, Neurobiology. **Computer lab/training:** The high school's computer lab has 16 Mac computers. Students are required to be computer proficient to graduate. **Grading:** Letter grades A-F. **Graduation requirements:** The graduation requirements are meant to exceed the UC requirements for admission. 4 years English, 4 years history, 3 years math, 3 years science, 3 years foreign language, 1.5 years electives, .5 year fine arts, 4 years P.E., computer keyboarding proficiency, health and safety, and 60 hours community service. **Average nightly homework:** G9-10: 30 min. per subject; G11-12: 40 min. or more per subject. **Faculty:** 33% male, 67% female. 33% of faculty hold bachelor's degrees as highest degree; 61% hold master's degrees; and 6% hold doctorates. **Faculty ethnicity:** 89% Caucasian (non-Latino); 9% Asian; 9% African-American; 5% Latino. **Faculty selection/training:** "Faculty are selected through administrative screening including placement agencies, resumes, interviews, etc. Professional development funding helps keep faculty professionally up-to-date. We have in-services twice a year." **Teacher/student ratio:** 1:10. **Teacher's daily student load in required academic subject:** 60-75 over 4-5 periods. **AP courses/exams:** 75% of students are currently taking one or more AP courses. Last year 214 students took 1083 AP exams. 86% scored 3 or above. (N/P # subjects) **Senior class profile (mean):** SAT Math 688, SAT Verbal 687. (SAT II: AH 657; BY 643; CH 660; FL 680; FR 702; LR 646; LT 654; M1C 653; M2C 675; PH 727; SL 680; WR 666; SP 690.) **GPA:** 3.38 unweighted; 3.68 weighted for UC honors classes (1 additional point each). **National Merit Scholarship Program:** Last year's graduating class included 20 commended, 9 semi-finalists, 8 finalists, and 2 winners. **College enrollment:** 100% of last year's graduating class enrolled in 4-year colleges, including: UC Berkeley (8), UCLA (6), U of Pennsylvania (4), UC Davis (4), UC Santa Cruz (4), Dartmouth (3), Princeton (3), MIT (3), Stanford (3), U of Virginia (3), Barnard, Duke (2), UC San Diego (2), Carleton (2), U of Colorado-Boulder (2), Harvard (2), USC (2), Wellesley (2), U of Arizona (2), Vassar (2), UC Santa Barbara, Brown, Yale, Wesleyan, Northwestern, RISD, Georgetown, Scripps, Tufts, Howard, Washington U, Northwestern, Colgate, U of Michigan, Claremont McKenna, Amherst, Columbia, Smith, CSU-SF, U of Denver, and U of Washington.

## Other Indicators the School is Accomplishing its Goals

"Alumni and parent feedback, college admissions, test scores."

## Campus/Campus Life

**Campus description:.** The campus consists of 14 acres in a canyon in the Oakland Hills with a view of the San Francisco Bay. Each of the three schools (Lower, Middle and Upper) has its own modern facilities. The campus includes an auditorium with a capacity of 320, a Creative Arts Center, and an eight-acre athletic complex with an outdoor swimming pool, three tennis courts, a regulation soccer field, baseball/softball diamond, two basketball courts, and a new gymnasium. **Library:** 2,261 sq. ft.; study space for 64 students; 64 periodical subscriptions; 18,000 print volumes; 6 computers (with Internet access); and an on-line catalog. Open to students from 7:45 a.m. to 3:45 p.m. **Open/closed campus:**

Closed, but juniors and seniors have off-campus privileges. **Classroom space per student:** N/P. **Lunches:** Most students bring their lunches. An outside vendor provides bag lunches for purchase. **Bus service:** A private bus service is available to students commuting from Orinda, Lafayette, Danville, and Walnut Creek. Current cost is $1,000/year. (AC Transit provides supplementary service from Berkeley and Oakland.) **Uniforms/dress code:** No specific requirements other than that clothing be clean and neat and not distracting or offensive to others. **Co-curricular activities/clubs:** Activities include community service, outdoor education (sea kayaking, high ropes courses, river rafting), debate, student newspaper, yearbook, drama, instrumental and vocal groups, Latin Club, Kaleidoscope Club (Multicultural), Recycling Club, Mountain Biking Club, Improv Club, Afro-American Student Club, Amnesty International, A.S.I.A. Club, Chess Club, The Earth Society, French Club, Gay Lesbian Awareness Group, Italian Club, Junior Statesmen, Reading & Poetry, Snowboarding Club, Spanish Club, Thespian Society, Video/Film. **Foreign exchange program:** The school has exchange programs with Bloxham School in England and American School in Paris. **Opportunities for community service:** Project Open Hand, SPCA, coaching little league, tutoring, outdoor clean-up, etc. **Typical freshman schedule:** Geometry (beginning at 8:33), 3D Art, homeroom, Physics, History, lunch (12:10-12:50), English 9, Spanish II, Drama (ending at 3:20).

## STUDENT SUPPORT SERVICES

**Counselor/student ratio (not including college counselors):** 1:300. **Counseling:** The school has a full-time school counselor who also advises the student community service board. Academic advising is done by faculty, deans, and the head of the upper school. Peer counseling also takes place. A full-time Director of College Counseling works actively with students and parents to coordinate college planning and help with the college admissions process. Meetings, workshops, and individual family meetings occur during the sophomore, junior, and senior years. **Learning differences/disabilities:** "We have a learning specialist to help us diagnose and support LD kids." **Career apprenticeship programs:** Job listings are posted in the spring.

## STUDENT CONDUCT AND HEALTH

**Code of conduct:** Students are expected to act responsibly and to actively support the goals of Head-Royce. In addition to abiding by the major school rules, all members of the Head-Royce community are expected to treat each other with courtesy and respect. The administration and faculty reserve the right to remove a student from Head-Royce whose behavior has been disruptive to the learning environment of the school, damaging to the school community, or to the school's reputation within the greater community. **How school handles drugs/alcohol usage**: The school's "likely response" to a first alcohol/drug use offense is, after due process, substance abuse counseling, 5-10 day suspension or expulsion, and on the second offense, expulsion. Students who use tobacco on or in the vicinity of the school grounds receive substance abuse counseling and may be suspended with repeated infractions. **Drug/alcohol abuse prevention/AIDS awareness program:** These issues are addressed in a sophomore course called Health and Safety. The course teaches skills to prevent, identify, and treat health problems and increase students' knowledge of safe and unsafe behavior. The course is team taught by the school counselor and a physical education teacher.

## SUMMER PROGRAMS

The school has summer programs for K-8 only.

## PARENT INVOLVEMENT

**Parent participation:** Parents are encouraged to contribute 16 hours per family per year. **Parent/teacher communication:** "Report cards, comments, and conferences as needed. Regular mailings about high school events." **Parent education:** "We offer in-services and programs for parents. This year we had Michael Thompson speak to parents about boy development and the college-admissions process." **Donations:** Donations are "voluntary but strongly encouraged." Each year parents are requested to participate in annual giving. The school seeks 100% participation from parents.

## SPORTS

Approximately 80-85% of students participate in at least one season of after-school sports. Students compete in the Bay Counties League in boys' soccer, cross-country, basketball, baseball, volleyball, tennis, and swimming, and in girls' volleyball, cross-country, tennis, basketball, soccer, swimming, and softball.

## OTHER

Recent Senior Projects include students working at internships at crisis intervention centers, the French Consulate, the San Francisco Museum of Modern Art, and KTVU; volunteering at the elementary schools and for AIDS services; creating photo essays; working as stagehands, park rangers, and athletic trainers; and painting murals.

## WHAT SETS SCHOOL APART FROM OTHERS

"Outstanding faculty, great facilities (gym, fields, performing arts center, fine arts studios, technology labs, library), two international programs, community service (required), accelerated high school program at [UC Berkeley], integrated technology curriculum including digital video, senior projects."

## How Parents/Students Characterize School
N/P.

# Holy Names High School
4660 Harbord Dr.
Oakland, CA 94618

(510) 450-1110 *fax (510) 547-3111*
www.hnhs.pvt.k12.ca.us/doors.html

Laura M. Held, President
Angela Schenone, Principal
Francis Bird, Director of Admission, (510) 450-1110 x119

## General

**Girls'** day high school. **Catholic** (44% Catholic). Founded in 1868 by the Sisters of Holy Names of Jesus and Mary. **Nonprofit. Enrollment:** Approximately 300. **Average class size:** 25. **Accreditation:** WASC (N/P re term). **School year:** 9-month calendar. (N/P re # of instructional days) **School day:** 8 a.m. to 2:35 p.m. (Students may arrive at 7:30 a.m. and stay until 4:30 p.m.) **Location:** Close to Highways 13 and 24, off Broadway Terrace, the school is accessible by AC Transit buses 59, 59A and 651 Supplementary; the Rockridge BART station is in the vicinity. Students car pool from Pinole, Fremont, Hayward, Dublin, Walnut Creek, and other areas.

## Student Body

**Geographical breakdown (counties):** 85% from Alameda County; 13% from Contra Costa. **Ethnicity:** Approximately 41% African-American; 31% Caucasian (non Latina); 11% Latina; 2% Asian; 11% other. **Foreign students (I-20 status):** 0. **Single parent/two f/t working parent families:** N/P. **Middle schools:** Of the most recent entering freshman class, 55% came from parochial schools; 31% came from public middle schools; 7% from private, non-parochial schools. (N/P re #)

## Admission

**Applications due:** Approximately January 23 (call for date). **Application fee:** $50. **Application process:** The school hosts an open house in October for interested families and an information night in January. To apply, parents submit an application form and fee. Applicants take the High School Placement Test (HSPT) at the school in Late January and submit the prior two years' report cards and standardized test results, assessments from an English teacher, math teacher, and principal/counselor. Parents and students submit statements, and an interview is scheduled. **No. of applications:** 179 applications were received for 90 places in prior year's class. (N/P re # new students admitted to upper grades) **Admission cut-off:** N/P. **Preferences:** N/P. **"We are looking for** demonstrated academic ability to benefit from the school curriculum, responsible citizenship, and reasons for enrolling which are compatible with school's philosophy. Though we look at a lot more than test scores, students admitted generally score in the 50th percentile or above on the [HSPT]." **What sort of student do you best serve?** (See above.)

## Costs

**Latest tuition:** $5,750 payable in 1 or 11 payments. **Sibling discount:** No. **Tuition increases:** 4-5% annually. **Other costs:** Books/co-curricular fees of approximately $400; uniforms approximately $100. **Financial aid:** Need-based grants. In addition, the school has a number of academic scholarships available. **Percentage of students receiving financial aid:** 27%. **Average grant:** $980. **No. of full-tuition grants:** None. **No. of half-tuition grants:** None. **Grants of half-tuition or more:** N/P.

## School's Mission Statement/Goals

"Holy Names High School was established on the shores of Lake Merritt in 1868 by the Sisters of the Holy Names of Jesus and Mary. Holy Names was the first secondary school in Oakland. Having outgrown its original campus, the school moved to its present site on Harbord Drive in 1931.

"The mission of Holy Names High School is to provide a quality college preparatory education for young women in a supportive environment which fosters a Christian life view, which promotes academic excellence, and which values each individual in its culturally and ethnically diverse student body. Holy Names has a strong belief in the unique advantages that an all girls' school gives young women; namely, to recognize and grow to their full potential. Holy Names commits itself to foster that growth in all aspects of school life. Through a rigorous academic program complemented by well-rounded co-curricular opportunities, Holy Names prepares young women for entering and succeeding in higher education, for citizenship in our global and technological society, and for assuming expanding responsibilities as women and leaders for the 21st century."

# ACADEMIC PROGRAM

"Holy Names provides its students with a rigorous academic program which meets the standards required for college and university entrance and prepares them for success in their chosen fields. Having the opportunity to take seven classes each semester, students are able not only to meet but also to exceed what is required for college entrance. This extra seventh class gives them the opportunity to augment a basic college preparatory curriculum with additional courses which strengthen their areas of primary emphasis, broaden the scope of their educational preparation, and enrich their personal lives. Our average class size is 25 students. This allows for more individual attention, cooperative learning, and educational enrichment." **Courses offered (AP=Advanced Placement, H=Honors, (AP)=AP option, (H)=Honors option): Computers:** Integrated Computer Applications/Keyboarding, Introduction to Structured Programming in Pascal AP, Introduction to Structured Programming in Basic; **English:** English 9, 10 (H), 11 (H), & 12 (AP); **Fine Arts:** Basic Fine Arts (Choral, Beginning Instrumental, Speech/Drama, Drawing and Design), Drawing, Color and Design, Painting and Advanced Drawing, Advanced Art Lab AP, World Arts, Choir, Vocal Ensemble, Piano, Orchestra, Drama, Graphic Arts/Yearbook Production; **Foreign Languages:** French 1-5, AP French, Spanish 1-5, AP Spanish; **Math:** Math 9, Algebra 1 (H), Advanced Algebra/Trigonometry 2 (H), Geometry, Pre-Calculus, Calculus AP, Trigonometry/Statistics; **P.E.:** P.E. 1-2; **Social Studies:** World Cultures 1, 2 (H), US History (H), US Government, Economics (H), Psychology (H); **Religious Studies:** Religions of the World and Introduction to Catholic Christianity (G9), Ethics and Decision Making (G10), Christian Scriptures and Christian Lifestyles (G11), Women's Spirituality and Social Justice (G12); **Science:** Health Science, Lab Biology, Chemistry (H), Physics, Physiology. **Computer lab/training:** The school has 2 computer labs as well as a library mini-lab with a total of 1 computer per 4 students, including Mac 550LCs, scanners, and integrated applications. Students have e-mail and access to the Internet. **Grading:** Report cards issued each quarter include A-F grades, teacher comments, conduct ratings, and attendance. Only semester grades appear on transcripts. **Graduation requirements:** 260 credits including 4 years English, 4 years religious studies, 4 years social science, 2 years science, 3 years math, 2 years foreign language, 2.5 years fine arts, 1 year P.E., and 1 semester computers. **Average nightly homework:** 3-4 hours. **Faculty:** 8% male, 92% female. 29% of faculty hold bachelor's degrees as highest degree; 70% hold master's degrees; and 1% hold doctorates. 5-6 religious on teaching faculty. **Faculty ethnicity:** N/P. **Faculty selection/training:** N/P. **Teacher/student ratio:** 1:18. **Teacher's daily student load in required academic subject:** N/P. **AP courses/exams:** In 1997, 18 students took 24 AP examinations in 5 subjects. 72% received scores of three or above. (N/P re % in AP classes) **Senior class profile (mean):** N/P. **GPA:** "Range and # of students falling in range: 4.0 (1); 3.99-3.75 (3); 3.74-3.50 (8), 3.49-3.25 (8), 3.24-3.0 (12), 2.99-2.75 (12), 2.74-2.5 (9), 2.49-2.0 (16)." **National**

**Merit Scholarship Program:** "In 1997, 2 students received outstanding scores on the National Merit Scholarship Qualifying Test." **College enrollment:** 94% of last year's graduating class enrolled in 4-year colleges, 2% in 2-year colleges. (N/P re colleges)

## OTHER INDICATORS THE SCHOOL IS ACCOMPLISHING ITS GOALS

"In 1985 and 1991, Holy Names received a Blue Ribbon Exemplary Award from the US Department of Education. Schools awarded this mark of excellence are evaluated primarily on evidence of superiority of their leadership, teaching, environment, curriculum, instruction, parent and community support, student achievement, and organizational vitality. In 1991, Holy Names was one among only 62 private schools nationwide that had received this distinction twice. In the summer of 1997, the school renovated, updated, and obtained new equipment for science labs."

## CAMPUS/CAMPUS LIFE

**Campus description:** The school sits on 5.78 acres in a wooded, residential section of the Upper Rockridge section of Oakland. The school building is a stately three-story building built in 1931, which includes classrooms, administration, a gym, cafeteria, and a gothic-style auditorium that seats 525. **Library:** 9,000 print volumes; 8 computers (4 with Internet access); 40 periodical subscriptions; open to students from 7:30 a.m. to 4 p.m. (N/P re sq. ft., study space) **Open/closed campus:** Closed. **Classroom space per student:** N/P. **Lunches:** Food may be purchased in the cafeteria from 7:45 a.m. to 12:45 p.m. **Bus service:** None. **Uniforms/dress code:** The school uniform includes a pleated or kilt-style skirt, navy blue twill pants, or navy shorts, with short- or long-sleeved collared polo shirts in white, red, or navy. **Co-curricular activities/clubs:** Activities include Ambassadors, Block Society (athletic honors), California Scholarship Federation, Campus Ministry, Class Government, Community Service Program, Dances, Drama, *Echoes* (Yearbook), Interscholastic Teams, Mock Trial, Model UN, Multicultural Club, National Honor Society, Student Council, World in Focus (environmental). Students are welcome to start their own clubs. **Foreign exchange program:** None. **Opportunities for community service:** Through Campus Ministry, students are required to perform on/off campus service for 20 hours each year enrolled. They volunteer at numerous social service agencies involved in helping the sick, elderly, homeless, AIDS patients, and children. These include Elizabeth House, Piedmont Gardens Rest Home, San Leandro Shelter, Glide Memorial Church, Alameda County Food Bank, and Habitat for Humanity. **Typical freshman schedule:** Religion 9, World Cultures I, foreign language, mathematics, P.E./Health Science, Freshman Fine Arts, English 9.

## STUDENT SUPPORT SERVICES

**Counselor/student ratio (not including college counselors):** N/P. **Counseling:** The school offers personal, academic, and college counseling. Each student is assigned one of three personal counselors to assist in any personal matters that may arise. In addition, each student has an academic counselor with whom she meets at least four times a year. Students take the PSAT in sophomore and junior years and may enroll in a SAT preparation program. Each spring, the school sponsors a California College Tour which allows juniors to visit 10 college campuses in California. **Learning disabilities/differences:** N/P. **Career apprenticeship programs:** N/P.

## STUDENT CONDUCT AND HEALTH

**Code of conduct:** Standard. No pagers or cell phones. **How school handles drugs/alcohol usage:** "The school has a no tolerance policy for alcohol/illegal drug use on campus." **Drug/alcohol abuse prevention/AIDS awareness program:** Included in 9th grade Health/Science class and in various assemblies.

## SUMMER PROGRAMS

None.

## PARENT INVOLVEMENT

**Parent participation:** Parents are asked to serve on a Parent Advisory Council and to volunteer for various events/projects. **Parent/teacher communication:** Progress reports and report cards four times a year. Additionally, parents receive a monthly parent newsletter. **Parent education:** The counseling department provides a grade-level event each year. **Donations:** Parents are expected to make contributions to the school.

## SPORTS

Students compete in the Alameda/Contra Costa Athletic League in volleyball, tennis, basketball, soccer, swimming, track, and softball.

## OTHER

All students participate in a yearly retreat with their class. The retreats are sponsored by Campus Ministry and focus on spiritual growth development and building community within the class and school. During mid-sessions (two-week period between semesters), students choose from 30 academic and enrichment classes and approximately 60 community service opportunities. Classes include African-American History, Cello, Intro to Law, Modern Jazz Dance, Math Games, SAT Preparation, Self-Defense, Voice, Sign Language, Driver's Ed, Money Management, Auto Mechanics, and Creative Writing. Career and service opportunities include internships in accounting, architecture, dentistry, child care, engineering, fire fighting, law, medical research, medicine, radio, television, and government. Trips are also planned during these sessions, including to Washington, D.C., and Mexico.

## What Sets School Apart From Others

"At Holy Names, we offer a rigorous academic program which supports and challenges the very best in each student of the school community. We are committed to teaching Catholic Christian values and to providing opportunities for each young woman to nourish her relationship with her God. Our Holy Names environment offers a commitment to developing leadership and to preparing young women for responsible and active participation in their world. Most significant to our heritage is our value for diversity. We celebrate the rich varied culture and backgrounds of our young women and we challenge them to learn together and from one another. Finally, our school offers students the opportunity to develop a sense of social responsibility and service in the broader community."

## How Parents/Students Characterize School

**Parent response(s):** N/P.
**Student response(s):**
"Holy Names is a place of acceptance, understanding, and individuality, preparing young women for a bright future; we are a caring community, building pride, prestige, and honor." "Excellence is in the school; pride is in the person." "Grow up, find yourself, have fun, be yourself. Holy Names is the place where all this happens and more." "Holy Names is the place where minds grow."

# THE INTERNATIONAL HIGH SCHOOL OF THE FRENCH-AMERICAN INTERNATIONAL SCHOOL

**Lycée International Franco-Américain**
150 Oak Street
San Francisco, CA 94102-5912

(415) 558-2084 *fax (415) 558-2085*

Jane Camblin, Head of School
Dan Harder, Director of Admission, danh@fais-ihs.org
Betsy Brody Albertazzi, Associate Director of Admission, betsyb@fais-ihs.org

## GENERAL

**Coed** day high school. **Nonsectarian.** The high school was founded in 1975.
The high school shares a campus with the French-American International School
("FAIS") (founded 1962), which has a lower school (preK-5) and a middle school
(G6-8). **Nonprofit**, member CAIS, NAIS, BAIHS. **Enrollment:** Approximately
250 (high school only). **Average class size:** 15-17. **Accreditation:** WASC/CAIS
(6-year term: 1996-01), International Baccalaureate Organization, French Min-
istry of Education. **School year:** 10-month calendar (184 instructional days).
**School day:** 8:25 a.m. to 4:05 p.m.

## STUDENT BODY

**Geographical breakdown (counties):** The majority of students live in San Francisco, others commute from Oakland/Contra Costa, Marin, San Mateo, and other
Bay Area locations. **Ethnicity:** 78% Caucasian (non-Latino); 9% African-American; 8% Asian; 3% Latino; 2% other. The student body is made up of students
from more than 50 countries speaking 34 different languages or dialects. **Percentage foreign students (I-20 status):** 15%. **Single parent/two f/t working
parent families:** N/P. **Middle schools:** 10% of the most recent entering freshman class came from public middle schools; 70% from private, non-parochial
schools; 20% from parochial schools. (Of these, 10% were from French schools.)
A good number of students come from Bay Area independent middle schools.
(N/P re # schools)

# ADMISSION

**Applications due:** Approximately January 20 (call for date). (Late applications are welcome but timely applications will be given priority.) **Application fee:** $60. **Application process:** Students visit the school and submit an essay, teacher's recommendations (BAIHS forms), transcripts, and results of a standardized test (CTBS, CTPII, CAT, SSAT, IC or STS). Each student is interviewed by an IHS representative. **No. of applications:** 220 applications were received for 75 places in prior year's class. Of these, 28 places were taken by FAIS middle school students. Two new students were admitted to G10, 2 to G11, 1 to G12. **Admission cut-off:** "None, although generally we expect students to have at least a B average and fairly strong standardized test scores (50% or above in independent school norms on SSATs, for example)." **Preferences:** Siblings, French nationals in the French program, and FAIS eighth graders who meet admissions standards. Note: Prior study of a foreign language is *not necessary* for admission to the international track of the high school. Classes in the international track are taught in English and students may choose from French, Spanish, German, or Mandarin as their foreign language (or another language via a tutor). (Study in Spanish, German, or Mandarin is at intermediate to advanced levels.) Applicants to the French section must be highly proficient in French (usually 6 years previous study of French). "**We are looking for** kids with curious, capable minds." **What sort of student do you best serve?** "Students with curious minds who are capable of doing a challenging program. Initiative, independent minds, and a lust for learning are unstated prerequisites."

# COSTS

**Latest tuition:** $15,250, payable in two installments or through payment plans. **Sibling discount:** None. **Tuition increases:** Approximately 6% annually. **Other costs:** Approximately $700-800 for two-week exchange trips to foreign country. **Financial aid:** Need-based. French government aid is available to French nationals. **Percentage of students receiving financial aid:** 40%. **Average grant:** $3,500. **No. of full-tuition grants:** 5. **No. of half-tuition grants:** "Some." **Grants of half-tuition or more:** N/P.

# SCHOOL'S MISSION STATEMENT/GOALS

The IHS seeks to provide students with a global perspective in everything that is taught. Science, literature, social sciences, geography, history, and art options (theater, art, music, computer science) are not taught as isolated subjects but as interconnected aspects of a broad world context. The purpose is to cultivate as many areas of interest as possible so that students can make responsible choices about their continuing education and mission in life. Learning in this tradition, students acquire understanding, an acceptance of differences, a personal sense of integrity, and compassion toward the community as a whole.

"Guided by principles of academic rigor and diversity, the IHS offers programs of study in French and English to prepare its graduates for a world in which the ability to think critically and to communicate across cultures is of paramount importance."

# ACADEMIC PROGRAM

Students participate in one of two honors baccalaureate programs: The International Baccalaureate (IB) or the French Baccalaureate. Both are internationally recognized and often earn students as much as one year college credit from American universities. "The IB is a holistic student-oriented educational experience which is designed to foster international understanding and individual initiative. The IB is the most comprehensive honors program taught in the US. As an internationally developed and monitored program recognized in the colleges and universities of over 90 countries, the IB also maintains the most consistently high reputation among competing honors programs." **Courses offered (AP=Advanced Placement, H=Honors, (AP)=AP option, (H)=Honors option):** Language A1, Language B, Individuals and Societies (history and economics), Experimental Sciences (biology, physics, and chemistry), mathematics (higher level math, math methods, math studies), electives (art and design, theater arts, computer science, music), Theory of Knowledge. **Computer lab/training:** Computer science options G9-12. (N/P re lab) **Grading:** Grades are given each semester, evaluations twice yearly. **Graduation requirements:** 4 years English and world literature, 4 years mathematics based on the IB curriculum (including algebra, transformational geometry, trigonometry, calculus, and computer science), 4 years sciences (physical science, biology, chemistry, physics), 4 years humanities, including world history, economics, geography, and US history, 4 years of a foreign language or foreign languages, 2 years theory of knowledge or philosophy, 2 years of the arts (art, music, drama) and 1 year of media studies. **Average nightly homework:** G9-10: 1-2 hours; G11-12: 1-4 hours. **Faculty:** Of the 38 full-time and 4 part-time teachers, 18 are male and 20 female, and they represent 10 nationalities. Six hold doctorate degrees and 95% have master's degrees or foreign equivalents. **Faculty ethnicity:** N/P. **Faculty selection/training:** N/P. **Teacher/student ratio:** 1:17. **Teacher's daily student load in required academic subject:** N/P. **AP courses/exams:** "Students seek college credit through the International or French Baccalaureate, making AP course work unnecessary. It is available, however. 95% of graduates receive college credit for their work at the IHS." **Senior class profiles (mean):** SAT Math 620 (including ESL students), 640 (excluding ESL students). SAT Verbal 550 (including ESL students), 610 (excluding ESL students). **GPA:** 3.03. **National Merit Scholarship Program:** One scholar, 3 semi-finalists, 6 commended in last class. **College enrollment:** 100% of last year's graduating class enrolled in 4-year colleges, including: Amherst, Boston U, Bowdoin, Brandeis, Brown, Clark Atlanta U, Dartmouth, Drexel, Harvey Mudd, McGill (Canada), Morehouse, National Taiwanese U, Stanford, UC Davis, UCLA, UC Santa Cruz, UC San Diego, U of Chicago, and Williams C.

## OTHER INDICATORS THE SCHOOL IS ACCOMPLISHING ITS GOALS

"Since 1990, more than 91% of graduates have been accepted to their first choice college or university. (Students who do not pass the entire IB diploma program have always passed individual tests and gotten what amounts to AP credit for each. In other words, it's a win/win situation. Students take the exams in June—after acceptances to college—and find out in July how much college credit they have received.)"

## CAMPUS/CAMPUS LIFE

**Campus description:** The IHS's new International Schools Campus, a site shared with FAIS as well as the Chinese American International School and the Institute for Chinese Language Learning, is a 180,000 sq. ft. campus in the heart of San Francisco's Civic Center and within blocks of the opera, ballet, symphony, main library, and government centers. The campus includes a library, gymnasium, science labs, technology center, rooftop deck, theater, and performing and fine arts studios. **Library:** 10,000 sq.ft; approx. 10,000 print volumes; 35 periodical subscriptions; 6 computers all with Internet access; 70 CD-ROMS; on-line catalog (OPAC); study space for 50; open to students 8:30 a.m. to 5:30 p.m.; 2 full-time librarians. **Open/closed campus:** Open. **Classroom space per student:** N/P. **Lunches:** Students bring their own lunches daily or visit nearby cafes. **Bus service:** The campus is 4 blocks from the BART station, one block from the MUNI streetcar station, and one block from the bus lines on Van Ness Avenue. **Uniform/dress code:** None. **Co-curricular activities/clubs:** Activities include drama club, literary magazine, speech and debate, photography club, student newspaper, multicultural alliance, film appreciation, student council, speech and debate, yearbook, etc. **Foreign exchange program:** The school will arrange semesters abroad for interested students. Each year, 10th graders visit a foreign country for two weeks and stay with families in order to use the foreign language they have been studying. Past trips have included Barcelona, Guadalupe, Montreal, Beijing, and Tahiti. **Opportunities for community service:** Required by the school and the International Baccalaureate. Students have assisted with Project Open Hand, Habitat for Humanity, senior centers, and have helped around campus, etc. **Typical freshman schedule:** 8:25 a.m. to 3:15 p.m., five 45-minute classes (classes vary depending on the day, often classes have double periods).

## STUDENT SUPPORT SERVICES

**Counselor/student ratio (not including college counselors):** (See below.) **Counseling:** Counseling is provided by staff/faculty who act as advisors with a 1:15 advisor/advisee ratio. Students are assigned faculty advisors to assist them in academic and nonacademic matters. The advisor stays with the students through the four years of high school. The school has a full-time psychological counselor and a college counselor. **Learning disabilities/differences:** N/P. **Career apprenticeship programs:** "[Assistance is provided] through our International Baccalaureate Coordinator."

## Student Conduct and Health

**Code of conduct:** N/P. **How school handles drugs/alcohol usage:** "Forbidden on campus." **Drug/alcohol abuse prevention/AIDS awareness program:** Provided at all grade levels as a part of the required health education curriculum.

## Summer Programs

None.

## Parent Involvement

**Parent participation:** Parents are required to give 12 hours per family per year. **Parent/teacher communication:** Parent/teacher conferences are held once a semester. **Parent education:** The Parents' Association sponsors seminars for parents; parents may attend monthly meetings with the principal; and parents may become involved in the Parents' Coalition of Bay Area High Schools. **Donations:** N/P.

## Sports

Through the Bay Counties League, IHS students compete in soccer, volleyball, basketball, swimming, tennis, baseball and softball.

## What Sets School Apart From Others

"The International High School is unique. We not only offer rigorous academics and an 'all-honors program,' but we are also the only local school which provides a truly multilingual, multicultural, and student-centered education. We view our graduates as key players in a future world which will be characterized by rapid change and fierce competition. The education offered at the IHS provides our students with a multicultural understanding and the tools for success in the global village of the twenty-first century."

## How Parents/Students Characterize School

**Parent response(s):** "I am impressed with the excited commitment both the students and the teachers have to the educational ideals of the International Baccalaureate. It's a deep, well-rounded education at a school that gives a lot of support."

**Student response(s):** "A few candid remarks from students in one multi-purpose room: 'Known for being more intense than a lot of schools.' 'Very diverse culturally, individually.' 'The teachers are willing to help you.' 'A small community, the students are friendly and smart, the assignments are problem-solving based.'"

# THE KING'S ACADEMY

562 Britton Ave.
Sunnyvale, CA 94086

(408) 481-9900 *fax (408) 481-9932*
www.tka.org

Steve Truesdell, Principal
Dannie Gober, Administrative Assistant

## GENERAL

**Coed** day high school and middle school (grades 6-12). **Christian.** Founded in 1991. **Nonprofit. Enrollment:** Approximately 580. **Average class size:** 22. **Accreditation:** WASC/ACSI (6-year term, 1997-03). **School year:** 10-month calendar (N/P re # instructional days). **School day:** 8:15 a.m. to 3:05 p.m. **Location:** Located off the Fair Oaks exit of Highway 101 (Wolfe Road exit off Highway 280), the school is accessible by CalTrain (Sunnyvale Station), and by bus.

## STUDENT BODY

**Geographical breakdown (counties):** 90% from Santa Clara; 10% from San Mateo. **Ethnicity:** N/P. **Foreign students (I-20 status):** N/P. **Single parent/two f/t working parent families:** N/P. **Middle schools:** N/P.

## ADMISSION

**Applications due:** Approximately January 3 (call for date). **Application fee:** $75. **Application process:** The applicant submits the application, provides three references, is tested and has an interview. **No. of applications:** 275 applications were received for 175 places in prior year. (N/P re middle schools, new students) **Admission cut-off:** N/P. **Preferences:** N/P. "**We are looking for** students with teachable hearts and coachable spirits." **What sort of student do you best serve?** (See above.)

# Costs

**Latest tuition:** $5,700 payable in 11 monthly payments. **Sibling discount:** $400. **Tuition increases:** 5% annually. **Other costs:** Student fee of $500 (covers books, yearbooks, academic field trips, graduation, retreats, etc.). **Financial aid:** Need-based; amounts vary each year. **Percentage of students receiving financial aid:** 10%. **Average grant award/no. of full/half-tuition scholarships:** N/P. **Grants of half-tuition or more:** N/P.

# School's Mission Statement/Goals

"The King's Academy is a Christ-centered college preparatory middle and senior high school for students who have teachable hearts and coachable spirits. We offer a loving family environment where students are encouraged to grow in their relationships with Jesus, their family, teachers, and others. We are committed to developing God's best for each student spiritually, academically, morally, and socially through every program and activity."

# Academic Program

**Courses offered (AP=Advanced Placement, H=Honors, (AP)=AP option, (H)=Honors option):** English 9-12 (H, AP), Geography, Algebra I, Geometry (H), Algebra 2 (H), Advanced Math (H), Business Math, Calculus AB/BC (AP), Introduction to Language Through Latin, Foreign Language 1-4 (Spanish, French, German, Sign Language), Bible, Basic Science, Biology (H, AP), Chemistry (H, AP), Physics, Anatomy & Physiology, P.E., Sports, World History (H), US History (H), Government/Economics, Introduction to Computers, Office Pro, Programming 1, Web Page Design, Upgrade 10, Logic Design and Program Techniques, Beginning Band, Production Drama, Stage Craft, Intermediate Band, Intermediate Drama, Yearbook, Creative Writing, Student Council, Student Store, Journalism, Speech & Debate, Writing for College, SAT Prep, Weight Training, Volleyball, Basketball, P.E., Art, Creative Endeavors, Arts in History, Musical Theater History, Basic Video Production, Guitar (Beg. & Adv.), Choir, Concert Choir, Performance Dance, Dance Workshop, Choir 1-2, Home Economics, Intro. to Journalism, Silent Reading, Missions, Staying in Tune, Communication, Teambuilding & Problem Solving, Intro to Engineering: Engines. **Computer lab/training:** Two computer labs with PCs and new software—computers are networked with access to Internet. One-half year computer training required. (N/P re # computers) **Grading:** Letter grades. **Graduation requirements:** 3 years math, 3 years science, 4 years English, 4 years history, 1 year fine arts, 2 years foreign language, .5 year computers, 2 years P.E., 4 years electives, 40 hours community service per year, plus one semester of Bible for each semester enrolled. **Average nightly homework:** 2-3 hours. **Faculty:** 46% male, 54% female. 64% of faculty hold bachelor's degrees as highest degree; 30% hold master's degrees, 6% hold PhDs. **Faculty ethnicity:** N/P. **Faculty selection/training:** "Interview process after applying. Teachers must keep their credentials current." **Teacher/ student ratio:** 1:20. **Teacher's daily student load in required academic subject:** N/P. **AP courses/exams:** "5." (N/P re exams, scores) **Senior class profile (mean):** SAT Math 595, SAT Verbal 591. **GPA:** N/P. **National Merit Scholarship Program:** "12." **College enrollment:** "98% attend college." (N/P re colleges)

## OTHER INDICATORS THE SCHOOL IS ACCOMPLISHING ITS GOALS

The school received WASC accreditation in May, 1997.

## CAMPUS/CAMPUS LIFE

**Campus description:** The school is located in a former Sunnyvale public high school building of 40,000 sq. ft. surrounding a large community area. The school's facilities include chemistry, biology, and physics labs; three computer labs; a gym, and a locker room and weight room. The grounds include a full track, soccer fields, three swimming pools, and baseball diamonds. **Library:** 4 computers; open to students from 8 a.m. to 4 p.m. (N/P re # volumes, sq. ft., study space, etc.) **Open/closed campus:** Closed (open for seniors). **Classroom space per student:** N/P. **Lunches:** Available in the student store. **Bus service:** N/P. **Uniform/dress code:** The dress code prohibits sweats, untucked shirts, clothing with heavy metal music group images, hats, short shorts, sleeveless/midriff shirts, and baggy pants. No earrings or facial hair for boys. No body piercings, dyed hair, or tattoos. **Co-curricular activities/clubs:** Activities include drama, sports, chess, missions, tech club, ping-pong club. **Foreign exchange program:** None. **Opportunities for community service:** "Service safari" to Mexico for high school students; alternate service plan. **Typical freshman schedule:** English 9 Honors, Geography, Geometry/Geometry Honors, foreign language 1 or 2, Bible, Biology/Biology Honors, P.E. or other elective.

## STUDENT SUPPORT SERVICES

**Counselor/student ratio (not including college counselors):** N/P. **Counseling:** "Men's and women's counselors are available for personal and academic counseling. College/career counseling is also available." **Learning differences/disabilities:** "Peer tutoring program." **Career apprenticeship programs:** "We post summer job opportunities as well as network with people who can offer students summer jobs."

## STUDENT CONDUCT AND HEALTH

**Code of conduct:** The school's behavior code, aside from standard provisions, requires students maintain a "Christ-like attitude," exercise common courtesy and respect, refer to adults by "Mr." and "Mrs." rather than by first names, and refrain from dating relationships while on campus. **How school handles drugs/alcohol usage:** Expulsion. **Drug/alcohol abuse prevention/AIDS awareness program:** Drug and alcohol issues are dealt with in Bible class as well as in chapel and family groups.

# SUMMER PROGRAMS

Varies each summer.

# PARENT INVOLVEMENT

**Parent participation:** 16 hours of service per year. **Parent/teacher communication:** Progress reports mid-quarter. **Parent education:** "Understanding Your Teenager" seminar. **Donations:** Encouraged but not required.

# SPORTS

Girls' soccer, volleyball, cross-country, basketball, track, and softball; boys' soccer, cross-country, basketball, wrestling, baseball, volleyball, and track; jr. high boys' flag football; boys' and girls' swimming.

# OTHER

The school offers a part-time high school program for students who are home schooled. The student attends the school two days a week to take advantage of programs such as sports and extracurricular clubs that are difficult to obtain in a home school environment. Other programs that support home schooling are also available.

# WHAT SETS SCHOOL APART FROM OTHERS

"We have a strong academic program in a Christian environment. While The King's Academy places high value on academic excellence, important growth occurs by building strong relationships in and out of the classroom."

# HOW PARENTS/STUDENTS CHARACTERIZE SCHOOL

**Parent response(s):** "Strong parent support for the school program."
**Student response(s):** "Students very much enjoy the school with all its activities."

*Illustration by Lick-Wilmerding student Sabra Saperstein*

# LICK-WILMERDING HIGH SCHOOL

755 Ocean Avenue
San Francisco, CA 94122

(415) 333-4021 *fax (415) 239-1230*

Dr. Albert M. Adams, Headmaster
Marcia Bedford, Director of Admissions

## GENERAL

**Coed** day high school. **Nonsectarian.** Founded in 1895. **Nonprofit**, member CAIS, NAIS, BAIHS. **Enrollment:** Approximately 360. **Average class size:** 13.5. **Accreditation**: WASC/CAIS (6-year term: 1999-05). **School year**: 9-month calendar (182 instructional days). **School day:** 8 a.m. to 3:15 p.m. (building opens at 7:00 a.m.). **Location**: In the southern part of San Francisco at the intersection

133

of Ocean Avenue and Highway I-280; L-W is across the street from City College, one block from the Balboa Park BART station, and on MUNI 15, 29, 36, 43, and 49 bus lines and the J, K, and M streetcar lines.

## Student Body

**Geographical breakdown (counties):** 78% from San Francisco; 15% from East Bay; 5% from San Mateo; 2% from Marin. **Ethnicity:** 64% Caucasian (non-Latino); 14% bi-racial; 11% Asian; 8% African-American; 3% Latino. **Foreign Students (I-20 status):** 0. **Single parent families:** N/P. **Two f/t working parent families:** 93%. **Middle schools:** 28% of the most recent entering freshman class came from 8 public middle schools; 52% from 18 private, non-parochial schools; 28% from 10 parochial schools.

## Admission

**Applications due:** Approximately January 21 (call for date). **Application fee:** $40. **Application process:** Open houses are held for applicants and parents on several Sundays in October through January. Students interested in the school should call to schedule a half-day visit and interview any morning or afternoon except Friday afternoons (October through January). Students "shadow" a student through a half day of classes and activities then interview with a member of the faculty. Lick uses the BAIHS recommendation forms. Current SSAT, ERB, CTBS, or SAT scores must be submitted. **No. of applications:** 731 applications were received for 94 places in prior year's class. **Admission cut-off:** "Lick-Wilmerding has a GPA cutoff of a B average. Because we accept a variety of standardized tests, we do not have a test score cutoff. Test scores are reviewed in conjunction with the applicant's 7th and 8th grade transcript to determine a student's qualifications." **Preferences:** N/P. **"We are looking for** students who (1) have strong academic ability, who are ready for independence, and are focused in the classroom; (2) have talents (or budding talents) and a broad range of interests, and who are generous-spirited and who can make a contribution to the school community; and (3) will take advantage of the many unique offerings of Lick." **What sort of student do you best serve?** N/P.

## Costs

**Latest tuition:** Flexible tuition ranges from $600 to $15,170 depending on a family's financial circumstances and full tuition is $15,170. Tuition is payable in 1, 3, or monthly installments. **Sibling discount:** None. **Tuition increases:** Approximately 5-7% annually. **Other costs:** $400 for books and supplies. **Financial aid:** Lick has a flexible tuition plan which reduces tuition to a range of $600 to $14,700 depending upon financial need. **Percentage of students receiving financial aid:** Approximately 38% of the current students are on this plan. **Aver-**

**age grant:** Average flexible tuition paid was $5,900 for the 1999-00 school year. **No. of full/half tuition grants:** One hundred students in the Flexible Tuition Program (out of 134 total) pay half or less than half of full tuition. **Grants of half tuition or more:** (See above.)

## School's Mission Statement/Goals

Mission: "Lick-Wilmerding High School inspires students to become self-directed, lifelong learners who contribute to our world with knowledge, skill, creativity, compassion, and can-do confidence. Toward this end, Lick-Wilmerding integrates a distinguished college preparatory curriculum with a distinctive program in the technical arts. As a private school with public purpose, Lick-Wilmerding encourages participation in community service and is committed to developing innovative educational programs that will benefit students and teachers throughout the Bay Area. Lick-Wilmerding's purpose, built on the foundation of a diverse and inclusive community, is to develop qualities of the head, heart, and hands that will serve students well throughout their lives.

"Lick-Wilmerding provides a non-competitive environment that enables students to take risks and encourages collaboration among students and faculty; the school maintains an unpretentious, supportive, and stimulating atmosphere, which inspires students to value who they are now and to envision unbounded futures; it seeks and develops well-rounded students with high academic potential who are excited about learning, self-motivated, resourceful, and respectful of others. The rigorous curriculum prepares students to think deeply, logically, critically, and creatively and presents a unique, hands-on opportunity to develop skills and confidence necessary for the practical tasks of life; it balances physical, cognitive, emotional, and aesthetic development and empowers students to be self-directed, life-long learners who take pride in themselves, their work, and their school. Lick-Wilmerding believes that a distinguished faculty is at the heart of a great school; such teachers contribute innovative skill and are committed to professional reflection, self-examination, and collegial interchange. Lick-Wilmerding values a community diverse in economic, ethnic, cultural, and educational backgrounds and supports critical inquiry from multiple perspectives into today's salient issues."

## Academic Program

Classes meet in a six day rotation, with each class meeting four times each rotation. **Courses offered (AP=AP option, H=Honors option): Counseling:** Issues and Choices, Peer Counseling, Peer Education Training and Teaching; **English:** English 1 (required for freshmen); sophomore choices: Literature of Self-Discovery, Tales of the City, Composition (required); junior choices (all H): Critical Thinking (composition), British Literature, Journey and Myth in Literature, Southern Literature, Multicultural Biography, Creative Writing; senior choices (all H): Shakespeare, Masterpieces of Western Literature, Greek Drama, American and British Poetry, Literature and Film, Pilgrimage and Escape; electives: Journalism, Literary Magazine; **Foreign Language:** French 1-5 (AP, H), French Literature (AP), Japanese 1-4, Spanish 1-5 (AP, H), Spanish Literature (AP); **History and Social Studies:** Discovery and Transition, US History, European History (AP), Topics in Modern US History, Topics in Modern World History; America: Another History, Asian History: Southeast Asia and India, Contemporary Asian History, 20th Century Revolutions, World Religions; **Math:** Algebra 1-2 (H), Inductive Geometry, Deductive Geometry, Pre-Calculus (H), Calculus AB (AP), Calculus BC (AP), Statistics (AP), Advanced Topics in Mathematics, Statistics and Probability, Topics in Discrete Mathematics; **Performing Arts: Dance:** Dance 1-2, Dance Production, Performance Workshop, Pandora's Dancers (repertory dance company); **Drama:** Acting Techniques 1-2, Directing/Dramatic Theory, Advanced Acting Workshop, Stage Design, Theatre Performance; **Instrumental Music:** Concert Band, String Orchestra/Advanced Chamber Music, Jazz Improvisation, Advanced Jazz Ensemble; **Vocal Music:** Singing/Voice, Men's/Women's Chorus, Chamber Singers, Music Theory (AP), Computer Music Composition; **P.E.:** Boys'/Girls' Physical Education, Advanced Physical Education, Mind/Body; **Science:** Conceptual Physics, Biology (AP), Chemistry (AP), Physics, Brain and Behavior (AP Psychology), Environment and Society; **Technology and Design:** Computer: Computing Foundations, Computer Science (AP), Computer Illustration, Digital Imaging, Video Technologies, Spreadsheets, Computer Animation; **Electronics Shop:** Electro-Fundamentals–including Robotics and Broadcast Radio (student-built and run radio station), Networks; **Fine Arts:** Design, Foundations: Painting and Drawing, Intermediate Art: Explorations in Visual Art, Selected Topics in Art, Art Studio (AP), Photography 1, 2, Advanced Photography, Yearbook; **Technical Arts:** Applied Technology, Drafting and Design, Senior Project (required), Architecture, Advanced Architecture, Machine Tool Process/Beginning Jewelry, Advanced Machine/Jewelry, Blacksmithing/Metalsmithing, Intermediate Metals/Jewelry, Intermediate Metal, Advanced Metal, Hot Glass, Mosaics/Sandblasting/Glass, Stained Glass, Chairmaking, Woodcarving, Intermediate Wood, Advanced Wood. **Special Programs:** Independent Study, Teaching Apprentices. **Computer lab/training:** Lick requires that students take two semesters of computer science. It has 3 computer labs—one with IBMs and 2 with Macs (including a new writing center). Computers are used throughout the curriculum. (N/P re # computers) **Grading:** Letter grades, A-F, are given at the end of the semesters. Narrative comments are given at the end of the first quarter of each semester. **Graduation requirements:** 4 academic courses in the freshman, sophomore, and senior years, and 5 academic courses in the junior year. Each student is required to complete at least 5 semesters in the Technology and Design Department (includes wood, metal, and machine shop, drafting and design), 2 semesters of fine or performing arts, 2 semesters of computer science, and a major independent project. **Average nightly homework:** N/P. **Faculty:** Of 57 teachers and administrators, 10 hold bachelor's degrees as their highest degree; 36 hold master's degrees; and 8 hold doctorates.

**Faculty ethnicity:** N/P. **Faculty selection/training:** "L-W faculty are selected based on their education, teaching experience, educational philosophy, recommendations, interviews, and teaching demonstration at L-W. In addition, candidates are assessed on their understanding of and desire to commit to the School's Mission and Vision. L-W teachers grow as educators by taking classes, through L-W's professional development program, by being active in a wide variety of professional organizations, etc." **Teacher/student ratio:** 1:8. **Teacher's daily student load in required academic subject:** 56-70. **AP courses/exams:** 90% of students are taking AP courses. In May of 1998, 171 students took 336 AP examinations; 89% of the exams received scores of 3 or above. Students are limited to two AP courses annually except with permission. **Senior class profile (mean):** SAT Verbal 680, SAT Math 660. **GPA:** 3.83. (See "Other Indicators" section below for SAT II scores.) **National Merit Scholarship Program:** The most recent graduating class had 13 finalists, 23 commended students, and 1 semifinalist in the National Achievement Scholarship Program for Outstanding Negro Students. **College enrollment:** 98% of 1999 graduates are enrolling in 4-year colleges, including UC Santa Cruz, UCLA, UC San Diego, Columbia, Pomona, Barnard, NYU, and Wesleyan. Graduates of the last four years are currently attending UC Berkeley (39), UC Santa Cruz (26), UCLA (18), Brown (10), UC San Diego (10), NYU (13), Stanford (11), Vassar (9), UC Davis (10), Wellesley (7), Yale (9), Columbia (7), Oberlin (7), Occidental (4), USC (5), Barnard (8), U of Oregon (5), SCU-Humboldt (4), Georgetown (3), Kenyon C (3), Smith (4), U of Chicago (5), Wesleyan (5), and others.

## OTHER INDICATORS THE SCHOOL IS ACCOMPLISHING ITS GOALS

SAT II Mean Scores (class of 1999): Biology 630, Chemistry 660, English Comp 660, Physics 670, Spanish 630, US History 680, Math 2C 680, Math I 620, French 710, English Lit 650.

## CAMPUS/CAMPUS LIFE

**Campus description:** L-W's campus consists of 6 buildings housing classrooms, a gymnasium, a performing arts theater, computer and science labs, a cafeteria, metal, wood, and machine shops, and dance and music studios. The McCullough Library/Herbst Arts and Humanities Center, a new 18,000 sq. ft. facility, opened in 1997 across the field from the main buildings. It houses a new library on the top floor, and the ground floor includes a humanities writing center and new studios for art, photography (with darkroom), drafting and design, and an electronics workshop. **Library:** 7,100 sq. ft.; "capacity for 25,000 volumes"; study space for 95 students; on-line catalog. Open to students 7 a.m. to 5 p.m. (N/P re subscriptions, etc.) **Open/closed campus:** Open. **Classroom space per student:** 103 sq. ft. **Lunches:** Students bring their lunches or purchase food from the school cafeteria, which is open from 7:30 a.m. to 2:30 p.m. **Bus service:** City buses, MUNI Metro, and BART. Van service is provided for a fee to Northern San Francisco and the Peninsula. **Uniform/dress code:** "Students are expected to be neat and clean and to use good judgment in matters of dress. Casual dress is acceptable but students should be mindful of the academic nature of the environment." **Co-curricular activities/clubs:** Activities include California Scholarship Federation, KCIL Radio, Hospitality Club, College Hosts, Multicultural Alliance, Environmental Club, N.O.W., A.S.I.A., Black Student Union, Chamber Singers, Jazz Ensemble, Orchestra, Yearbook, Literary Magazine, *Paper Tiger* (school newspaper), JSA (Junior Statesmen of America), World Wide Web Club, Pandora's Dancers, Juggling Club, Gay/Lesbian/Bisexual Alliance, Student Council. **Foreign exchange program:** N/P. **Opportunities for community service:** Based on the belief that "volunteerism should be voluntary," students are encouraged but not required to participate in community service. The school's community service office assists students in finding projects that match their interests and maintains on-going programs and extensive involvement with many community organizations, including several tutoring programs with local elementary schools. **Typical freshman schedule:** (55-minute periods, 5 minutes between, 30-minute lunch) English 1, P.E., Deductive Geometry, Biology, French 1 H, Drafting and Design, Issues and Choices, Computing Foundations, Orchestra, and Discovery and Transition.

# Student Support Services

**Counselor/student ratio (not including college counselors):** 1:217. **Counseling:** Freshmen are assigned an advising group of approximately 11 students. A faculty advisor moderates the group, overseeing each student's progress for the full four years and serving as the first point of contact for parents. The counseling program also includes peer counseling groups, and personal/family counseling is available. Formal **college counseling** begins in the junior year with individual and family meetings; 1-1/2 counselors serve each typical class of 85-90 students; the College Counseling Center has a library of resources and makes use of computer software for college searches and financial aid research. The Center also offers SAT prep classes each year at a minimal cost. **Learning disabilities/differences:** "The Learning Services program, directed by a professional specialist, offers resources to support students with diagnosed learning disabilities and students with learning differences who have not yet been diagnosed but struggle with some aspect of learning. These services include: consultation with students and parents on learning challenges; referral for assessment, tutoring, and organizational coaching; consultation with teachers on classroom and assessment practices to meet the needs of students with diverse learning styles; and, new this year, a peer support group for students with learning differences." **Career apprenticeship programs:** The school has a summer opportunities coordinator who keeps a bulletin board on opportunities for summer employment. The school also hosts talks from various summer employment agencies and programs, such as Enterprise.

## STUDENT CONDUCT AND HEALTH

**Code of conduct:** The school has standard rules regarding drugs, alcohol, tobacco, stealing, lying, plagiarism, and harassment. It also prohibits rudeness and insists on civility. Students elect a Student Judicial Board to assist the Dean of Students in assessing disciplinary situations. **How school handles drug/alcohol usage:** Students will not possess or use illegal drugs or alcohol at school or during school events or sell or distribute drugs or alcohol at any time. Students using drugs or alcohol who seek help from the counselors or the Dean of Students will receive counseling and helpful intervention to the extent that the school is able to provide it. However, violation of this rule will be treated as a serious disciplinary matter and will elicit disciplinary action fitting to the circumstances. **Drug/alcohol abuse prevention/AIDS awareness:** Freshmen are required to take Issues and Choices, a course that addresses issues including self-esteem, decision-making, and sexuality. The course covers AIDS education and prevention as well as drug and alcohol abuse prevention. AIDS education, and a wide range of health-related topics, is also taught in a five-week health unit that is part of the required P.E. class.

## SUMMER PROGRAMS

Each summer the school offers alternating foreign language trips to France, Spain, and Japan. Each provides a cultural immersion opportunity with touring and family homestays. Students on the Flexible Tuition Program are assisted with the cost of these trips. On-campus, classes are offered in wood, architecture, photography, and ceramics.

## PARENT INVOLVEMENT

**Parent participation:** Lick encourages parents to attend student activities and to volunteer through the Parents' Association and the Annual Fund. **Parent/teacher communication:** Annual parent conference; bi-annual written comments; progress reports upon request; access to students' advisors. **Parent education:** The Parents' Association holds monthly meeting which spotlight a certain topic, often concerning parenting a teenager. Topics have included, "Teen Nutrition and Body Image," "Teens, Drugs, and Alcohol," and sessions at the beginning of the year which introduce what parents can expect at each grade level, both academically and socially. L-W parents also are invited to participate in the Bay Area Coalition of Parents and are regularly mailed the "Parenteen" newsletter. **Donations:** Parents are expected to make a contribution to the Annual Fund, which supports the annual operating budget of the school. L-W's goal is 100% participation in the Annual Fund.

## Sports

L-W students compete on 27 interscholastic teams in the Bay Counties League (BCL) including girls' tennis, basketball (frosh/soph, jv, v), volleyball (jv, v), and soccer (jv, v); boys' basketball (frosh/soph, jv, v), soccer (jv, v), tennis (jv, v), volleyball, baseball, and lacrosse (not in BCL); boys' and girls' cross-country, track & field, and swimming; and coed badminton. Over the course of the year, more than 60% of the student body participates on sports teams.

## What Sets School Apart From Others

"L-W is best known for the economic, racial, and cultural diversity of its student body and its commitment to a well-rounded education for the 'Head, Heart and Hands.' Having been tuition-free for 77 of its 102 years, L-W takes its mandate to be accessible to students from all walks of life very seriously. The earnings on its large endowment are dedicated almost exclusively to making the school more financially accessible. As a result, 37% of families participate in L-W's unique Flexible Tuition Program, 33% of its students are of color, and nearly 50% of the student body comes from public and parochial middle schools. L-W is genuinely a Bay Area school, with its current 380 students representing 88 middle schools, including every San Francisco zip code, 15% from the East Bay and many from the Peninsula. Lick is often described as being 'a down-to-earth, unpretentious and unusually friendly place.'

"L-W is the only independent school in the nation which, in addition to its rigorous college preparatory program, also requires extensive work in the wood, metal, and machine shops and in drafting/design and architecture. Three philosophical pillars support this historic technical arts program: (1) an understanding of and appreciation for fine craftsmanship (*e.g.*, furniture making, wood carving), (2) the blending of the fine and technical arts (*e.g.*, jewelry, sculpture, stained glass) and (3) the integration of science and technology (*e.g.,* building telescopes, robotics, electronics). The school's 'Head, Heart, Hands' philosophy is further animated by first-rate programs in theater, choral and instrumental music, dance, and fine arts."

## How Parents/Students Characterize School

**Parent response(s):** "L-W impressed me, my wife, and two daughters (one a 9th grader, one a recent alumna) as a welcoming, collaborative, and socially responsible learning environment with an outstanding curriculum from top to bottom and a unique heritage in the technical arts. What we wanted their teachers to encourage in our girls—a lifelong love of learning, self-confidence, and a commitment to bettering society—we have found at L-W."

"The L-W community is friendly, informal, and very high-energy. Walk around the campus and you may hear a lively discussion emanating from an English seminar in the new classroom/library building, a Duke Ellington tune being played by the Advanced Jazz Ensemble, and the hum of a circular saw being used in a Tech Arts workshop. You may also find students sitting in the hallway studying for a chemistry test or discussing the agenda for the Multicultural Alliance meeting later in the day. It's a school where learning takes place on many levels and people smile a lot."

**Student response(s):** "Lick-Wilmerding has a non-traditional, creative learning environment, with a large focus on personal attention, writing across the curriculum, and immersing yourself in whatever you choose to do."

"L-W is a very challenging place with a good variety of people to meet. There's a relaxed environment even though the academics are so challenging."

"You get a 'snap shot' of life at Lick with real-life situations and applications in the classroom wherever possible. The great tech arts program that all students are involved in, plus two years of P.E., helps to round out your academics. In whatever you do–sports, performing arts, or math–you learn to work in a group and as part of a team. Also, the field is a nice part of campus where you can just relax during the busy day."

# LYCÉE FRANÇAIS LA PÉROUSE, THE INTERNATIONAL FRENCH SCHOOL

755 Ashbury Street
San Francisco, CA 94117

(415) 661-5232 *fax (415) 661-0246*
www.lelycee.org

Patrick Frébet, Principal
Sophie Drozek, Director of Admissions, (415) 661-5401 x122
*fax (415) 661-0945,* admissions@lelycee.org

## GENERAL

**Coed** French day high school. (All courses are taught in French with the exception of US History, English Literature, Spanish and German.) Founded in 1967. **Nonsectarian. Nonprofit**, provisional member CAIS (expected completion, 1999-2000). The San Francisco campus includes a lower school which is preschool (beginning at age 3) through G12; the Corte Madera (Marin County) campus includes preschool through G5. **Enrollment:** Approximately 86 students in the high school; total San Francisco campus enrollment is approximately 410. **Aver-**

age class size: 18-20. **Accreditation:** Accredited by the French Ministry of Education. **School year:** 9-month calendar (174 instructional days). **School day:** 8:15 a.m. to 3:50 p.m. **Location:** Between Frederick and Waller Streets on Ashbury at the site of the old St. Agnes School. Accessible by MUNI bus lines 33, 6, 7, 71, and MUNI Metro N.

## STUDENT BODY

**Geographical breakdown (counties):** 71% from San Francisco; 14% from San Mateo and South Bay; 10% from Marin and other North Bay counties; 5% from East Bay. **Ethnicity:** "The high school has 11 nationalities represented (19 in the total campus) including approximately 58% French; 25% French-US; 5% US; 4% US-other; and 7% other." **Foreign students (I-20 status):** 15%. **Single parent/two f/t working parent families:** N/P. **Middle schools:** Most recent entering freshman class came from: 10% French educational systems around the world, 90% from the Lycée middle school.

## ADMISSION

**Applications due:** February (call for date). **Application fee:** $100. **Application process:** Visits by appointment. Students coming from other French schools or the French system are automatically admitted in their own grade level based on their report cards. **No. of applications:** N/P. **Admission cut-off:** None. **Preferences:** Students from French educational backgrounds, Lycée middle school students and siblings of Lycée students. **"We are looking for** students coming from a French educational system. French fluency is required for entering the high school (as well as the lower schools beyond kindergarten)." **What sort of student do you best serve?** N/P.

## COSTS

**Latest tuition:** $9,440 (G9), $10,360 (G10-12), payable in one payment or in 10 payments through Smart. A $100 discount is allowed for full payment in advance. **Sibling discount:** 10% for second child, 20% for third, and 30% for fourth. **Tuition increases:** Approximately 4-5% per year. **Other costs:** $50 registration fee; $950 one-time building fund fee per family; $500 deposit to enroll a sibling (deducted from tuition); fee of approximately $70 for field trips and overnights (varies by grade and by teacher). **Financial aid:** French national scholarships are need-based and available to students of French nationality. A limited number of need-based scholarships are made by the school to students ineligible for French national scholarships. **Percentage of students receiving financial aid:** 25%. **Average grant:** $1,000. **No. of full/half tuition scholarships:** None. **Grants of half-tuition or more:** 60% of French government grants, 5% of Lycee grants.

# School's Mission Statement/Goals

"The Lycée provides a challenging educational environment emphasizing academic achievement leading to the French standardized test (Baccalaureat) as well as the American high school diploma. We provide our students with a structured, well-assimilated body of general knowledge while encouraging the development of analytical and critical skills, with the enrichment of language, culture, and the arts. The curriculum fosters autonomy, initiative, self-respect and the respect of others, cooperation, and responsibility. In addition, by becoming not only bilingual, but also bi-cultural, our students become aware of and respect cultural differences."

# Academic Program

The academic program is based on the French national curriculum augmented by courses in American history and English literature. **Courses offered (AP=Advanced Placement, H=Honors, (AP)=AP option, (H)=Honors option):** French H, Mathematics H, French History, Geography, Economics, English Literature (AP, H), ESL, US History, Physics/Chemistry H, Biology/Geology H, Technology/Computer Science, Arts (Visual Art, Theater, Music), Spanish, German, Latin, P.E. **Computer lab/training:** The new campus is equipped with both a computer lab and a teaching center dedicated to teaching on the Internet and taking advantage of the many French educational programs available through the Internet. (N/P re # computers, training.) **Grading:** The Lycée uses the French system of grading on a scale of 0 to 20, complemented by brief written evaluations. "The French system is more rigorous than American grading and is known and respected by American colleges and universities." **Graduation requirements:** "Set by French Ministry plus SF Unified School district." **Average nightly homework:** G9-11: 2 hours, G12: 2.5+ hours. **Faculty:** N/P. **Faculty ethnicity:** 99% Caucasian; 1% Middle Eastern. **Faculty selection/training:** "The French Ministry of Education sends certified teachers from France for one to four years, while other French teachers are hired locally. Yearly evaluations are held by French officials. English and US History teachers hold California teaching credentials. In-service days are held on an on-going basis as well as continuing education." **Teacher/student ratio:** 1:5. **Teacher's daily student load in required academic subject:** N/P. **AP courses/exams:** 55% of students are currently taking AP courses. In fall, 1997, 21 students took AP examinations in French, English, and Calculus. 95% received scores of 3 or above. **Senior class profile (mean):** SAT Math 638, SAT Verbal 627. **GPA:** 3.76 (only calculated for the students going on to UC universities; weighted for honors courses A=5, B=4, C=3, D=2). **National Merit Scholarship Program:** N/P. **College enrollment:** 80% of last year's graduating class enrolled in 4-year colleges, 20% in 2-year colleges, including: Johns Hopkins, UC Berkeley, UCLA, and French universities (Classes Preparatoires, la Sorbonne, Université de Grenoble, Université de Paris).

## OTHER INDICATORS THE SCHOOL IS ACCOMPLISHING ITS GOALS

"The Lycée offers only the college preparatory track of the French educational system. At the end of the 12th grade students take the French Baccalaureat exam (with an International option), allowing them to continue on with excellent university studies in France, in other European countries, or in the US. Lycée students have a 93% pass rate (students in France have a 60% pass rate). Students entering the US university system also take the PSAT and SAT exams and AP courses for their high school diploma. Lycée students often are given as much as one year's college credit for their scores on the Bac. The Lycée's goal is to awaken the desire for learning and equip the child with the tools to earn self-esteem through personal achievement."

## CAMPUS/CAMPUS LIFE

**Campus description:** In 1996, Lycée moved into a 42,000 sq. ft. building at the site of the old St. Agnes School. The building has been extensively remodeled to include three floors of classrooms, computer and biology labs, music rooms, an extensive library with a rooftop terrace (open only to the upper grades), and a greenhouse. **Library:** The secondary school library, with a balcony overlooking the courtyard, houses more than 10,000 print volumes, has computers with Internet access, and a videotheque. (N/P re periodicals, study space, etc.) **Open/closed campus:** High school students may leave campus at lunch if they have written permission from a parent at the beginning of the school year. **Classroom space per student:** N/P. **Lunches:** Hot lunches may be purchased. **Bus service:** From the Peninsula, North Bay, and East Bay, $1,500-$1,800/year. **Uniform/dress code:** "No uniform." **Co-curricular activities/clubs:** Activities include drama club, yearbook, multimedia (Internet), music, orchestra, dance, roller hockey, basketball and volleyball, table tennis, and student government. **Foreign exchange program:** N/P. **Opportunities for community service:** Each class carries out a project such as volunteering at the Hamilton Center and the Haight-Ashbury Food Program, helping at the Randall Museum, visiting seniors in retirement homes, fundraising and clothing collection for projects in Latin America, Amnesty International. **Typical freshman schedule:** Seven periods of 55 minutes each. A freshman would study, over the course of a week, Music, Art, Computer Science, Dramatic Art, US History, Biology, Physics/Chemistry, Latin (an elective), History-Geography, foreign language, P.E., Math, French Literature, and English Literature.

## STUDENT SUPPORT SERVICES

**Counselor/student ratio (not including college counselors):** 1:30. **Counseling:** A full-time American college counselor and part-time psychologist are on staff. An optional study hall supervised by faculty is offered and tutoring is available from other students upon parental request. **Learning disabilities/differences:** A part-time school psychologist is available at the request of teachers or parents. **Career apprenticeship programs:** "None, however, French and US advisors are available on an individual basis for any student."

## STUDENT CONDUCT AND HEALTH

**Code of conduct:** Standard. **How school handles drugs/alcohol usage:** N/P. **Drug/alcohol abuse prevention/AIDS awareness program:** Students and teachers undergo a substance abuse awareness program at the beginning of each year.

## SUMMER PROGRAMS

Lower grades only on Marin County campus.

## PARENT INVOLVEMENT

**Parent participation:** Parents are expected to participate in fundraising by contributing financially to the Annual Appeal and volunteering 10 hours a year, by assisting in tasks such as gardening and painting, or by lodging or sponsoring a student. Parents are encouraged to serve on committees of the Board of Directors and to seek election to the Board or School Council. Other volunteer opportunities include a French market in June at the Marin campus, translating, library help, and newsletter publication. **Parent/teacher communication:** Students receive five report cards a year. Two conferences between parents and teachers are held on a one-on-one basis. One class council per trimester is held with all teachers, student delegates, parent delegates, and the administration. **Parent education:** Cross-cultural workshops; US college panel discussions with alumni; a French educational system counselor from France available annually; lectures/discussions on bilingualism, communication, safety and other issues. **Donations:** Parents are asked to participate in the annual giving campaign and several fundraisers.

## SPORTS

The regular sports curriculum includes roller hockey, table tennis, gymnastics, swimming, basketball, and soccer. The Lycée participates in city-wide private school games with teams in basketball and volleyball.

## OTHER

"Consistent with the French system of education, in high school, Lycée students choose one of three general areas of study, corresponding to the three most prestigious Baccalaureat diplomas: Literature (14 hours of humanities, philosophy, and languages), Economics and Sociology (6 hours of economics), or Sciences (18 hours of mathematics and sciences)."

## WHAT SETS SCHOOL APART FROM OTHERS

"The Lycée belongs to a network of over 400 French schools worldwide and receives financial support from the French government. Founded in 1967 by parents, the Lycée is an academic institution accredited by the French Ministry of Education. The Lycée's students have access to any other French school at their own grade level. As a result of the high quality English curriculum, students are also qualified to enter an American school at or above their grade level and are fully prepared to enter European or North American colleges and universities."

## HOW PARENTS/STUDENTS CHARACTERIZE SCHOOL

**Parent response(s):** "I believe that the Lycée is educating tomorrow's world leaders. Who else can be better prepared to face this international world than our own children, who at age eight can already tell us how a French person's approach is different from an American's and that neither one is better, they are just different."—Canadian parent

"The environment is so positive. It's obvious that the instructors have a vision. They are well prepared to carry out their mission, and they are secure in their role. I like the fact that my son's teachers have such excellent morale."—American parent

**Student response(s):** "The Lycée's students are winners in the intellectual arena; the Baccalaureat scores every year are remarkable. In the social arena the Lycée's theater workshop is always admired and congratulated by the American and French art communities. I realize that many doors were opened to guarantee me a successful future. A graduate of the Lycée enters the world of work or higher education with incomparable potential ... and the Lycée gives us the keys to fully realize that potential."—Argentinean graduate

"It was at the Lycée that I discovered learning is wonderful. Just last year in my master's program at Stanford University I noticed I often used the methods of analysis that I learned at the Lycée in philosophy class. Where else can you play the saxophone in a jazz group with the director, garden with the history/geography professor, spend hours arguing with the philosophy professor in a café, and finish school with 100% on the Baccalaureat."—French student

*Illustration by Marin Academy student Rashida Lorell*

# MARIN ACADEMY

1600 Mission Ave.
San Rafael, CA 94901

(415) 453-2808 *fax (415) 453-8905*
www.ma.org/admissions

Bodie Brizendine, Head of School
Tony Krackeler, Director of Admissions and Financial Aid

# GENERAL

**Coed** day high school. Founded in 1971. **Nonsectarian. Nonprofit**, member CAIS, NAIS, BAIHS. **Enrollment:** 375. **Average class size:** 15. **Accreditation:** WASC (6-year term: 1999-05). **School year:** 9-month calendar. (N/P instructional days) **School day:** 8 a.m. to 3 p.m. **Location:** Near downtown San Rafael, a small urban city 12 miles north of San Francisco in Marin County. Accessible from Highway 101 to San Francisco and 580 from the Richmond Bridge to the East Bay.

# STUDENT BODY

**Geographical breakdown (counties):** 60% from Marin; 20% from East Bay; 15% from San Francisco; 5% from Sonoma. **Ethnicity:** 80% Caucasian (non-Latino); 10% Asian; 6% African-American; 4% Latino. **Foreign students (I-20 status):** 0. **Single parent/two f/t working parent families:** N/P. **Middle schools:** 62 of the latest freshman class came from 21 private non-parochial schools; 25 from 10 public middle schools; 15 from 7 parochial schools.

# ADMISSION

**Applications due:** Mid-January (call for exact date). **Application fee:** $50. **Application process:** At the beginning of their child's eighth grade year, parents should contact the school to be put on the admissions mailing list. Visits are scheduled from October through early January. By mail parents on the mailing list receive information regarding open houses, "Parent Coffees," and other events. Applications include parent and student sections, recommendations from current math and English teachers, a Principal/Guidance Counselor Recommendation (BAIHS forms), transcripts, and test scores (SSAT, ERB/ISEE, or CTBS/Stanford Achievement Test). Parent portions of applications are due in December; student interviews are then scheduled. **No. of applications:** More than 500 applications were received for 100 places. Four new students were admitted to G10; 1 to G11. **Preferences:** None. **"We are looking for** students who want to be challenged, who want to think, question and explore. We seek to enroll students who demonstrate a love for learning and the ability to pursue a demanding college preparatory curriculum balanced by participation in extracurricular activities, including athletics, the arts and outdoor education—students with passion, who are willing to become fully involved in the life of their school and to make a contribution." **Admission cut-off:** None. **What sort of student do you best serve?** "Academically able active learners—motivated students who are interested in school and the world around them."

# Costs

**Latest tuition:** $15,990. **Sibling discount:** None. **Tuition increases:** Approximately 6% annually. **Other costs:** Books, minicourses. **Percentage of students receiving financial aid:** 21%. **Average grant award:** $9,700. **No. of full tuition grants:** 8. **Grants of half-tuition or more:** 70%.

# School's Mission Statement/Goals

"Marin Academy asks every individual to think, question, and create in an environment of encouragement and compassion, and challenges each person to accept the responsibilities posed by education in a democratic society."

# Academic Program

"The curriculum is rigorously college preparatory with highly developed requirements in all academic areas, plus the arts and physical education." **Courses offered (AP= advanced placement, H=Honors, (AP)= AP option, (H)=Honors option): English:** English I, English II, Power of the Word: The Impact of the English Language on Our Lives, Journalistic Writing, Newswriting, Editing and Production, The 19th Century British Novel & Play: Literature of the Victorian Era, British Literature from the 14th to the 18th Century: Classics in Poetry & Prose, 20th Century American Fiction, Literature and Philosophy, Race, Redress and Recovery: A Look at the Relationship Between Blacks and Whites in the US, Shakespeare—Survey, Reading and Writing Poetry, Writing Workshop, Real-World Writing, The Sublime and Gothic, Pacific Crossing: Asian American Literature, Brave New Worlds: Utopias and Dystopias in Literature, Voices: Studying Society and Self Through Literature, Writing Workshop, Short Story, Performance Writing (+ frequently offered electives such as After Armageddon, Autobiographical Writing, Fiction by Women, Search for Eden, Southern Fiction); **Math:** Algebra I, Algebra II (H), Geometry (H), Finite Mathematics, AP Statistics, Precalculus (H), AP Calculus AB, AP Calculus BC; **History:** World Civilizations, US History (AP), Modern World History: From the Great Depression to the Millennium, Modern American History, Art History from 1848-1998, Asian History: Migrations to California, European History I—Biography, Asian Art History: India and China, Middle East Studies, Latin American Studies, European Studies II, (+ frequently offered electives such as African Studies, AP American Government, Classical Studies: Greece, and Classical Studies: Rome, Senior Seminar); **Computer Science:** Computer Applications, Introduction to Computer Programming, AP Computer Science; **Science:** Biology (AP), Geology, Environmental Studies, Astronomy H, Chemistry (AP), Oceanography H, Biochemistry & Physics, Physics (AP), Psychology, Individual Investigation in Advanced Science; **Foreign Language:** Spanish I, Spanish II (H), Spanish III (H), Spanish IV-Theater and Acting, Spanish IV AP Language, Spanish V AP Literature, French I, French II (H), French III (H), French IV Conversation and Theater, French IV AP Language, French V AP Literature, Japanese I, Japanese II-IV H; **Art/Performing Arts:** Modern Art History from 1848-1998, Asian Art History: India and China, Introduction to Animation, Music of the World, Chorus/Vocal Workshop, Classical Guitar, Chamber Ensemble, Advanced Chamber Ensemble H, Jazz Band, Rock/Blues Ensemble, Guided Study in Music, Visual Arts I, Visual Arts II: Drawing and Painting, Visual Arts III: Drawing H, Visual Arts III: Painting H, Visual Arts IV: Drawing H, Visual Arts IV: Painting H, Visual Arts II: Ceramics, Visual Arts III: Ceramic Hand-building, Visual Arts III: Ceramic Wheel-throwing, Visual Arts IV: Advanced Ceramics, Visual Arts II: Photography, Visual Arts III: Photography, Visual Arts IV: Photography H, Theater I: Acting, Theater II: Advanced Acting and Playwriting, Theater III: Advanced Acting, Theater History III: Design and Directing, Theater IV: Independent Study, Dance I-IV; **P.E.:** Intramural Sports Program, Freshman Core Human Development, Aikido, Dance, Outdoor Education & Skills; **Other:** Peer Teaching Assistant Program, Independent Study. **Special programs:** Students may seek to graduate with an International Studies Emphasis. This requires they take specific classes with a non-US focus; take four years of French or Spanish or three years of Japanese; perform 20 hours of international studies outside the classroom; and, in their senior year, write a thesis or present a project. The school's mini-courses (one a year required) include 30-40 offerings for week-long experiential learning, often involving travel or community service. The school also has an Outings Program involving weekends participating in various outdoor activities including backpacking, skiing, scuba, and rock climbing. Through the High School Honors Program, juniors and seniors, with approval, may take one course per semester at nearby Dominican College at a reduced rate. **Computer lab/training:** Computers and multimedia technology are available to faculty and students in most classrooms and in four labs located throughout campus. 100 computers are available to students, and all faculty are assigned laptops. E-mail accounts, digital storage services and web publishing are provided for students. The school supports a fiber optic network and a T-1 connection to the Internet. The school has a full-time Director of Educational Technology and a full-time technology specialist. **Grading:** Letter. **Graduation requirements:** (Designed to exceed UC admission requirements.) 4 years English, 3 years math (through Algebra II), 3 years history, 3 years lab science, 3 years of one foreign language or 2 years of two, 2 years fine arts, 2 years P.E., 60 hours community service, one mini-course each year. **Average nightly homework:** G9-12: 45 min.-1 hour per class meeting. (Classes meet every other day.) **Faculty:** Of the 56 faculty members, 50% are male, 50% female; 1/3 of faculty hold bachelor's degrees as highest degrees; 2/3 hold master's degrees. Students address faculty and administrators by their first names. **Faculty ethnicity:** 16% of color. **Faculty selection/training:** "Faculty selection is based on subject area expertise, reflected in the field, etc. The school is deeply interested in the professional growth of the faculty. Support is given for faculty to attend professional workshops, conferences, and seminars; continuing education for faculty including course work and advanced degrees; encouragement of faculty participation and leadership in local, regional, and national professional groups and task forces; professional in-service programs; the E.E. Ford Fellowship; professional development via curriculum expansion and development." **Teacher/student ratio:** 1:10. **Teacher's daily student load in required academic subject:** N/P. **AP courses/exams:** In 1998, 89 students took 148 AP exams in 12 subjects. 91% scored 3 or above. (N/P % in AP courses) **Senior class profile (mean):** SAT Math 639, SAT Verbal 657. **GPA:** 3.5 (highest 4.388, lowest, 2.405). **National Merit Scholarship Program:** In most recent year's class, 3 students were winners; 7 were semi-finalists; 7 were commended. **College enrollment:** 98% of last year's graduating class (81 graduates) enrolled in 4-year colleges, 2% in 2-year colleges. Graduates from the last two years are attending: U of Arizona, Barnard, Bates, Berklee C of Music, Boston C, Boston U, Brandeis, Brown, Bucknell, Calif. CC, Calif. Culinary Academy, CSU campuses (Long Beach, San Diego, San Luis Obispo), UC campuses (Berkeley, Davis, LA, Riverside, San Diego, Santa Barbara, Santa Cruz), Carleton, Claremont McKenna, Clark, U of Colorado-Boulder, Colorado C, Columbia, Cornell, U of Denver, Evergreen State, U of Florida, Franklin & Marshall, Georgetown, George Washington, Glasgow (UK), Hampshire, Hartwick, Harvard, Howard, Lehigh, U of Maryland, McGill (Canada), U of Miami, U of Michigan, U of Missouri-Columbia, Mt. Holyoke, NYU, Northwestern, Occidental, U of the Pacific, Pacific U, U of Pennsylvania, Pomona, Reed, RISD, U of San Diego, USF, Sarah Lawrence, Skidmore, Smith, USC, U of Southern Oregon, St. John's (NM), Stanford, Tufts, Vassar, Washington State, Wesleyan, Whittier, Willamette, and Yale.

## OTHER INDICATORS THE SCHOOL IS ACCOMPLISHING ITS GOALS

N/P.

## CAMPUS/CAMPUS LIFE

**Campus description:** The school is situated on a 10-acre campus on a hillside in San Rafael, the former site of a military school. The campus's eight buildings include Foster Hall, a three-story former private home circa 1870, which houses administration, college counseling offices, classes and cafeteria. The Thacher Hall of Science has four lab-classrooms, a science library, a computer lab and an observation platform for experiments. A newly refurbished Founders Hall includes computer labs, classrooms and an audio-visual lecture room with each seat wired for laptops and Internet connections. The Fine Arts Center includes dance studios, a photo lab, and ceramics studio; the Music Building includes practice rooms and a 175-seat theater. (Construction of a new performing arts center, which will eventually house the theater, dance, and music programs, is planned to begin in 2000.) A new Athletic Center, completed in 1998, has a gym, locker rooms, and training rooms. The old gym continues to be used as a gym, and also a student lounge. The school grounds include a pool, tennis courts, and two fields for soccer, softball, lacrosse and baseball. Classrooms are arranged in seminar-style. **Library:** 7,000 print volumes; 40-50 periodical subscriptions (+ Pearlquest on-line periodical access service); 5 computers (all with Internet access); on-line catalog; study space for 40 students. Open to students from 7:30 a.m. to 5 p.m.; full-time librarian. (N/P sq. ft.) **Open/closed campus:** Open. **Classroom space per student:** N/P. **Lunches:** Hot lunches are available daily. **Bus service:** A private company provides van service to/from the East Bay, Southern Marin and San Francisco. **Uniforms/dress code:** "Marin Academy expects that students will dress in a manner that is appropriate for a school setting and that is not disruptive of the educational process. If a dispute over the appropriateness of clothing arises, the decision of the Head will be final." **Co-curricular activities/clubs:** Yearbook, athletics, school newspaper, literary magazine, Trust Council, Student Senate, dramatic and musical productions, senior projects, forensics, filmmaking, Model UN, Japanimation, Technology Club, Thespian Society, Multicultural Action Coalition and many others. **Foreign exchange program:** None. **Opportunities for community service:** 25 hours per year are required; up to 10 hours per year and 20 hours overall may be served on campus. A Community Service Coordinator helps students find placement at Bay Area agencies ranging from food kitchens to beach clean-up, to tutoring at local schools. Some students organize their own projects such as food, book, and clothing drives and recently, an Oxfam banquet. **Typical freshman schedule:** 7 periods of approximately 80 minutes each (classes meet every other day), including English, math, World Civilizations, human development, foreign language, science, and an elective.

## Student Support Services

**Counselor-student ratio: (not including college counselor)** 1:10. **Counseling:** The School Counselor offers one-on-one counseling for students and consults with parents. The Director of Counseling (Michael Riera, Ph.D.) oversees the counseling program and the general counseling environment of the school and also provides individual counseling. In addition, group counseling is provided from time to time as the students request it. Both the Director of Counseling and the School Counselor hold advanced degrees in social work or psychology. All students are matched with an advisor and are part of an Advising Group. The advisor is an advocate for the students and advises them on the culture, standards, rules and academic and social lives of the school, and monitors the students' progress throughout the year. The class deans work closely with the advisors to help ensure the academic and personal well-being of each student. Marin Academy has a Director and Associate Director of **College Counseling** who work with students all four years. The assigned college counselor meets individually with each student and family beginning in the spring of the junior year. In addition, the school hosts a Junior College Night for students and parents, plus two college nights for seniors and their families. Approximately 90 colleges visit Marin Academy each year. Teachers are available for **tutorials** every other day to help students on an individual basis. **Learning disabilities/differences:** "No learning specialist on staff. The school works with several independent learning specialists. Students with special learning needs are granted extended time on tests if they have submitted documentation of educational testing by an approved specialist or institution, specifically indicating the need for additional time." **Career apprenticeship programs:** None.

## STUDENT CONDUCT AND HEALTH

**Code of conduct:** Standard. **How school handles drug/alcohol usage:** "The sale or distribution of all illegal drugs or alcohol will result in immediate expulsion, barring extraordinary circumstances. A student found in the presence of, using, or in possession of an illegal drug or alcohol will not be allowed to attend school until he or she has undergone a clinical assessment for substance abuse with a mutually agreed upon professional counselor. The student and his or her family will further be required to follow the recommendations of the assessment in order for the student to reenter Marin Academy. A second instance of use or possession of an illegal drug or alcohol will result in immediate expulsion, barring extraordinary circumstances." **Drug/alcohol abuse prevention/AIDS awareness programs:** The human development curriculum is structured to provide students with up-to-date pertinent information about social issues, especially those that directly affect adolescents.

## SUMMER PROGRAMS

The school offers two 3-week sessions for middle school students (8:30 a.m. to 2 p.m. with extended a.m. and p.m. hours) and a Multicultural Leadership Program for incoming 8th graders; two high school programs (week-long intensive all day workshops and a 6-week summer school session); as well as Musical Theater Production, Driver's Education, and Wilderness Outings. The middle school program offers students entering grades 5-8 extensive courses in academics and fine arts. (Approx. $595 per session; extended care from 7:30 a.m. and to 5:30 p.m. costs $5/hr.) The high school program includes review and development courses in math, English, and foreign language, and intensive workshops, this year in marine biology and astronomy. ($400 per class—two classes max.) Both middle school and high school summer students may participate in an afternoon musical theater program (12:30 p.m.-3:30 p.m.) culminating in a performance ($450). Driver's ed, individual tutoring, and SSAT prep classes are also offered. (Courses, offerings, and prices are subject to change from summer to summer.)

# Parent Involvement

**Parent participation:** Not required, though the Marin Academy Parents' Association seeks the involvement of all interested parents. The Association holds monthly meetings with educational opportunities for parents; sponsors a scrip program; trains guides for admission tours; hosts gatherings for new parents; and assists with other events throughout the year. **Parent/teacher communication:** Advisors, who meet with students once a week (each Advisor is responsible for 10-12 students) are the first link between school and home. Advisors are in communication with the parents and will inform a student's teacher, if necessary, of any difficulties the child is having and any support that should be offered. Parents meet with the Advisors on Parent Conference Day. Parents are also welcome to call individual classroom teachers (whom they will all meet at Back-to-School Night) at any time, as well as class deans, the Academic Dean, and the Dean of Students. (All faculty and staff have voice mail.) **Parent education:** The Director of Counseling, Dr. Michael Riera, conducts at least one seminar a year to which all school parents are invited. The seminars address the challenges and issues facing teenagers in general and school students in particular, and have included what parents of incoming freshmen can expect, and the separation process for parents of graduating seniors. **Donations:** None.

# Sports

Girls' and boys' varsity teams in volleyball, tennis, cross-country, water polo, basketball, softball, swimming, soccer, and track and field; girls' and boys' junior varsity volleyball; boys' varsity lacrosse, and baseball. Boys' and girls' sailing; boys' golf; girls' softball and soccer (jv and v). More than 90% of students participate in sports. Most teams compete in the Bay Counties League; teams have won 30 League titles.

# What Sets School Apart From Others

"While we believe that the preparation for college and adult life must begin in the classroom with a demanding academic curriculum, we are as much concerned with our students' personal growth as we are with their intellectual growth, and this concern is reflected in our commitment to the variety of challenging experiences which, taken as a whole, constitute a Marin Academy education. First and foremost, we are committed to academic excellence. In addition, our commitment to experiential education is reflected in everything we do outside the classroom at Marin Academy. We believe that many adolescents in our society are information rich and experience poor and that they need challenging experiences which will help them discover their sense of self and their essential humanity. We believe that students learn best in a relaxed, open, friendly, school community—one based on respect and trust, where they are encouraged to take responsibility for their education and to be an integral part of the school's decision-making process."

## How Parents/Students Characterize School

N/P.

# Marin Catholic High School

675 Sir Francis Drake Blvd.
Kentfield, CA 94904

(415) 461-8844 *fax (415) 461-7161*
www.marin.k12.ca.us/~marcath/

Monsignor Stephen Otellini, President
William Isetta, Principal
Theresa Groshong, Director of Admissions, (415) 461-0757

## General

**Coed** day high school. **Catholic parochial** (70% Catholic). Founded in 1949. **Nonprofit. Enrollment:** Approximately 740. **Average class size:** 24. **Accreditation:** WASC (6-year term: 1999-06). **School year:** 9-month calendar. (N/P re # instructional days) **School day:** 7:55 a.m. to 2:55 p.m. **Location:** On Sir Francis Drake Boulevard, a main thoroughfare in Marin County, accessible by Golden Gate Transit buses. (Approximately 15 minutes by car from the Golden Gate Bridge and 20 minutes from the Richmond-San Rafael Bridge.)

## Student Body

**Geographical breakdown (counties):** 94% from Marin; 2% from San Francisco; 2% from Sonoma; 2% from Alameda. **Ethnicity:** Approximately 82% Caucasian (non-Latino); 8% multi-racial; 4% Latino; 4% Asian; 1.5% Asian-American; 1% Native American. **Foreign students (I-20 status):** N/P. **Single parent/two f/t working parent families:** N/P. **Middle schools:** 52% of the most recent entering freshman class came from Marin County parochial schools; 11% from private schools; 37% from public schools. (N/P re # schools)

# ADMISSION

**Applications due:** Early January (call for date). **Application fee:** $50. **Application process:** From September through January, the school schedules student and parent visits. An open house is held in November. Applications submitted by early January (call for date) receive priority. The HSPT is given on two dates in January. Interviews of parents and student are held in February and decisions are mailed out mid-March. **No. of applications:** 425 applications were received for 200 places in prior year's class. **Admission cut-off:** N/P. **Preferences:** N/P. **"We are looking for"** N/P. **What sort of student do you best serve?** "Marin Catholic students are college-bound young people interested in developing themselves as a 'whole person.' Marin Catholic seeks students who wish to become positive contributors to the school community, bringing with them their own unique talents and individual interests."

# COSTS

**Latest tuition:** $7,250 payable in 1, 2, or 11 payments. **Sibling discount:** None. **Tuition increases:** Approximately 4% annually. **Other costs:** Approximately $300 for books when purchased new; used books are also available at a discounted price. **Financial aid:** Aid from the Archdiocese of San Francisco is available to students living within the San Francisco Archdiocese who demonstrate financial need. Aid from the school is available to Catholics and non-Catholics demonstrating need; they are required to make a 40-minute-a-day work contribution to the school for one or two semesters. **Percentage of students receiving financial aid:** 20%. **Average grant:** N/P. **No. of full/half-tuition scholarships:** N/P. **Grants of half-tuition or more:** N/P.

# SCHOOL'S MISSION STATEMENT/GOALS

"Marin Catholic serves young men and women in the Catholic tradition. Consistent with our Gospel values, we are committed to the education of the whole person. We provide a spiritual, academic, and extracurricular environment dedicated to imparting knowledge, values, and vision.

"We expect our students, through their experiences in the classroom and as active members of the school community, to develop the attributes of an educated person: responsibility, both personal and social; critical ability; appreciation for the beauty and complexity of the world around us. We hope to instill in our students the confidence that will empower them, as informed and compassionate individuals, to effect change in that world. We are committed to learning as a lifelong process."

# ACADEMIC PROGRAM

**Courses offered (AP=Advanced Placement, H=Honors, (AP)=AP option, (H)=Honors option): Computer Education:** Keyboarding, Computer Applications, Graphic Design and Desktop Publishing, Computer-Aided Design/Drafting, Advanced Business Skills, Computer Programming, Multimedia Design and Production; **English:** English 9, English 10 (H), American Studies: Literature, American Literature H, California Writers, Senior Composition, Imaginative Literature, AP English; **Visual and Performing Arts:** Art I-II, Drawing and Painting, Advanced Art and Portfolio Preparation, Ceramics I-II, Ceramics, Photography I-II, Beginning Drama, Play Production, Dramatic Literature, Speech, Chorus I-II, Concert Band, Band, Jazz Ensemble; **Foreign Language:** French I-III, French IV (H), AP French, Italian I-IV, Spanish I-IV, AP Spanish; **Math:** Introduction to Algebra, Algebra I, Geometry (H), Advanced Algebra (H), Introduction to Probability and Statistics, Pre-Calculus (H), AP Calculus (H); **P.E.:** Freshmen P.E., Fitness, Weight Training for Individual Needs, P.E. Assistant; **Religious Studies:** Religious Studies 9-Introduction to Faith and Catholicism, Religious Studies 10-The Bible, Religious Studies 11-Christian Morality and Social Justice, Religious Studies 12-Relationships and Contemporary Issues, Religious Studies 12 (H)-Introduction to Theological Investigations: A Catholic Approach; **Science:** Integrated Science I-II, Chemistry, Physics (H), Honors Physiology/AP Biology, Marine Science, Physiology, Chemistry (H), Science Lab/Teaching Assistant; **Social Studies:** World Geography, Western Civilization (H), American Studies: US History, AP US History (H), US Government (H), Economics, Law, Psychology (AP). **Computer lab/training:** All students are required to take 1 year computer education including electronic writing and computer applications. The school has a newly upgraded computer center that includes PowerPCs. (N/P # computers) **Grading:** Letter grades and progress reports. **Graduation requirements:** 260 credits including 4 years English, 4 years religious studies, 3.5 years social studies, including world geography, western civilization, US history and US government, 2 years foreign language, 1 year fine/performing arts, 2 years science, 3 years math, 1 semester computer education including electronic writing and computer applications, 1 semester P.E., 100 hours Christian Service (transfer students, 25 hours for each year enrolled at Marin Catholic) and a retreat for each year enrolled at Marin Catholic. **Average nightly homework:** 2-3.5 hours. **Faculty:** 61 faculty members including 2 Archdiocesan priests, 1 Dominican Sister, and 1 Franciscan Sister. 50% hold master's degrees. (N/P remaining faculty information.) **Faculty ethnicity:** N/P. **Faculty selection/training:** N/P. **Teacher/student ratio:** 1:19. **Teacher's daily student load in required academic subject:** N/P. **AP courses/exams:** "12/12." **Senior class profile (mean):** SAT Math/Verbal combined 1123. **GPA:** 3.15. **National Merit Scholarship Program:** "8." **College enrollment:** 85% of last year's graduating class enrolled in 4-year colleges, 15% in 2-year colleges, including: American, Arizona State, Boston C, Boston U, Bowdoin, Cal Lutheran, Chapman, Claremont McKenna, Colby, C of Notre Dame, Colorado State, Connecticut C, Cornell, CSU campuses (Cal Poly-SLO, Cal Poly-Pomona, Chico, Fullerton, Humboldt, Long Beach, Maritime, Monterey, Sacramento, San Diego, San Francisco, San Jose, Sonoma), Dominican, Embry Riddle, George Washington, Georgetown, Gonzaga, Harvard, Hawaii Pacific, Holy Cross, Ithaca C, Johns Hopkins, Knox C, Lehigh, Lewis & Clark, Loyola Marymount, Macalester C, Middlebury, Mills, Moore C, NYU, Northern Arizona, Northwestern, Occidental, Oregon State, Penn State, Pepperdine, Philadelphia C of Textiles and Science, Pitzer, Purdue, Randolph-Macon Women's C, Reed, Regis, RISD, Santa Clara, Sarah Lawrence, Savannah School of Design, Seattle U, St. Louis U, St. Mary's, Stonehill C, Syracuse U, Texas A & M, Thomas Aquinas, Tufts, Tulane, US Air Force Academy, US Coast Guard Academy, U of Notre Dame, U of Arizona, UC campuses (Berkeley, Davis, Los Angeles, Riverside, San Diego, Santa Barbara, Santa Cruz), U of Colorado-Boulder, U of Hawaii-Hilo, U of Illinois-Champain, U of Massachusetts, U of Miami, U of Michigan, U of Nebraska, U of Nevada-Las Vegas, U of North Carolina-Charlotte, U of Oregon, UOP, U of Pennsylvania, U of Portland, U of Puget Sound, U of San Diego, USF, USC, U of the Incarnate Word, U of Virginia, U of Washington, U of Western Michigan, Utah State U, Vanderbilt, Villanova, Westmont C, Wheaton C, Whitman, Whittier, Willamette, Woodbury U, and Wyoming Tech.

## Other Indicators the School is Accomplishing its Goals

N/P.

## Campus/Campus Life

**Campus description:** The school has a 14-acre campus at the base of Mt. Tamalpais in Kentfield, a suburb 15 miles north of San Francisco in Marin County. The school includes a two-story school building, football field, performing arts center, gym, baseball field, community park, and chapel. **Library**: 3,000 sq. ft.; 10,000 print volumes; 26 computers (all with Internet access); 16 periodical subscriptions (as well as Ebsco); CD-ROM with 60 full text journals and index to 600 journals; on-line catalog; study space for 75 students; open to students from 7:30 a.m. to 5:30 p.m. **Open/closed campus:** Closed. **Classroom space per student:** N/P. **Lunches:** The school cafeteria serves breakfast and lunch. Open from 7:45 a.m. to 3:15 p.m. **Bus service:** N/P. **Uniforms/dress code:** No caps, facial hair, extreme haircuts or hair coloring; no T-shirts with offensive slogans, "grunge-look" clothing, athletic sweats, or gym shorts; no tight or extremely baggy clothing, no midriff blouses, halter or tank tops. **Co-curricular activities/clubs:** Activities include Academic Decathlon (ACADEC), California Scholarship Federation, Cheerleading, Washington, D.C. Close-up, Drama Club, Earth Awareness Club, *Emcee Echoes* Student Newspaper, French Club, Intramural Sports, Italian Club, Mock Trial Team, National Honor Society, Rotary Interact Club,

Scuba Diving Club, Student Government, Wilderness Club, and Women's Science and Math Club. **Foreign exchange program:** N/P. **Opportunities for community service:** Canal Child Care Center, Marin Head Start, Boy Scouts/Girl Scouts, CYO Camp Armstrong, Little League, Marin YMCA, Big Brother/Big Sisters, SADD, AIDS Interfaith, St. Vincent Dining Room, Family Service Agency, Hillhaven Convalescent, Marin Suicide Prevention, Salvation Army, Catholic Charities, California Marine Mammal Center, La Familia de Marin, and others. **Typical freshman schedule:** English 9, Religious Studies, Algebra I or Advanced Algebra Honors, foreign language (French, Italian, or Spanish), World Geography, Integrated Science I, P.E. or performing arts elective.

## STUDENT SUPPORT SERVICES

**Counselor/student ratio (not including college counselors):** 1:255. **Counseling:** The school assigns each student a personal and academic counselor with whom the student meets individually on a regularly-scheduled basis during the year. Parents, advisors, and students do academic planning each spring. A full-time College Admission Advisor staffs the College and Career Center. Junior and seniors receive systematic individual and small group college counseling. **Learning disabilities/differences:** N/P. **Career apprenticeship programs:** N/P.

## STUDENT CONDUCT AND HEALTH

**Code of conduct:** In addition to proscribing illegal activity, the Code of Behavior provides sanctions for profanity/vulgarity/insolence, verbal harassment, denigrating speech and name-calling, and physical intimidation. **How school handles drugs/alcohol usage:** If a student is found in possession of illegal substances, the substance and the student's car keys (if applicable) are confiscated, and parents/guardians are immediately notified. The student is subject to expulsion and possibly immediate suspension pending a meeting of the Disciplinary Review Board. Should the student be allowed to remain, he or she may be subject to random drug testing, an after-care program, and other disciplinary actions. The school may randomly use a "breathalizer" at school-sponsored events to ensure safety and sobriety. **Drug/alcohol abuse prevention/AIDS awareness program:** These issues are discussed in Religious Education classes; in addition, counselors are trained to identify problem behavior and make referrals as necessary.

## SUMMER PROGRAMS

The school hosts a month-long summer session (mid-June to mid-July) consisting of academic classes, fitness courses, and private tutoring. Incoming freshmen may take a class in study skills. Cost: Approximately $225 per class.

# Parent Involvement

**Parent participation:** None required, though parents are very active in the school. **Parent/teacher communication:** Formal report cards each semester and progress reports at six-week intervals. **Parent education:** N/P. **Donations:** Parents are asked to give to the annual fund.

# Sports

Students compete in the Marin County Athletic League in more than 14 sports. Boys compete in football (frosh, jv, v), soccer (frosh, soph, v), basketball (frosh, jv, v), wrestling, baseball (frosh, jv, v), tennis, and volleyball (frosh, v). Girls compete in field hockey (jv, v), tennis, volleyball (frosh, jv, v), soccer (jv, v), softball (jv, v), and basketball (frosh, jv, v). Girls and boys compete in cross-country (frosh, jv, v), water polo, spirit/cheerleading, swimming/diving, track (v), and golf.

# What Sets School Apart From Others

"Marin Catholic High School is a Catholic, coeducational college preparatory school. As a school community we strive to provide opportunities for growth academically, spiritually, and socially. The Marin Catholic curriculum is designed to provide a challenging and stimulating academic experience for all of our students. ... The spiritual program at Marin Catholic is the foundation of all our school programs. Students are required to complete four years of Religious Studies, participate in a retreat each year, and complete 100 hours of Christian Service. Our Campus Ministry Program invites students to become involved in the planning of liturgies, retreats, and other prayer services.

"The athletic and extracurricular program is as diverse and interesting as our student body, providing students with tremendous opportunities to enhance their high school experience. Over 90 percent of our student body participate in athletic or extracurricular activities."

# How Parents/Students Characterize School

N/P.

# MAYBECK HIGH SCHOOL

2362 Bancroft Way
Berkeley, CA 94704

(510) 841-8489 *fax (510) 548-1907*

Jonathan Martin, Director
Gretchen Griswold, Education Director

## GENERAL

**Coed** day high school. **Nonsectarian.** Founded in 1972. **Nonprofit. Enrollment:** Approximately 105. **Average class size:** 12. **Accreditation:** N/P. **School year:** 9.5 month calendar. (N/P re # instructional days) **School day:** 8 a.m. to 5 p.m. (varies). **Location:** Located near the UC Berkeley campus, the school is several blocks from the Berkeley BART station and accessible by AC Transit buses 51, 64, 40, and 52.

## STUDENT BODY

**Geographical breakdown (counties):** 95% from Alameda; 5% from Contra Costa. **Ethnicity:** 80% Caucasian (non-Latino); 10% African-American; 5% Asian; 5% Latino. **Foreign students (I-20 status):** 2%. **Single parent/two f/t working parent families:** N/P. **Middle schools:** Of freshmen students, 50% came from public schools; 40% from private non-parochial schools; and 10% from parochial schools. (N/P re #) The schools draws a good number of students from Willard, King, Claremont, and Montera public schools as well as East Bay Science & Arts, Community School of the East Bay, St. Paul's and Berkeley Montessori.

## ADMISSION

**Applications due:** Rolling admissions process beginning in December. **Application fee:** $25. **Application process:** Interested students visit classes, preferably for a full day, take a placement test, and are interviewed. Math and English placement tests are given. **No. of applications:** 35 applications were received for 25 places in prior year's class. Eight new students were admitted to G10, 5 to G11 and 3 to G12. **Admission cut-off:** None. **Preferences:** None. **"We are looking for** students at or above grade level dedicated to learning for its own sake while preparing for college." **What sort of student do you best serve?** "Students who feel most comfortable in small schools; students who enjoy outdoor experiences; students committed to learning in a rigorous but supportive environment; students who feel they don't fit in elsewhere."

# Costs

**Latest tuition:** $8,800, payable monthly or semi-annually. **Sibling discount:** N/P. **Tuition increases:** N/P. **Other costs:** Class materials cost approximately $330/year; spring special programs vary from $75-$1,500. **Financial aid:** Need-based; the school dedicates 17% of its annual operating budget to financial aid. Travel grants are available to 3rd and 4th year students who have not been able to afford a travel experience through Special Programs. **Percentage of students receiving financial aid:** 31%. **Average grant:** $3,900. **No. of full tuition grants:** 0. **Half-tuition grants:** N/P. **Grants of half-tuition or more:** Normally 5-10%.

# School's Mission Statement/Goals

"Maybeck High School is a small community dedicated to learning, where all forms of diversity can flourish amid mutual support, respect and responsibility. Through our small classes, high expectations, academic excellence, and programs outside the school, students prepare for college and acquire the tools to engage actively and creatively in the wider world."

# Academic Program

**Courses offered (AP=Advanced Placement, H=Honors, (AP)=AP option, (H)=Honors option): Math:** Algebra I, Geometry, Algebra II/Trig, Calculus; **Science:** Conceptual Physics, Biology, Chemistry, Advanced Biology, Computer Science, Electronics Lab, Field Botany, Invertebrate Anatomy, Ornithology; **English:** Composition, Intermediate Composition, Literature, Reading, 20th Century African-American Writing, Advanced Composition, The Bible as Literature, Comparative Literature, The English Romantics, The Essay, European Modernism, Folktales and Fables, Greek Classics, Modern Novel, Philosophy and Literature, Poetry, Shakespeare; **Foreign Language:** Spanish I-IV; **Social Studies:** World History, US History, Government, American Identity, Civil Rights, International Relations, On Revolution, Origins of the Holocaust, Race and Gender, World Religions, American Legal Systems, Psychology, Thinkers in Harmony & Conflict; **Arts:** Painting, Advanced Drawing and Painting, Environmental Design, Figure Drawing, Printmaking, Music, Photography, Watercolor, 2- and 3-D Studio Arts, Animation, Dynamics, Filmmaking, Drama Production; **P.E.:** Health, Commute Bicycling. **Computer lab/training:** 1 lab with 5 PCs running Windows 95. (N/P re training) **Grading:** A-F. **Graduation requirements:** 4 years English, 3 years math (Algebra I, Geometry, and Algebra II/Trig), 2.5 years science, 3 years social studies, 2 years foreign language, 1 year art, 2 years P.E., 60 hours community service. **Average nightly homework:** G9: 2 hours; G10: 2.5 hours; G11-12: 3 hours. **Faculty:** 40% male, 60% female. 40% hold bachelor's degrees as highest degrees; 55% hold master's degrees; and 5% hold doctorates. **Faculty ethnicity:** 86% Caucasian (non-Latino); 7% Latino; 7%

African-American. The average tenure of faculty is 16 years. **Faculty selection/ training:** N/P. **Teacher/student ratio:** 1:8. **Teacher's daily student load in required academic subject:** 48. **AP courses/exams:** N/P. **Senior class profile (mean):** "Maybeck does not use standardized tests in admitting students to the school, nor do we rank our graduates. Fifteen of the 18 graduates of 1998 took the SAT: median scores were 650 verbal and 600 math." **National Merit Scholarship Program:** N/P. **College enrollment:** 60% of last year's graduating class enrolled in 4-year colleges, 10% in 2-year colleges (almost all others intend to enroll in fall 2000 in 4-year colleges). Colleges include: UC Santa Cruz, UC Santa Barbara, Mills, Stanford, USF, U of Puget Sound, CSU-SF, Scripps, Norwich U (VT), Evergreen State (WA), and Beloit C (WI).

## OTHER INDICATORS THE SCHOOL IS ACCOMPLISHING ITS GOALS

N/P.

## CAMPUS/CAMPUS LIFE

**Campus description:** The school has eight classrooms and four offices in Trinity Hall of the United Methodist Church across from the UC Berkeley campus. Though not affiliated with the church, the school uses its chapel, social hall, and courtyard for school functions. **Library:** The school uses the Berkeley Public Library, which is four blocks away. **Open campus. Classroom space per student:** N/P. **Lunches:** N/P. **Bus service:** Public only. **Uniforms/dress code:** None. **Co-curricular activities/clubs:** Drama Club, Student Activities Committee, Bicycling Club, Backpacking Club. **Foreign exchange program:** Groups travel abroad annually. The school has a foreign exchange program to France. **Opportunities for community service:** Students arrange their own community service with guidance. **Typical freshman schedule:** Algebra I, World History, Composition, Conceptual Physics, Spanish/French I or II, Art, P.E.

## STUDENT SUPPORT SERVICES

**Counselor/student ratio (not including college counselors):** N/P. **Counseling:** No personal counselors. The school provides academic and college/career counseling; each student is provided a contact advisory teacher. **Learning differences/disabilities:** No special programs or resources. **Career apprenticeship programs:** None.

## STUDENT CONDUCT AND HEALTH

**Code of conduct:** Standard. Smoking is prohibited. **How school handles drugs/alcohol usage:** Immediate expulsion upon evidence of usage or possession at school or on school trips. Upon suspicion of use outside school, intervention with parents and teacher advisors. **Drug/alcohol abuse prevention/AIDS awareness program:** Part of required health class.

## SUMMER PROGRAMS

Students may take two semesters of US History and a semester course in English. Cost: Approximately $450 per semester.

## PARENT INVOLVEMENT

**Parent participation:** None required. Parents serve on a Parent Advisory Board and help with fundraising, building improvement, recruitment, and special events. **Parent/teacher communication:** Two midsemester narrative reports; semester grades; conferences are scheduled as needed or as requested. **Parent education:** "Three or four times a year grade level parents meet to share concerns and strategies in a peer education approach." **Donations:** Parents are requested to participate in annual giving.

## SPORTS

P.E., bicycling and backpacking clubs.

## OTHER

"Students have many opportunities for outdoor experiences: optional monthly backpacking trips, and two week-long camping trips in the mountains with all school students and faculty at the beginning and end of the school year.

"The school is very small and intimate—100 students, with an average classroom size of 12. All staff and faculty are on a first name basis. The school has a unique and diverse student body with enormous freedom for and acceptance of self-expression: No dress code, little peer pressure."

Each year the school has special programs. They have included trips to China, Guatemala, Cuba, France, and Ecuador, a mural painting course, a Bay Area cultures workshop, a California coastline bike tour, a book design workshop, fencing, skiing, and a "breakfast club"—sewing (flannel pajamas) and baking.

## WHAT SETS SCHOOL APART FROM OTHERS

"Lean organization—little bureaucracy, little administration, dedicated to teaching as the core of what we do. Teacher-run school, collectively governed by the faculty. Highly affordable relative to other secular private schools. Not a lot of trappings—just enormous dedication to learning."

## HOW PARENTS/STUDENTS CHARACTERIZE SCHOOL

**Student response(s):** "There is a strong teacher-student bond." "The quality of the education is high above the education I could get anywhere else." "Maybeck likes you to be unique and yourself." "A supportive environment is offered here." "I like the small classes." "Maybeck is a really nice community; people accept one another well." "I like the relaxed nature and the great education." "I feel that I received an education that is incomparable to anything else I could have gotten." "I like it that it's hard." "It simulates a college-type style of learning." "Everybody can be an individual and not have to worry about what anybody else says." "I like the diversity of people and ideas that exists in such a close personal environment." "I like being able to dress and look how I choose." "I like being able to be myself." "Maybeck really wants you to use your mind and really think." "I like the small community, the atmosphere for learning, small classes and diverse choices—Hell, I just like the school!"

# MENLO SCHOOL

50 Valparaiso Avenue
Atherton, CA 94027

(650) 688-3856 *fax (650) 325-0223*

Norman Colb, Headmaster
Glen Pritzker, Director of Admissions, (650) 688-3866

## GENERAL

**Coed** high school and middle school. **Nonsectarian**. Founded in 1915. **Nonprofit**, member CAIS, NAIS, BAIHS. **Enrollment:** 532 (high school only). **Average class size:** 14-18 in 90% of academic classes. **Accreditation:** WASC/CAIS (6-year term: 1999-05). **School year:** N/P. **School day:** 8 a.m. to 3 p.m. **Location:** In Menlo Park, a suburb just north of Palo Alto. A school shuttle takes students to and from the Menlo Park CalTrain station.

## STUDENT BODY

**Geographical breakdown (counties):** 40% from San Mateo; 40% from Santa Clara; 1% from San Francisco. **Ethnicity:** Approximately 60% Caucasian (non-Latino); 20% Asian; 10% Latino; 5% African-American; 5% other. **Foreign students (I-20 status):** N/P. **Single parent/two f/t working parent families:** N/P. **Middle schools:** N/P.

## ADMISSION

**Applications due**: Approximately January 20 (call for date). **Application fee:** $50. **Application process:** "Application, essay, visit, test (STS)." **No. of applications:** 320 applications were received for 130 places in prior year's class. Of these, 65 places were taken by school's middle school students. (N/P re new students admitted to G10-12.) **Admission cut-off:** "Top 20% on standardized tests—3.5 or better GPA." **Preferences:** N/P. **"We are looking for** bright students with a special talent." **What sort of student do you best serve?** N/P.

## COSTS

**Latest tuition:** $15,625 payable in 1 or 10 payments. **Sibling discount:** No. **Tuition increases:** 5% annually. **Other costs:** $350 for books. **Financial aid:** In the last year, the school awarded $1,029,000 in financial aid to 15% of the student body. **Percentage of students receiving financial aid:** 15%. **Average grant:** $6,000. **No. of full-tuition grants:** 0. **No. of half-tuition grants:** N/P. **Grants of more than half-tuition:** 15%.

## SCHOOL'S MISSION STATEMENT/GOALS

"Menlo School is dedicated to providing a challenging academic curriculum complemented by outstanding fine arts and athletic programs. The school helps students develop positive values and nurtures character development in a supportive environment that upholds the highest moral and ethical standards. Menlo's program encourages students to reach their fullest potential and to develop the skills necessary to respond intelligently and humanely to the complexities of a diverse world."

## ACADEMIC PROGRAM

**Courses offered (AP=Advanced Placement, H=Honors, (H)=Honors option, (AP)=AP option):** English 1-4, including college-level electives such as British Literature, College Writing, Creative Writing, In a Different Voice, Poetry, Rites of Passage, Shakespeare, 20th Century American Fiction, Comparative Literature, Detective Literature, Introduction to History, Western Studies, US History,

History and Social Science Electives (including Russian History, Asian History, Political Ideologies, Introduction to Law, Supreme Court Cases, Economics, Psychology, Modern Ethical Dilemmas), Algebra 1, Algebra 2 (H), Geometry (H), Pre-Calculus, Foundations of Calculus H, Computer Science AP, Computer Science II, Statistics, AB Calculus (AP), BC Calculus (AP), Physics, Integrated Chemistry & Biology, AP Physics B, AP Physics C, Electronics and Robotics, Chemistry (AP), Marine Biology, Human Physiology, Bio-Tech/Science Research, French 1-3, French 4 H, AP French Language, AP French Literature, Spanish 1-3, Spanish 4 H, AP Spanish Language, Spanish 5 Literature, Japanese 1, Latin 1, Latin 2-4 (H), AP Vergil, AP Latin Literature, Introduction to the Arts, Freshman Seminar, Public Speaking, Writing with Computers, Studio Art, Advanced Art, AP Art Portfolio, Drama, Advanced Drama, Chorus, Select Chorus, Chamber Orchestra, Jazz Band, Music Theory AP, Jazz Dance, Advanced Jazz Dance. **Computer lab/training:** N/P. **Grading:** Letter grades. **Graduation requirements:** 4 years English, 1.5 years fine arts, 3 years foreign language, 3 years history, 3 years math, 3 years science (physics, biology, chemistry). Beginning with the class of 2002, 20 hours of community service will be required each year. **Average nightly homework:** N/P. **Faculty:** Of the 80 full-time and 10 part-time faculty members, 48 hold master's degrees, 9 hold Ph.Ds and 3 hold JDs. (N/P re gender) **Faculty ethnicity:** 94% Caucasian (non-Latino); 2% Latino; 2% Asian. **Faculty selection/training:** "National searches are conducted. Advanced degrees are encouraged. Rigorous teacher evaluation process." **Teacher/student ratio:** N/P. **Teacher's daily student load in required academic subject:** N/P. **AP courses/ exams:** 60% of students are currently taking AP courses. In 1998, 163 students took 371 AP examinations. 89% scored 3 or above. **Senior class profile (mean):** SAT Verbal 619, SAT Math 640 (for the class of 1999 as of June 1998). Same class's mean SAT II scores: Writing 614; Lit 585; Math 1C 617; Math 2C 641; Am Hist 604; Bio 616; Chem 596; Phy 677; French 650; Latin 611; Spanish 594; Japanese listening 750. **GPA:** 3.3 (for same class calculated using all courses except P.E.). **National Merit Scholarship Program:** In the class of 1998, 6 students were semi-finalists; of these 5 became finalists. Thirteen were commended. Eleven from the class of 1999 were named semi-finalists, 16 commended. **College enrollment:** Over the past 3 years, 3 or more Menlo graduates have attended the following colleges: UC Davis (93), UC Berkeley (77), San Diego (73), UCLA (60), UC Santa Barbara (60), U of Colorado (43), UC Santa Cruz (38), U of Oregon (36), USC (35), Santa Clara (28), U of Arizona (27), Stanford (23), Occidental (23), SMU (19), Cornell (18), Lewis & Clark (18), U of San Diego (13), NYU (12), Duke (12), Princeton (11), Claremont McKenna (10), Tufts (10), Bucknell (9), Vassar (9), Washington U (9), Brown (8), MIT (8), U of Michigan (8), Cal Poly-SLO (8), Willamette (7), Yale (6) Amherst (5), Foothill C (5), Dartmouth (5), Cal Poly-Pomona (3), and Harvard (3).

# OTHER INDICATORS THE SCHOOL IS ACCOMPLISHING ITS GOALS

N/P.

# Campus/Campus Life

**Campus description:** N/P. **Library:** N/P. **Open/closed campus:** N/P. **Classroom space per student:** N/P. **Lunches:** N/P. **Bus service:** N/P. **Uniform/dress code:** N/P. **Co-curricular activities/clubs:** Multicultural Awareness Club, Junior Statesmen of America, Junior Classical League, Literary Magazine, Video Club, Chess Club, Interact, Debate Club, Friends Club, The Neighborhood, Political Action Awareness Club, Photography Club, Spanish Club, *Menlo Modern Language Journal*, Four From Earth, Indus Club, French Club, TEAM, Student Council, Art Club, Model United Nations. **Foreign exchange program:** N/P. **Opportunities for community service:** N/P. **Typical freshman schedule:** "Five solids/ arts rotation."

# Student Support Services

**Counselor/student ratio (not including college counselors):** 1:125. **Counseling:** Personal, academic, and college counseling. The school has two full-time college counselors. **Learning disabilities/differences:** "No formal programs." **Career apprenticeship programs:** Career day only.

# Student Conduct and Health

**Code of conduct:** N/P. **How school handles drugs/alcohol usage:** "Zero tolerance." **Drug/alcohol abuse prevention/AIDS awareness program:** N/P.

# Summer Programs

Please contact the school for information on its summer programs.

# Parent Involvement

**Parent participation:** N/P. **Parent/teacher communication:** N/P. **Parent education:** A school counselor runs seminars for parents on typical adolescent issues. **Donations:** N/P.

# Sports

Through the Bay Counties League, girls compete in cross-country, water polo, tennis, volleyball, basketball, soccer, golf, track, lacrosse, softball, and swimming; boys compete in cross-country, football, water polo, basketball, soccer, baseball, golf, swimming, tennis, track, volleyball, and lacrosse.

## OTHER

"Outwardly rigorous, inwardly informal."

## WHAT SETS SCHOOL APART FROM OTHERS

"Strong academics with emphasis in sports and arts."

## HOW PARENTS/STUDENTS CHARACTERIZE SCHOOL

N/P.

# MERCY HIGH SCHOOL

2750 Adeline Drive
Burlingame, CA 94010

(650) 343-3631 *fax (650) 343-2316*
mercyhsb@aol.com

Rosann Fraher, RSM, Principal
Mrs. Betty Duran, Admission Director, (650) 343-1414

## GENERAL

**Girls'** day high school. **Catholic** (freshman class 80% Catholic). Founded in 1931. **Nonprofit. Enrollment:** 445. **Average class size:** 25. **Accreditation:** WASC (6-year term: 1997-03). **School year:** Mid- to late August to early June. 10-month calendar (180 instructional days). **School day:** 8 a.m. to 3 p.m. **Location:** Located between Highways 101 and 280, accessible by bus (SamTrans). CalTrain to SamTrans bus connections are also a possibility. Car pools arranged.

## STUDENT BODY

**Geographic Breakdown:** 97.8% from San Mateo; 1.6% from San Francisco; .5% from Alameda. **Ethnicity:** 52% Caucasian (non-Latina); 16.1% Latina; 8.5% Asian; .7% African-American; 22.7% other. **Foreign students (I-20 status):** 0. **Single parent families:** 20%. **Two f/t working parent families:** 80%. **Middle schools:** Based on 141 freshman students, 60% are from parochial (Catholic) schools; 31% from public schools; and 9% from private non-Catholic schools. (N/P re #) "Typically, each freshman class includes students from 40-50 middle schools in the area."

# ADMISSION

**Applications due/fee:** Priority admission for freshmen by mid-December (priority admission fee, $55); regular admission for freshmen after mid-December (fee, $65), Spring admission for freshman after mid-January (fee, $75). Freshmen applying after June 5 may be considered on a space-available/wait list basis (fee, $85). (Ed. Note: Check with school for exact cutoff dates.) **Application process:** The Admission Committee reviews each applicant based upon her (1) 7th and 8th grade report cards—for consistency and academic promise; (2) principal, 8th grade teacher, or counselor recommendation; (3) entrance examination results (exam given twice in January); (4) personal interview; and (5) clergy recommendation. The Admission Committee meets in late February and finalizes acceptance in mid-March. **No. of applications:** More than 300 applications were received for 125 places in prior year's class. Two new students were admitted to G10, 1 to G11. **Admission cut-off:** "Mercy accepts students with average GPAs and above." **Preferences:** Catholic students. **"We are looking for** well-rounded students willing to commit to the Mercy tradition of excellence in education. Mercy High School encourages students interested in a college prep curriculum to apply. Our idea of community will be enhanced because families are involved in their daughters' education from the beginning. This initial and continued contact allows the student to reach her highest potential. We are able to accommodate students from varying academic backgrounds." **What sort of students do you best serve?** N/P.

# COSTS

**Latest tuition:** $6,700 payable annually, bi-annually, quarterly, or monthly. First payment due in July of each year. **Sibling discount:** None. **Tuition increases:** 3 - 5% annually. **Other costs:** $350 registration fee, books $300 to $600 annually, uniforms, approx. $150. **Percentage of students receiving financial aid:** 20%. **Average grant:** $800. **No. of full/half-tuition awards:** 0. **Grants of half-tuition or more:** N/P. **Academic scholarships:** Those incoming freshmen who score in the top second percentile on the HSPT given in January are awarded The Board of Directors Scholarship. Those incoming freshmen who score in the top tenth percentile on the same test are awarded the Principal Recognition Scholarship. These students also must have maintained an excellent academic record and have contributed to their school communities.

# SCHOOL MISSION STATEMENT/GOALS

"Mercy High School, sponsored by the Sisters of Mercy, in collaboration with the faculty and staff, is a Catholic college preparatory school which provides the opportunity for young women of all cultures to realize their potential as productive and responsible members of society.

"Within a Christian community supporting the dignity and respect of each person, Mercy High School's staff is dedicated to the education of its young women, challenging them to compassionate service, leadership, and lifelong education."

## ACADEMIC PROGRAM

Mercy High School offers a comprehensive college preparatory curriculum. **Courses offered (AP=Advanced Placement, H=Honors, (H)=Honors option, (AP)=AP option): Counseling:** Introduction to Counseling; **English:** English I (H), English II (H), English III (AP), English IV (AP), CORE, Drama, Yearbook; **Fine/Performing Arts:** Art I, Art II, Art III H, Ceramics I-II, Ceramics III H, Chorale, Advanced Chorale, Dance I-III; **Foreign Language:** French I, French II (H), French III Honors, French IV AP, Spanish I, Spanish II (H), Spanish III (H), Spanish IV (AP, H); **Math:** Integrated Math I (H), Integrated Math II (H), Trigonometry/Analysis, Analysis/Calculus H, AP Calculus, Computer Science I, Computer Science II, Computer Science III AP; **P.E.:** P.E. I; **Religious Studies:** Religious Studies I-IV; **Science:** Environmental Science, Biology (H), Chemistry (H), Physics (H); **Social Science:** Social Studies, World History, US History (AP), American Government/Economics, AP American Government. **Computer lab/training:** The school has 2 computer labs, each with 25-30 IBM PCs. The Math Center, English Center, and Foreign Language Center each has 5-6 Macs. The library has IBMs. Every classroom has an IBM for the teacher's use. All freshmen take Computer Science I, which covers word processing, graphics, spreadsheets, databases, multimedia, and on-line communications through a project-based approach. Students produce a final interdisciplinary project assimilating all their computer skills and knowledge. **Grading:** A-F. **Graduation requirements:** 4 years English, 4 years religion, 3.5 years social studies, 1 year fine arts, 3 years math, 1 year P.E., 2 years foreign language, 1 semester computer science I, 3 years science. 20 hours of community service per year. **Average nightly homework:** G9-12: 3-4 hours. **Faculty:** 11% male, 89% female. 57% of faculty hold bachelor's degrees as highest degree; 39% hold master's degrees. **Faculty ethnicity:** 86% Caucasian (non-Latino); 17% Latino; 3% Native American. **Faculty selection/training:** "100% of our teachers have credentials or master's degrees. All are required to take 3 semester units of continuing education every 3 years." **Teacher/student ratio:** 1:11. **Teacher's daily student load in required academic subject:** N/P. **AP courses/exams:** 18% of students are currently taking AP courses. In 1998, 59 students took 100 AP examinations in 6 subjects. 92% received scores of 3 or above. **Senior class profile (mean):** SAT Math 524, SAT Verbal 590. (ACT composite, 21.3) **GPA:** N/P. **National Merit Scholarship Program:** One scholar, 2 commended. **College enrollment:** 69% of last year's graduating class enrolled in 4-year colleges, 30% in 2-year colleges. "In the last four years our graduates have been accepted to: Stanford, Harvard, Duke, Mt. Holyoke, Smith, Boston U, Notre Dame, Goucher C, George Washington, U of Chicago, Emory, Pomona C, Chapman, Loyola Marymount, U of Washington, U of Miami, UOP, U of Colorado, U of Arizona, UC Berkeley, UC Davis, UCLA, UC San Diego,

UC Santa Barbara, St. Mary's C, Santa Clara, Cal Poly-SLO, Cal Poly-Pomona, California State, U of Oregon, RISD, Pratt Institute, Cal Arts, and the San Francisco Art Institute." (N/P re: last year's college enrollment.)

## OTHER INDICATORS THE SCHOOL IS ACCOMPLISHING ITS GOALS

"Mercy High School is true to the school's roots in the Mercy tradition of excellence in education. The Mercy student is more prepared and eligible to take AP classes and honors classes because of the Mercy tradition of excellence in education. The Class of 1996 holds the distinction that all the students who took the University of California Subject A Examination, passed it."

## CAMPUS/CAMPUS LIFE

**Campus description:** Nestled in the Burlingame hills, the school is located on a 40-acre campus. Facilities in the high school complex include: the historic Kohl Mansion, the two-story classroom wing, Russell Hall, the Multi-Purpose Room, the swimming pool, tennis courts, three Resource Centers which supplement the large library in Russell Hall, the Multi-Media Lab, and the Physics, Chemistry, and Biology Labs. **Library:** 4,850 sq. ft.; study space for 70 students; 11 computers with Internet access; card catalog; 60 periodical subscriptions; 14,000 print volumes; open to students 7:45 a.m.-4 p.m. **Open/closed campus:** Closed. **Classroom space per student:** N/P. **Lunches:** Hot lunch service is provided in student cafeteria. **Bus service:** Public bus, SamTrans. Cost: approximately $.75 (one-way trip). **Uniform/dress code:** The required school uniform consists of a blue/black plaid knife pleat skirt, a polo shirt (long or short sleeve) with the school logo, pullover sweater, vest, or jacket. Options include navy walking shorts or pleated slacks, Dockers, school sweatshirt, and navy or white turtleneck. **Co-curricular activities/clubs:** California Scholarship Federation, National Honor Society, National Spanish Honor Society, National French Honor Society, Ambassador Club, Earthwatch, Heritage Club, Girls' Athletic Association, Junior Statesmen of America, PACE (Promoting a Christian Environment), Roving Ambassador Club, Service Club. **Foreign exchange program:** None. **Opportunities for community service:** Community service includes visiting the elderly, tutoring, coaching sports teams, donating blood, outdoor education, peer counseling and education camp counseling volunteering at parish festivals, community service agencies, political campaigns, soup kitchens, or a local hospital. **Typical freshman schedule:** Computer Science I, CORE, English I, foreign language, science, math, P.E., Religious Studies, social studies.

# Student Support Services

**Counselor/student ratio (not including college counselors):** 1:220. **Counseling:** All students are assigned a personal counselor and normally remain with the same counselor for four years. Students meet with counselors individually at least once a semester. Counselors also meet with students in groups as appropriate. **Academic Counseling:** The Counseling Department, faculty, and staff collaborate in academic counseling. Faculty may approach counselors with concerns about specific students. Meetings are set up between counselors, teachers, and students. Mercy's flexible schedule gives students some unscheduled time during the school day to see their counselors for drop-ins or scheduled appointments. **College Counseling/Career Guidance:** Students are provided yearly with information and guidance about the college selection process (including how to calculate their GPA), and about college requirements and college entrance tests. In junior year students take a semester class of "Introduction to College." They are encouraged to visit colleges, and they receive instruction about writing college essays. Parents and students are invited to these on-site college presentations. **Learning disabilities/differences:** The school has a Learning Assistance Program that "works with students of average, above average, and gifted intelligence exhibiting disorder(s) in one or more of the basic psychological processes involving or in using spoken or written language. ... They include conditions which have been referred to as perceptual handicaps, minimal brain dysfunction, dyslexia, developmental aphasia, etc. [The program] does not work with the mentally retarded, emotionally disturbed, or the physically handicapped." **Career apprenticeship programs:** None.

# Student Conduct and Health

**Code of conduct:** While at Mercy or off-campus, students are expected to be respectful of themselves and others, and of the property of others. They are expected to show pride in Mercy by exhibiting considerate behavior and respect for Mercy. A student can expect that disciplinary action will be taken if she is reported for misconduct on her way to or from school, at another school, or at a school function. **How school handles drug/alcohol usage:** (1) Suspension, probation, and participation in the diversion program at Mills-Peninsula Hospital or (2) expulsion from school. **Drug/alcohol abuse prevention/AIDS awareness program:** Mercy's Substance Abuse Program began in the 1994-95 school year as an in-service to both the students and faculty. This program is part of an outreach program with Mills/Peninsula Hospitals to educate parents, students, faculty, and staff. It is also designed for intervention and referral on an individual basis by students, teachers, parents, or counselors so that the school can support "at risk" students. The school community is provided with up-to-date information regarding the causes, effects, and prevention of HIV infection, AIDS, and AIDS Related Complex (ARC).

## SUMMER PROGRAMS

For grades 6-12, Mercy offers a summer sports camp in four one-week sessions (mid-June-mid-July). Students choose from half or full days including volleyball, Tae Kwon Do, basketball, swimming, water safety, and water polo. Pre-high school and high school academic courses are also offered in half or full days for one month during the summer. High school students may take credit courses in math, computers, and writing. Cost: Sports, full day, approximately $500 for 4 weeks; academic, approximately $200 per three-hour course.

## PARENT INVOLVEMENT

**Parent participation:** Parents are expected to give 30 hours per year for two-parent households; 15 hours per year for one-parent households. **Parent/teacher communication:** Reports cards are issued quarterly; progress reports are issued quarterly as needed; conferences involving student and/or family may be initiated by faculty and/or family at any time deemed necessary. **Parent education:** Two to three evening seminars each year for parents, touching upon areas of youth/parent interest, such as college planning and stress reduction. **Donations:** Parents are asked to give $600 per year.

## SPORTS

Sixty percent of the student body participates in sports. Mercy students may try out for 25 athletic teams in 13 sports.

## OTHER

"What every young woman needs to know for college and adult life isn't necessarily found between the covers of a book. Attitude and environment are just as important in forming the self-confidence and independence that drives successful women. Mercy seeks to develop these qualities in its young women as well."

## WHAT SETS SCHOOL APART FROM OTHERS

"Mercy High School is one of thirty-nine Mercy schools throughout the United States sponsored by the Sisters of Mercy. It is a single-gender college preparatory school that has always promoted an atmosphere of encouragement and high expectations for its students. The school is dedicated to providing young women with a strong foundation in the Mercy tradition of Catholic values, academics, the arts, and athletics."

## How Parents/Students Characterize School

**Parent response(s):** "Our expectations have not only been met, but greatly exceeded in a wide variety of ways. Our daughter has acquired maturity, self-confidence, and the desire to do well. ... [T]he college prep program is outstanding. We are extremely pleased and impressed with the well-rounded curriculum."

**Student response(s):** "Mercy has given me a taste of the various things the world has to offer. Because of this, I look upon my upcoming college experience with an anticipation to explore any realm of interest. Mercy has prepared me for the university lifestyle by showing me how to be independent, [how] to take the first step, and [that] a young woman can follow her dreams."

# Mercy High School

3250 19th Avenue
San Francisco, CA 94132-2000

(415) 334-0525 *fax (415) 334-9726*
www.mercyhs.org
mercysf@ix.netcom.com

Dotty McCrea, Principal
Liz Belonogoff, Admission Director, (415) 584-5929

## General

**Girls'** day high school. **Catholic parochial** (60% Catholic). Founded in 1952. **Enrollment:** Approximately 550. **Average class size:** 25. **Accreditation:** WASC (Term: N/P). **School year:** 10-month calendar (180 instructional days). **School day:** 8 a.m. to 3 p.m. **Location:** Mercy is located on 19th Avenue, a main northwest artery on the west side of San Francisco, across from Stonestown Galleria and several blocks north of San Francisco State University. It is accessible by MUNI Metro K and M, and MUNI bus lines 17, 18, 28, and 29.

## Student Body

**Geographical breakdown (counties):** 76% from San Francisco; 20% from San Mateo; 1% from Santa Clara; 1% from Alameda; 1% from Contra Costa; 1% from other Cal. **Ethnicity:** Approximately 32% Caucasian (non-Latina); 26% Asian; 22% Filipina; 14% Latina; 6% African-American. **Foreign students (I-20 status):** 1.5%. **Single parent/two f/t working parent families:** N/P. **Middle

**schools:** The most recent entering freshman class came from 54 schools—75% from Catholic elementary schools, 13% from private, non-parochial schools, and 11% from public schools. (N/P #)

# ADMISSION

**Applications due:** Mid-December (call for date). **Application fee:** $55. **Application process:** School visits and open houses are held in October and November. The HSPT is administered twice in January. Notification letters are mailed mid-March. Each applicant is reviewed on the basis of 7th and 8th grade transcripts and standardized test results, the HSPT, confidential recommendations from the teacher/counselor/principal, a math assessment from the current math teacher, a writing sample, and, as needed, a personal parent/student interview. **No. of applications:** N/P. "Limited openings in upper grades." **Admission cutoff:** "We evaluate each student academically, socially, spiritually, and personally." **Preferences:** None. **"We are looking for** college/university-bound, academically accomplished, socially aware young ladies." **What sort of student do you best serve?** "Girls who are interested in spiritual, intellectual, and creative growth opportunities. Girls who want to develop skills to become strong, independent women who can make a difference in the world."

# COSTS

**Latest tuition:** $6,150. "Payment plans are available." **Sibling discount:** None. **Tuition increases:** N/P. **Other costs:** Registration fee ($350), book rental fee ($150), various intersession fees, arts/ceramics ($25), AP classes ($80), uniforms ($200+). **Percentage of students receiving financial aid:** 30%. **Average grant:** $1,000. **No. of full-tuition grants:** 0. **No. of half-tuition grants:** 0. **Grants of half-tuition or more:** None. **Academic scholarships:** Academic scholarships are awarded at entrance, based on HSPT results and overall academic achievement.

# SCHOOL'S MISSION STATEMENT/GOALS

"The mission of Mercy San Francisco is to educate women to serve in leadership roles and to instill the Mercy values of compassion, respect, and service. A Mercy education both challenges and fosters each student to share her gifts with the community, celebrate diversity, and defend social justice with competence and conscience."

# ACADEMIC PROGRAM

**Courses offered (AP=Advanced Placement, H=Honors, (AP)=AP option, (H)=Honors option): Computer/business:** Keyboarding, Word Processing, Introduction to Computer Programming, Computer Literacy, Creative Writing on the Computer, PageMaker/Lotus, Accounting; **English:** (sequential study of language and literature including British and American Literature, World Literature, writing, reading, and grammar—all college prep, Honors and AP option for juniors and seniors); **Fine Arts:** Beginning Art A & B, Intermediate Art, Advanced Art, Beginning Ceramics A & B, Intermediate Ceramics, Advanced Ceramics, Beginning Dance A & B, Intermediate & Advanced Dance, Dance Ensemble, Acting Techniques A, Acting Techniques B, Acting in Production, Theater Production, Mercy Chorus, Concert Choir, Musical Theater Workshop; **Foreign Language:** French I-III, French IV (AP), Spanish I-III, Spanish IV (AP), Spanish for Native Speakers I-II, III (H), IV (AP), Spanish Literature, American Sign Language; **Mathematics:** Integrated Math I-III (H) (includes Algebra I and II, and Geometry), Problem Solving, Trigonometry, Pre-Calculus, AP Calculus; **P.E.:** Fitness Walking/Jogging, Physical Fitness for Life, Self-Defense, Tennis, Teaching Assistant; **Religion:** Religion I, Ethics, Electives, including World Religions, Old Testament Personalities, Life after Life, Jesus in Word and World, Relationships, and Prayer and Meditation; **Science:** Environmental Science, Chemistry (H), Physics (AP), Biology (H), Physiology; **Social Science:** Freshman Social Science, World History (H), US History (AP), American Government, Contemporary World Issues. **Computer lab/training:** The school has two computer labs with more than 60 networked Pentium computers (connected to the Internet) with 15" Super VGA monitors, laser printers, color printers, and scanners. Students use software designed for areas such as English, social studies, math, religion, counseling, business, and foreign language. All students are required to take keyboarding. **Grading:** A-F. **Graduation requirements:** 240 credits including 4 years English, 2 years math, 1.5 years US government/history, 1 year life science, 1 year physical science, 2 years foreign language, 1 year visual and performing arts, 3.5 years electives, 3 years religion, 1.5 years social science, 1 year P.E., 1 semester keyboarding. **Average nightly homework:** G9-10: 2-3 hours; G11-12: 2-4 hours. **Faculty:** 98% female, 2% male. 27% of faculty hold bachelor's degrees as highest degree; 70% hold master's degrees; and 3% hold doctorates. Four members of teaching faculty are Sisters. **Faculty ethnicity**: "Call for current information." **Faculty selection/training:** Faculty are kept current "through in-service and continuing education." (N/P selection) **Teacher/student ratio:** 1:20. **Teacher's daily student load in required academic subject:** 130-150. **AP courses/exams:** "Please contact school's admission office." **Senior class profile (mean):** "SAT Math: 400-650 range; SAT Verbal 400-650 range." **GPA:** "Please contact school's admission office." **National Merit Scholarship Program:** The last graduating class had one finalist and one commended student. **College**

**enrollment:** 70% of last year's graduating class enrolled in 4-year colleges, 30% in 2-year colleges (with plans to transfer to 4-year colleges and universities). "For a list of colleges, contact the admission office or see the school's brochure."

## OTHER INDICATORS THE SCHOOL IS ACCOMPLISHING ITS GOALS

"Ninety-eight percent of graduates go on to college. Mercy has more than 7,800 alumnae; 40-45 return for Career Day."

## CAMPUS/CAMPUS LIFE

**Campus description:** The Mercy campus extends from 19th Avenue to Junipero Serra Blvd. and includes a three-story school building, outdoor basketball courts, and gardens. In addition to classrooms, the building houses a chapel, resource center, cafeteria, and counseling center. The building's fine arts wing has studios for ceramics, drawing, and dance, as well as a 470-seat theater. A multi-purpose athletic facility is scheduled for completion in 1999. **Library:** 2,772 sq. ft.; 8,000 print volumes; 7 computers (with Internet access); 65 periodical subscriptions (plus full-text CD-ROMs); study space for 95 students. Open to students from 7:30 a.m. to 3:30 p.m. **Open/closed campus:** Closed. **Classroom space per student:** N/P. **Lunches:** Hot lunches are available daily in the cafeteria. **Bus service:** City bus only. **Uniform/dress code:** White blouse or polo shirt, plaid skirt, navy twill slacks, navy sweater or polar fleece. Occasional casual and dressy free dress days. **Co-curricular activities/clubs:** California Scholarship Federation (CSF), Campus Ministry, National Honors Society (NHS), Green Team Environmental Club, Kaleidoscope (International), Literary Magazine, Math Club, Mercy Web Club, Performing Arts Association, Photo Club, The Talking Heads (Speech Club), Yearbook Staff, Service Club. **Foreign exchange program:** No formal programs. **Opportunities for community service:** 60 hours of community service is required through religion classes. "Many opportunities are available through campus ministry." **Typical freshman schedule:** (8 a.m. to 3 p.m.) English, Religion I, foreign language, fine arts elective or P.E., lunch, Integrated Math I, Environmental Science or Social Science, Computer Keyboarding or Word Processing, academic advising.

## STUDENT SUPPORT SERVICES

**Counselor/student ratio (not including college counselors):** N/P. **Counseling:** Each student is assigned a counselor to assist in academic, personal, and college/career counseling. Students, parents or guardians, and teachers or counselors may request counseling appointments. **Learning disabilities/differences:** No special programs or resources. **Career apprenticeship programs:** Career counseling through the counseling office.

# Student Conduct and Health

**Code of conduct:** The student handbook requires reverence and respect for self and others; prohibits racism and/or prejudiced behavior and harassment of any kind; prohibits smoking on campus and within a half-mile of the school. No headphones, cell phones, and pagers. **How school handles drugs/alcohol usage:** "Any student found dealing in or selling drugs or alcohol will be expelled. Any student involved in possession or use of drugs or alcohol at school or during a school function will be sent home immediately in the company of a parent or guardian and is subject to expulsion." (The Principal makes the final decision following consultation with counselors, the Dean of Students, the student and parents/guardians.) **Drug/alcohol abuse prevention/AIDS awareness program:** Drug and alcohol abuse prevention along with AIDS awareness programs are sponsored by the counseling department, the religion department, and student government.

# Summer Programs

Mercy offers a five-week coed academic summer program for students in G6-12. The G6-8 program offers academic courses as well as enrichment activities including field trips. The high school program is for students wishing to review, makeup, or preview an academic course. It includes math, English, science, foreign languages, driver's education, Internet Research, Study Skills, Introduction to High School Math and English, and SAT prep. Cost: $150 per class plus $50 registration.

# Parent Involvement

**Parent participation:** Parents are encouraged to participate in the Parent Guild, which supports Mercy with volunteers as needed and with various annual fundraisers. **Parent/teacher communication:** Report cards twice a semester, including grades, credits, and teachers' comments. Progress reports mid-quarter for those experiencing difficulty. Parent/teacher conferences upon request. **Parent education:** The Parents Guild sponsors Parenting Teen information talks. **Donations:** Parents are asked to give $300 annually.

# Sports

Students compete in the Girls' Athletic Association in volleyball, tennis, cross-country, basketball, soccer, track & field, and softball.

# OTHER

Mercy sponsors a week-long intersession every other year. Participation in two sessions is a graduation requirement. The purpose is to enrich the curriculum beyond the walls of the classroom into the greater community. Offerings have included theater performances, trips to Washington, D.C., backpacking trips, Oregon Shakespeare Festival, Northern California college campus tours, equestrian camp, shadowing a professional (medicine, business, education), foreign film study, off-shore marine life and biology. Each course has a separate fee; scholarships are available.

## WHAT SETS SCHOOL APART FROM OTHERS

"Mercy High School-San Francisco is a small, safe, and caring environment with a college preparatory curriculum, extensive fine arts program, advanced technology department, and an outstanding library. Mercy students can choose from over 40 elective courses, diverse club activities, and competitive athletic teams. The beautiful Mercy campus is easily accessible by public transportation."

## HOW PARENTS/STUDENTS CHARACTERIZE SCHOOL

**Parent response(s):** "In a recent parent survey, 95% of all parents surveyed rated Mercy good to excellent in meeting the spiritual, academic, and social needs of their daughters."

**Student response(s):** "In a recent student survey, 75% of Mercy students rated both their educational experiences and student services (library, computer, and science labs, Resource Center, clubs, student government, assemblies) as good or higher."

# MOREAU CATHOLIC HIGH SCHOOL

27170 Mission Boulevard
Hayward, California 94544

(510) 881-4300 *fax (510) 582-8405*
mariner.moreau.pvt.k12.ca.us

Mrs. Patricia Geister, Principal
Mr. Tony Guevara, Vice Principal: Admission, (510) 881-4320

## GENERAL

**Coed** day high school **Catholic parochial** (75% Catholic). Sponsored by Brothers of the Holy Cross. Founded in 1965. **Enrollment:** Approximately 1,200. **Average class size:** 30. **Accreditation:** WASC (6-year term: 1994-00). **School year:** 9-month calendar (185 instructional days). **Location:** South Hayward. The school is located on Mission Boulevard in Hayward and is accessible by public transportation. Buses to and from the Hayward and South Hayward BART stations stop near the school.

## STUDENT BODY

**Geographical breakdown (counties):** 100% from Alameda County. **Ethnicity:** 45% Filipino; 25% Caucasian (non-Latino); 14% Latino; 11% Asian; 3% African-American; 2% other. **Foreign students (I-20 status):** 0. **Single parent families:** N/P. **Two f/t working parent families:** 76%. **Middle schools:** 50% of most recent entering freshman class came from 10 public middle schools; 50% from 18 parochial schools.

## ADMISSION

**Applications due:** Approximately January 15 each year (call for date). **Application fee:** $50. **Application process:** Applications are available October 31. An open house is held in November, and a parent information night in early January. The STS HSPT is administered the last Saturday of January, and notifications are sent mid-March. **No. of applications:** 400 applications were received for 290 places in prior year's class. Six new students were admitted to G10; 2 to G11; and 0 to G12. **Admission cut-off:** N/P. **Preferences:** Siblings, legacies, and students whose families support the school. **"We are looking for ..."** "Entrance requirements are not necessarily based on solely intellectual ability, but also on a combination of character, willingness to learn and study, and a concern for others." **What sort of student do you best serve?** N/P.

# Costs

**Latest tuition:** $6,072 payable in 12 or 10 monthly installments. **Sibling discount:** None. (Family grants are available for families with two or more children.) **Tuition increases:** 2-4% annually. **Other costs:** Books cost approximately $275, and are sold back to the school at the end of the year. **Financial aid:** Need-based financial aid and merit scholarships are available. **Percentage of students receiving financial aid:** 20%. **Average grant:** N/P. **No. of full-tuition grants:** None. **No. of half-tuition grants:** "A maximum of half of the tuition can be granted as aid." The school also offers the Father Moreau Catholic Scholarship, which is merit-based, and the Brother Gary Stone Scholarship which is merit- and need-based. **Grants of half-tuition or more:** N/P.

# School's Mission Statement/Goals

"Moreau Catholic is a college preparatory high school sponsored by the Brothers of Holy Cross. Our school exemplifies excellence and caring in the spirit of Father Basil Moreau, the founder of the Congregation of Holy Cross. We affirm the traditions and values of Christianity and the Catholic Faith. Moreau Catholic is a special community which strives to meet the life needs of the individual student."

# Academic Program

**Courses offered:** N/P. **Computer lab/training:** 2 computer labs with 150 computers for students, one teacher technology lab with 6 computers. One semester computer science required. **Grading:** Letter grades. **Graduation requirements:** 240 units, including 4 years English, 3.5 years theology, 3 years social studies, 2 years math, 2 years science (life and physical), 2 years P.E., 2 years foreign language, .5 year computer science, 80 hours community service. In addition, 12th graders must demonstrate achievement on the 12th grade level or above on a standardized achievement test in the areas of reading, language arts, and math. Students are tested in October and retested in January. Those not demonstrating proficiency receive an "amended diploma" indicating this area of deficiency. **Average nightly homework:** 2 hours. **Faculty:** 49% male, 51% female. 40% of faculty hold bachelor's degrees as highest degree; 57% hold master's degrees; and 3% hold doctorates. **Faculty ethnicity:** N/P. **Faculty selection/training:** N/P. **Teacher/student ratio:** 1:22. **Teacher's daily student load in required academic subject:** N/P. **AP courses/exams:** 46% of students are currently taking AP courses. In April 1998, 188 students took 338 AP examinations in 13 subjects. 70% received scores of 3 or above. **Senior class profile (mean):** SAT Math 523, SAT Verbal 528. **GPA:** 3.3. **National Merit Scholarship Program:** N/P. **College enrollment:** 71% of last year's graduating class enrolled in 4-year colleges, 27%

in 2-year colleges. (N/P re colleges) **Typical freshman schedule:** English, fine, applied, and performing arts, foreign language or study skills, math, P.E., theology, world history.

## OTHER INDICATORS THE SCHOOL IS ACCOMPLISHING ITS GOALS

"Moreau Catholic was founded and is sponsored by the Congregation of Holy Cross. This religious congregation came to the United States and began its educational mission by starting a college in South Bend, Indiana—College of Notre Dame. The goal for every Holy Cross school is to educate the *whole* person. This means not only the intellect, but also the artistic, physical, social, and spiritual as well. Moreau Catholic continues that tradition by meeting the life needs of every individual student."

## CAMPUS/CAMPUS LIFE

**Campus description:** Situated on 14 acres in Hayward, the school has seven buildings. Besides the main building, which houses classrooms and the library and chapel, there are two gymnasiums, a student center, a center for the fine arts, and an auditorium dedicated solely to fine arts performances. **Library**: 1,026 sq. ft.; study space for 75; 14 computers; on-line catalog; 75 periodical subscriptions, 15,000 print volumes; Internet access. Open to students 7:30 a.m. to 3:30 p.m. **Open/closed campus:** Closed. **Classroom space per student:** 18 sq. ft. **Lunches:** N/P. **Bus service:** None. **Uniforms/dress code:** The school's dress code allows jeans but not cutoffs, shorts, sweats, or tights; boys' shirts must have collars or turtleneck; no T-shirts or shirts with words or graphics; skirts no more than 3" above knee. **Co-curricular activities/clubs:** Activities include African American Alliance, Amnesty International, Asian Student Union, Aviation Club, Band and Color Guard, California Scholarship Federation, Chess Club, Computer and Math Club, Equestrian Club, Environmental Club, Filipino American Cultural Exchange Club, Film Threat, Friday Night Live, Hiking Club, Interact Club, Junior Statesman, National Honor Society, Newspaper, Portuguese Club, Academic Challenge Team (Quiz Bowl Club), Ski Club, Students Against Drunk Driving, Student Government, Theater Club, Yearbook, Young United Latin American Association. **Foreign exchange program:** Foreign exchange program with Funibashi, Japan. **Opportunities for community service:** 80-hour requirement fulfilled by providing service to nonprofit agencies. **Typical freshman schedule:** N/P.

## STUDENT SUPPORT SERVICES

**Counselor/student ratio (not including college counselors):** 1:301. **Counseling:** Four full-time counselors provide academic, personal, and college and career counseling. **Learning disabilities/differences:** N/P. **Career apprenticeship programs:** N/P.

## STUDENT CONDUCT AND HEALTH

**Code of conduct:** In addition to proscribing illegal conduct, the school prohibits habitual profanity or vulgarity and persistent violation of the dress code. In addition, students may be suspended or expelled for violations of the law or "actions or attitudes directly contrary to the mission of [the school]." **How school handles drugs/alcohol usage:** "In the case of a discipline violation concerning drugs, including alcohol, the students may be required to undergo a professional assessment. Failure to undergo the assessment will result in the student's dismissal. The result of this assessment will be among the factors considered to determine the student's continued enrollment. ..." **Drug/alcohol abuse prevention /AIDS awareness program:** The school has a Student Assistance Impacts Life (SAIL) program that provides health awareness activities, early intervention for students troubled by alcohol and other drugs, or whose behavior interferes with their education or safety. The school depends on the Diocese of Oakland to supply materials for AIDS awareness. It also has had Kaiser give its "Secrets" presentation.

## SUMMER PROGRAMS

A summer school program is provided to incoming students who need to strengthen a skill such as math or English. There are a limited number of class offerings for current students needing to make up a course because of a non-passing grade. Cost: $245 per class.

## PARENT INVOLVEMENT

**Parent participation:** Parents are not required to give hours to the school; all such participation is voluntary. **Parent/teacher communication:** Grades are sent to parents at the end of each quarter (academic year is two semesters consisting of two quarters each). If an academic deficiency exists, parents are notified by a progress report sent mid-quarter. In November, parents may meet with teachers to discuss their child's progress at Student Progress Evening. Appointments can be made to meet with teachers at any other time during the year as well. **Parent education:** N/P. **Donations:** Parents are expected to make donations to the annual fund.

## SPORTS

Seventy percent of the student body participates in the school's sports program which includes 41 teams staffed by 59 coaches. Teams include, for boys, football, cross-country, rally squad, basketball, wrestling, soccer, badminton, baseball, golf, track and field, swimming, tennis, and volleyball. For girls, tennis, cross-country, rally squad, volleyball, basketball, soccer, softball, badminton, and track and field.

## WHAT SETS SCHOOL APART FROM OTHERS

"A Holy Cross education seeks to achieve three specific, but integrated goals: information, formation, and transformation. Information is comprised of the knowledge and skills communicated to students which is aimed at preparing them for life and work in the future. By formation, it is meant that the intellectual, social, and spiritual development of students is found in every aspect of school life. Finally, transformation is where the values and qualities of life which students are taught and encouraged to embrace will eventually lead the individual student to be an agent of change for the common good."

## HOW PARENTS/STUDENTS CHARACTERIZE SCHOOL

N/P.

# NORTH BAY MARIN SCHOOL

70 Lomita Drive
Mill Valley, CA 94941

(415) 381-3003 *fax (415) 381-3055*

Barbara J. Schakel, Principal and Director of Admissions

## GENERAL

**Coed** day high school. **Nonsectarian**. Founded in 1980. **Nonprofit**, seeking CAIS membership. **Enrollment:** 93. **Average class size:** 8. **Accreditation:** WASC (currently up for renewal). **School year:** 10-month calendar (approx. 180 instructional days). **School day:** 9 a.m. to 3:25 p.m. **Location:** In Mill Valley, a suburb 10 miles north of San Francisco in Marin County. Just off Highway 101.

## STUDENT BODY

**Geographical breakdown (counties):** 85% from Marin; 10% from San Francisco; 5% from Sonoma. **Ethnicity:** "7% minority." **Foreign students (I-20 status):** 0. **Middle schools:** 50% of the latest freshman class came from the school's middle school; 40% from public middle schools; 10% from private non-parochial schools. (N/P re #) The school draws a good number of its students from Delmar, Mill Valley Middle, and Brandies Hillel Day School.

# ADMISSION

**Applications due:** Early March (call for exact date). **Application fee:** $35. **Application process:** The application includes personal statements from both students and parents, three recommendations (from the student's current English and math teachers as well as one additional teacher or counselor), transcripts from current schools (sent directly to NBMS from the current school's registrar), and a placement exam to be taken after all application materials have been received and an interview has taken place. Parents should call to arrange for an interview upon application. With advance notice parents and students may attend and observe classes. Decisions will be mailed April 1 and tuition agreements and deposits are due by April 15. **No. of applications:** N/P. **Preferences:** N/P. **Admission cut-off:** None. **"We are looking for ...** students who have strong academic potential and would benefit from and enjoy an environment where they will receive a lot of personal attention, where their individuality is valued, and where they learn responsibility and organizational and study skills." **"What sort of student do you best serve?** "Students with academic potential—often unrealized potential—who have the ability to achieve academic success through increased accountability and structure."

# COSTS

**Latest tuition:** $12,800 payable in one or two payments (includes textbooks). Monthly payment plans or loans are available through an outside source. **Other costs:** Parent association dues, yearbook, graduation, and curriculum related activities. **Sibling discount:** 10%. **Tuition increases:** Approximately 5-7% annually. **Percentage of students receiving financial aid:** 10%. **Average grant:** Approx. 1/2 tuition. **No. of full tuition grants:** 0. **No. of half tuition grants:** 7. **Grants of half-tuition or more:** 66%.

# SCHOOL'S MISSION STATEMENT/GOALS

"We at North Bay Marin School are committed to the development of the academic, creative, and social skills of every child in our care. Our hope is that each student will discover a love of learning, will build a set of personal, moral and ethical values, and will develop an interest in and appreciation for the diversity of our multi-cultural world and all that it has to offer. A vital part of this endeavor includes fostering critical thinking skills, a cooperative learning environment, and a sense of academic and personal responsibility in all members of our school community. We celebrate the unique qualities of every child, and assist each in reaching his or her full potential as a confident, self-reliant individual."

# ACADEMIC PROGRAM

**Courses offered (AP=Advanced Placement, H=Honors, (AP)=AP option, (H)=Honors option): English:** Survey/Mythology, World Literature, American Literature (H), Advanced Composition, European Literature, Writers' Workshop 1&2, Senior English; **Math:** Pre-Algebra, Elementary Algebra 1&2, Geometry, Algebra 1, Algebra 2/Trigonometry (H), Pre-Calculus, Calculus; **Social Sciences:** Geography, Western Civilizations, US History (H), Civics, Economics, "Resistance/Rebellion/Revolution," Leadership; **Science:** Health, Physical Science, Biology, Physics, Chemistry, SF Bay Ecology; **Foreign Language:** Spanish 1-4, French 1-3; **Computer:** Word Processing and Applications (no credit), Computer Programming 1&2; **Fine Arts:** Studio Art A&B, Intermediate Art, Advanced Art, Art History; **Performing Arts:** Drama, Jazz Band. **Special programs:** Students seeking to study in other academic areas may sometimes arrange for independent study. **Computer lab/training:** The school has a computer lab with 12 PCs. Students have e-mail accounts. (N/P re training) **Grading:** Letter grades 2 times a year. **Graduation requirements:** (Designed to meet UC admission requirements.) 4 years English, 3 years math, 3.5 years history/social science, 2 years lab science, .5 year health, 2 years foreign language, 1 year drama/fine arts, 2 years P.E., 5 years additional electives, 80 hours community service. **Average nightly homework (Mon-Th):** G9-10: 1.5 to 2 hours; G11-12: 2-3 hours. **Faculty:** Of the 13 full-time faculty members, 62% are male, 38% female. 60% of faculty hold bachelor's degrees as highest degrees; 40% hold master's degrees. Faculty, students, and staff address each other by first-names. Classrooms are arranged in a seminar style. **Faculty selection/training:** "Teachers must hold valid teaching credentials. They are selected based upon experience, personality, talents and their ability to interact one-on-one with students. The school requires both in-service training and continuing education." **Faculty ethnicity:** 92% Caucasian (non-Latino); 8% Latino. **Teacher/student ratio:** 1:7. **Teacher's daily student load in required academic subject:** 45. **AP courses/exams:** 31% of the most recent year's class took AP exams. In 1998-99, 5 students took 5 AP exams in 3 subjects. 60% scored 3 or above. **Senior class profile (mean):** SAT Math 534, SAT Verbal 560. **GPA:** 2.8. **National Merit Scholarship Program:** N/P. **College enrollment:** 80% of last year's graduating class enrolled in 4-year colleges, 20% in 2-year colleges (many with the goal of transferring to a 4-year college). (N/P re colleges)

# OTHER INDICATORS THE SCHOOL IS ACCOMPLISHING ITS GOALS

"The school's increasing enrollment indicates it is successfully fulfilling a need in the community."

# Campus/Campus Life

**Campus description:** The school building is a one-story, 10,000 sq. ft. building with a mezzanine study hall and with an inner courtyard where students eat lunch. The building includes classrooms, labs, offices, library, an art room and study rooms. The grounds include a field where students play basketball, soccer, street hockey, and football. **Library:** 300 sq. ft.; 5 periodical subscriptions; 1 computer; study space for 12 students. Open to students from 9 a.m. to 3:10 p.m. (N/P re print volumes, etc.). **Open/closed campus:** Closed campus except for students with privileges who may leave for 50 minutes (walking, not driving) for lunch. **Classroom space per student:** N/P. **Lunches:** Students bring their lunches daily. Students with privileges may walk off campus for 50 minutes for lunch. **Bus service:** Public transportation. **Uniforms/dress code:** Clothing must be in good taste. Students are allowed to express their individuality so long as it is school-appropriate and not offensive to others. **Co-curricular activities/clubs:** Newspaper, yearbook, student council, literary publications, intramural sports, basketball, and various academic and cultural clubs. **Foreign exchange program:** Each year students and teachers spend two weeks to a month in a foreign country engaging in travel and sometimes performing community service. Trips have included Mexico, Spain, France and Ghana. **Opportunities for community service:** 80 hours required for graduation. Sophomores engage in a service project with their class members; juniors work on assorted service projects; and seniors work with social service agencies for an extended period of time. **Typical freshman schedule:** Six periods of approximately 50 minutes each, including 5 core classes, P.E., art or drama.

# Student Support Services

**Counselor-student ratio (not including college counselor):** 1:8. **Counseling:** Each teacher works with 8-9 students as advisees. Advisors communicate with parents on a regular basis. With a 1 to 8 student-teacher ratio, student work is monitored closely by teachers. Teachers work individually with students each day to ensure all assignments are completed to 100% satisfaction by the end of each day. Students earn privileges (such leaving campus at lunchtime) if they meet the daily expectation. All teachers meet daily to discuss the progress of each student in the school. Study periods are scheduled each day to enable students to meet with each of their teachers and get any additional help needed. Each student's weekly assignment schedule is posted in a study room. Each week, the school honors a "Student of the Week." Staff member acts as **college counselors**. **Learning disabilities/differences:** No special programs. **Career apprenticeship programs:** The school has a senior internship program to help students explore career options.

## STUDENT CONDUCT AND HEALTH

**Code of conduct:** "We focus on rights for all members of our community: students, teachers, and staff. These are related to issues of respect, safe environment, and community." **How school handles drug/alcohol usage:** For possession on campus, immediate expulsion. For use off campus, mandatory referral to an outside counseling program. **Drug/alcohol abuse prevention/AIDS awareness programs:** These subjects are covered in a required health course; in addition the school brings speakers to the campus on a regular basis, including former substance abusers.

## SUMMER PROGRAMS

Each summer students may participate in a 2-4 week trip to a foreign country where students travel and sometimes engage in service. Cost varies.

## PARENT INVOLVEMENT

**Parent participation:** Parents are expected to participate in the school but no formal requirement is in place. **Parent/teacher communication:** Parents receive biweekly report cards on their children's progress. Teachers meet to discuss each student's progress every day, and parents are notified whenever necessary. Advisors keep parents apprised as well. Parent-teacher conferences are held at the end of the semester. Students are required to attend. Advisors contact parents on a regular basis, daily if needed, and a newsletter is published monthly. **Parent education:** The parent association holds monthly meetings which feature speakers of interest to the parent group. **Donations:** "Not required but expected."

## SPORTS

Boys compete with other independent schools in basketball through the North Coast Section. The school has plans to add girls' basketball or soccer. Students also engage in running, basketball, volleyball, soccer, football, and street hockey through the P.E. program and intramural sports program.

## WHAT SETS SCHOOL APART FROM OTHERS

"The school offers a unique opportunity for students who need more individualized attention and a smaller school and class setting to achieve their potential. Since they must complete their assignments to 100% each day, students experience academic success daily. The school offers a structured supportive environment and helps students with academic potential develop the self-discipline and organizational skills they need to succeed. Because of the school's small size, it can respond to the needs of each student. It also offers extensive outdoor and field trip opportunities including raft trips, rope courses, Shakespeare festival, museum visits, and outward bound."

## How Parents/Students Characterize School

"North Bay Marin School's small class size, intimate student-teacher relation-ships, and immediate work assessment/correction system, help children to be successful. Rewards and consequences are built into the academic and behavioral programs, which create a solid structure for learning."—Stacy Bischoff, parent
"North Bay gives each of its students what every young adult deserves: support, stimulation and an environment that encourages both self-expression and intel-lectual growth. Students leave our community knowing they can succeed."—Louisa Finberg, parent of graduate
"North Bay Marin School provides my son with the 'free' structure and gentle discipline that he needs to succeed in his academics. It seems a contradiction in terms, but it works, and the combination is unbeatable."—John Fraine, parent
"North Bay Marin School's unique educational methods provide our son with the individual attention he needs to be enthused about school and excited about learning."—Wayne Dennis, parent

# North Bay Orinda School

19 Altarinda Road
Orinda, CA 94563

(925) 254-7553 *fax (925) 254-4768*

Ronald Graydon, Director

## General

**Coed** day high school with middle school (G7-12). **Nonsectarian.** Founded in 1982. **Nonprofit. Enrollment:** 100. **Average class size:** 9. **Accreditation:** WASC (6-year term: 1993-99). **School year:** 10-month calendar (180 instructional days). **School day:** 8:45 a.m. to 3:15 p.m. **Location:** Approximately one-third of a mile from the Orinda Exit of Highway 24 and the Orinda BART Station.

# Student Body

**Geographical breakdown (counties):** 65% from Contra Costa; 35% from Alameda. **Ethnicity:** 80% Caucasian (non-Latino); 10% Asian; 5% African-American; 5% Latino. **Foreign students (I-20 status):** 5%. **Single parent families:** 20%. **Two f/t working parent families:** 46%. **Middle schools:** 50% of the most recent entering freshman class came from North Bay Orinda School's middle school; 25% from public middle schools; 25% from private schools. (N/P re #) The school draws a good number of students from Stanley Middle School, Orinda Intermediate, Joaquin Moraga Intermediate, Montera Middle, Concordia School and Berkeley Montessori.

# Admission

**Applications due:** Call for date. **Application fee:** $35. **Application process:** A parent wishing to enroll a student should contact the Director, Mr. Ron Graydon, at (925) 254-7553. Mr. Graydon will send the parent two recommendation forms to be answered by former teachers or educators with knowledge of the student's abilities. Transcripts must also be submitted. Upon review of this information, Mr. Graydon will arrange an interview with the parents and the student. Parents should bring any information they have regarding academic progress of their child to the interview, including transcripts, standardized tests, psychological testing, and report cards. Following the interview, a date is set for student testing. When the parents, student, and officials of the school are satisfied that placement in the school is appropriate, the student is enrolled or placed on a waiting list if enrollment is full. The entrance exams are the Science Research Associates Level F for middle school students, Science Research Associates Level H for high school students. **No. of applications:** 100 applications were received for 35 places in the most recent class following re-enrollment. Seven new students were admitted to G10, 9 to G11, 1 to G12. **Admission cut-off:** "We look for students with a C average or better who test at or above grade level." **Preferences:** N/P. **"We are looking for** students who have the desire to learn. The range of academic skill levels extends from students with minor learning disabilities to gifted students. Grades are used in the selection process; however, they are not the sole criterion, as grades do not always reflect the ability of a student. The school prefers students with a 'C' average or above. The ability of a student to follow basic rules and guidelines of the school is an essential requirement for entrance. If the school can meet the educational needs of the student and the student's presence benefits the school community, the student will be acceptable." **What sort of student do you best serve?** "North Bay is not an exclusive school. We ask for a 'C' average minimum. We can serve students with minor learning disabilities as well as accelerated students. Students who want to learn and be successful are well served at North Bay."

# Costs

**Latest tuition:** $11,000. Tuition payment plans available through FACTS allow 10 monthly payments of $1,140 or 12 monthly payments of $950. A semester payment plan is also available with a deposit of $1,120 and an additional payment of $5,040 by the first day of each semester. **Sibling discount:** 10%. **Tuition increases:** N/P. **Other costs:** $350 for books. **Percentage of students receiving financial aid:** 8%. **Average grant:** $5,500. **No. of full-tuition grants:** None. **Grants of half-tuition or more:** 75%.

## School's Mission Statement/Goals

History and Philosophy: "North Bay Orinda School is a small private school serving grades 7-12 which provides a group standard for students while maintaining an understanding of individual needs. The school was conceived by a group of credentialed teachers and administrators whose interest was in creating a quality school which meets the needs of parents and students alike, while providing a positive environment in which to learn. We feel that it is the relationship between the student and teacher, as well as joint communication with the parent or guardian, that makes the difference between a mediocre school and an excellent one. North Bay Orinda School is an academically oriented school that has an overall goal that each student be a success and work to full potential. It is the task of the school to encourage and secure self-management and self-esteem in each student in order to assume responsibility.

"In order to achieve our goals North Bay maintains an overall student-teacher ratio of nine to one and employs both individualized and small classroom techniques. Parents are sent bi-weekly progress reports and are frequently contacted by phone. Both students and parents are made to feel a part of the school."

Mission statement: "North Bay Orinda School is committed to the development of the academic, creative, and social skills of every child in our school.

"Our hope is that each student will discover a love of learning, will build a set of personal, ethical values, will develop a respect for the natural environment and foster an appreciation for the diversity of our multi-cultural world.

"A vital part of this endeavor includes engendering a healthy lifestyle, critical thinking skills, a cooperative learning environment, and a sense of academic and personal responsibility in all members of our school community.

"To reach these goals, the parents are actively involved in this mission; hence our logo of three interlocked circles—parents, students and teachers working together. We honor the unique qualities of each child, and assist each in reaching his or her full potential as a confident, successful, self-reliant individual."

# ACADEMIC PROGRAM

The school day, from 8:45 a.m. to 3:15 p.m., is broken into eight periods. Most courses are taught five days a week, while some courses and electives are offered two or three days per week. Student progress is monitored on a daily basis. Most students will have two study periods a day to complete a portion of "homework" at school under teacher supervision. One-to-one tutoring is an essential element of the school day. All work is corrected and returned with feedback to insure each student is able to proceed successfully to the next assignment. **Courses offered (AP=Advanced Placement, H=Honors, (AP)=AP option, (H)=Honors option):** English 1-3, Advanced Composition, Reading, Literature 1-2, American Literature, British and Western Literature (H), Women's Literature, English as a Second Language, General Math, Pre-Algebra, Math A, Math B, Algebra, Geometry, Algebra and Trigonometry, Advanced Mathematics, Calculus, Life Science, General Science, Biology, Health, Environmental Science, Ecology and Advanced Biology, Physics, Chemistry, Social Studies, Geography, US History, Civics, Western Civilization, Economics, Spanish I-III, French I-III, Coed P.E., Visual/Performing Arts, Chorus, Art, Drama, Typing, Word Processing. **Computer lab/training:** One computer lab with 10 Power Macs, 1 computer work room with 4 IBM compatibles and 2 PowerMacs, and 1 resource room with an Apple LCII (IBM compatible), and a Power Mac. (N/P re training) **Grading:** Letter grades determined by percentage. **Graduation requirements:** Students may choose a course of study to prepare for college or to obtain a regular diploma. All students must complete 40 hours of community service to graduate. College Prep graduation requirements are: 4 years English, Advanced Composition, 2 years foreign language (3 recommended), Algebra I or Math A & B, Geometry, Intermediate Algebra, Health, Biology, Physics or Chemistry, Civics, US History, plus additional social science, 4 additional courses in social science, language, science, math, or history, 3 years P.E., visual or performing arts. Standard graduation requirements are: 4 years English and 2 years composition or an advanced composition course, 3 years math, 1 year social science, health, biology, 3 years P.E., 1 year foreign language or fine arts. **Average nightly homework:** G9: 1 hour; G10-12: 1-2 hours. **Faculty:** Eleven full-time and 4 part-time teachers and administrators. Six staff members have been with the school for 10 or more years, 3 for 8 years, 2 for 5 years, 2 for 4 years, and 2 for 2 years. The faculty is 60% male, 40% female. 40% hold master's degrees. **Faculty ethnicity:** 100% Caucasian (non-Latino). **Faculty selection/training:** "All teachers are fully credentialed. The school leadership and staff are qualified for their assigned responsibilities, are committed to the school's purpose and engage in ongoing professional development that promotes student learning." **Teacher/student ratio:** 1:9. **Teacher's daily student load in required academic subject:** N/P. **AP courses/exams:** N/P. **Senior class profile (mean):** SAT Math 602, SAT Verbal 630. **GPA:** 2.89. **National Merit Scholarship Program:** N/P. **College enrollment:** 47% of last year's graduating class (8 graduates) enrolled in 4-year colleges, 53% (9 graduates) in 2-year college including: SCU-Chico, SCU-Humboldt, Drew U, Oregon State, UCLA, UC Santa Barbara, U of Denver, Diablo Valley C, and Heald Business College.

# OTHER INDICATORS THE SCHOOL IS ACCOMPLISHING ITS GOALS

"The small size of North Bay Orinda School allows a family atmosphere. Our graduates keep in close contact. We follow our students' activities well beyond high school. The overwhelming majority of North Bay Orinda graduates not only are accepted to colleges of their choice, they succeed in college. Along with the academic skills necessary for post high school success, North Bay also stresses the behavioral skills necessary for equal success."

# CAMPUS/CAMPUS LIFE

**Campus description:** The newly renovated campus overlooks the East Bay hills separating Contra Costa and Alameda Counties. The site contains eight classrooms, two study halls, two student resource rooms, administrative offices, and a student lounge/cafeteria. The campus also has an outdoor picnic/study area, and half court and full court outdoor basketball facilities. Additional classroom space and outdoor field space are utilized at the adjacent John F. Kennedy University. The school rents a local indoor basketball facility for team practices and games. **Library**: The school's library resources are spread throughout the school. The school has seven periodical subscriptions, as well as Ebsco Middle Search Plus, which provides articles from an additional 100+ magazines on CD. The CDs are available to students in two locations on campus—one with two Apple computers, the other, four PCs, and both with Internet access (all campus computers have ISDN Internet access). A computer lab with 10 PowerMacs is also available for student use. (N/P re hours, # volumes, study space, etc.) **Open/closed campus:** Closed campus for 7-11th grades. Twelfth grade students may earn the privilege to leave campus during lunch. **Classroom space per student:** N/P. **Lunches:** Students may purchase hot lunch and snacks. **Bus service:** N/P. **Uniforms/dress code:** Clothes referring to or depicting drugs, sex, alcohol, violence, or obscenities are not allowed. No spikes. **Co-curricular activities/clubs:** North Bay has an active Student Council which organizes events and club activities throughout the school year. The small size of the school allows flexibility to reorganize the club program on an annual basis to fit the needs of the current year. The most recent clubs include chess, Japanese animation, computer, and music. **Foreign exchange program:** None, although an ESL program is offered. **Opportunities for community service:** 40 hours of community service are required for graduation. **Typical freshman schedule:** Literature 1, Algebra 1, World Geography, French or Spanish, Earth Science, elective, P.E.

# Student Support Services

**Counselor/student ratio (not including college counselors):** 1:10. **Counseling:** Each teacher is the advisor to 10 students. The advisor maintains close personal contact with the student and parents. A minimum of three conferences per year are held with the advisor, student, and parent. Most academic and college/career guidance counseling occurs at the parent-student-advisor conferences. The advisors are available on a daily basis to provide additional counseling. The school provides an Academic Dean to supervise counseling operations and review the academic progress of each student. The Academic Dean also assists with counseling and college/career guidance. **Learning disabilities/differences:** "While North Bay has no special program for students with learning differences/disabilities, many students with mild learning disabilities prosper in our setting of small classes with the opportunity for more individualized help. The school attempts to make reasonable accommodations, within our means, for students with learning differences/disabilities." **Career apprenticeship programs:** No special programs. Students are encouraged to explore future career options through their community service.

# Student Conduct and Health

**Code of conduct:** The school rules prohibit, in addition to illegal activities, lying, profanity toward staff, cheating on any test or assignment, and other inappropriate behavior. **How school handles drugs/alcohol usage:** Any student found in possession of drugs or alcohol on campus or at a school function will be expelled from the school. North Bay Orinda School is a small school in which every teacher has personal contact with each student; each teacher is trained in recognizing drug use and strategies to help students avoid or cease drug use. It is the policy of the school that if the majority of the staff believes a student is abusing drugs or alcohol, an immediate mandatory conference will be held with the student, parent, and school personnel to remedy the situation. If the parents are unable to recognize or remedy the situation, the school will require an approved substance use evaluation and lab test within 24 hours of notification. If the tests reveal drug or alcohol use, the student will be required to complete a substance abuse program designed to free the student of chemical abuse. If the parents or student refuse to participate in an evaluation or program, the student will not be allowed to continue in the school. **Drug/alcohol abuse prevention/AIDS awareness program:** AIDS prevention is taught as a unit in the 10th grade health class.

# Summer Programs

Students may take a full-year class or two semester classes during two morning (9 a.m.-1 p.m.) summer school sessions running late June through early August. A Junior High Basic Skills Review course is also offered. Costs range from $525 to $950 depending on courses.

## Parent Involvement

**Parent participation:** No parent hours required. The school requests that parents attend the monthly parent group meeting. **Parent/teacher communication:** Parents keep informed of a child's progress at three conferences per year as well as from report cards sent home every two weeks describing the quality of work performed during the two-week period. **Parent education:** "The North Bay Orinda Parent Group ... determines issues of relevance and the school administration offers avenues to address the issues." **Donations:** Parents are not expected to make donations. There is no annual donation fund. The school does have two fundraising activities during the year for which parent input and help are appreciated.

## Sports

The school has a basketball team which competes in interscholastic competition. The team plays about 20 games per year including a local, regional, and national tournament. North Bay provides intramural tournaments in softball and basketball for students not interested in interscholastic sports, and offers a diverse physical education program which includes yoga, hiking, mountain bike riding, weight training, and traditional team sports as well as hiking, skiing and river rafting trips.

## Other

(See below.)

## What Sets School Apart From Others

"North Bay has a unique system combining the traditional classroom with a Mastery Learning System designed to allow each student to reach full potential. Mastery Learning requires a student to work on a task until achieving a specified competency level before continuing to the next task. This provides the necessary foundation for educational growth. In addition to homework assignments, students are able to do a high percentage of work at school, with quality feedback on the day of assignment. Classroom discussions are reinforced by one-on-one tutoring sessions with teachers in study hall surroundings. One-on-one tutoring is a valuable resource for achieving desired goals. As a small private school, North Bay is able to provide a group standard while maintaining an understanding of the individual. The goal of North Bay is to have each student reach potential by utilizing close interaction between the school, the parents, and the student, thereby providing a structure and support system for the student."

## How Parents/Students Characterize School

**Parent response(s):** "It is a wonderful, small private school with an excellent program for college preparation, a truly gifted staff, and a diverse student population."

"I think that the clear expectations, consistency, support, and inspiration [my son] experienced with all of you at North Bay was just what he needed, and provided a definite turning point in his life."

"I think [my son] has greatly benefited from his years at North Bay. The small classes, good teachers, and emphasis on academics should give him a strong foundation for the years ahead. ... [H]e seems much more motivated and responsible than last year. ... [H]e seems to have improved his work habits. He has enjoyed school."

**Student response(s):** "I am graduating from [UC Santa Barbara] on June 17th with a BA in Environmental Studies. I am sending you my graduation announcement to say thank you for everything you did for me while I was at NBOS! I did it thanks to all of you supporting me and encouraging me! You gave me the tools I needed to succeed in college." —1991 graduate

# Notre Dame High School

1540 Ralston Avenue
Belmont, CA 94002-1995

(650) 595-1913 *fax (650) 595-2643*

Rita Gleason, Principal
Maureen Velasquez, Director of Admissions

## General

Girls' day high school. **Catholic** (78% Catholic). Founded in 1851. **Nonprofit**, member BAIHS. **Enrollment:** Approximately 740. **Average class size:** 24.3. **Accreditation:** WASC (6-year term: 1999-05). **School year:** 9-month calendar (180 instructional days). **School day:** 8 a.m. to 2:50 p.m. **Location:** Located on Ralston Avenue between Highways 101 and 280, the school provides free shuttle service in the morning between the school and SamTrans bus stops on El Camino Real and Ralston, and Ralston and Alameda de las Pulgas, and to the Belmont CalTrain Station. (The stops are a 10-minute walk from the school.) Students who drive are assigned parking spaces.

## STUDENT BODY

**Geographical breakdown (counties):** 96% from San Mateo; 2% from Marin; 1% from San Francisco; 1% from Santa Clara. **Ethnicity:** "28% minority." **Foreign students (I-20 status):** 0. **Single parent/two f/t working parent families:** N/P. **Middle schools:** 27% of the most recent entering freshman class came from 18 public middle schools; 6% from 7 private, non-parochial schools; 67% from 17 parochial schools.

## ADMISSION

**Applications due:** January 16 (call for date). **Application fee:** $50; transfer/late fee $100. **Application process:** "Please request brochure." The school requires the HSPT. **No. of applications:** 425 applications were received for 185 places in prior year's class. Seven new students were admitted to G10, 5 to G11. **Admission cut-off:** "We do not accept students with Ds/Fs on 8th grade transcripts." **Preferences:** Catholics, siblings, legacies. **"We are looking for** young women who demonstrate an aptitude and motivation to commit to a college preparatory program with a willingness to participate in religious and extracurricular activities." **What sort of student do you best serve?** (See above.)

## COSTS

**Latest tuition:** $7,437 payable in 12 payments. **Sibling discount:** None. **Tuition increases:** 3%-7% annually. **Other costs:** $300-$400 for books; $300 for uniforms. **Financial aid:** Notre Dame offers merit scholarships, citizenship scholarships, and need-based financial aid. **Percentage of students receiving financial aid:** 25% receive need-based financial aid in awards ranging from $500 to $3,500. Students reapply annually and recipients must maintain satisfactory academic performance. **Average grant:** $1,000. **No. of full/half-tuition scholarships:** N/P. **Grants of half-tuition or more:** 16%. **Academic scholarships:** Honors at Entrance scholarships are based upon standardized test scores and strong academic records. They are renewable if the student maintains a 3.2 GPA. Citizenship scholarships (nonrenewable) are awarded Catholic students from elementary schools who exemplify the values of the co-foundresses of the Sisters of Notre Dame. Incoming alumnae daughters scholarships (nonrenewable) are available to daughters of alumnae.

## SCHOOL'S MISSION STATEMENT/GOAL

"Dedicated to the mission of the Sisters of Notre Dame de Namur, Notre Dame High School is an independent Catholic school committed to developing responsible women of vision, hope, and prayer. Notre Dame is a caring, compassionate community, concentrating on the education of the whole person. We strive to provide a quality Catholic education which encourages each individual to achieve her full potential. At Notre Dame, we seek to help our students not only to master the skills needed to succeed in college and beyond, but also to discover within themselves a love of learning, a love of service for others, and a love for the spiritual life.

"The school community seeks: (1) to encourage, in a spirit of mutual acceptance and trust, a common searching for a deeper realization of truth, learner and teacher growing together in their awareness and expression of new insights; (2) to lead each student through innovative education to develop her unique capacities for reflection, discovery, creative and critical thinking, and responsible choice; (3) to create a climate of joy in the school for the experiencing and building of a Christian community; (4) to extend the influence of Christian community beyond the school, preparing and motivating students to build structures consistent with justice and charity in the society to which they belong; (5) to challenge students to respond with the fullness of Christian hope, compassion, and the commitment of Christ Himself to suffering and injustice in their own immediate world as well as the global world."

## ACADEMIC PROGRAM

Students take a minimum of six classes each semester. In addition to classes offered at Notre Dame, students may take part in a tri-school program, attending classes at Mercy High School Burlingame (girls), and Junipero Serra High School in San Mateo (boys). Students may also take classes at the College of Notre Dame, on the same campus as Notre Dame High School. **Courses offered (AP=Advanced Placement, H=Honors, (AP)=AP option, (H) Honors option): English:** English I (H), English II-American Literature (H), English III-British Literature (AP), English IV-World Literature (AP), Creative Writing; **Math:** Pre-Algebra, Algebra I (H), Geometry (H), Advanced Algebra (H), Statistics, Functions/Statistics/Trigonometry, Pre-Calculus (H), AP Calculus A/B; **P.E.:** P.E., Body Conditioning, Self Defense; **Religious Studies:** Scripture, Living the Gospel, Moral Decision Making, Signs & Symbols/World Religions, Social Justice, Church History, Women in Relationships, Peer Ministry, Bioethics, Senior Seminar; **Science:** General Science, Biology (H, AP), Physical Science, Chemistry (H), Physics (H); **Social Science:** World History (H), Modern World History, US History (AP), US Government, AP US History/Government/Politics/Economics, Economics, Psychology; **Creative Arts:** Art I-III, Art IV H, Art History (AP), Music History, Photography I, AP Art Studio, Ceramics I-II, Theatre Workshop I-III, Theatre Workshop IV H, Chorus I-III, Chorus IV H, Dance I-III, Speech; **Computers:** Computer Education, Computer Applications, Programming-Basic, Independent Study; **Foreign Language:** French I-III, French IV H, AP French, Spanish I-III, Spanish IV H, AP ; **Other:** Yearbook, Journalism, Driver's Ed. In addition, students may take Art I (UC approved), Photography, Advanced Level Spanish IV, Anatomy and Physiology at Mercy High School, Burlingame; at Junipero Serra High School in San Mateo: Beginning Instruments, Jazz Band,

Advanced Band (UC approved), Creative Writing (UC approved), Journalism, German I-IV, Architectural Design, Business Accounting, Leadership, and Advanced Biology. "Mini course" week, offered every other year, provides students with on- and off-campus experiences such as Yosemite Institute, Outdoor Education, Family Trips, and other activities. **Computer lab/training:** The school has two computer labs with 25 PowerMacs each. The library has 31 IBM computers with Internet access. One-half year computer education is required. **Grading:** Letter grades A-F. **Graduation requirements**: (Graduation requirements are designed to meet UC Berkeley admission requirements.) 240 credits are required including 4 years English, 3 years math, 1 year P.E., 3 years science (general science, biology, and chemistry, physics, or physical science), 3 years social science (world history, US history, American government, economics), 4 years religious studies, 1 year creative arts, .5 years computer education, 2.5 years electives, 2 years foreign language, 100 hours community service. **Average nightly homework:** 1.5 to 3 hours. **Faculty:** 37% male, 63% female (including 1 Sister). 38% of faculty hold bachelor's degrees as highest degree; 62% hold master's degree. **Faculty ethnicity:** 92% Caucasian (non-Latino); 6% Latino; 2% Asian. **Faculty selection/training:** The school requires faculty members to hold a teaching credential in their subject area and to attend 4 in-services per year. The school has a cooperative arrangement with the College of Notre Dame for high school teachers to take graduate courses. **Teacher/student ratio:** 1:18. **Teacher's daily student load in required academic subject:** N/P. **AP courses/exams:** In May, 1998, 131 students took 217 AP examinations in 8 subjects. 109 scored 3 or above. (N/P re % in AP courses) **Senior class profile (mean):** SAT Math 570, SAT Verbal 580. **GPA:** 3.0 (unweighted, includes all courses except P.E. and Computer Education). **National Merit Scholarship Program:** Five students in the most recent class were recognized. "Over the past 9 years, 32 students have received recognition for outstanding scores on the PSAT/NMSQT." **College enrollment:** 87% of last year's graduating class enrolled in 4-year colleges, 13% in 2-year colleges. Acceptances include: Agnes Scott C, American, Arizona State, Boston U, Bryn Mawr, California C of Arts and Crafts, Cal State campuses (Chico, Fullerton, Hayward, Humboldt, LA, Long Beach, Sacramento, San Diego, San Francisco, San Jose, Sonoma, Cal Poly-SLO), Canada CC, Carnegie Mellon, C of the Holy Cross, C of San Mateo, Cornell, Creighton, DeAnza CC, Dominican, Duke, Foothill C, Johnson and Wales U, Lewis & Clark, Loyola Marymount, Mount Holyoke, Northern Arizona U, Northwestern, NYU, Oregon State, Otis C of Art and Design, Pepperdine, Samuel Merritt C, Santa Clara, Santa Barbara City C, Savannah C of Art and Design, Scripps, Seattle U, Smith, St. Edward's C, St. Mary's, Stanford, Tufts, US International U, U of Arizona, UC campuses (Berkeley, Davis, Irvine, LA, Riverside, San Diego, Santa Barbara, and Santa Cruz), U of Chicago, U of Colorado at Boulder, U of Mass-Amherst, U of Miami, U of Minnesota, U of North Carolina-Chapel Hill, UOP, U of Puget Sound, U of Rochester, U of San Diego, USC, Virginia Polytechnic Institute, Wentworth Institute of Technology, Westmont C, Whittier, and Whitworth.

## OTHER INDICATORS THE SCHOOL IS ACCOMPLISHING ITS GOALS

"100% of graduating seniors enroll in college; 6-year WASC accreditation."

## CAMPUS/CAMPUS LIFE

**Campus description:** The school occupies a three-story building (built in 1928) on the former Ralston-Sharon Estate in Belmont, a suburban community between San Francisco and San Jose. The building, surrounded by 11.6 acres including expansive lawns and wooded areas, borders the Notre Dame Elementary School and the College of Notre Dame. The high school building includes Dining Room/Soda Fountain, Technology Center, gymnasium, an outdoor swimming pool (in a courtyard), and a garden courtyard off the cafeteria where students can eat their lunch. The grounds include a new softball and soccer field. The school uses the auditorium at the College of Notre Dame, on campus. **Library**: 3,850 sq. ft.; study space for 95 students; 64 periodical subscriptions; 8,480 print volumes; 21 computers (with Internet access); on-line catalog. Open to students 7 a.m. to 6 p.m. **Open/closed campus:** Closed. **Classroom space per student:** N/P. **Lunches:** Hot lunches are available daily in two locations on campus. **Bus service:** Van pick-up at El Camino/Ralston every morning (no cost). **Uniform/dress code:** Everyday uniforms: navy skirts, khaki walking shorts or pants, white tops (polo or Oxford shirts), or navy polo shirts, navy fleece vest, school sweatshirt, tennis shoes. Formal dress consists of navy blue skirt, long-sleeved white Oxford blouse, navy sweater, black, blue or brown shoes. No more than two piercings per ear, no other visible body piercings and no visible tattoos allowed. No shaved heads or unnatural dye colors. **Co-curricular activities/clubs:** The school shares social and other activities with two other area Catholic schools— Mercy High School in Burlingame (girls) and Junipero Serra High School in San Mateo (boys). This tri-school program provides coeducational experiences in academics, Campus Ministry, athletics, performing arts, and student activities. Approximately 65% of students are involved in student leadership. Clubs include Admission Club, Amnesty International, Campus Ministry, CSF, Dance Club, Ecology Club, Fencing Club, Friday Nite Live, International Club, Junior State of America, Library/Technology, Math-Science Club, Millard Fillmore Contest, National Honor Society, Service Club, and Tri-Music Honor Society. In addition, students participate in Chorus, Tri-School Mixed Chorus, Literary Magazine, Yearbook, and Newspaper. **Foreign exchange program:** No. **Opportunities for community service:** A weekly bulletin lists opportunities. Three times each semester group opportunities are provided by the Campus Ministry staff. **Typical freshman schedule:** Beginning at 8:10: Scripture/Living Gospel, English, World History, mathematics, General Science, foreign language, elective. Classes end at 2:50 on M-Th, 1:05 on Friday.

# STUDENT SUPPORT SERVICES

**Counselor/student ratio (not including college counselors):** 1:180. The school has four full-time counselors, two-full time and one part-time campus ministers, an administrative assistant, and student peer tutors. **Counseling:** Freshmen meet in small groups during their first quarter with a counselor or member of the Campus Ministry to ease the transition to high school and to learn of campus resources. Personal crisis counseling is available to students in need; the department also makes available printed materials on issues relating to adolescence, referrals to outside agencies, and counseling and mediation. **Academic counseling:** Students meet once a year with a counselor to plan their schedule for the following year, and meet during the year on an as-needed basis. **College counseling/career guidance**: A college counselor and a scholarship coordinator assist students with college planning through visits with college representatives, college catalogs, and on-line college and scholarship information. **Learning disabilities/differences:** The school admits five students to the 9th grade each year who have learning disabilities. These students have their own counselor for their four years at Notre Dame to assist them through the school's academic program. Individual learning style compensations are also given. No accommodations are given, however, in terms of requirements. (In other words, all students in the school, with or without learning disabilities/differences, are expected to complete all graduation requirements.) **Career apprenticeship programs:** Through the counseling department students can obtain information from a local business job board.

# STUDENT CONDUCT AND HEALTH

**Code of conduct:** The school has a policy of academic honesty adopted from Stanford's Honor Code. **How school handles drugs/alcohol usage:** On the first offense, the student is suspended for 3 days minimum and placed on probation. Student and parents must agree to a drug evaluation and mandatory drug testing; the student may not return to school until results are received by the school. For second offenses, the student is liable for immediate expulsion. Knowingly being present where alcoholic beverages or intoxicants are being used is prohibited by the school. Selling or dealing drugs on campus or at school-sponsored trips or activities results in immediate expulsion and police involvement. **Drug/alcohol abuse prevention/AIDS awareness program:** Campus Ministry presents Friday Nite Live, which promotes healthy living and drug and alcohol education. AIDS education is provided in religion classes.

# SUMMER PROGRAMS

Notre Dame offers coed summer school for students entering G9-12 from approximately June 16 to July 18. Classes include pre-high school courses in English and math, driver's ed, computers, and sports camp. The academic courses are designed for students who need remediation, review, or to preview certain courses and are not for credit unless previously approved. Students may take two courses (each meeting 2.5 hours per day). Cost: Approximately $250 per academic course, $175 for P.E. courses.

The school also offers a summer enrichment program for girls and boys entering G6-8. The morning program includes art, computers, English, math, science, study skills and tutorials. (Approximately $600 for a 5-week session.)

# Parent Involvement

**Parent participation:** The Parent Association provides opportunities for parents to be involved in a volunteer capacity. **Parent/teacher communication:** Report cards are distributed 3 times each semester (6 per year). Only the semester grades are recorded on the permanent transcript of academic record. Parents may request mid-grading period progress reports. **Parent education:** Monthly parent meetings on a wide range of topics relating to teenagers; grade level college planning evening meetings. **Donations:** "Although there is no mandatory donative commitment, parents are encouraged to make up tuition shortfall on a yearly basis."

# Sports

The school competes in the Girls' Private School League on the varsity, junior varsity, and freshman levels in cross-country, tennis, volleyball, water polo, basketball, crew, golf, soccer, softball, swimming, and track and field. There are more than 500 roster spots available for students on 23 teams.

# What Sets School Apart From Others

"As a single-gender institution, Notre Dame, Belmont is committed to the development of responsible women of vision, hope, and prayer. In our challenging academic environment, our young women separate academic concerns from social concerns; learn from a greater number of same gender academic role models; and assume leadership positions without fear of upsetting gender stereotypes."

# How Parents/Students Characterize School

"At NDB, we are taught to value and celebrate creativity. I've learned so much and gained so much self-confidence through being involved in the arts, and it's wonderful knowing that my teachers and classmates are so supportive."—Elyse Regan, '98

"It wasn't until I started NDB that I actually decided to play a sport of my own accord. I went out for the crew team, and it ultimately changed my life. I discovered aspects of athleticism within myself such as focus, determination, and competition which I had always possessed in my intellectual pursuits and academic endeavors but had never been able to apply to athletic arenas." —Amy Stoddard, '97 (student at Yale)

"Our daughter's years at Notre Dame gave her a rare opportunity to attend a school that is as wholesome as it is rigorous, as supportive as it is challenging. From choral and art activities to campus ministry and the classrooms, she thrived at Notre Dame."—parents, Schuyler and Yvonne Moore

# NOTRE DAME HIGH SCHOOL

596 South Second Street
San Jose, CA 95112

(408) 294-1113 *fax (408) 288-8185*

Mary Lou Schoone, Principal
Mary Beth Riley, Admissions, Rileynd@hotmail.com

## GENERAL

**Girls'** day high school. **Catholic** (79% Catholic). Founded in 1851. **Nonprofit**, sponsored by the Sisters of Notre Dame de Namur. **Enrollment:** 525. **Average class size:** 27. **Accreditation:** WASC (6-year term: 1997-03). **School year:** 10-month calendar (approx. 170 instructional days). **School day:** 7:50 a.m. to 2:40 p.m. (dismissal is 1:25 p.m. on Friday). **Location:** In downtown San Jose, near Highways 280 and 101, 5 blocks from San Jose State University.

## STUDENT BODY

**Geographical breakdown (counties):** 92% from Santa Clara; 7% from East Bay; 1% from San Benito. **Ethnicity:** 42% Caucasian (non-Latina); 19% Filipina; 17% Latina; 8% Vietnamese; 4% Chinese; 2% African-American; 1% Japanese. **Foreign students (I-20 status):** 0. **Single parent/two f/t working parent families:** N/P. **Middle schools:** 53% of the latest freshman class came from 27 parochial schools; 45% from 55 public middle schools; .07% from 10 private nonparochial schools. The school draws a good number of students from St. John Vianney, St. Victor, St. Leo, Chaboya and Quimby.

# ADMISSION

**Applications due:** Late January (call for exact date). **Application fee:** $50. **Application process:** Shadow dates may be scheduled for October through April. In early November the school holds an 8th Grade Day when interested students may visit the campus. An open house is held in early December for families of students currently in G6-8. Applicants may take the HSPT at Notre Dame in early to mid-January (or at any other school in the Diocese). The school does not use a clergy recommendation form though the application asks for religion and baptism dates, if applicable. The school uses the Diocese 7th and 8th grade student report. Decisions are mailed mid-March. **No. of applications:** 357 applications were received for 140 places in most recent freshman class. Four new students were admitted to G 10, 3 to G 11. **Admission cut-off:** "B average and grade equivalency or higher on HSPT. Transfer students must have a B average and be able to meet the requirements for graduation. Students are accepted to 12th grade only if they are moving to the area and were enrolled in a Catholic school." **Preferences:** Catholic, daughters of alumnae, siblings. **"We are looking for..."** N/P. **What sort of student do you best serve?** N/P.

# COSTS

**Latest tuition:** $6,200 (payment options available). **Sibling discount:** None. **Tuition increases:** Approximately 6% annually. **Other costs:** $250 registration fee, additional cost for uniforms, student body fees, class dues, and Parents' Assn. dues ($25). **Percentage of students receiving financial aid:** 10%. **Average grant:** $1,035. **No. of full tuition grants:** 0. **Grants of half-tuition or more:** 0. **Other scholarships:** The Julie Billiart Scholarship is available for applicants with outstanding junior high academic records and who demonstrate superior ability on the HSPT; students with a 2.0 GPA and financial need may apply for Notre Dame financial assistance; Catholic students with financial need who reside in the Diocese may apply for Diocesan Scholarships.

# SCHOOL'S MISSION STATEMENT/GOALS

"Established in 1851, Notre Dame High School is a Catholic secondary school which educates young women in the tradition of the Sisters of Notre Dame de Namur, founded by St. Julie Billiart. Our primary mission is expressed in her words: 'Teach them what they need to know for life.'

"We provide a challenging college-preparatory curriculum which integrates classroom learning with downtown educational opportunities in culture, science, and technology. We maintain an enrollment that allows faculty to know each student and to give special attention to individual, academic, and personal needs.

"We encourage students to participate in varied activities to discover skills and talents in the arts, athletics, student leadership, and community service.

"In our richly diverse student body, young women develop a respect and appreciation for other individuals and cultures. Together, faculty and students create a supportive, open-minded environment in which each young woman is encouraged to explore her creative potential, develop self-esteem, strengthen her relationship with God, enjoy nurturing friendships and grow in her ability to work with others and serve her community.

"We educate young women for success and leadership in a global and technological society. We prepare them to live as well-educated, self-confident and socially responsible women, sustained by religious faith and guided by spiritual values."

# ACADEMIC PROGRAM

In addition to the academic program offered by the school, juniors and seniors may, with permission, take classes at San Jose State University. 23 students currently do. **Courses offered (AP=Advanced Placement, H=Honors, (AP)=AP option, (H)=Honors option): English:** English I-IV (H), Shakespeare: The Comedies, Shakespeare: The Tragedies, Writing Workshop, Writing for Publication; **Math:** Pre-Algebra, Algebra I-II, Geometry, Trigonometry/Pre-Calculus, AP Calculus, Practical Statistics, Geometric Art and Advanced Constructions; **Religious Studies:** Hebrew Scriptures, Christian Scriptures, Faith, Values, and Lifestyles, Decision Making, Spirituality and Self, Women, Creativity, and Spirituality, World Religious, Peace and Justice, Spiritual & Liturgical Leadership; **Social Studies:** Modern World History, US History (AP), US Government (H), Psychology I and II, The Law, Economics, Conflict in the Modern World; **Technology:** Internet & Applications, Web Design: The Vega Project; **Science:** Biology, Biology II, Chemistry (H), Physics, Earth Science; **Foreign Language:** Spanish I, Spanish II-III (H), Spanish IV AP, French I-IV, Advanced College Level French or Spanish; **Art/Performing Arts:** Introduction to Art, Drawing and Design Fundamentals, Pen, Paint, and Pastels, Advanced Pen, Paint and Pastels, Photography, Ceramics, Advanced Ceramics, Yearbook I & II, Chorus, Foods and Nutrition, International Foods; **P.E.:** Physical Education, Fitness for Life. **Special programs:** Docent Program (at San Jose museums), Business Internship, Senior Honors Project, Peer Counseling Training. Students participate in NASA Ames research projects and the Nuclear Science summer program for women at San Jose State University. **Computer lab/training:** The school has two computer labs each with Pentium PCs. The school's computers are networked. (N/P re #) **Grading:** A-F. **Graduation requirements:** 4 years English, 2 semesters fine arts, 2 semesters P.E., 2 years foreign language, 3 years math (including geometry), 6 semesters religious studies, 2 years lab science and 1 year social science, 3.5 years social studies, 1 semester computers, community service. **Average nightly homework (Mon-Th):** G9-10: 2 hours; G11-12: 2.5-3. **Faculty:** Of the 36 full-time faculty members, 26% are male, 74% female. 40% of faculty hold bachelor's degrees as highest degrees, 60% hold master's degrees. **Faculty ethnicity:** 83% Caucasian (non-Latino); 14% Latino. **Teacher selection/training:** N/P. **Teacher/ student ratio:** 1:12. **Teacher's daily student load in required academic subject:** 125. **AP courses/exams:** 24% of the most recent year's class took 3 AP courses. In 1997-98, 54 students took 73 AP exams in 5 subjects. 75% scored 3 or above. **Senior class profile (mean):** SAT Math 520, SAT Verbal 530. **GPA:** 3.1. **National Merit Scholarship Program:** In most recent year's class, 3 students were semi-finalists, 5 were commended. **College enrollment:** 78% of last year's graduating class enrolled in 4-year colleges, 22% in 2-year colleges, including: UC campuses (Berkeley, Davis, Irvine, San Diego, Santa Barbara, Santa Cruz, and UCLA), Carnegie Mellon, Columbia, Cornell, Princeton, De Paul, CSU campuses (Humboldt, Long Beach, San Diego, San Francisco, Hayward, Northridge, Cal Poly-Pomona, and Cal Poly-SLO), Loyola Marymount, Santa Clara, Scripps, St. Andrew's U (Scotland), St. John's U (NY), St. Mary's, Stanford, U of Colorado Boulder, USF, USC, U of Rochester, Western Oregon State, and Whitman.

## OTHER INDICATORS THE SCHOOL IS ACCOMPLISHING ITS GOALS

"Notre Dame students have been selected for state and national honors including Tandy Technology Scholars (class of '98); Santa Clara County Olympiad of the Arts awards; Santa Clara County Salute to Youth Awards for Leadership; and Community Service."

## CAMPUS/CAMPUS LIFE

**Campus description:** The school occupies a one-square block campus in downtown San Jose. The campus currently consists of two three-story buildings housing offices and classrooms, two computer labs, science labs, cafeteria and a gym, and a separate one-story student life center with a student lounge, courtyard, counseling offices, art studios (ceramics studio, painting/drawing studio, photography lab), and a chapel. Most classrooms have desks arranged in clusters to advance cooperative learning. The grounds include a grassy area with picnic tables. The school plans to replace the three-story buildings with a new building by 2002. This building will include upgraded science labs, a new library, new classroom space, and computer lab(s). The school uses the swimming pool at San Jose State University and nearby parks for soccer, and uses Bellarmine's facilities for track and field. **Library:** 1,800 sq. ft.; 17,000 print volumes; 23 periodical subscriptions; 15 computers (Mac 575s, Mac Centris 610, Mac 5400 Power PC,

Packard Bell Windows '95, all with Internet access); 25 CD-ROMs; study space for 75 students. Open to students from 7:30 a.m. to 5 p.m.; card catalog (on-line for research); full-time credentialed Library Media Specialist. **Open/closed campus:** Closed. **Classroom space per student:** 750 sq.ft. **Lunches:** Morning snacks and hot lunches are available daily. **Bus service:** Public only. **Uniforms/dress code:** Gray skirts, white school logo shirts, gray school sweatshirts for everyday; free dress on Fridays (jeans permitted), formal dress for liturgy days. No unnatural hair colors; pierced ears only. **Co-curricular activities/clubs:** The school's location permits students, on organized field trips, to walk to the San Jose museums, the Technology Center, Performing Arts Center, and other downtown cultural venues. Clubs include: The American Technology Honor Society, Amnesty International, The Animal Liberation League, Because Animals Really Count, California Scholarship Federation, Gospel Choir, Interact, Library Service Club, National Honor Society, Notre Dame Ambassadors, Peer Counseling, Peer Tutoring, Students Against Destructive Decisions, African American Student Union, Filipino Student Association, French Club, Indo Student Association, Japan Club, Latinas Unidas, Portuguese American Club, Vietnamese Sisterhood, Astronomy Club, Elizabethan Club, Environmental Club, Future Business Leaders of America, Odyssey of the Mind, Food Lovers Club, Lights, Camera, Action (film club), Ski Club. **Foreign exchange program:** The school is currently arranging for a summer program in Uruguay in conjunction with students at Bellarmine. **Opportunities for community service:** The school's Community Service Learning Program involves 10 hours of service in the freshman year, 15 hours sophomore year, 18 hours junior year and a senior project presented to the community. Students fulfill the requirement through work with local agencies. During Easter Break, students may travel to Tijuana where they live with a family and help build homes. **Typical freshman schedule:** Students take six classes. Class periods are approximately 45 minutes each. English I, Algebra I or Geometry, homeroom/break, Spirituality & Self/Hebrew Scripture, Modern History, Intro to Art, P.E., lunch, French I or Spanish I, resource period.

## STUDENT SUPPORT SERVICES

**Counselor-student ratio (not including college counselor:** 1:250. **Counseling:** The school also has a full-time licensed Marriage and Family therapist for students requesting help with personal concerns. The **personal counselor** facilitates support groups, and trains and supervises peer counselors. She meets with every 9th grader during her first year at the school. Each student is assigned a teacher to act as **mentor/advisor** throughout her four years. The mentor meets with the groups of 20 students each week for 15 minutes, and each month for an extended period. In addition, an Academic Counselor is available to provide support for students who have special learning needs or who may be academically at risk. **Tutoring** in math is available daily in a math lab staffed by a teacher or an advanced senior student. The school has a full-time **college counselor** who begins assisting students in their sophomore year. All students use the college, career and scholarship computer program; students can access their files from any computer on campus. **Learning disabilities/differences:** "Testing and classroom accommodations are provided, as appropriate, for diagnosed students. An academic support class is available for freshmen." **Career apprenticeship programs:** The academic/career counselor posts information regarding local jobs and job fairs. Students are also informed of and encouraged to participate in a number of volunteer and internship programs, both locally and out-of-state. Local programs include NASA, Tech Museum, Art Museum, and tutoring programs.

## STUDENT CONDUCT AND HEALTH

**Code of conduct:** "The code of conduct is commensurate to the expectations of a college preparatory Catholic high school." **How school handles drug/alcohol usage:** For first offenses, suspension, parent conference, behavior probation, referral to school counselor or a drug and alcohol education program, possible expulsion, police may be called. Second offenses will result in parent conference and ordinarily in expulsion. **Drug/alcohol abuse prevention/AIDS awareness programs:** Issues are addressed through the mentoring program along with other women's health issues.

## SUMMER PROGRAMS

None.

## PARENT INVOLVEMENT

**Parent participation:** No required hours, though the Parent Club is open to all parents—its main function is to support the school. Through the Club parents assist with a variety of school functions, including drama, field trips, and sports. **Parent/teacher communication:** As needed. **Parent education:** The personal counselor facilitates a monthly parent education class that is open to all parents. The counseling department schedules annual parent nights for each grade level that address development and parenting issues. **Donations:** Parents are encouraged to participate in the Parent Giving Program and the Annual Fund Drive, along with other development/school events.

## SPORTS

The school is a member of the Private School Athletic League and competes with other South Bay schools of a similar size in volleyball (frosh, jv, v), tennis (jv, v), cross-country (v), water polo (v), basketball (frosh, jv, v), soccer (jv, v), softball (v), track & field (jv, v), swimming (jv, v), and golf (v).

## WHAT SETS SCHOOL APART FROM OTHERS

"148-year tradition in downtown San Jose; diverse student body; excellent fine arts; lab science program; proximity to SJSU."

## HOW PARENTS/STUDENTS CHARACTERIZE SCHOOL

"Academic excellence/rigor; caring school community; responsive faculty and administration; creativeness of student work."

# PINEWOOD SCHOOL

26800 Fremont Road
Los Altos Hills, CA 94022

(650) 941-1532 *fax (650) 941-4727*
www.pinewood.edu
info@pinewood.edu

Mark Gardner, Principal
Laurie Wilson, Admissions Coordinator and Registrar, lwilson@pinewood.edu

## GENERAL

**Coed** day high school. **Nonsectarian.** (N/P re year founded) **Nonprofit. Enrollment:** 300 (grades 7-12; approx. 50 students per grade level). **Average class size:** 15-20. **Accreditation:** WASC (6-year term: 1995-01). **School year:** 9-month calendar (approx. 170 instructional days). **School day:** 8 a.m. to 3 p.m. **Location:** The campus is in a wooded area of rolling hills in the suburban residential community of Los Altos Hills, just south of Palo Alto, off Highway 280 (40 miles south of San Francisco, 15 miles north of San Jose).

## STUDENT BODY

**Geographical breakdown (counties):** 75% from Santa Clara; 25% from San Mateo. **Ethnicity:** N/P. **Foreign students (I-20 status):** 1%. **Single parent/two f/t working parent families:** N/P. **Middle schools:** 66% of the latest freshman class came from the school's middle school; 24% from public middle schools; 8% from private nonparochial schools; 1% from parochial schools. (N/P re #)

# ADMISSION

**Applications due:** Approx. February 1 (call for exact date). **Application fee:** $50. **Application process:** Prospective students and parents may visit the campus on Mondays beginning October 1. They may observe classes and meet and talk with students, teachers, and the school administration. Campus informational tours are given at 9 a.m. and 10:30 a.m. No appointment is necessary, but visitors need to check-in with the main office upon arrival. If Monday is not convenient, appointments may be scheduled for Wednesday-Friday. Prospective students must take Pinewood's admission test; scores from other tests may be submitted as additional information, but will not be accepted in lieu of school test. The admission test assesses English and math skills only and is untimed. Open testing is held on three Saturdays in December, January, and February. Prospective students are encouraged to spend a day shadowing a current student, going to classes and experiencing school life. Shadowing may be done November - March, Tuesday through Friday. **No. of applications:** 65 applications were received for 20 places in the most recent freshman class. Five new students were admitted to G 10, 2 to G 11, 1 to G12. **Preferences:** None. **Admissions cut-off:** "No specific cut-off—combination of grades, scores, and recommendations." **"We are looking for** those students who are strong academically, but who also want to be part of an educational environment that values and encourages creative expression, athletic participation and community involvement. The school motto is 'Pinewood is the Difference,' and faculty and students take pride in making this a reality. All students are expected to accept and support a standard of behavior that stresses commitment, honesty, kindness, conservative standards of dress, appearance, language and moral conduct." **What sort of student do you best serve?** "The student who is a willing, positive and active participant in the opportunities provided—students who want personal involvement with their education, their teachers and their fellow students do best at Pinewood. Students who are most comfortable being part of the 'background' will not be happy at Pinewood."

# COSTS

**Latest tuition:** $10,900. **Sibling discount:** N/P. **Tuition increases:** N/P. [Ed. note: Approx. 7% in past year.] **Other costs:** $700 book/activity fee. **Percentage of students receiving financial aid:** N/P. **Average grant:** N/P. **No. of full-tuition grants:** N/P. **Grants of half-tuition or more:** N/P.

## SCHOOL'S MISSION STATEMENT/GOALS

"Pinewood School seeks to create an educational environment where students may acquire academic stamina, intellectual maturity, self-esteem and a high standard of behavior. Our goal is to provide students with the skills necessary for success in school and beyond through a strong college preparatory curriculum that emphasizes the importance of reading, writing, computation, communication, critical thinking and problem solving skills.

"We believe learning should be a positive and rewarding experience that challenges students to achieve their highest potential. Classes are small, allowing for individual instruction and attention and promoting student diversity and self-expression. This fosters open communication and rapport between students and teachers. Outside the classroom students are given opportunities to express themselves through a number of extracurricular activities designed for both group and individual involvement. The importance of these activities is stressed and student participation is actively encouraged and supported.

"At Pinewood, it is our hope that students will take advantage of the opportunities afforded so that they become self-motivated, disciplined, responsible citizens prepared to lead a life of purpose, dignity and concern for others."

## ACADEMIC PROGRAM

"As a college preparatory school, Pinewood's standard curriculum path is designed to meet the minimum course requirements of the UC system and other highly selective colleges and universities. Many students, however, follow the school's honors and AP curriculum paths." **Courses offered (AP=Advanced Placement, H=Honors, (AP)= AP option, (H)=Honors option; \*= required for freshmen): English:** English I (Genre of Literature), English II (American Literature), English III (British Literature) (H), English IV (World Literature), AP English Literature and Composition, Writing Techniques I\*, Writing Techniques II, College Writing, Yearbook, Journalism, Creative Writing; **Math:** Algebra I-II, Geometry (freshmen will take either Algebra I, II or Geometry), Probability and Statistics, Mathematics-Selected Topics, Pre-Calculus with Trigonometry (H), AP Calculus I (AB), AP Calculus II (BC); **Speech:** Oral Communication; **History:** World History I\*-II, US History (AP), American Government (H), World Geography, Economics; **Computer Science:** Computer Applications\*, Advanced Computer Literacy, AP Computer Science, Computer Programming, Web Page Design; **Science:** Biology (AP), General Chemistry, Honors Chemistry, General Physics, AP Physics, Astronomy; **Social Science:** Introduction to Psychology, Sociology, Leadership; **Foreign Language:** Spanish I or II\*, Spanish III, Spanish IV (H), Spanish V (H, AP), French I-or II\*, French III, French IV (H), French V (AP); **Art/Performing Arts:** Art History (AP), Studio Art I-II, Basic Drawing, Theater Arts; **P.E. Computer lab/training:** The school has a computer lab with 20 PowerMac G3s and a big screen teaching monitor. The Yearbook and Journalism offices have 5 additional computers; science labs and math classes each have at least one computer (physics lab has 6, chemistry lab has 3). All students are required to take keyboarding and computers. **Grading:** Letter grades (4.0 scale + for honors/AP courses). **Graduation requirements:** 4 years English/literature, 2.5 years writing, 3 years foreign language, 4 years history (including 1 semester of art history), 3 years mathematics, 3 years science, .5 year oral communication, 2 years P.E., .5 year computer literacy, .5 year music appreciation, .5 year economics, .5 year world geography. **Average nightly homework (Mon-Th):** G9: 3 hours; G10-12: 3 hours (plus additional homework for honors and AP courses). **Faculty:** 30% are male, 70% female. 65% hold bachelor's degrees as highest degrees; 15% hold master's degrees. **Faculty ethnicity:** N/P. **Faculty selection/ training:** "Faculty members are selected based on their resumes, recommendations, personal interviews with members of the administration, and in-class teaching demonstrations. Teaching credentials are not required; all faculty members are expected to teach in their major field. Pinewood holds several in-service meetings throughout the year and teachers are encouraged to pursue continuing studies often with the financial support of the school administration." **Teacher/student ratio:** 1:8. **Teacher's daily student load in required academic subject:** 70-80. **AP courses/exams:** In 1998-99, 73 students took 187 AP exams in 17 subjects. 76% scored 3 or above. (N/P re % in AP courses) **Senior class profile (mean):** SAT Math 626, SAT Verbal 603. **GPA:** 3.56. **National Merit Scholarship Program:** In most recent year's class, 3 students were semi-finalists, 3 were commended. **College enrollment:** 96% (43) of last year's graduating class (45 graduates) enrolled in 4-year colleges, 4% (2) in 2-year colleges, including: MIT, Pomona, Brown, Wheaton, Whitman, Carnegie-Mellon, SMU, USC, Pepperdine, UC Santa Barbara, UC Santa Cruz, UCLA, UC Riverside, Sarah Lawrence, Whittier, U of Michigan, Vassar, U of Colorado, Azusa Pacific, Santa Clara, Mills, Boston U, Cal Lutheran, Cal Poly-SLO, Point Loma Nazarene U, Westmont C, U of Arizona, Ricks, and C of San Mateo.

## OTHER INDICATORS THE SCHOOL IS ACCOMPLISHING ITS GOALS

N/P.

## CAMPUS/CAMPUS LIFE

**Campus description:** The campus, housing grades 7-12, consists of one two-story building and several one-story buildings arranged around a wide open area of playing fields. Classrooms, offices, labs (biology, chemistry, and physics), an art studio, and a small theater open onto the courtyard area; the two-story building houses the gym and a student "union"/study hall and additional classrooms. The outdoor area includes 4 tennis courts, basketball standards, and a soccer field. **Library:** 1,090 sq. ft.; 5,000 print volumes; 20 periodical subscriptions; 5

computers (all with Internet access); on-line catalog; study space for 35 students. Open to students from 7:45 a.m. to 4:15 p.m.; full-time librarian. **Open/closed campus:** Closed campus except for seniors who may leave for lunch. **Classroom space per student:** N/P. **Lunches:** A lunch truck provides hot lunches and bag lunches; miscellaneous snacks are also available. **Bus service:** None. **Uniforms/ dress code:** Dress code. (No clothes advertising drugs, alcohol, etc.; no visible non-ear piercings; no midriffs, tanks, etc.) **Co-curricular activities/clubs:** Interact Club (affiliated with Rotary International), National Honor Society, French Honor Society, Spanish Honor Society, Art Honor Society, speech and debate team, yearbook and newspaper, plays, musicals, student government, service clubs. **Foreign exchange program:** None. **Opportunities for community service:** N/P. **Typical freshman schedule:** 8 periods of approximately 45 minutes each, including English, Writing (1 semester), History (1 semester), math, science, French or Spanish, computers (1 semester), communications, music (1 semester), P.E.

## Student Support Services

**Counselor-student ratio:** N/P. **Counseling:** In junior high, **college counseling** begins with students and parents becoming acquainted with general college requirements and planning high school classes to meet those requirements. Starting the junior year of high school, the college advisor assists in all phases of the college admission process. Juniors take a semester-long college preparation class. Teachers offer **tutoring** throughout the day and after school for students who wish to pay for the service. A math lab, staffed by a math teacher and selected students from the National Honor Society or a Math Honor Society is open daily to students. The school also has a Foreign Language Workshop staffed by teachers and honor students. Regarding personal counseling, students are encouraged to talk to members of the administration or their teachers. **Learning disabilities/differences:** "Students with *mild* diagnosed learning differences function well at Pinewood. They are permitted to have extended testing time and to take oral exams as deemed necessary by an educational counselor. Pinewood does not offer any special programs for students with learning differences." **Career apprenticeship programs:** N/P.

## Student Conduct and Health

**Code of conduct:** Standard. **How school handles drug/alcohol usage:** "Depends on specific circumstances. Zero tolerance for drug/alcohol use at school functions. Other interventions/counseling will depend on student and situation." **Drug/alcohol abuse prevention/AIDS awareness programs:** Discussed in depth in various class curricula.

## Summer Programs

The Pinewood summer program is open to the public. A six-week session includ-ing enrichment and academics is offered from approximately early July through mid-August. It may be required for students admitted to Pinewood condition-ally. Cost: Approximately $995 for academics, $695 for enrichment.

## Parent Involvement

**Parent participation:** N/P. **Parent/teacher communication:** No scheduled con-ferences; conferences may be requested by parents, teachers or the administration at any time during the year. Parents are invited to communicate with all teachers and administrators in person, by phone, and by e-mail; they also have access to their child's grades and attendance through the Internet. **Parent education pro-grams:** None. **Donations:** None.

## Sports

Girls' volleyball, tennis, soccer, basketball, softball and golf; boys' soccer, basket-ball, volleyball, tennis, golf, and baseball.

## What Sets School Apart From Others

"Small size, caring attitude, friendly environment, relaxed, pleasant environment where students seems happy to be a part of it."

## How Parents/Students Characterize School

(See above.)

# PRESENTATION HIGH SCHOOL

2281 Plummer Ave.
San Jose, CA 95125

(408) 264-1664 *fax (408) 266-3028*
www.pres-net.com

Mary Miller, Principal
Pauline Newton, Director of Admissions (408) 264-1664, pnewton@pres-net.com

## GENERAL

Girls' day high school. **Roman Catholic** (74% Catholic). Founded in 1962. **Nonprofit.** Operated by the Sisters of the Presentation. **Enrollment:** 712. **Average class size:** 28. **Accreditation:** WASC (6-year term: 1995-01). **School year:** 9-month calendar (approx. 180 instructional days). **School day:** 7:30 a.m. to 2:10 p.m. Early morning classes are offered which begin at 7:30 a.m. **Location:** In the Willow Glen residential neighborhood of San Jose, near Highways 280, 101 and 87.

## STUDENT BODY

**Geographical breakdown:** N/P. **Ethnicity:** 66% Caucasian (non-Latina); 12% Latina; 4% Filipina; 4% Chinese; 3% Vietnamese; 1.5% Japanese; 1% African-American; 1% Korean; .5% American Indian; .5% Pacific Islander; 5% other non-Caucasian. **Percentage of foreign students (1-20):** N/P. **Single parent/ two f/t working parent families:** N/P. **Middle schools:** Presentation students come from more than 90 feeder schools, 58% of which are Catholic, 13% non-Catholic private, and 27% public. (N/P #) Among the represented feeder schools are St. Christopher, St. Francis Cabrini, St. John Vianney, Holy Family, St. Martin (San Jose), St. Mary's Gilroy, and Almaden Country School.

## ADMISSION

**Applications due:** Late January (call for exact date). **Application fee:** $50. **Application process:** Presentation offers an admissions open house during which parents and prospective students may visit the campus and meet faculty, coaches and students. On Eighth Grade Day, eighth grade students "shadow" a current Presentation student, attend Mini-Classes and a special assembly produced by Presentation students, and have an ice cream social. Placement tests are held in

January. Eighth grade transcripts are due in early February and acceptance letters are mailed mid-March. **No of applications:** In 1998, 595 applications were received for 180 places. Three students were admitted to G10, 1 to G 11. **Admission cut-off:** N/P. **Preferences:** N/P. **"We are looking for..."** N/P. **What sort of student do you best serve?** N/P.

## Costs

**Latest tuition:** $5,920. Tuition may be paid annually, each semester, quarterly, or monthly. **Sibling discount:** None. **Tuition increases:** Approx. 4% annually. **Percentage of students receiving financial aid:** 13%. **Average grant award:** 50%. **No. of full-tuition grants:** N/P. **No. of half-tuition grants:** 95. **Grants of half-tuition or more:** N/P.

## School's Mission Statement/Goals

"... Presentation High School strives to permeate the entire educational process with the vision of life found in the Gospels. It endeavors to enable each student to integrate the acquisition of human knowledge and skills with her total development as a Christian person. The school recognizes that it shares with the family and the Church and the state in the total work of education. In particular with the family, which is the primary educator, the school must enter a fruitful partnership. The school, however, assumes responsibility for using its own unique resources to bring about its shared purpose. In order to be faithful to its purposes, the school recognizes the following beliefs must be the foundation upon which all goals, objectives, programs, and procedures are developed and are continually evaluated: That education consists in the harmonious development of the whole person—her religious, intellectual, volitional, aesthetic, emotional, and physical powers [; that] although faith is a gift from God, it is capable of growth and must be nurtured to maturity in harmony with the stages of human development[; that] Gospel values are best taught and internalized in the supportive atmosphere of a Christian community where the professional educators and staff along with the students evidence commitment to school goals and Gospel values[; that] the work of education is the work of empowering individuals to reach their full potential as human beings, to make responsible decisions as individuals and members of the human community and to assume their full stature in today's society[; and that] the school is an active institution which must be a dynamic force in bringing about the implementation of Christian principles in the social sphere."

## Academic Program

Students take a minimum course load of five classes a semester, though early morning classes beginning at 7:30 a.m. allow students to take seven. Presentation graduation requirements are designed to satisfy those of the state of California and the UC and CSU systems. **Courses offered (AP=Advanced Placement, H=Honors, (AP)=AP option, (H)=Honors option): Computers:** Computer Technology, Advanced Computers, Computer Basics, Computer Programming, Computer Programming C++, Desktop Publishing; **English:** English 9, English 9 Accelerated, English 10, English 10 (H), Beginning Speech, Intermediate Speech (10), The Adolescent in Literature, American Literature (H), British Literature, Creative Writing, Death in Literature, Ethnic Literature, Expository Writing, God in Modern Literature, Law in Literature, Literary Biographies, Classical Literature H, Poetry H, World Literature H; **Fine and Applied Arts:** Introduction to Drawing, Introduction to Painting, Advanced Art, Drawing with Computers, Photography, Yearbook I and II, Ceramics, Art Appreciation, Introduction to Music, Film Study, Drama Workshop, Choir; **Math:** Introduction to Algebra, Algebra I, Accelerated Algebra I, Geometry (H), Algebra II, Honors Algebra II/Trigonometry, Statistics, Trigonometry, Math Analysis, Calculus I (H), Honors Calculus II; **Modern Language:** French I, II (H), III (H), Honors French IV, V, Spanish I, II (H), III (H), Honors Spanish V; **P.E:** Step Aerobics/Conditioning, Weight Training/Conditioning, Beginning Tennis, Physical Education/Health, Indoor Sports; **Religion:** Religious Studies for 9th and 10th Grades, Understanding Your Faith/Religion 9A and 9B, Jesus of the Gospels/Religion 10, Religious Studies Electives for 11th and 12th Grades, Christian Ethics (graduation requirement), Christian Marriage, Contemporary Catholic, Prayer, Scripture, Christian Values and the Media, Church History, Women of Faith, World Religions; **Science:** Biology I (H), Biology II (H), Chemistry (H), Earth Science, Environmental Science, Physics (H); **Social Studies:** World History, Cultures, and Geography 9A and 9B, US History 10A and 10B (H), Civics (H), California History, Economics (H), Modern History, Peace and Justice, Psychology (H), Ethnic Studies, Global Women's Studies. **Computer lab/training:** Pres-Net, a system developed in partnership with IBM, is a local area token-ring network integrating fiber optic technology. It consists of an IBM Windows NT file server with 256 megabytes of memory and 60 gigabytes of disk storage, two CD-ROM towers featuring 28 networked CDs, and a daily backup system. The network features: A ratio of 1 computer for every 4 students; Internet access in all classrooms and computer labs utilizing a T-1 line; Internal e-mail and Internet e-mail for all faculty, staff, and students; a computer in every classroom with a link to the classroom TV for student and instructional presentations; 3 computer labs featuring Pentium computers in each, laser printers, scanners, and color laser printers; a new high-tech science lab with 16 Pentium computers with scientific instruments for lab experiments and HP calculators connected to every computer; LCD projectors in 3 computer labs and 1 classroom for large screen presentation of computer software, as well as video. **Grading:** N/P. **Graduation requirements:** 200 credits minimum. Presentation strongly recommends that students acquire 220-240 credits. .5 year computer basics, 4 years English, 1 year fine/applied arts, 2 years same foreign language, 3 years mathematics (Algebra II strongly recommended), 1 year P.E., 3.5 years religious studies (including .5 year ethics), 1 year lab science and 2 years other science, 3.5 years social studies including .5 year civics. (A minimum of 5 classes per semester is required.) **Average nightly homework (Mon-Th):** G9: 2 hours; G10-11: 3-4 hours; G12: 3 hours. **Faculty:** Of the school's 63 faculty members, 84% are female, 16% are male. 50 faculty members hold master's degrees. **Faculty ethnicity:** 90% Caucasian (non-Latino); 9% Latino; 1% Asian. **Faculty selection/training:** All faculty have California state credentials and are teaching in their subject area. Thirty professional growth units each year for each faculty member are required. (N/P re faculty selection) **Teacher/student ratio:** 1:28. **Teacher's student load in required academic subject:** N/P. **AP courses/exams:** In 1998 students took 139 AP exams in 15 subjects. 63% received scores of 3 or better. (N/P # takers, % in classes) **Senior class profile(mean):** SAT Math 541, SAT Verbal 560. **GPA:** N/P. **National Merit Scholarship Program:** Last year, 6 scholars; 5 scholars with honors; 3 scholars with distinction. **College enrollment:** 100% of last year's graduates enrolled in college—88% in 4-year colleges, 12% in community colleges. 69% were accepted to their first choice college. (N/P colleges)

## OTHER INDICATORS THE SCHOOL IS ACCOMPLISHING ITS GOALS

N/P.

## CAMPUS/CAMPUS LIFE

**Campus description:** The campus consists of a one-story building containing classrooms and offices; an athletic complex with a gym, weight room, dance studios and locker room; and a Christian Life Center with a chapel. The outdoor area includes tennis courts and a softball field. The school uses a pool at a Willow Glen public high school. **Library:** Open to students from 7:30 a.m. to 4 p.m. The library has a satellite computer lab and electronic access to the Santa Clara County Libraries. (N/P sq. ft., volumes, etc.) **Open/closed campus:** Campus is closed during lunchtime for freshmen and sophomores. Juniors and seniors may leave campus at lunchtime or during a free period. **Classroom space per student:** N/P. **Lunches:** A breakfast and lunch service is provided. **Bus service:** Public only. **Uniforms** required. **Co-curricular activities/clubs:** Dance, Drama, Speech and Debate, Campus Ministry, Student Government, and over 20 other clubs. **Foreign exchange program:** N/P. **Opportunities for community service:** N/P. **Typical freshman schedule:** N/P.

## STUDENT SUPPORT SERVICES

**Counselor-student ratio (not including college counselor):** 1:4. **Counseling:** Each student has an **advisor** with whom they meet regularly. Advisors help students prepare for college, aid in career education, and provide personal counseling as needed. At the beginning of her freshman year, each student is assigned a **mentor** with whom she will work over her four years at Presentation. Mentoring groups—28 to 35 students—meet once a week for general information, study skill instruction, and college and scholarship information. Mentors also meet with each of their mentees at least once a semester to discuss the student's academic progress, goals, abilities and interests, and to provide guidance in these areas.

## STUDENT CONDUCT AND HEALTH
N/P.

## SUMMER PROGRAMS
N/P.

## PARENT INVOLVEMENT
N/P.

## SPORTS
Presentation competes in the Blossom Valley Athletic League. Teams include basketball, cross-country, golf, soccer, softball, swimming and diving, tennis, track & field, volleyball, and water polo. (A 1998 grad was named Gatorade's Athlete of the Year—the first woman to hold the title.)

## WHAT SETS SCHOOL APART FROM OTHERS
N/P.

## HOW PARENTS/STUDENTS CHARACTERIZE SCHOOL
N/P.

# SACRED HEART CATHEDRAL PREPARATORY

1055 Ellis Street
San Francisco, CA 94109

(415) 775-6626 *fax (415) 931-6941*

Mr. John Scudder, Jr., Principal
Timothy M. Burke, Director of Admission

## GENERAL

**Coed** day high school. **Catholic** (72% Catholic). Founded in 1874 as Sacred Heart High School—in 1987, the boys' school merged with Cathedral High School, a girls' school, founded in 1852. Owned by the Archdiocese of San Francisco and directed by the Christian Brothers and Daughters of Charity. **Nonprofit. Enrollment:** Approximately 1,216 (600 males, 616 females). **Average class size:** 28. **Accreditation:** WASC (6-year term. N/P years). **School year:** 10-month calendar. (N/P re: # instructional days) **School day:** 8:15 a.m. to 2:10 p.m. **Location:** In the northern part of San Francisco near the Civic Center, opposite St. Mary's Cathedral near Van Ness Avenue. It is accessible by three MUNI bus lines running along Van Ness Avenue.

## STUDENT BODY

**Geographical breakdown (counties):** Approximately 80% from San Francisco; 18% from San Mateo; 5% from Marin; 1.5% from Contra Costa. **Ethnicity:** 37.6% Caucasian (non-Latino); 18% Chinese; 18% multi-racial; 14% Filipino; 6.6% Hispanic; 2.3% other Asian; 2% African-American; 1.4% Japanese. **Foreign students (I-20 status):** 0. **Single parent/two f/t working parent families:** N/P. **Middle schools:** 80% of most recent entering freshman class came from 53 parochial schools; 20% from public and private, non-parochial middle schools. (N/P re #)

## ADMISSION

**Applications due:** Approximately December 10 (call for date). **Application fee:** $50. **Application process:** The school holds an open house in November. Half-day visits are scheduled for potential applicants from mid-September through late November. Applicants take the HSPT in January. Notifications are mailed mid-March. Decisions are based on grades in G7-8, test scores, and teacher/principal recommendations. **No. of applications:** Approximately 1,000 applications were received for 300 places in prior year's class. Five new students were admitted to G10. **Admission cut-off:** None. **Preferences:** Siblings, legacies, and Catholics. **"We are looking for** young men and women of excellent character who show promise of benefiting from and succeeding in the school's challenging program of academics and activities." **What sort of student do you best serve?** "SHCP serves the student who is interested in a well-rounded college preparatory education built on the philosophy and vision of our founders, St. John Baptist De La Salle and St. Vincent De Paul. As is stated in our mission statement, we 'strive to provide each student with the means to develop relationships founded on mutual respect and the belief in the intrinsic dignity of all people.' To be able to accomplish this we must have students who come from diverse communities and backgrounds."

# COSTS

**Latest tuition:** $6,650 payable in 1, 2, or 10 payments. **Sibling discount:** None. **Tuition increases:** 2-3% annually. **Other costs:** Approximately $675-750 in fees. **Financial aid:** The two religious orders offer approximately $280,000 in financial aid and scholarships. **Percentage of students receiving financial aid:** In 1998-99, 212 students applied for and 168 students received need-based assistance totaling $198,000. (Normally families earning more than $55,000 do not qualify.) **Average grant:** Approximately $1,200; largest award $1,800. **No. of full-tuition grants:** None. **Grants of half-tuition or more:** None. **Other aid:** In addition to need-based assistance, the school offers the De Paul Scholar Program—a $3,150 scholarship based upon students' "standardized test results, overall intellectual ability and achievement, potential, grade point average, and teacher/counselor recommendations that include considerations of how the applicants might thrive in the SHCP community dedicated to the principles of its founders. The De Paul Scholar Program culminates in the 12th grade with the senior seminar, a course offered for three hours one evening each week where students discuss readings from the Great Books. The course is taught by Dr. Kenneth W. Hogarty, who also teaches at a local 4-year college."

# SCHOOL'S MISSION STATEMENT/GOALS

"Inspired by and grounded in the philosophy and vision of St. John Baptist De La Salle and St. Vincent de Paul, respective founders of the Brothers of the Christian Schools and the Daughters of Charity, this school's mission is to help students live the Gospel, build a faith community, and serve others. Thus, faculty and staff provide each student with a quality college preparatory education and an opportunity to grow in his or her relationship with God. They strive to provide each student with the means to develop relationships founded on mutual respect and the belief in the intrinsic dignity of all people. They endeavor to nurture in each student a positive and realistic sense of pride and self-esteem."

# ACADEMIC PROGRAM

**Courses offered (AP=Advanced Placement, H=Honors, (AP)=AP option, (H)=Honors option): Religion:** Scripture 1-2, Christian Life 1, Church History 1-2, Morality 1, Senior Religion Electives (one each semester), Comparative Religion 1, Human Sexuality 1, Life after Life 1, Social Justice and Spirituality 1-2; **English:** English 1-2, English 3-4 (H), English 5-6 (H), English 7-8 (H, AP), Journalism 1-2, Speech 1-2 (after school); **Math:** Pre-Algebra 1-2, Algebra 1- 2 (H), Geometry 1-2, Advanced Algebra 1-2, Advanced Algebra and Trigonometry 1-2, Advanced Math 1-2 (Trigonometry and Analytical Geometry), Math Analysis 1-2, AP Calculus 1-2, AP Calculus 3-4 (Independent Study pending); **Science:** Biology 1-2 (H), Chemistry in the Community, Chemistry 1-2 (H), Physiology 1-2, Physics 1-2 (H); **Social Science:** World History 1-2 (H), US History 1-2 (H, AP), Civics 1 (H), American Government (AP), Economics 1, Psychology 1, Psychology AP 1-2, Sociology 1, Modern America 1, Vietnam 1; **Visual and Performing Arts:** Introduction to Art, Art 1-2, Art 3-4, Art 5-6, Introduction to Drama, Drama 1-2, Drama Production, Advanced Drama Production, Technical Theater, Chorus 1-2, Concert Choir 1-2, Music Appreciation 1-2; **Business and Practical Arts:** Accounting 1-2, Business Math 1-2, Computer Applications 1-2, Library Skills 1-2; **P.E./Health:** P.E./Health 1; **Foreign Languages:** French 1-6, AP French 7-8, Spanish 1-8, Spanish 1-6/Honors, AP Spanish 7-8, Japanese 1-8. **Computer lab and training:** The school has a computer lab with 37 IBM terminals. Students are required to take 1 semester of computer applications. **Grading:** Grades (letter grades) are sent to parents three times a semester, or approximately every six weeks. Parents may request informal progress reports from the student's counselor. **Graduation requirements:** 4 years English, 3 years math, 4 years religion, 2 years science (including biology), 2 years foreign language (requirement may be waived by proven ability in another foreign language), 3 years social science, 1 year visual and performing arts, 1 semester health/P.E., 1 semester computer applications. **Average nightly homework:** 2-3 hours. **Faculty:** The school has 77 lay teachers, 7 Christian Brothers, and 3 Daughters of Charity. The faculty is 58% male, 42% female. 31 faculty members hold bachelor's degrees as highest degree; 44 hold master's degrees (6 more are candidates); and 4 hold doctorates (2 more are candidates). **Faculty ethnicity:** N/P. **Faculty selection/training:** All faculty hold BA degrees and teaching credentials. **Teacher/student ratio:** 1:15. **Teacher's daily student load in required academic subject:** N/P. **AP courses/exams:** 22% of students are currently taking AP courses. In 1998, students took 250 AP exams in 8 subjects. 70% passed with a score of 3 or above. (N/P # takers) **Senior class profile (mean): SAT/ACT:** 1036.2 (SAT Math 526.6, Verbal 509.6); ACT Composite Score: 23.8. **GPA:** 2.98 (unweighted). **National Merit Scholarship Program:** N/P. **College enrollment:** 98.56% of last year's graduating class plan to attend college with 79.42% planning to attend 4-year colleges and universities (23% Catholic institutions), and 19.14%, 2-year colleges, including: CSU-SF (47), CSU-San

Jose (35), USF (22), San Francisco City C (21), St. Mary's (13), UC Davis (12), UC Santa Barbara (10), City C of San Mateo (10), Santa Barbara City C (8), Santa Clara (7), Cal Poly-SLO (6), UC Riverside (6), CSU-Long Beach (6), UC Irvine (5), CSU-Chico (5), UC Berkeley (4), Seattle U (4), Loyola Marymount (3), CSU-San Diego (3), Canada C (3), Skyline C (3), Diablo Valley C (3), CSU-Sonoma (2), Chabot C (2), UC San Diego (2), UCLA (2), UC Santa Cruz (2), MIT (2), Northeastern (2), US Naval Academy (2), Stanford, Emerson, Arizona State, Gonzaga, Regis, Academy of Art, U of Michigan, U of Oregon, Boston Conservatory, Menlo C, C of Notre Dame, Cornell, Pratt, Boston U, C of Wooster, CSU-Maritime, C of Marin, Foothill C, CSU-Humboldt, Cal Poly-Pomona, and Santa Rosa JC.

## OTHER INDICATORS THE SCHOOL IS ACCOMPLISHING ITS GOALS

"SHCP has an increasingly high applicant base, a very low attrition rate, and an innovative administration and faculty."

## CAMPUS/CAMPUS LIFE

**Campus description:** The campus occupies a city block. Its four buildings house classrooms, two chemistry and four biology labs, a computer lab, a library, a 2,300 sq. ft. weight room, a gymnasium and multipurpose playing field, and chapel. **Library**: 12,000 sq. ft.; 18,000 print volumes; 92 periodical subscriptions; study space for 176 students; 50 computer work stations; and an on-line catalog. Open to students from 7 a.m. to 5 p.m. (4 p.m. on Fridays). **Open/closed campus.** Closed. **Classroom space per student:** N/P. **Lunches:** Students may purchase lunches daily from the school cafeteria. **Bus service:** Public only. **Uniform/dress code:** No dyed hair or tattoos, no earrings for boys. Girls may wear the school skirt or pants that are not jeans. Boys wear school pants or shorts or other pants other than jeans. **Co-curricular activities/clubs:** Art Club, Block Club, Bowling Club, California Scholarship Federation (CSF), Chess Club, CLASS (Altar Servers), Earth Action, *Emerald* (newspaper), Junior Statesmen of America (JSA), International Thespian Society, Internet Club, Language Club, Model Building Club, *Oracle* (literary journal), Outdoors Club, Peer Educators, Peer Helpers, Photo Staff, Rally Board, Science Club, Ski Club, Speech Team, Sports Information, Sports Medicine, Step Team, Student Council, Yearbook, Yell Leaders. **Foreign exchange program:** Through an endowed scholarship program, students may travel and study abroad with faculty members during the summer and Christmas and Easter vacations. **Opportunities for community service:** Through the Campus Ministry program and religion classes, students choose from a variety of opportunities. The school also offers to juniors and seniors, through Campus Ministry, Venaver, a program to increase knowledge of social and economic problems of the world through travel to a Third World country where students interact with people in need. **Typical freshman schedule:** A typical school day includes seven 45-minute class periods, from 8:15 a.m. to 2:10 p.m.

## STUDENT SUPPORT SERVICES

**Counselor/student ratio (not including college counselors):** N/P. **Counseling:** The school's Counseling Department provides academic, personal, and college counseling to all students. Peer counseling is done by a small, select group of students under the direction of a faculty member. In conjunction with college counseling, the school provides career counseling to assist students in developing realistic career plans and means of implementing them. **Learning disabilities/ differences:** No special resources or programs. **Career apprenticeship programs:** N/P.

## STUDENT CONDUCT AND HEALTH

**Code of conduct:** N/P. **How school handles drugs/alcohol usage**: "Selling any controlled, mood-altering substance (alcohol, drugs, etc.) may be dealt with by immediate expulsion from the school. ... Regarding the possessing or being under the influence of any controlled, mood-altering substance ... the first offense will bring immediate suspension. The student will not be readmitted until there has been a drug education conference with the Dean of Students or Drug Counselor, the parents, and student. The second offense may be dealt with by immediate expulsion or may necessitate the student's enrollment in either an in-patient or out-patient treatment group depending on the seriousness of the chemical dependency. The determination will be made after consultation and evaluation of professional testing at an appropriate agency or institute. Failure to enroll and to participate in the designated program will result in expulsion. The third offense will bring immediate expulsion." **Drug/alcohol abuse prevention/AIDS awareness program:** Through the "IDEAS" program, students are taught drug/ alcohol abuse prevention at each grade level. AIDS awareness is part of the required P.E./health curriculum.

## SUMMER PROGRAMS

The school has a summer school for high school and pre-high school students. Cost: $210 per course for high school students (+ $35 registration); $150-300 for pre-high school students depending on number of courses taken (+ $25 registration).

## PARENT INVOLVEMENT

**Parent participation:** No required hours, but parents are encouraged to be involved in the Parents' Association, Boosters Club, and a variety of activities. **Parent/teacher communication:** Parents receive student grades three times a semester, or approximately every six weeks, and may request informal progress reports from the student's counselor. **Parent education:** Programs are offered through the counseling office, including single parent events, etc. **Donations:** Parents are asked to be involved in the Parents' Pledge Program.

## SPORTS

Students compete through the West Catholic Athletic League and the Girls Private School League in boys' basketball, baseball, cross-country, football, soccer, tennis, track and field, volleyball, and wrestling, and girls' basketball, cross-country, soccer, softball, tennis, track and field, and volleyball. The school also has a coed golf team and offers coed intramural volleyball, soccer, and basketball.

## WHAT SETS SCHOOL APART FROM OTHERS

"We have a nurturing and caring environment where individual respect is fostered on a daily basis. This is based on the teachings of St. John Baptist de la Salle and St. Vincent de Paul."

## HOW PARENTS/STUDENTS CHARACTERIZE SCHOOL

**Parent response(s):** "I truly believe that Sacred Heart Cathedral Prep is genuinely concerned with the overall growth of its students—academically, morally, and spiritually." "Good communication with students and parents." "Dedication of faculty and staff." "Because of their positive philosophy, my son wakes up every day happy and eager to go to school." "Heads are not 'buried in the sand'—the school deals with today's problems related to teens." "Discipline and a good environment." "Continuing the Christian education from the family environment." "High standards of academic studies and a clean and healthy environment for the students."

**Student response(s):** "I now feel prepared for college, especially academically, but I'll really miss my friends. The teachers would always help you after school whenever you needed it. I feel ready for college and have a sense of direction in my college science classes." —SHCP Alumnus now a UC Davis engineering major

"If I had to do it all over again, I would definitely go to SHCP. My experience with other high schools has made me see how well-rounded we are here and what a good job the faculty does working with the students. Some of my friends went to all-girl schools, and I think they are good schools, but I feel coeducational high schools are important to prepare for college. I think men and women should work together and learn about each other because that's what must happen in the outside world."—Alumna now a psychology major at UC Berkeley

*Illustration by Sacred Heart student Roger Royce*

# Sacred Heart Preparatory

150 Valparaiso Ave.
Atherton, CA 94027

(650) 322-1866 *fax (650) 322-7151*

www.schools.org
admission@schools.org

Richard Dioli, Principal
Carl Dos Remedios, Admission Director
Betsy Burdick, Assistant Director of Admission

## General

**Coed** day high school. **Independent Catholic** (70% Catholic). Founded in 1887. (The school shares a campus with St. Joseph's, a preK-8 school.) Founded in 1898 by the Religious of the Sacred Heart. **Nonprofit**, member CAIS. **Enroll-**

ment: 430. **Average class size:** 15. **Accreditation:** WASC/CAIS (6-year term: 1999-05), Sacred Heart Network. **School year:** 9-month calendar (approx. 173 instructional days). **School day:** 7:45 a.m. to 3 p.m. **Location:** At the border of Menlo Park and Atherton, 33 miles south of San Francisco, 2 miles north of Palo Alto.

# STUDENT BODY

**Geographical breakdown (counties):** 94% from San Mateo; 4% from Santa Clara; 2% from East Bay. **Ethnicity:** 79.9% Caucasian (non-Latino); 10.7% Asian; 6.1% Latino; 3.4% African-American. **Foreign students (I-20 status):** 0. **Single parent/two f/t working parent families:** N/P. **Middle schools:** 104 of the latest freshman class who applied came from public middle schools; 101 from private non-parochial schools; 61 from parochial schools; 28 from the school's middle school. (N/P re # schools) A good number of students come from St. Joseph's and from Menlo Park middle schools.

# ADMISSION

**Applications due:** Mid-January (call for exact date). **Application fee:** $50 (non-refundable). (An application fee waiver is available for those students for whom the application fee would be a hardship.) **Application process:** Applications are available on the school's web site. (Adobe Acrobat is required to download them.) Financial aid applications must be obtained through the admission office. Open houses are held in the fall and winter for students and their families. Interested families should call the school early in the fall to schedule a full day campus shadow visit for the applicant (these dates fill up quickly—it is important to call early). Applications must be on file prior to the shadow visit as applicants are interviewed on that day. Applicants must register for and take the HSPT, which the school administers twice in January. (The test is administered at many Catholic high schools throughout the Bay Area and may be taken at a location other than Sacred Heart with a request to forward results to Sacred Heart.) Students are also strongly encouraged to submit a writing sample (the HSPT test given at Sacred Heart include a writing sample), though it is not required. The school uses BAIHS recommendation forms for Principal/Counselor and Math/English teacher recommendations. Up-to-date middle school transcripts are also required. **No. of applications:** 345 applications were received for 105 places in the last freshman class. Four new students were admitted to G10; 2 to G11; 3 to G12. **Admission cut-off:** N/P. **Preferences:** Catholics, Alumni, siblings. "**We are looking for** very well rounded hardworking enthusiastic students who will appreciate the gift that their parents are giving them with a Sacred Heart education." **What sort of student do you best serve?** N/P.

# Costs

**Latest tuition:** $13,965. Tuition payment plans are available. **Sibling discount:** None. **Tuition increases:** Approx. 3-6% annually. **Financial aid:** Need-based financial aid is available. Some merit-based scholarships are available to incoming freshman. **Percentage of students receiving financial aid:** 35%. **Average grant:** $5,000. **No. of full tuition grants:** 0. **Grants of half-tuition or more:** 15%.

# School's Mission Statement/Goals

"Every Sacred Heart School offers an education that is marked by distinctive spirit, an education concerned for each student's total development: spiritual, intellectual, aesthetic, emotional, and physical. As a Sacred Heart School, Sacred Heart Preparatory emphasizes serious study, social responsibility, and lays the foundations of a strong faith. Five goals and criteria encompass the holistic nature of a Sacred Heart education. We seek to educate students toward: 1) a personal and active faith in God; 2) a deep respect for intellectual values; 3) a social awareness which impels to action; 4) the building of community as a Christian value; 5) personal growth in an atmosphere of wise freedom. These goals seek the development of persons who are knowledgeable, questioning, thoughtful and integrated. A Sacred Heart education provides students with a cognitive sense of values, allowing students to develop leadership skills, a knowledge of responsibility, and a sense of community based on mutual respect."

# Academic Program

**Courses offered (AP=Advanced Placement, H=Honors, (AP)=AP option, (H)=Honors option): Religious Studies:** Introduction to Religious Studies, Christian Scriptures, History of Christianity, Personal Ethics: Moral Decision-Making, Social Ethics: The Search for Justice, Christian Ministry and Leadership, Ethics and Technology, Prayer and Meditation, World Religions: The Search for Meaning, Relationships; **English:** English 1-Literary Genius, English 2-US Literature, English 3-World Literature & British Classics, Creative Literature, Expository Writing, Literature & Cinema, Myth to Literature, The Short Story, Literature of Renaissance and Revolution, Exploring Poetry: The Craft and Creation, AP English; **Social Science:** History I-Global Studies, History 2-History of the US, AP History of the US, History 3-World Civilization, Comparative Political Systems, Economics (H), Art History, Introduction to Russian History H, Comparative Constitutional Law Since 1945, History of American Foreign Policy, Revolution in Theory and Practice H, Society and the Individual, Psychology (AP), Model United Nations; **Math:** Algebra I, Geometry (H), Algebra

2, Algebra 2/Trig H, Functions, Statistics and Trigonometry, Pre-Calculus (H), AP Calculus AB, AP Calculus BC, AP Statistics; **Science:** Integrated Lab Science, General Biology, Biology H or AP, Chemistry (H, AP), Marine Biology, Anatomy and Physiology, Physics (H); **Foreign Language:** French 1-3 (H), French 4, French AP Language, Latin 1-4, Spanish 1, Spanish 2 (H), Spanish 3 (H), Spanish 4, Spanish AP Language; **Fine Arts:** Introduction to Art, Art 1, Advanced Art, Ceramics, Introduction to Sculpture, AP Art, Photography, Advanced Photography, Concert Choir, Chamber Choir, Applied Music, Drama 1-Acting Techniques/Scene Studies, Drama 2-6, Technical Theater & Design, Drama & Performance, Directing Project, Modern Dance, Yearbook; **Technology:** Computer Basics and Keyboarding, Introduction to Computer Technologies, Technology and Communications, The Internet and the World Wide Web, AP Computer Science-A, AP Computer Science -AB, Network Management, Technology Internship, Yearbook, Journalism 1-2; **P.E.:** Freshman P.E., Weight Training/Court Sports, Aerobics, Field Sports, Golf; **Media:** Intensive Reference Skills, Advanced Research Skills. **Special programs:** "Opportunities for interdisciplinary course work of independent projects are encouraged." Programs include the Freshman Interdisciplinary Honors Program, the Sophomore Symposium Project, and the Independent Honors Program for seniors. Exchange opportunities also exist within the network of 17 Sacred Heart schools in the United States. **Computer lab/training:** The school has 2 computer labs with NT stations and Macs. All classrooms have computers with Internet access and all students have e-mail accounts. (N/P re #, training) **Grading:** Letter grades two times a year. **Graduation requirements:** (Designed to meet UC requirements) 4 years English, 3.5 years religious studies, 4 years social science, 3 years math, 3 years science, 1.5 years fine arts, 3 years of the same foreign language, 1 year P.E., 100 hours of community service. **Average nightly homework (Mon-Th):** G9-12 3 hours. **Faculty:** 24% of faculty hold bachelor's degrees as highest degrees, 76% hold master's degrees. (N/P re gender) **Faculty ethnicity:** 87% Caucasian (non-Latino); .5% Latino; .5% African-American; 3% Asian. **Faculty selection/training:** "We have a professional growth budget, recently supplemented by funds from our recent Capital Campaign, which allows teachers to attend workshops, conferences, symposia, seminars and university extension courses. Many faculty also receive grants from outside organizations (NEH, Klingenstein, etc.) to pursue summer work connected with their teaching. While most of our faculty already have master's degrees and/or teaching credentials, teachers are encouraged and supported in their endeavors to earn these degrees while they are on the staff at SHP. There are also numerous occasions during which issues of pedagogy are addressed on campus by the entire teaching community: early-morning meetings, summer workshops, in-service days, department retreats, etc." **Teacher/student ratio:** 1:15. **Teacher's daily student load in required academic subject:** 70. **AP courses/exams:** In 1998, students took 168 AP exams in 17 subjects. 127 students achieved a score of 3 or better. All students enrolled in AP courses are required to take the AP test. (N/P re % in AP classes.) **Senior class**

**profile(mean)** (Class of 1999) SAT Math 610, SAT Verbal 627. **GPA:** 3.24 (Class of 1999) **National Merit Scholarship Program:** In the latest senior class, 7 students were commended, 1 was a finalist and a scholarship recipient. One National Hispanic Scholar Finalist. **College enrollment:** "95-100% of graduating seniors continue their education at 4-year institutions, 0-5% attend 2-year colleges with the intent of continuing as transfer students to 4-year programs." Last year's graduates are attending: American U, Boston C, Boston U, Brown, C of Santa Fe, Cal Poly-Pomona, Cal Poly-SLO, Clark U, Colorado C, Colorado State, Cornell, SCU-Chico, Davidson U, Duke, Embry Riddle, Georgetown, Harvey Mudd, MIT, Montana State-Bozeman, Oberlin, Occidental, Pitzer, Pomona, SCU-San Diego, Santa Clara, Scripps, Smith, SMU, Stanford, U of Arizona, U of Denver, U of Edinburgh (Scotland), U of Michigan, U of Oregon, U of Pennsylvania, U of Puget Sound, U of San Diego, USC, St. Andrew's (Scotland), UC Berkeley, UC Davis, UC Santa Barbara, UC San Diego, UC Santa Cruz, Vanderbilt, Villanova, Wake Forest, Wheaton, Whitman, and Willamette.

## Other Indicators the School is Accomplishing its Goals

(See Mission Statement, above.)

## Campus/Campus Life

**Campus description:** At the center of the 62-acre campus is the main building, built in 1897 as a girls' boarding school and convent. The three-story building houses offices, classrooms, a chapel, choir room, and a library. Across a courtyard (the Palm Court, where graduation is held) is the Little Theater and a separate wardrobe building. The Sports Center contains a gym, a dance studio, weight room and locker rooms. The campus also includes a new Aquatic Center with an Olympic-sized pool and a new football field. Three other buildings house classrooms, science, physics, math and chemistry labs, campus ministry, a library, computer labs, counseling offices and a 400-seat auditorium. **Library:** 11,000 print volumes; on-line periodical subscriptions; 12 computers (all with Internet access); on-line catalog; study space for 44 students. Open to students from 7:30 a.m. to 5 p.m.; full-time librarian (N/P sq. ft.). **Open/closed campus:** Closed. **Classroom space per student:** 900 sq. ft. **Lunches:** The cafeteria offers an extensive hot lunch menu daily provided by an outside caterer. **Bus service:** A shuttle service to/from the CalTrain station. **Uniforms/dress code:** Girls and boys may wear pants, including jeans (but not including athletic pants), walking shorts, t-shirts (absent inappropriate messages). Girls are required to wear dresses or skirts on liturgy days. They are not allowed to wear at any time, halter tops, tank tops, or midriff tops. Boys, for liturgy days, wear dress pants, collared shirt, and tie. Boys' hair may not extend over the collar and they may not have beards or moustaches. Only one ear stud is allowed for boys. Neither sex may wear hats or thong-sandals. No extreme dyed hair, tattoos, or piercings other than ears. **Co-curricular activities/clubs:** More than 30 clubs are represented on campus— all with faculty moderators or student representatives. **Foreign exchange program:** The school has a network exchange program with Sacred Heart Schools in the US and abroad. **Opportunities for community service:** 100 hours of community service are required for graduation. Students fulfill this requirement through various programs including 3-day trips to San Francisco to assist in homeless shelters and other services; house-building in Mexico; environmental justice programs in Yosemite. Students act as tutors in Redwood City elementary schools, and on a literacy project in East Palo Alto and intern with social service agencies such as the Boys' and Girls' Club and Packard Children's Hospital. Students choose projects that interest them at a volunteer fair held each September. **Typical freshman schedule:** Religion, math, English, history, science, P.E., fine arts, foreign language.

## STUDENT SUPPORT SERVICES

**Counselor-student ratio (not including college counselor):** 1:215. **Counseling:** The school has two college counselors who, along with the class advisors, work with students in college planning. Class advisors meet monthly with faculty to monitor academic progress and work individually with students on course selection, skills building and academic planning. **College counseling** begins freshman year with a parent/student college night. Some freshmen take the SAT II subject exams. Sophomores take the PSAT; some take the SAT IIs. Students are encouraged to attend a Case Study Workshop and College Fairs. Juniors are required to meet monthly in the spring to develop college and career options. Parents and students meet on a college night in the fall, and a Case Study Workshop is held in the Spring. Students take the PSAT/National Merit Scholarship Qualifying Test in the fall and the SAT I and II, ACT and AP exams in the spring. Seniors have required individual meetings and class meetings all year to assist in college and career choices. They take the entrance exams in the fall and AP exams in the spring. One full-time **personal counselor. Learning disabilities/differences:** "We have a full-time learning specialist." **Career apprenticeship programs:** None.

## STUDENT CONDUCT AND HEALTH

**Code of conduct:** The school requires students and parents to sign an honor code promising to "maintain honest, respectful relationships with all members of the Sacred Heart community; not copy/share homework; never plagiarize another's work; and uphold the policies and goals of Sacred Heart Prep." **How school handles drug/alcohol usage:** Zero tolerance (immediate dismissal) for using or selling drugs or alcohol. **Drug/alcohol abuse prevention/AIDS awareness:** "A health education program for freshmen will be part of the physical education curriculum and will focus on nutrition, body awareness, drug and alcohol awareness, and HIV/AIDS awareness."

## SUMMER PROGRAMS

Sports camp, drama camp.

## PARENT INVOLVEMENT

**Parent participation:** No required hours. **Parent/teacher communication:** The school has parent-teacher conferences at the end of the first quarter. **Parent education:** "The Parents' Association has a networking program for parents." **Donations:** N/P.

## SPORTS

More than 80% of the student body participates in competitive sports including tennis, cross-country, volleyball, water polo, basketball, soccer, softball, track, football, golf, and swimming.

## WHAT SETS SCHOOL APART FROM OTHERS

"Sacred Heart Preparatory places an emphasis on spiritual and moral development as much as academic excellence."

## HOW PARENTS/STUDENTS CHARACTERIZE SCHOOL

"The teaching profession is not merely conveying information. It is sharing a part of one's life, that education is based not just on facts but upon imparting values and understanding the importance of relationships."—Sacred Heart teacher

*Illustration by Saint Francis student Adam Worsham*

# SAINT FRANCIS HIGH SCHOOL

1885 Miramonte Avenue
Mountain View, CA 94040-4098

(415) 968-1213 *fax (415) 968-1706*
www.sfhs.com

Kevin J. Makley, President
Patricia I. Tennant, Principal
Bill Delaney, Director of Admissions, ext. 430

## GENERAL

**Coed** day high school. **Catholic.** (% Catholic: N/P.) Founded in 1955. Sponsored by the Brothers of Holy Cross, South-West Province, Saint Francis High School was originally a school for boys until 1972 when it merged with Holy Cross High School, an all-girls school administered by the Sisters of the Holy Cross. **Enrollment:** 1,455. **Average class size:** 30.5. **Accreditation:** WASC (6-year term: 1994-00). **School year:** Two 18-week semesters (N/P re # instructional days). **School day:** 7:50 a.m. to 2:30 p.m. **Location:** On the border of Mountain View and Los Altos, a suburb on the San Francisco Peninsula just south of Palo Alto.

# STUDENT BODY

**Geographical breakdown (counties):** N/P. **Ethnicity:** N/P. **Foreign students (I-20 status):** None. **Single parent/two f/t working parent families:** N/P. **Middle schools:** The school draws students from more than 80 middle schools. (# students: N/P)

# ADMISSION

**Applications due:** Usually third-fourth week in January (call for date). **Application fee:** $55. **Application process:** The school hosts an open house in December for interested families. Applicants must take the HSPT entrance/placement exam, submit 7th and 8th grade reports from their current school, and provide a Religious Affiliation form from their church. Applicants and parents must attend an interview/workshop in February. Decisions are sent out mid-March. **No. of applications:** 1,000-1,100 for 385 places in freshman class. (N/P: # new students) **Admission cut-off:** "Admission criteria include 1) 7/8th grade grades; 2) entrance exam; 3) teacher recommendation; 4) activity profile; and 5) interview." **Preferences:** Siblings, legacies, and Catholics. **"We are looking for"** N/P. **What sort of student do you best serve?** N/P.

# COSTS

**Latest tuition:** $5,875. **Sibling discount:** None. **Tuition increases:** 2-6%. **Percentage of students receiving financial aid:** 8+%. **Average grant:** $2,800. **No. of full-tuition grants:** 2. **Grants of half-tuition or more:** 42.

# SCHOOL'S MISSION STATEMENT/GOALS

"Saint Francis High School educates the whole person in the tradition of the Holy Cross. Saint Francis provides an environment which encourages students to achieve their highest potential through spiritual development, which imparts Christian values and promotes community service; through intellectual development, which fosters academic achievement and lifelong learning; and through social development, which provides exposure to a broad range of activities and experiences."

# ACADEMIC PROGRAM

"The Saint Francis curriculum is an academically challenging college preparatory program. Accelerated and honors classes are offered in all the traditional disciplines. An extensive elective program in the visual and performing arts and a state-of-the-art technology curriculum offer a variety of courses to meet the needs of our diverse and talented student body." **Courses offered (AP=Advanced Placement, H=Honors, (H)=Honors option, (AP)=AP option): History:** World History & Geography, World History & Geography-X, US History (AP), US Government (AP); **English:** English 1, 1-X, 2, 2-X, 3-H, British Literature/Advanced Writing, AP English 4, Senior English electives (Irish Literature; Sports in Literature), Speech 1 and 2 and Journalism 1 and 2; **Math:** Algebra 1, 1-X, 1-A, 1-B, Geometry, Geometry-S, Geometry-X, Intermediate Algebra, Algebra 2, Advanced Algebra/Trig/H, Trig/Analytic Geometry, Pre-Calculus, AP Calculus AB (H), AP Calculus BC (H), Applied Mathematics, Statistics; **Foreign Language:** French 1-3, 4-AP, 5-AP, German 1-4, 4-AP, Spanish 1-3, 4-AP, 5-AP, 2-A; **Computer Science:** Beginning Computer Science, Typing/Word Processing, Computer Literacy, Information Technology, Systems Technology; **Social Science:** Economics 1 and 2, Senior Economics, Psychology 1 and 2, Leadership, The Arab World and the West, Contemporary American Issues, Contemporary World Problems/World Cultures; **Religious Studies:** Religious Studies 1, Church and Sacrament, New Testament, Social Justice, Moral Issues, Christian Vocation, World Religions, Contemporary Christian Spirituality, Christianity and Philosophy; **Advanced Visual/Performing Arts:** Drama 3 and 4, Three-Dimensional Design, Oil, Watercolor, Printmaking, Computer Graphics, Symphonic Band 2, 3 and 4, Technical Drawing 1 and 2. **Computer lab/training:** The school has a fiber optic computer network (SFNet) that connects all buildings on campus and allows for cross-campus communication, access to the school library, a port into the Internet and the power to create multimedia applications. Over 250 computers on campus are dedicated solely to student use. Experience is offered on both the Pentium PC and Macintosh G3 platforms. In addition, the school provides 8 separate labs where different applications are taught. Each student receives an e-mail address. **Grading:** Letter grades A-F. **Graduation requirements:** 230 semester units, including 4 years religious studies, 4 years English, 3 years math, 3 years social studies, 2 years foreign language, 2 years science, .5 year health, 1.5 years P.E., 3 years electives, demonstrated computer literacy, and 50 hours community service. **Average nightly homework:** N/P. **Faculty:** 88 faculty members; 58% have advanced degrees. (N/P re gender) **Faculty ethnicity:** N/P. **Faculty selection/training:** N/P. **Teacher/student ratio:** N/P. **Teacher's daily student load in required academic subject:** N/P. **AP courses/exams:** In 1998, 278 students took 546 exams, the largest number in the school's history. (N/P re scores) **Senior class profile (mean):** (1998) SAT Math 563, SAT Verbal 564. **GPA:** 3.172 (Class of 1999 mean GPA, non-weighted, includes all subjects except P.E. during the freshman and sophomore years and service courses.) **National Merit Scholarship Program:** In 1998, the school had 13 finalists, 13 semifinalists, and 17 commended students. **College enrollment:** 86% of last year's graduating class enrolled in 4-year colleges, 14% in 2-year colleges, including: Santa Clara (17), UC Berkeley (12), Cal Poly-SLO (15), Harvard, Princeton, Tufts, Vanderbilt, Vassar, Yale, Stanford, and USC. (76 enrolled in the UC system; 52 in Catholic colleges and universities; 48 in California State universities; 18 in private schools in California; 44 in community colleges; and 63 in out-of-state schools.)

# OTHER INDICATORS THE SCHOOL IS ACCOMPLISHING ITS GOALS

Twice recognized since 1991 by Department of Education as a "National School of Excellence."

# CAMPUS/CAMPUS LIFE

**Campus description:** The school's campus is spread over 26 acres alongside a creek at the Los Altos/Mountain View border, in a residential neighborhood. The school buildings (including a new fine arts building) surround a large "quad"planted with grass and flowering plum trees. Outdoor facilities include a new Olympic-size pool, three baseball/softball/soccer fields, a football field and an all-weather track. **Library:** The school library is open from 7:30 a.m. - 5 p.m. The circulation system is fully automated with electronic catalog. Access to research databases. (N/P re study space, # volumes, sq. ft. etc.) **Open/closed campus:** Closed. **Classroom space per student:** N/P. **Lunches:** N/P. **Bus service:** N/P. **Uniform/dress code:** Dress code. **Co-curricular activities/clubs:** Activities include ASB, Band, Chess Club, CSF, Drama, Foreign Language Honor Society, Forensics, International Club, Intramurals, JSA, Monogram, Multicultural Art Club, NHS, newspaper, Peer Helpers, Poetry Club, Radio Club, Students Against Driving Drunk (SADD), Service Club/Interact, Shakespeare Club, Spirit Commission, Spirit Groups, Stock Market Club, Technology Club, Voices of Hope, Yearbook. **Foreign exchange program:** The school has a program with a sister school in Santiago, Chile. **Opportunities for community service:** N/P. **Typical freshman schedule:** N/P.

# STUDENT SUPPORT SERVICES

**Counselor/student ratio (not including college counselors):** 1:175. **Counseling:** "Student support services include those provided through Campus Ministry, the Guidance and Counseling Department and Peer Helpers." **Learning disabilities/differences:** N/P. **Career apprenticeship programs:** N/P.

# STUDENT CONDUCT AND HEALTH

N/P.

# SUMMER PROGRAMS

N/P.

# PARENT INVOLVEMENT

**Parent participation:** Parents are invited to become involved in the school's Men's and Women's Clubs. Parents organize and participate in events including the Father-Son Communion Breakfast, the Lancer Auction, and the Twilight Retreat held each spring. They work on projects from monthly mailings to concessions for sporting events and serve on committees in areas such as technology. **Parent/teacher communication:** N/P. **Parent education:** "The school offers several seminars each year to help educate parents. They include a special speakers' series which the Women's Club oversees; example topics this year include 'Ten Successful Keys to Parenting Teens,' and 'Goal Setting.' The Guidance and Counseling Department sponsors several seminars throughout the year including: a freshman/sophomore parent evening discussing choosing appropriate courses with an eye toward college; a sophomore parent meeting discussing appropriate curfews, peer pressure and teen parties; and a junior college parent night explaining the application process for various categories of colleges." **Donations:** N/P.

# SPORTS

Boys' cross-country, football, water polo, basketball, soccer, wrestling, baseball, swimming, tennis, track, volleyball. Girls' cross-country, field hockey, tennis, volleyball, water polo, basketball, soccer, gymnastics, softball, swimming, track. Coed golf. Holy Cross Aquatic Center, completed in October, 1998, has a 50-meter Olympic size pool.

# OTHER

"Saint Francis High School respects and promotes the dignity and worth of each individual, promoting Christian values and challenging students to take those values and apply them in their lives outside of the classroom."

# WHAT SETS SCHOOL APART FROM OTHERS

"Saint Francis High School was founded in the Holy Cross tradition of educating the hearts and minds of young people to serve the world. This heritage of education and service continues today as the school strives to develop the well-rounded individual who grows spiritually, intellectually and socially."

# HOW PARENTS/STUDENTS CHARACTERIZE SCHOOL

N/P.

# St. Ignatius College Preparatory

2001 37th Avenue
San Francisco, CA 94116

(415) 731-7500
www. siprep.org

Mr. Charles Dullea, Principal
Mr. Kevin M. Grady, Director of Admissions

## General

**Coed** day high school. **Catholic** (Jesuit) (82% Roman Catholic; 12% other Christian; 6% non-Christian). Founded in 1855. **Nonprofit. Enrollment:** Approximately 1,415. **Average class size:** 28. **Accreditation:** WASC (6-year term: 1994-2000). **School year:** 10-month calendar (180 instructional days). **School day:** 8:30 a.m. to 2:15 p.m. **Location:** Located at 37th Avenue and Quintara, one block west of Sunset Blvd., in the Sunset District, the school is accessible by the 29 MUNI bus line and the L-Taraval streetcar.

## Student Body

**Geographical breakdown (entering freshman class, counties):** Approximately 51% from San Francisco; 12% from Marin; 33% from San Mateo; 2% from East Bay. **Ethnicity (latest entering class):** Approximately 52% Caucasian (non-Latino); 12% Latino; 12% Filipino; 12% Asian; 6.5% African-American. **Foreign students (I-20 status):** 0. **Single parent/two f/t working parent families:** N/P. **Middle schools:** 75% of the most recent entering freshman class came from parochial schools; 12% from public middle schools; 13% from private, non-parochial schools. (N/P re #)

## Admission

**Applications due:** December 10 (call for date). **Application fee:** $50. **Application process:** St. Ignatius holds one Sunday afternoon open house in the fall. Students must take the HSPT. **No. of applications:** 1,100 applications were received for 350 places in prior year's class. Two new students were admitted to G10, 2 to G11. **Admission cut-off:** N/P. **Preferences:** Qualified Catholics, legacies, siblings, and poor. **"We are looking for** academically talented, spiritually open and active participants." **What sort of student do you best serve?** "We best serve students who are looking for the total package—a rigorous college preparatory school, a Catholic school, and a school with a wide range of co-curricular activities. Students must be open to the spiritual dimension of the school."

## COSTS

**Latest tuition:** $7,245 payable in 10 monthly payments. **Sibling discount:** None. **Tuition increases:** N/P. [Ed. Note: last increase 5.2%.] **Other costs:** Registration fee of $295, approximately $275 for books. **Financial aid:** Need-based. **Percentage of students receiving financial aid:** 18%. **Average grant:** $2,400. **No. of full-tuition grants:** N/P. **Grants of half-tuition or more:** N/P.

## SCHOOL'S MISSION STATEMENT/GOALS

N/P.

## ACADEMIC PROGRAM

Saint Ignatius offers a college preparatory curriculum representing "a combination of courses fundamental to the Ignatian spirit of education, and including every aspect of the St. Ignatius experience: religious, social, and psychological, as well as academic. The kind of student St. Ignatius is striving to form is open to growth, intellectually competent, religious, loving, committed to doing justice, and capable of leadership." Students are required to enroll in six classes each semester. **Courses offered (H=Honors, AP=Advanced Placement, (H)=Honors option, (AP)=AP option): Computer Education:** Computer Applications, Computer Science AP; **English:** English 100, English 103 H, English 200, English 203 H, English 300, English 303 H, English 403 AP, English 462-From Page to Screen, English 430-Modern American Authors, English 440-Shakespeare, English 450-Mythology, English 460-Fiction into Film, English Short Fiction, English 472-Asian American Literature, English 492-Poetry, English 407-Writing for College, English 487-Creative Writing; **Fine Arts:** Art and Architecture I-II, Studio Art 1-2, Sculpture: 3-dimensional Mixed Media, Photography I, Dance I-II, Acting: Scene Study, Advanced Acting, Music Appreciation, Survey of Early American Jazz, Beginning Band/Orchestra, Intermediate Band, (by audition: Acting/Drama Workshop, Musical Theater Workshop II, Dance Workshop, Mixed Chorus, Advanced Vocal Ensemble, Symphonic Orchestra, Jazz Band, String Quartet, Dixieland Band, Independent Study: Music Ensemble); **Foreign Language:** French 1-4, French 1 Accelerated, French 2 H, French 3 H, French 4 AP, Spanish for Spanish Speakers, Spanish 1-4, Spanish 1 Accelerated, Spanish 2 H, Spanish 3 H, Spanish 4 AP, Spanish 5 AP Literature, Latin 1-4, Latin 3 H, Latin 4 AP, German 2, Japanese 1-3, Japanese 4 H; **Math:** Algebra I, Algebra I H, Algebra 2 H, Geometry (H), Algebra 2, Pre-Calculus A H, Pre-Calculus B H Math Analysis, Problem Solving Strategies, Intro. to Trigonometry, Calculus (AP),

Calculus AB; **P.E.:** P.E. 100-General Physical Education, P.E. 200- Weight Training and Fitness, P.E. 300- Recreational Sports, P.E. 400-Competitive Sports, P.E. 500-Beginning/Intermediate Aquatics; **Religious Studies:** Religious Studies 110-Hebrew Scriptures, Religious Studies 111-Christian Scriptures, Religious Studies 210-Sacraments & Relationships, Religious Studies 310-Morality and Social Justice, Religious Studies 440-The Gospel & Jesus, Religious Studies 442-The Search for Spiritual Meaning, Value and Belief, Religious Studies 444-Liturgy and Worship, Religious Studies 445-History of the Church, Religious Studies 446-Ministry, Religious Studies 447-Faith: A Universal Reflection (Major World Religions); **Science:** General Science, Biology (H, AP), Chemistry (AP), Science Research Project, Physics (H, AP), Human Anatomy & Physiology; **Social Sciences:** World History I (to 1914), World History 2 (20th Century), American History (AP), American Government (H, AP), Asian History in the 20th Century, History of California, European History, Economics, Intro. to Psychology, AP Psychology, AP Introductory Psychology. **Computer lab/training:** N/P. **Grading:** A-F. **Graduation requirements:** 100 hours community service, 4 years English, 3 years math, 2 years same foreign language, 2.5 years science, 3 years social science, 3.5 years religious studies, 1 year fine arts, 1 year P.E., 4 years college prep electives. **Average nightly homework:** G9: 2.5 hours; G10: 3.5 hours; G11-12: 4.5 hours. **Faculty:** 64% male, 36% female. 49 faculty members hold bachelor's degrees as highest degree; 59 hold master's degrees; and 6 hold doctorates. **Faculty ethnicity:** N/P. **Faculty selection/training:** N/P. **Teacher/student ratio:** 1:16.4. **Teacher's daily student load in required academic subject:** 140 students per day. **AP courses/exams:** In 1998, 526 students took 1,054 AP examinations in 16 subjects. 77% received scores of 3 or above. (St. Ignatius was ranked 19th in the nation this year in size of its AP program. Many students take and pass AP exams without having taken the corresponding AP course.) **Senior class profile (mean):** SAT Math 586, SAT Verbal 598. **GPA:** N/P. **National Merit Scholarship Program:** Six finalists in latest year's class. **College enrollment:** 100% of last year's graduating class enrolled in college; 94% in 4-year colleges, 6% in 2-year colleges. Of the 90%, 38% enrolled in UC universities and 16% in Jesuit universities. Colleges/universities included: American U (2), Auburn U, Bethamy C, Boston U (2), Brown, Bryn Mawr, Cal Poly-SLO (7), Cal Poly-Pomona, SCU-Long Beach, SCU-Sacramento, Canada C (2), CSU-Chico (3), SF City C (10), C of Marin (3), C of San Mateo (5), Columbia C, Cornell, Cuesta C (2), Dartmouth, Fairfield U (3), Foothill C (2), Fordham, Georgetown (4), Gonzaga (2), Harvard (2), Howard (2), Loyola Marymount (22), MIT, Marymount C, Morehouse C, Northern Arizona U, NYU (2), Northeastern (2), Occidental C, Pomona, Princeton, Purdue (2), Reed, Regis U (4), CSU-San Diego (3), CSU-SF (11), CSU-San Jose (6), Santa Barbara CC (2), Santa Clara (16), Santa Monica CC, Seattle U (4), Skyline C (2), CSU-Sonoma (5), St. Mary's, Stanford (10), Syracuse (2), Tulane, U of Arizona (6), U of Colorado, U of Maryland, U of Nevada, Notre Dame, U of Oregon, Oregon State, U of Pennsylvania, U of Portland (2), U of Puget Sound, U of San Diego (11), U of Virginia, U of Washington (2), UC Berkeley (33), UC Davis (26), UC Irvine (2), UCLA (21),

UC Riverside (2), UC San Diego (15), UC Santa Barbara (27), UC Santa Cruz (8), US Air Force Academy, USC (5), USF (14), Vanderbilt, Villanova, Wellesley, West Valley JC (2), Willamette and Yale.

## OTHER INDICATORS THE SCHOOL IS ACCOMPLISHING ITS GOALS

N/P.

## CAMPUS/CAMPUS LIFE

**Campus description:** The 11.5 acre campus includes three buildings housing classrooms, administration, an indoor swimming pool, two theaters, a gymnasium, cafeteria, and chapel. The grounds consist of a full-size football field, four tennis courts, baseball diamond and practice cages, soccer field, and track. **Library**: 18,000 print volumes; 80 periodical subscriptions; 12 Macintosh computers (one with Internet access); study space (32 desks wired for laptops); 3 librarians. It is available to students daily from 7:30 a.m. to 5 p.m. Monday-Thursday and until 3:30 p.m. on Friday. (N/P. re sq. ft.) **Open/closed campus:** Closed. **Classroom space per student:** N/P. **Lunches:** May be purchased at the school cafeteria. **Bus service:** Charter service available from San Mateo and Marin Counties. Cost: N/P. **Uniform/dress code:** Dress code allows shirts with sleeves, school T-shirts, pants or walking shorts but not jeans, tights, or sweats, skirts/sleeved dresses no shorter than 4" above kneecap. Two earrings per ear are allowed but no other facial or body piercings; no spiked hair, unnaturally dyed hair, or facial hair. **Co-curricular activities/clubs:** All freshman are required to choose at least one activity (*=those that satisfy freshman requirement). Clubs and activities include: A.A.A.S. (Association of African American Students), Ambassador Club, Asian Students Coalition, Art & Publicity Committee*, Band*, Big Brothers & Sisters, Cycling Club, Block Club, California Scholarship Federation, Cheerleaders, Chess Club, Christian Life Community*, Computer Club*, Democratic Youth Rally, Drama Club*, *Ignatian* (Yearbook), *Inside SI* (newspaper), Irish Club, Italian Club, Junior Statesmen of America, Latino Club, Liturgy Club, Orchestra*, Social Justice, Rally Committee, Science Club*, Service Club, Speech and Debate*, Spirit Club, Student Council, Video Yearbook*, Wildcat Welcoming Club, and Young Republican Club. **Foreign exchange program:** No formal programs. **Opportunities for community service:** The community service program has two directors and offers hundreds of community service opportunities including in parishes, hospitals, day care and recreation centers, convalescent homes, and summer schools and camps. At least 50 hours must be spent working with a disadvantaged segment of society. **Typical freshman schedule:** English 100, Algebra I, French 1, P.E., Religious Studies 110, General Science, Beginning Band (5 periods of 50 minutes each, 50-minute lunch).

# STUDENT SUPPORT SERVICES

**Counselor/student ratio (not including college counselors):** N/P. **Counseling:** The school has 11 counselors, including a full-time academic support service coordinator, and three college counselors. The counselors provide individual and academic counseling, alcohol and drug counseling, assistance with transition to high school, assistance with SAT, SAT II and AP exam preparation, and career and college counseling. **Learning disabilities/differences:** "The school accepts some gifted students with mild, documented learning disabilities. Through its Academic Support Services program, such students are given reasonable accommodations such as extra time on major exams, etc." **Career apprenticeship programs:** N/P.

# STUDENT CONDUCT AND HEALTH

**Code of conduct:** N/P. **How school handles tobacco/drugs/alcohol usage:** No smoking within five blocks of campus. For a first violation of rules against possession, use, or sale of alcohol, illegal drugs or controlled substances at school or at school sponsored event or activity, the student is automatically suspended, placed on disciplinary probation for at least three months, and required to undergo alcohol/drug assessment, substance abuse counseling, and a treatment program; the student is also required to perform work for the school. Any subsequent violation within the student's four years may result in expulsion. (All athletes and fine arts participants who are found to have been using alcohol or drugs on or off campus during season are prohibited from further participation.) **Drug/alcohol abuse prevention/AIDS awareness program:** The required freshman P.E. course includes drug and alcohol education components.

# SUMMER PROGRAMS

SI offers academic summer school (1/2 day) for students entering G8-9 (English, math, computer skills, and electives). Limited high school course offerings.

# PARENT INVOLVEMENT

**Parent participation:** N/P. **Parent/teacher communication:** Report cards are sent to parents twice each semester. Parents may arrange parent-teacher conferences with an individual teacher or a conference with the student's counselor at any time. **Parent education:** N/P. **Donations:** The school has a parent pledge program. Parents who are able to make tax deductible contributions to offset the difference of approximately $1,800 in the cost of education versus the tuition are asked to do so.

# SPORTS

More than 60 interscholastic teams including boys' cross-country, football, water polo, volleyball, tennis, basketball, soccer, wrestling, baseball, crew, golf, lacrosse, swimming, diving, tennis, track & field, and volleyball; girls' cross-country, water polo, field hockey, volleyball, tennis, basketball, soccer, softball, crew, swimming, diving, lacrosse, and track & field. In addition, intramural sports are played during the lunch period.

# OTHER

"SI's retreat program presents students with special opportunities for personal growth, spiritual reflection, and community building. We have retreats for all levels of students, and the vast majority of them attend a retreat each of the four years at SI. Junior and senior retreats are not mandatory, yet over 90% of both classes still choose to attend these events. The senior year retreat is a privately directed, three-day encounter with God based upon the Spiritual Exercises of St. Ignatius of Loyola. Students often describe this intense experiential retreat as one of their most important experiences at SI."

# WHAT SETS SCHOOL APART FROM OTHERS

"Jesuit philosophy, total education, and forming, to paraphrase the words of Father Pedro Arrupe, S.J., 'men and women for and with others.'"

St. Ignatius High School's "Profile of the Graduate at Graduation" is a statement of academic abilities and personal characteristics the school seeks to instill in its students by the time of graduation. The school seeks to graduate students who are open to growth, intellectually competent, religious, loving, and committed to doing social justice, and who are committed to the pursuit of leadership growth.

# HOW PARENTS/STUDENTS CHARACTERIZE SCHOOL

**Parent response(s):** "SI offers something for every student."
**Student response(s):** Students describe SI as a "family," with a great sense of community.

# St. Joseph Notre Dame High School

1011 Chestnut Street
Alameda, CA 94501

(510) 523-1526

Anthony V. Aiello, Principal
Kathie Montserrat, Director of Admission

## GENERAL

**Coed** day high school. **Catholic** (76% Catholic). Founded in 1881. **Nonprofit.**
**Enrollment:** 560. **Average class size:** 28. **Accreditation:** WASC (6-year term:
1994-00). **School year:** 9.5 month calendar (181 instructional days). **School
day:** 8:15 a.m. to 3 p.m. **Location:** In central Alameda on Chestnut St. between
Encinal and San Jose. Accessible from the Fruitvale BART Station on AC Transit
50 to Encinal and San Jose Ave., and from the 12th Street BART Station on AC
Transit 51A to Santa Clara and San Jose Ave.

## STUDENT BODY

**Geographical breakdown (counties):** 99% from Alameda. **Ethnicity:** 37%
Caucasian (non-Latino); 28% Asian; 18% African-American; 16% Latino; 1%
other. **Percentage foreign students (I-20 status):** 0. **Single parent/two f/t working parent families:** N/P. **Middle schools:** 70% of the most recent entering
freshman class came from 12 parochial schools; 23% from 13 public middle
schools; 7% from 5 private, non-parochial schools.

## ADMISSION

**Applications due:** Approximately January 20 (call for date). **Application fee:**
$50. **Application process:** An open house is held on a Sunday afternoon in
October. Information Night is in mid-January. The HSPT is given at end of
January. Interviews with prospective students and parents take place at the end of
February. Decisions are mailed out in March. Decisions are based on several
criteria: test score, 7th and 8th grade performance, and recommendations from
current principal, math, and English teachers. **No. of applications:** 238 applications were received for 160 places in prior year's class. **Admission cut-off:** "Generally speaking, we will consider students who score above the 50% nationally."
**Preferences**: Alameda Catholic middle school students, other Catholic students,
non-Catholic students from surrounding areas. "**We are looking for** students
who wish to pursue a rigorous college prep academic program in a Catholic-

Christian environment; who are well-rounded with interests in athletics, drama or stage craft, art, and/or music; students willing to work to their full potential and who wish to be an active member of the SJND community." **What sort of student do you best serve?** "SJND serves best those students who are motivated to prepare themselves for acceptance at a 4-year university in a high school environment supportive of Catholic/Christian values. Our program is designed to challenge the gifted student and to develop the skills of the average to above-average student to meet that goal. Students who have athletic, artistic, leadership, and musical talent are valued for those skills as well."

# Costs

**Latest tuition:** $4,800 for St. Joseph Basilica parishioners; $5,150 for other Catholic families; $6,000 for non-Catholics. Tuition is payable in 10 monthly payments. **Sibling discount:** None. **Tuition increases:** 5-8% annually. **Other costs:** Registration fee $400; misc. fees (parents' club, yearbook, subject materials, graduation, etc.) $75-$150; textbooks $200-$400; uniforms $100-$200 (uniform exchange and assistance is available). **Percentage of students receiving financial aid:** 21%. **Average grant:** $972. **No. of full-tuition grants:** None. **Grants of half-tuition or more:** 12-15%.

# School's Mission Statement

"St. Joseph Notre Dame is a Catholic, coeducational, college preparatory parish high school which is dedicated to the development of the whole person. St. Joseph Notre Dame and the parish communities have a rich tradition and long history of Catholic secondary education in Alameda. Our program of instruction emphasizes academic excellence, teaches moral values, and encourages service within the context of a faith community."

# Academic Program

**Courses offered (AP=Advanced Placement, H=Honors, (AP)=AP option, (H)=Honors option): Computer Science**: Computer Literacy, Computer Graphics & Multimedia, Personal Keyboarding; **English:** English Workshop, English 1 & 2 (required for freshmen & sophomores), English I H, English 2 H, English 3 (H), English 4 (AP), World Literature & Electives in: Literature of the British Isles, Magical Realism, The 'Isms: Literary Movements as Responses to Politics and World Views, Yearbook, Journalism; **Foreign Language:** French 1, 2, 3, AP French 4, Spanish 1A & 1B, Spanish 1, 2, 3 (H), AP Spanish 4; **Math:** Pre-Algebra, Algebra 1, Geometry (H), Finite Math/Algebra 2, Algebra 2, Algebra 2/Trigonometry H, Math Analysis, Pre-Calculus, AP Calculus AB or BC, Accounting; **P. E.:** P.E. 1, P.E. 2; **Religion:** (all are semester-length classes) Christian Life & the Teenager, Introduction to Hebrew Scriptures, Jesus in The Christian Scriptures, Sacraments & Worship, Christian Morality, Justice & Peace: The Christian in Society, World Religions, Christian Life Styles, Religious Themes in Literature and Film, History of the Catholic Church, Catholic Traditions; **Science:** Biology (H, AP), Integrated Physical Science, Chemistry (H), Physics (AP), Anatomy & Physiology, Environmental Biology; **Social Studies:** World History, US History (AP), American Government, Economics, Ethnic Studies, Leadership, Peer Support, Psychology; **Visual & Performing Arts:** Introduction to Art, Art 2: Drawing & Painting, Art 3: Portfolio Seminar, AP Art Studio, Drafting 1, 2, 3, Introduction to Drama, Drama 1, Beginning Band, Concert Band, Choral 1 & 2. **Computer lab/training:** SJND has a one-semester freshman computer literacy requirement and offers electives in Personal Keyboarding, and Graphics & Multimedia Production. (N/P re lab) **Grading:** Letter grades A-F are given quarterly and at semesters. **Graduation requirements:** "SJND's graduation requirements exceed all of the State of California High School Graduate requirements." Semester units (5 per course) are taken as follows: 4 years English, 4 years religion, 3 years social studies, 2 years math, 2 years foreign language, 2 years science, 1 year P.E., .5 year computer literacy, 1 year fine arts, 4 years electives, minimum 40 hours Christian Service. **Average nightly homework:** G9: 1.5-2 hours; G10: 2-2.5 hours; G11-12: 2-3 hours. **Faculty:** 62% male, 38% female. Of 45 teachers and administrators, 20 hold bachelor's degrees as highest degree; 24 hold master's degrees; and 1 holds a doctorate. **Faculty ethnicity:** 75% Caucasian (non-Latino); 13% Latino; 5% African-American; 3% Filipino; 3% Asian. **Faculty selection/training:** Faculty are selected by a 3-person committee made of the Principal, Assistant Principal, and Department Chair for the position open. All teachers are required to have a teaching credential or be in the process of obtaining one. Six units of continuing education are required for all faculty every 3 years. **Teacher/student ratio:** 1:15. **Teacher's daily student load in required academic subject:** N/P. **AP courses/exams:** 13% of students are currently taking AP courses. In 1998, 63 students took 85 AP examinations in 9 subjects. 88% received scores of 3 or above. **Senior class profile (mean):** N/P. **National Merit Scholarship Program:** In 1998, 1 semi-finalist and 5 commended. **College enrollment:** 83% of last year's graduating class enrolled in 4-year colleges, 15% in 2-year colleges. 4-year schools include: UC campuses (Berkeley, LA, Davis, Irvine, Riverside, Santa Cruz,), CSU campuses (Hayward, San Francisco, San Jose, Sonoma, Cal Poly-SLO), USC, U of Pennsylvania, USF, U of Houston, Arizona State U, Stanford, Gonzaga, St. Mary's C, Notre Dame C.

## OTHER INDICATORS THE SCHOOL IS ACCOMPLISHING ITS GOALS

N/P.

# CAMPUS/CAMPUS LIFE

**Campus description:** SJND's campus includes four buildings housing classrooms, a counseling center, music room, and a gymnasium. It has a substantial quad area with lawn, trees, and picnic tables. It is situated in a quiet residential neighborhood and is part of a larger Catholic parish plant including a church and separate elementary school. **Library:** 1,600 sq. ft.; 4,000 print volumes; 20 computers, all with Internet access; 15 print periodical subscriptions; study space for 35 students. Open to students from 7:30 a.m. to 4 p.m. **Open/closed campus:** Closed. **Classroom space per student:** N/P. **Lunches:** Hot lunches available—approx. $2. **Bus service:** Public only—AC Transit Lines 50 and 51A. **Uniforms/dress code:** Uniform wardrobe, moderate jewelry, makeup, and hairstyles. **Co-curricular activities/clubs:** Together, the six student body officers, class officers (seven from each Division) and ten Campus Ministers form the Campus Life Team which works to provide both social and spiritual opportunities for the students of SJND. Additionally, students may join the Outdoor Club, Academic Team, Computer Club, Latino Club, FASO (Filipino American Student Organization), African-American Student Association, Social Justice Committee, California Scholarship Federation, and National Honor Society. **Student Publications:** *Prisms* (literary magazine), *Kaleidoscope* (newspaper), *Reflections* (yearbook). **Foreign exchange program:** N/P. **Opportunities for community service:** All students are required to volunteer a minimum of 10 hours each academic year as their Christian Service graduation requirement. Students select activities at an annual "Service Fair," to which service providers and agencies are invited. **Typical freshman schedule:** (7-period day, 45-minute classes, 5 minutes passing, 35-minute lunch) English, Algebra 1, Spanish/French 1, Religion, Computer Literacy, World History, P.E.

# STUDENT SUPPORT SERVICES

**Counselor/student ratio (not including college counselors):** 1:140. **Counseling:** SJND has a staff of four full-time counselors. Academic and preparatory **college counseling** begins in the freshman year and proceeds in scope and direction as the student advances. Formal college counseling begins in junior year. The Counseling Center has both print and electronic resources for college searches and financial aid research. **Personal counseling** with referral service is also provided. **Learning disabilities/differences:** No special programs or resources. **Career apprenticeship programs:** "Counselors provide information about special programs to all students in 11th and 12th grades and assist students in applying for such programs."

## STUDENT CONDUCT AND HEALTH

**Code of conduct:** In addition to standard provisions, students are expected to conduct themselves as ethical young men and women. Courteous and respectful behavior toward faculty and their peers as well as respect for the personal property of others is expected at all times. **How school handles drugs/alcohol usage:** Violation of laws regarding the use of alcohol, narcotics, and other drugs is treated as an extremely serious disciplinary problem. Consequences may include referral to counseling, suspension, and/or expulsion from school. **Drug/alcohol abuse prevention/AIDS awareness program:** In conjunction with the freshman P.E./health component, a Chemical Dependency certified counselor conducts a weekly workshop for a full quarter focusing on all chemical dependency issues. Additionally there is a Chemical Dependency Support Group which meets with a counselor. SJND participates in "Red Ribbon Week" and SADD (Students Against Drunk Driving) Week preceding the Junior-Senior Prom.

## SUMMER PROGRAMS

Three types of classes are offered: skill development in math and English for incoming freshmen, review classes in math and foreign language for current students, and electives such as drama and computer literacy for current students. Cost: $175-$200 per class.

## PARENT INVOLVEMENT

**Parent participation:** All parents are members of the Parent Association which raises funds for school enhancement and provides ongoing social and clerical support for the school. Additionally, parents are required to volunteer one evening each school year to assist with Bingo, a fundraiser which keeps the school's tuition affordable, or they may choose to make a donation of $80 in lieu of that obligation. **Parent/teacher communication:** Written progress reports are sent to parents of students whose grade in any class is C- or lower at mid-quarter of each grading period. Report card nights are held at the first and third quarter grading periods to allow parents to meet with teachers and discuss the progress of their daughter/son. Parents may schedule additional individual conferences with teachers as needed. **Parent education:** "The Parents' Association from time to time offers speakers who address parents' areas of interest/concern." **Donations:** "Parents are asked to volunteer an annual gift of $125 to the Parents' Progress Fund."

## SPORTS

SJND is a member of the Alameda-Contra Costa Athletic League (ACCAL), the North Coast Section (NCS), and the California Interscholastic Federation (CIF). Girls compete in volleyball (jv, v), tennis, cross-country (frosh-soph, jv, v); basketball (jv, v), soccer (jv, v), softball (jv, v), golf, track (frosh-soph, jv, v), and swimming. Boys complete in: cross-country (frosh-soph, jv, v); basketball (frosh, jv, v), soccer (jv, v); tennis, baseball (jv, v), golf, track (frosh-soph, jv, v), swimming, and volleyball.

# OTHER

SJND provides a coordinated four-year retreat program which is co-curricular and culminates in senior year with a 4-day, 3-night Kairos Retreat. In association with the Close Up Foundation, SJND provides students the opportunity for a week-long study trip to Washington, D.C., annually. Additionally, study tours are generally offered each year to other locations such as Costa Rica, England, France, as well as expanded European tours.

# WHAT SETS SCHOOL APART FROM OTHERS

"SJND is unique in its size, its broad academic mission, and its Catholicity. Because we are limited to 560 students, SJND is a close-knit community where people know and care for each other and students do not 'fall through the cracks.' Although SJND is small, it offers significant numbers and levels of college preparatory classes. Traditional Catholic moral and social values are both taught in the classroom and lived through regular liturgies and prayer services, a coordinated four-year retreat program which involves *all* students, Christian Service, and Social Justice activities."

# HOW PARENTS/STUDENTS CHARACTERIZE SCHOOL

**Parents response(s):** "St. Joseph Notre Dame High School was the perfect choice for our son. You have given him the academic challenges he needed to prepare for success in his university career and, perhaps just as importantly, his self-confidence has grown through his participation in cross-country and as a Retreat Leader."

"We love SJND! You're more than a school; you're a community; you're a family."

"Our daughter was beaming when she announced that she had been accepted into the National Honor Society. She did it, but not without the investment of time and care that she has had from the faculty of SJND."

**Students response(s):** "If you want to accomplish something, you can do it at St. Joe's! I never thought I would have the courage to lead a rally or be able to stay on the Honor Roll for all four years, but I did and I have!"—Senior

"Yes, there's a lot of work. I'm taking two AP classes and one honors class this year, but the teachers make everything interesting and fun."—Junior

"I like St. Joseph Notre Dame because it's a small school and everyone knows each other and there is a lot of diversity. It's kind of like a small town or a small version of the United Nations. Plus, academically, I feel like I'm getting everything I need to be successful in the future."—Freshman

# ST. LAWRENCE ACADEMY

2000 Lawrence Court
Santa Clara, CA 95051

(408) 296-3013 *fax (408) 296-3794*
www.saintlawrence.org
slacad@saintlawrence.org

Ron Modeste, Principal
Gail Z. Harrell, Associate Principal and Admission Director

## GENERAL

**Coed** day high school (with elementary and middle school on shared campus). **Catholic** (60% Catholic). Founded in 1975. **Nonprofit,** operated by Saint Lawrence Parish in the Diocese of San Jose. **Enrollment:** 310. **Average class size:** 25. **Accreditation:** WASC (6-year term: 1994-00). **School year:** 10-month calendar (approx. 180 instructional days). **School day:** 8:25 a.m. to 2:50 p.m. **Location:** The St. Lawrence campus, shared with the elementary school, middle school and St. Lawrence Parish, is located in an urban residential area a few blocks from the main arteries St. Lawrence Expressway and El Camino Real.

## STUDENT BODY

**Geographical breakdown (counties):** 90% from Santa Clara; 5% from East Bay; 1% from San Mateo; 3% from other areas. **Ethnicity:** Approximately 80% Latino; 12% Caucasian (non-Latino); 8% African-American. **Foreign students (I-20 status):** 1%. **Single parent/two f/t working parent families:** N/P. **Middle schools:** 79 members of the latest freshman class came from 20 other parochial schools; 19 from 19 public middle schools; 16 from the school's middle school; and 6 from 6 private non-parochial schools.

## ADMISSION

**Applications due:** Mid-February (call for exact date). **Application fee:** $50. **Application process:** An open house is held in December for students and parents. Interested students may schedule a shadow visit for a morning during November - February. Students submit the application by mid-February (call for date) for priority consideration and an entrance exam registration form. In January, students may take the Diocese admission examination at any of the schools in the Diocese he or she is considering. The Diocese 7th and 8th grade school report is sent to the elementary/middle school; teacher evaluations are optional.

Students applying for the school's special program for students with learning disabilities should contact the school for additional admission information. **No. of applications:** 250-300 applications were received for 90 places in the most recent freshman class. Seven new students were admitted to G11. **Admission cut-off:** C average. Most students falling in the 50th percentile will be considered for admission. **Preferences:** Eighth grade graduates of St. Lawrence Middle School; students whose parents are parishioners of St. Lawrence the Martyr Church; students who have attended other Catholic elementary schools in the Diocese of San Jose; students whose applications are received first. **"We are looking for** average-achieving students with the potential and desire to attend college." **What sort of student do you best serve?** "We seem to serve average students who need some nurturing and guidance to achieve their best. Also, they usually have very supportive parents."

## Costs

**Latest tuition:** $6,150. **Sibling discount:** None. **Tuition increases:** Approximately 7% annually. **Other costs:** Uniforms, textbooks, materials. **Percentage of students receiving financial aid:** 7%. **Average grant:** $1,000. **No. of full-tuition grants:** 0. **No. of half-tuition grants:** 2. **Grants of half-tuition or more:** .5%.

## School's Mission Statement/Goals

"Philosophy: St. Lawrence Academy is a Catholic college preparatory community committed to the mission of Jesus Christ. Striving to create a caring family environment, we share our Christian beliefs with all students regardless of race or creed. We nurture our community through prayer, worship and service.

"In cooperation with students and parents, we seek to encourage our students' moral and spiritual potential; to recognize the uniqueness and dignity of the individual; to develop intellectual, emotional, social and physical growth; to instill a sense of integrity, self esteem, and self-discipline; and to encourage them to achieve to their fullest potential.

"Throughout the curriculum we promote the growth of the whole student in a school with a diverse population. We empower the students to become responsible leaders who will fully share their gifts and talents with family, church and their immediate and global communities."

## Academic Program

Academically, the Academy follows the guidelines of the University of California in addition to the guidelines established by the Diocese. **Courses offered (AP=Advanced Placement, H=Honors, (AP)=AP option, (H)=Honors op-**

tion): **English:** English I-II, American Literature, World Literature, English H (AP), Publications (Yearbook); **Math:** Introduction to Algebra, Algebra I-II, Geometry, Pre-Calculus, Calculus AB (AP), Computer Math, Accounting, Business Math; **Religion:** I Christian Morality/Sacraments; II Hebrew Scriptures/ Christian Scriptures, III Church Life/Social Justice, IV Christian Lifestyles; **Social Sciences:** World History, US History (AP), Government, Economics, Psychology; **Science:** Integrated Science, Biology, Chemistry (H), Physics, Life Science; **Foreign Language:** Spanish I-III, Spanish IV-V H, French I-III, French IV-V H; **Fine and Applied Arts:** Keyboarding/Computers, Chorus, Drama/ Theater Arts, Studio Arts, P.E., Business Law, Careers, Leadership. **Special programs:** The school offers the Zacchaeus Program, a special program for students with learning disabilities (see Student Support Services, below). **Computer lab/ training:** The school has a computer lab with 25 Mac LCIIIs. All students are required to take keyboarding and computers. **Grading:** Letter grades, 4.0 system. **Graduation requirements:** (Note: graduation requirements are designed to meet UC minimum admission requirements.) 4 years English, 4 years mathematics, 3 years social science including world history, US history, government and economics, 2.5 years science, .5 year keyboarding, 1 year visual and performing arts, 3 years of one foreign language or 2 years of two languages, 3.5 years religion, 1 year P.E. **Average nightly homework (Mon-Th):** G9: 1-1.5 hours; G10: 2 hours; G11: 2-2.5 hours; G12 2.5-3 hours. **Faculty:** 37% male; 73% female. 40% of faculty hold master's degrees. **Faculty ethnicity:** 88% Caucasian (non-Latino); 1.5% Latino; .07% Asian; 10% other. **Faculty selection/training:** "The school follows the Diocese guidelines on teacher credentials. They must complete 30 hours of in-service per year and must follow state guidelines for continuing education—150 hours every 5 years." **Teacher/student ratio:** 1:19. **Teacher's daily student load in required academic subject:** N/P. **AP courses/ exams:** N/P. **Senior class profile(mean):** SAT Math 510, SAT Verbal 510. **GPA:** "51% of student body maintain a GPA of 3.0 or higher." **National Merit Scholarship Program:** N/P. **College enrollment:** "97% of graduates go on to colleges—whether 4-year or 2-year."

## OTHER INDICATORS THE SCHOOL IS ACCOMPLISHING ITS GOALS

N/P.

## CAMPUS/CAMPUS LIFE

**Campus description:** The high school is housed in a one-story building with two wings of classrooms and labs. One wing was recently retrofitted, and the other is planned for retrofit, including new science labs. The school has a new gym and two outdoor pools in a courtyard. **Library:** N/P. **Open/closed campus:** N/P. **Classroom space per student:** N/P. **Lunches:** Hot lunches are available daily. **Bus service:** Public transportation only. **Uniforms/dress code:** Uniforms. **Co-curricular activities/clubs:** Student Government and Leadership, Associated Student Body & Government Class Officers, Homeroom Representatives, Clubs: National Honor Society, California Scholarship Federation, Christian Faith Community, Chess Club, Drama Group, Interact Club, International Club, Math Club, Science Club, Science Fiction Club, Service Corps. **Foreign exchange program:** N/P. **Opportunities for community service:** N/P. **Typical freshman schedule:** (6 periods of 50 minutes each) English, Algebra I, Christian Morality and Sacraments, Spanish or French, Keyboarding/Integrated Science, either P.E., Drama, Chorus, or Art.

## STUDENT SUPPORT SERVICES

**Student-counselor ratio (not including college counselors):** 1:160. **Counseling:** Two full-time counselors plus 2 part-time. The principal, vice principal, and campus minister all provide **personal, academic, college** and **career** guidance. **Learning disabilities/differences:** The Academy offers the Zacchaeus Program, a distinctive program for students with mild learning disabilities. The program accepts 15 students per year. Students are offered additional help for up to two years (freshman and sophomore) before being mainstreamed into the school community. Please contact the school for more information. **Career apprenticeship programs:** None.

## STUDENT CONDUCT AND HEALTH

**Code of conduct:** Standard. **How school handles drug/alcohol usage:** Zero tolerance for selling/dealing drugs or alcohol. The first offense for drug/alcohol use is treated as an illness involving intervention, counseling, probation, drug testing, and parent involvement. **Drug/alcohol abuse prevention/AIDS awareness programs:** Part of health/religion curriculum.

## SUMMER PROGRAMS

None.

## PARENT INVOLVEMENT

**Parent participation:** Parents are required to give 10 hours of their time to the school each year. **Parent/teacher communication:** Report cards 4 times a year; progress reports 4 times a year; parent meetings as needed. Teachers are available through phone, voice, and e-mail. Monthly newsletter of Parent-Teacher Group.

**Parent education:** Once a year, the Parent-Teacher Group puts on a college finance workshop and college applications workshop for parents. The school also hosts ADD (attention deficit disorder) workshops. **Donations:** The school asks that parents contribute the equivalent of one year's tuition over the four years their child attends the school.

## SPORTS

The school offers girls' varsity teams in basketball, soccer, softball, swimming, track & field and volleyball; boys' varsity teams in baseball, basketball, football, soccer, swimming, track & field and volleyball. Cross-country and track are also offered. The school is a member of the Christian Private School Athletic League and is eligible for Central Coast Section Playoffs.

## WHAT SETS SCHOOL APART FROM OTHERS

"St. Lawrence Academy is the most ethnically diverse high school in the Diocese of San Jose. It is unique in its provision of a program especially for students with learning disabilities. The school is a success-oriented high school that values the individual. We are committed to a college prep curriculum with academic excellence as well as diversity in the classroom. Through the educational process we attempt to inspire and instill positive values in our students. Our learning environment provides excellent student support: strong academic program, small class sizes, math and reading labs with study skills emphasis, before and after school Study Hall, four counselors on staff, crisis intervention team, disciplinary review board, extra curricular activities, student community outreach program, fully accredited."

## HOW PARENTS/STUDENTS CHARACTERIZE SCHOOL

"Caring, family-oriented, small."

# Salesian High School

2851 Salesian Avenue
Richmond, CA 94804

(510) 234-4433 *fax (510) 236-4636*

Fr. Christian Woerz, SDB, Director
Mr. Timothy Chambers, Principal
Dina Trombettas, Admission Director

## General

**Coed** day high school. **Catholic** (68% Catholic). Operated by Salesians of Don Bosco. Founded in 1960 (the school was originally all boys; it became coed in 1989). **Nonprofit. Enrollment:** 500. **Average class size:** 26. **Accreditation:** WASC (6-year term: 1998-04). **School year:** 10-month calendar (approx. 180 instructional days). **School day:** 8 a.m. to 2:40 p.m. **Location:** On the border of the urban communities of San Pablo and Richmond, the school, a former Salesian seminary, is located on an 11-acre park-like campus at the end of cul-de-sac. It is 6 miles from the Richmond Bridge leading to Marin County, and 14 miles north of the San Francisco Bay Bridge.

## Student Body

**Geographical breakdown (counties):** 95% from Contra Costa; 4% from Alameda; 1% from San Francisco. **Ethnic breakdown:** 24% Latino; 23% Filipino; 23% European-American; 20% African-American; 8% Asian/Pacific Islander; 2% Native American. **Foreign students (I-20 status):** 1%. **Single parent/two f/t working parent families:** N/P. **Middle schools:** N/P. A good number of students come from Juan Crespi Junior High, Pinole Middle School, Adams Middle School, and Helms Middle School.

## Admission

**Applications due:** Mid-January (call for exact date). **Application fee:** $40. **Application process:** Applications are available in October. An open house is held in November, and a parent information night in January. Applicants take the HSPT in January at the school. Recommendations from principal, math, and English teachers are due in February. Applicants and their parents are jointly interviewed in February - March. **No. of applications:** 240 applications were received for 150 places in most recent freshman class. Three new students were

admitted to G10, 2 to G11, 2 to G12. **Preferences:** N/P.
**Admission cut-off:** None. **"We are looking for..."** N/P. **What sort of student do you best serve?** N/P.

# Costs

**Latest tuition:** $4,750. **Sibling discount:** None. **Tuition increases:** Approx. $100/year. **Other costs:** $450 registration fee. **Percentage of students receiving financial aid:** 25%. **Average grant award:** $1,000. **No. of full tuition grants:** 1. **No. of half tuition grants:** "Up to 28." **Grants of half-tuition or more:** 13%.

# School's Mission Statement/Goals

School vision: "The students, parents, faculty, and staff of Salesian High School work together to create a community of faith that spreads the Good News of Jesus Christ. We foster life-long learning in a family atmosphere of love and safety where friends are made and joy is celebrated. With these essential qualities of church, school, playground and home, we are guided by the principles of Don Bosco's Preventive System of reason, religion, and loving kindness."
School Philosophy: "...We, the faculty and staff of the school strive to fulfill the charism of the Salesian Community, that is, to be joyful signs and bearers of God's love for the young. We provide college preparatory and general education for students from diverse socioeconomic backgrounds, with efforts to aid those who are poor, needy or at risk.

"Recognizing the importance of a sound, holistic education in a rapidly changing world, we seek to nurture the physical, emotional, intellectual, social, technological, cultural, artistic, moral, and spiritual potential of all students. We acknowledge the innate worth and dignity of all students and work to help them develop the respect for themselves and for one another within a Christian community of faith and love. We assist them in their efforts to become mature and self-disciplined citizens, responsive to local, national, and world issues. We strive to guide their personal growth, encouraging them to value and develop their unique talents and gifts.

"The Salesian educational system of reason, religion, and loving kindness animate the spirit of the school and guide us toward our goals. Recognizing parents as the primary educators of their children, we embrace St. John Bosco's vision of community as an ever-widening family; and, therefore, see the collaboration of the total Salesian family—students, parents, administrators, teacher, and staff—as essential for the achievement of our spiritual and academic goals."

# ACADEMIC PROGRAM

**Courses offered (AP=Advanced Placement, H=Honors, (AP)=AP option, (H)=Honors option): English:** English I-III, Junior Honors English, English IV (AP); **Math:** Intro to Algebra, Algebra I-II, Geometry, Algebra with Trigonometry H, Intro to Calculus H, AP Calculus AB, AP Calculus BC Independent Study, Statistics; **Religion:** Path Through Catholicism, The Hebrew and Christian Scriptures, Sign and Symbol, Christian Morality, Social Justice, History of Christianity, World Religions, Christian Lifestyles; **Social Sciences:** World History, US History (AP), Government (H), Economics (H), Psychology; **Science:** Biology (AP), Chemistry (H), General Science, Physics, Anatomy, Environmental Science; **Foreign Language:** Spanish I-III, Spanish A (accelerated), AP Spanish, French I-IV; **Fine Arts:** Art I-II, Art Appreciation, AP History of Art; **Computer education:** Introduction to Computers; **P.E.:** Health, P.E. **Computer lab/training:** The school has two computer labs with IBM PCs. (N/P re #) All students are required to take Introduction to Computers. **Grading:** Letter grades. **Graduation requirements:** 230 semester credits including 4 years religion, 4 years English, 3 years math, 3 years social science, 2 years foreign language, 2 years science, 2 years P.E./Health, 1 year fine arts. (Students seeking UC and CSU admission are advised to complete 3 years foreign language, 4 years math, and 3 years science.) In addition, students must complete 20 hours community service per year. **Average nightly homework (Mon-Th):** G9-10: 2 hours; G11-12: 3 hours. **Faculty:** N/P. Faculty complies with a dress code which requires male teachers to wear ties. **Faculty ethnicity:** 91% Caucasian (non-Latino); 8% Latino; 1% Filipino. **Faculty selection/training:** N/P. **Teacher/student ratio:** 1:25. **Teacher's daily student load in required academic subject:** 125. **AP courses/exams:** 25% of the most recent year's class took 6 AP courses. In 1998, 80 students took 109 AP exams in 8 subjects. 55% scored 3 or above. **Senior class profile (mean):** SAT Math 500, SAT Verbal 500. **GPA:** N/P. **National Merit Scholarship Program:** In the most recent class, 1 student was a semi-finalist, 1 was commended. **College Enrollment:** 75% of last year's graduating class enrolled in 4-year colleges, 24% in 2-year colleges. Acceptances included: UC campuses (Berkeley, Davis, Irvine, LA, Riverside, Santa Barbara, Santa Cruz, San Diego), CSU campuses (Maritime, Cal Poly-Pomona, Cal Poly-SLO, Chico, Fresno, Hayward, Sacramento, San Diego, San Francisco, San Jose, Sonoma), Cal Baptist College, St. Mary's, Santa Clara, Stanford, USF, Westmont, Canisius C, Dillard U, Fordham, Georgetown, Eastern New Mexico State, Humber C of Toronto, Keio U (Japan), Liberty U, Marymount (NY), Spelman, Stevens Institute of Technology, U of Arizona, U of Loyola (MD), U of North Carolina-Chapel Hill, Utah State U, and Villanova.

# OTHER INDICATORS THE SCHOOL IS ACCOMPLISHING ITS GOALS

N/P.

# CAMPUS/CAMPUS LIFE

**Campus description:** The main building of the campus is a three-story art deco building (former seminary building circa 1927) housing classrooms, offices, and science labs. At one end of the building is an addition with a recently refurbished gymnasium and locker rooms. The four additional campus buildings include a library/multimedia center/cafeteria/college placement office; the Salesian Brothers residence; and the Salesian Boys' and Girls' Club. The outdoor area includes a soccer field, baseball field and football field. (The school uses the Contra Costa College swimming pool.) Future capital improvements include upgrading the science labs. **Library:** 1,000 sq. ft.; 10 computers with Internet access; study space for 25; open to students from 9 a.m. to 5 p.m.; full-time librarian. (N/P re # print volumes, catalog, etc.) **Open/closed campus:** Closed. **Classroom space per student:** N/P. **Lunches:** Breakfast and hot lunches are served in the cafeteria which opens at 7:15 a.m. **Bus service:** None. **Uniforms/dress code:** The dress code prohibits jeans, sweats, clothes with drug, alcohol, etc. messages, hooded clothing, denim, camouflage, midriff shirts, etc. No visible tattoos, beards or goatees, no more than one ear piercing per ear (two for girls), no bandannas, hats, or excessive unnatural hair colors are allowed, no beepers or personal stereos. **Co-curricular activities/clubs:** N/P. **Foreign exchange program:** None. **Opportunities for community service:** N/P. **Typical freshman schedule:** (6 periods of 46 minutes each) Religious Studies, English, World History, math, P.E., Health, foreign language.

# STUDENT SUPPORT SERVICES

**Counselor/student ratio (not including college counselors):** 1:167. **Counseling:** Students receive **college counseling** beginning in 9th grade. **Personal counseling** is also available. After-school math labs are open to all students. **Learning disabilities/differences:** N/P. **Career apprenticeship programs:** N/P.

# STUDENT CONDUCT AND HEALTH

**Code of conduct:** Standard. **How school handles drug/alcohol usage:** Zero tolerance. **Drug/alcohol abuse prevention/AIDS awareness programs:** N/P.

## SUMMER PROGRAMS

N/P.

## PARENT INVOLVEMENT

**Parent participation:** Parents are required to give 40 hours of their time to the school each year. **Parent/teacher communication:** Two parent-teacher conferences are scheduled during each year. Additional conferences are available upon teacher or parent request. **Parent education:** N/P. **Donations:** N/P.

## SPORTS

Teams compete in cross-country, water polo, basketball, soccer, tennis, baseball, softball, swimming, and track. The school is a member of the California Interscholastic Federation (CIF) and a charter member of the Alameda Contra Costa Athletic League (ACCAL).

## WHAT SETS SCHOOL APART FROM OTHERS

N/P.

## HOW PARENTS/STUDENTS CHARACTERIZE SCHOOL

N/P.

# SAN DOMENICO UPPER SCHOOL

1500 Butterfield Road
San Anselmo, CA 94960-1099

(415) 454-0200 *fax (415) 258-9197*
www.sandomenico.org

Sister M. Gervaise Valpey, O.P., Head of School
John Bowermaster, Upper School Principal
Liz Leone, Director of Admission, (415) 258-1905, lleone@marin.k12.ca.us

# GENERAL

Girls' day and boarding high school (with pre-K-8th grade coed day school). **Dominican Catholic** (50% Catholic). Founded in 1850. **Nonprofit**, member CAIS, NAIS, BAIHS. **Enrollment:** Approximately 130 (40% board). **Average class size:** 12. **Accreditation:** WASC/CAIS (6 year term: 1995-01). **School year:** 9-month calendar (182 instructional days). **School day:** 8:10 a.m. to 3:30 p.m. **Location:** 626-acre campus in Marin County, approximately 20 miles north of San Francisco. The Golden Gate Transit bus stops at campus; private bus service is available from the East Bay, San Francisco, and Marin Counties.

# STUDENT BODY

**Geographical breakdown (counties):** 37% from Marin; 14% from Alameda; 10% from San Francisco; 2% from Contra Costa; 1% from San Mateo; 1% from Santa Clara; 10% from other California; 25% from out-of-state. **Ethnicity:** 52% Caucasian (non-Latina); 31% Asian; 7% Latina; 6% African-American; 4% other. Girls come from 10 states and 12 foreign countries. **Foreign students (I-20 status):** 20%. **Single parent families:** 15%. **Two f/t working parent families:** 85%. **Middle schools:** 30% of the most recent entering freshman class came from public middle schools; 60% from private, non-parochial schools; 10% from parochial schools (N/P re #s).

# ADMISSION

**Applications due:** Approximately January 21 (call for date). **Application fee:** $65. **Application process:** Open houses are held in October. Student tours are held in late September through early January. The tours, which take place weekday mornings from 8:30 a.m. to noon, involve groups of applicants and parents visiting classes and individual interviews with the Admission Director. SSAT, Catholic School Test, and ERB test results are accepted. **No. of applications:** 155 applications were received for 36 places in the prior year's class. Of these, 7 places were taken by San Domenico middle school students. Six new students were admitted to G10, 4 to G11. **Admission cut-off:** N/P. **Preferences:** N/P. **"We are looking for** academically motivated students who value the advantage of a small school setting, diversity of student body, and involvement in school life and activities." **What sort of student do you best serve?** N/P.

# COSTS

**Latest tuition:** $16,132 for day tuition (includes lunches, transportation and books); $28,528 for resident tuition, payable in 1, 2, or monthly payments. **Sibling discount:** Yes. **Tuition increases:** Approximately 4-5% annually. **Other costs:** Tuition insurance if paying tuition in installments (1.8% of tuition); approximately $150 for freshman wardrobe. **Financial aid:** Need-based. **Percentage of students receiving financial aid:** N/P. **Average grant:** $7,000. **No. of full-tuition grants:** 8. **No. of half-tuition grants:** 34. **Grants of half-tuition or more:** N/P.

## SCHOOL'S MISSION STATEMENT/GOALS

"In the Dominican tradition of truth, we celebrate diversity, recognizing God's presence in ourselves and all of creation. We explore and develop the unique gifts of each individual in mind, heart, body, and spirit. We inspire inquiry and provide a strong academic foundation for lifelong intellectual growth. We recognize what it means to be human in a global community and respond with integrity to the needs and challenges of our time."

## ACADEMIC PROGRAM

"All courses are college preparatory and many courses present advanced study opportunities. San Domenico's graduation requirements exceed minimum admission requirements for UC Berkeley. All freshmen take Freshman Foundations, which integrates the study of literature, history, religion, writing, computer skills, art, and drama." **Courses offered (AP=Advanced Placement, H=Honors, (AP)=AP option, (H)=Honors option):** Art 1 (part of Freshman Foundations), Art 2-3, Ceramic Art, Advanced Ceramics, Drawing/Painting, Advanced Drawing/Painting, Printmaking, Studio Art (AP, H), Visual Arts, History of Art and Music, Drama 1-3, Performance Art Workshop, Introduction to Dance, English 9 (Freshman Foundations), English 10 (H), Literature and Composition 1-2, The Newcomers: Ethnic Voices in American Culture, 20th Century American Literature, 20th Century Writers of the American South, 20th Century British Literature (H), Writing California in the 20th Century, Modern American Drama and Poetry, Survey of the English Poetic Tradition, 19th Century British Literature (AP), Classical American Literature (H), American Literature and the American Cultural History, English Literature and Composition (AP), Senior Seminars on: Modern European Drama, The American Novel at the Turn of the Century, and Fantasy Literature; 20th Century Literature: The Magic in Ordinary Life, The Story of Fiction, Contemporary Fiction by Women Writers: The Family, Senior Seminar on Modern European Drama, ESL (4 levels); French 1-5 (AP); Spanish 1-5 (AP); Japanese 1-2/3 (Latin, German, Russian on independent study basis); Integrated Mathematics 1-2 (H), Geometry, Algebra 2, Algebra 2/Trigonometry, Pre-Calculus (H), Calculus (AP), Introduction to Computers and Keyboarding, Computer and Technology Skills; P.E. 1-2, Independent Study Fitness, P.E. Dance, Riding, Tennis, World Religion (Freshman Foundations), World Religion and the Arts, The Nature of Religious Experience, Hebrew and Christian Scriptures, Ethics: Survey of Philosophy, Social Justice, Integrated Science 9, Biology (AP), Chemistry (AP, H), Physics (H), Ecology and Environmental Biology (H), Human Biology, Teacher Assistant in Sciences, World History, History 10 (Modern Europe, area studies—two non-European areas), US History and Government, US History (AP), Issues in American Democracy, International Relations, Music Conservatory Program (private musical instrument instruction in piano, harpsichord, voice, recorder, harp, guitar, violin, viola, cello, bass, clarinet, flute, oboe, and bassoon) (fee of $520-$800/semester), Orchestral Conducting, Flute Choir, String Quartet, Orchestra de Camera, Virtuoso Program, San Domenico Singers, San Domenico Chamber Singers, Journalism, P.E. (hiking, folk and jazz dance, hip-hop, step aerobics, yoga, karate, body conditioning, swimming, and health). **Computer lab/training:** All students learn computer skills as part of Freshman Foundations. The school's computer lab is equipped with 18 PowerMacs and several IBM PCs. **Grading:** Letter grades. Progress reports are issued mid-first quarter and at any time the teacher feels concern or extra praise is in order. Tri-weekly or weekly reports are provided if a student is having difficulty. **Graduation requirements:** 4 years English, 3 years math (Algebra 1 & 2, Geometry), 2 years foreign language, 3 years social studies, 2 years lab science, 4 years theology, 1 semester computer science, 1.5 years fine arts including History of Art and Music (1 semester), 2 years P.E., 100 hours community service. **Average nightly homework:** G9-10: 30 min. per course; G11-12: 40 min. per course. **Faculty:** 40% male, 60% female; of 35 faculty members, 15 hold advanced degrees in their fields. One religious on the faculty. **Faculty ethnicity:** N/P. **Faculty selection/training:** "We have a very strong professional development program. All teachers are required to have at least one professional development experience each year, such as classes, seminars, etc." **Teacher/student ratio:** 1:9. **Teacher's daily student load in required academic subject:** N/P. **AP courses/exams:** In the last academic year, 35 AP exams were taken by 24 students; 75% were scored 3 or higher. (N/P re % in AP courses) **Senior class profile (mean):** SAT Verbal 530, SAT Math 572 (includes ESL students). (See "Other indicators" section, below, for SAT II scores.) **GPA:** 3.29 (unweighted). **National Merit Scholarship Program:** N/P. **College enrollment:** 100% of last year's graduating class enrolled in 4-year colleges. Graduates from 1996-98 have enrolled in the following colleges: UC Berkeley (7), UC Irvine (5), UC Santa Cruz (4), Instituto de Tecnología(4), USC (3), UC Davis (3), UCLA (3), SCU-Humboldt (3), U of Chicago (2), U of Hong Kong (2), USF (2), Wellesley (2), Whitman (2), Parsons (2), Boston U (2), Lewis & Clark (2), Marymount (2), Boston U, Bowdoin, BYU, Cal Poly-SLO, Cleveland Institute of Music, C of San Mateo, SCU-Sonoma, DePauw, Fordham, Hamilton, Hawaii Pacific, Marymount Manhattan, Mills, Mt. Holyoke, Muhlenberg, Oberlin Conservatory, Otis, Peabody Conservatory, Princeton, Rensselaer Polytechnic, RISD, SF Conservatory, Spelman, St. Mary's, St. Olaf, Stanford, SUNY Buffalo, Trinity, Tulane, Universidad Iberoamericano (Mexico City), Universidad de Monterey (Mexico), U of Colorado, U of Montana, U of Pennsylvania, U of Puget Sound, UC San Diego, Wheaton, Willamette, and Yale.

# Other Indicators the School is Accomplishing its Goals

SAT II and # takers: Writing 540 (17), Math I 526 (14), Math II 631 (10), US Hist 540 (5).

# Campus/Campus Life

**Campus description:** The school, spread over 626 acres in the hills of Marin County, has the feel of a college campus, with separate buildings housing the library, chapel, music conservatory and art room, dining hall, classrooms, three residence halls, and administration buildings. A creek runs through the campus. The campus also includes an Olympic-sized swimming pool, riding stables, six tennis courts, equestrian center, basketball courts, softball diamond, jogging trails, hiking, biking, and riding trails, and a vegetable and herb garden. The school plans to build new gym, theater and technology center in the next few years. **Library:** The library is a separate building of 20,500 sq. ft.; 15,000 current print volumes; on-line and card catalog; 80 print periodical subscriptions (and access to an unlimited number of electronic periodicals); study space for 120 students; 12 computers, 3 with Internet access; 1 full-time and 3 part-time librarians. Open to students from 8 a.m. to 5 p.m. **Open/closed campus:** Closed. Seniors and second-semester juniors with parental permission have off-campus privileges after 11:20 a.m. but must sign in and out. **Classroom space per student:** N/P. **Lunches:** Included in tuition. The school has a separate dining hall. **Bus service:** Private bus service is available from the East Bay, San Francisco, and points in Marin County. **Uniforms/dress code:** Students choose from a casual wear wardrobe that includes skirts, khaki pants and shorts, polo shirts, and sweatshirts. **Co-curricular activities and clubs:** Activities include *Veritas*, the school yearbook, *Verities*, the literary magazine, *Panther Press*, the student newspaper, student council, English riding, Model U.N., Junior Statesmen, Environmental Club, Drama Club, Girls Athletic Assn., International Club, Tour Guides, Poetry Club, Guitar Club, Spanish Club, Resident Council, Photography Club, Arts & Design. Students are encouraged to organize new clubs. **Foreign exchange program:** The school has exchange programs providing opportunities for study in Germany, Japan, and France. **Opportunities for community service:** 100 hours are required for graduation. **Typical freshman schedule:** Ninth grade students take "Freshman Foundations," a program integrating literature, history, religion, writing, computer skills, and art and providing students with the foundational knowledge and skills for further study. The first three hours of each day are reserved for these classes, which divide the different aspects of study into four thematic units: Problems & Solutions, Order & Anarchy, Magic & Science, and Tradition & Innovation. The remainder of the day, students study math, foreign language, science, P.E., and art, music, or drama.

## STUDENT SUPPORT SERVICES

**Counselor/student ratio (not including college counselors):** 1:90. **Counseling:** Academic counseling begins in ninth grade with the assignment of a faculty advisor with whom students meet once a week (1:5 advisor to student ratio). College counseling begins in tenth grade with a parent evening and general information. The school has a college counselor. Girls seeking help with personal issues may consult with the school's full-time counselor. **Learning disabilities/ differences:** No special programs or resources. **Career apprenticeship programs:** None.

## STUDENT CONDUCT AND HEALTH

**Rules of conduct:** School rules apply at school and at school-sponsored events. **How school handles tobacco/drugs/alcohol usage:** Smoking on school grounds is punishable by probation; violation of the rule against drug/alcohol use/sale/ possession is punishable by dismissal. Students "merely present where alcoholic beverages, non-prescribed drugs, or tobacco are being used" are liable for disciplinary action as well. **Drug/alcohol abuse prevention/AIDS awareness:** All freshman are required to take P.E. 1, which includes a health component covering human sexuality, substance abuse (alcohol, tobacco, and drugs), eating disorders, general health, and nutrition.

## SUMMER PROGRAMS

None.

## PARENT INVOLVEMENT

**Parent participation:** No participation hours are required, but parents are asked to donate to the annual fund. Parents may participate in the Parent Service Association, Parent Information Nights, and a Speaker Series. **Parent/teacher communication:** "Parents and faculty are in close contact, either by phone or personal appointments. Report cards and progress reports are used for academic reporting. Each students has a faculty advisor who also keep parents informed." **Parent education:** N/P. **Donations:** N/P.

## SPORTS

Girls compete in volleyball, basketball, soccer, tennis, swimming, track & field, softball, cross-country, badminton, water polo and riding. San Domenico is a member of the Bay Counties League.

# OTHER

Fifty percent of students study a musical instrument through the school's Music Conservatory Program. San Domenico's Virtuoso Program prepares highly advanced instrumental musicians who wish to work toward a career in professional performance with an academic program individually tailored to her needs and abilities designed by the student, parents, faculty advisor, and director of music.

Each class attends a retreat sponsored by the campus ministry that consists of a day of reflection at a specific site—for freshman and sophomores, the Dominican Residence at Bolinas, California; for juniors, Alliance Redwood Center in Occidental; and, for seniors, the U.C.C.R. facility in Cazadero, California.

All students are required to participate in Spring Discovery, a week-long alternative learning experience involving extensive hands-on study of topics not normally taught in the conventional classroom. Freshman do community service; sophomores attend the Yosemite Institute; and juniors and seniors choose from activities such as photography workshops, car maintenance workshop, cross-country ski trips, self defense, gourmet cooking, DNA lab, creative writing, film study, a trip to Washington D.C., or the Yucatan, and other offerings.

# WHAT SETS SCHOOL APART FROM OTHERS

"San Domenico is the oldest independent school in California, offering a coeducational program for pre-kindergarten through eighth grade, and a day and boarding program for young women at the high school level. Established in 1850 by the Dominican Sisters, San Domenico draws students from many religious and cultural backgrounds from around the United States and the world. In additional to the school's superior college preparatory curriculum, San Domenico offers a music conservatory featuring a nationally renowned Virtuoso Program, drama, dance, studio art, and equestrian center, and more, all located on a picturesque 626-acre campus in Marin County."

# HOW PARENTS/STUDENTS CHARACTERIZE SCHOOL

N/P.

# SAN FRANCISCO UNIVERSITY HIGH SCHOOL

3065 Jackson Street
San Francisco, CA 94115

(415) 447-3100 *fax (415) 346-7522*

Jeanne E. Amster, Head of School
Lorri Hamilton, Director of Admissions

## GENERAL

**Coed** day high school. **Nonsectarian.** Founded in 1973. **Nonprofit**, member CAIS, NAIS, BAIHS. **Enrollment:** Approximately 389. **Average class size:** N/P. **Accreditation:** WASC/CAIS (6-year term. N/P years). **School year:** 9-month calendar. (N/P re instructional days) **School day:** N/P. **Location:** Pacific Heights, a residential neighborhood in the northern part of San Francisco, accessible by the 1 and 24 MUNI bus lines.

## STUDENT BODY

**Geographical breakdown (counties):** "San Francisco, Marin County, East Bay and Peninsula." **Ethnicity:** "Students of color comprise 30% of the student body." **Foreign students (I-20 status):** "I-20 forms are only available to students who are accepted and enrolled." **Single parent/two f/t working parent families:** N/P. **Middle schools:** "This year, University received applications from 110 different schools. The class of 2003 has students from 39 different schools in the Bay Area."

## ADMISSION

**Applications due:** Mid-January (call for date.) **Application fee:** N/P. **Application process:** Open houses are held in the fall for families. School visits run September through mid-January. The application process includes the student's completion of an essay, submission of transcripts and past test scores, the Secondary School Admission Test, a parent statement, and teacher recommendations. Applicants are also required to visit classes and to be interviewed by a member of the Admissions Committee. Decisions are mailed mid-March (BAIHS schedule). **No. of applications:** N/P. **Admission cut-off:** N/P. **Preferences:** N/P. **"We are looking for** highly motivated students who have demonstrated the ability to pursue an academically demanding secondary school program. Successful applicants will have a combination of intellectual skills and personal qualities which will enable them to become effective members of the School community. While we value academic skills and innate talent, we also look for a desire to learn, a willingness to take risks, a curiosity about the world, a seriousness of purpose, a sense of compassion, a concern for others, a dedication to the service of democracy, and a commitment to the life of the mind. Successful applicants will be able to demonstrate that their education is not something that they are coming to obtain, but something that they are willing to create." **What sort of student do you best serve?** N/P.

# Costs

**Latest tuition:** $16,175 payable in 1 or 2 payments (10-payment plan available through outside company). **Sibling discount:** N/P. **Tuition increases:** 5-7%. **Financial aid:** Need-based. **Percentage of students receiving financial aid:** Approximately 20% of the student body receives financial aid totaling $791,600. **Average grant:** N/P. **No. of full/half-tuition** grants: N/P. **Grants of half-tuition or more:** N/P.

# School's Mission Statement/Goals

Philosophy: "San Francisco University High School, a college preparatory secondary school, offers an intellectually stimulating, personally enriching, and academically challenging program in the liberal arts and sciences to an able and diverse student body. Standards of excellence guide all aspects of our program and the people engaged in it. We seek to instill in students the skills and attitudes of the lifelong learner and the responsible, engaged, and productive citizen. The School is committed to the welfare and development of the total student, to his or her emotional, moral, physical, and social as well as intellectual growth. We seek to maintain a nurturing and supportive learning environment, characterized by warmth, friendliness, and a spirit of equity and inclusion, which is sensitive to issues of gender, ethnicity, sexual orientation, and socioeconomic background. We endeavor to balance seriousness and fun. While emphasizing the aspiration of community, we seek to accommodate individual student needs as well as to foster mutual respect, a sense of humor, and the joy of life. A city school, we wish to reflect, learn from, and contribute to the richness of our urban environment."

# Academic Program

**Courses offered (AP=Advanced Placement, H=Honors, (AP)=AP option, (H)=Honors option): Arts:** Western Civilization, Studio Art AP, Art History AP, Beginning Instrumental Camerata, Jazz Ensemble, Chamber Orchestra, Ceramics I-III, Design 2-D, Drawing I-II, Film I-II, Painting I-III, Photography I-

III, Chorus, Electronic Music Studio, Jazz Combo, Acting I-II, Theater Production I-II, Dance Explorations, Music Theory AP, Technical Theater, Musical Theater Productions; **Computer Science:** Problem Solving and Programming, Integrated Computer Studies, Computer Science AB AP; **English:** English I-II, Freshman Humanities, Literature & Culture of America, African American Literature, American Communities, American Writers of the South, Choice/Circumstance, Innocence and Evil, Latin American Literature, Literature of World War I, Modern American Drama, Modern British Fiction, Poetry, Shakespeare, Indian Literature, Literature of American Immigration, Modern Poetry, Native American Literature, Short Story, Singing About Dark Times, Symbolic Reality, Toni Morrison, What We Carry: Vietnam, Journalism, Writing Workshop; **Interdepartmental Offerings:** Intro to Philosophy, Psychology; **Independent Programs** (Career Internships, Teaching Assistants, Tutorials, Alternative Education, Off-Campus Volunteers, Research Projects, Senior Seminars, Senior Project); **Foreign Languages:** French I-III, Spanish I-III, Latin I-II, Japanese II-V, French AP Language, French AP Literature, Advanced French Seminar, Spanish AP Language, Spanish AP Literature, Advanced Spanish Seminar, Advanced Latin: Catellus AP; **History:** Cultures and Civilizations, Freshman Humanities, US History AP (required), Modern European History AP, American Lives, Asian Studies, I-II, Gender in US History, Africa, San Francisco and American Urban; **Math:** Mathematics I, Mathematics II (H), Mathematics III (H), Math 101 (H), Mathematics 102 (H), Mathematics 103, Mathematics 110, Mathematics 112, Mathematics IV-A, IV-B; **Science:** Integrated Science I-II, Physics, Chemistry AP, California Natural History, Marine Biology, Advanced Physics, Physics-C AP, Advanced Biology: Physiology, Advanced Biology: Microbiology, Advanced Biology: Genetics, Advanced Chemistry. **Computer lab/training:** Two computer labs with Macintosh and PC/Windows computers. Students are required to take one semester computer science. (N/P # computers) **Grading:** A-F (grades and written comments). **Graduation requirements:** 4 years English, 3 years math, 3 years foreign language, 2 years lab science, 2 years history, .5 year computer studies, 2 years art, 4 years P.E., 20 hours community service each year and participation in a class project. (Requirements are designed to match UC admission requirements.) **Average nightly homework:** N/P. **Faculty:** 70 faculty members, 47 of whom hold advanced degrees. 32 women, 30 men. **Faculty ethnicity:** N/P. **Faculty selection/training:** "We conduct national searches for qualified candidates. University has attracted and retained a faculty of the highest caliber, equipped with outstanding skills in teaching, motivating and inspiring their students. Fully dedicated to the development of their students, faculty members possess a thorough knowledge of their subject matter and work to foster their students' intellectual, emotional and moral development. Ours is a highly committed and professional faculty. Over three-quarters hold advanced degrees, and virtually all have substantial previous teaching experience. In addition to their myriad duties as teachers, advisors, club leaders, coaches, and committee members, University faculty members systematically take time for their own professional growth. With the assistance of a sizable professional development fund, faculty attend and present papers at regional and national conferences, travel abroad during the summers and remain actively involved in their own study and scholarship. The 30 men and 32 women of the University faculty serve as living examples to the students in their continual quest for knowledge and personal growth. Teachers are readily available to students for informal advice and counsel outside the classroom." **Teacher/student ratio:** 1:8. **Teacher's daily student load in required academic subject:** N/P. **AP courses/exams:** In May 1998, 323 examinations were written by 180 students in 18 subjects; 88% percent scored 3 or above. (N/P re % in AP courses) **Senior class profile (mean):** Junior Year, Spring 1998—SAT Verbal 666, SAT Math 647. **GPAs:** 3.26 (unweighted). **National Merit Scholarship Program:** In the class of 1999, 14 students are expected to be NMSQT semi-finalists, and 37 are expected to be commended. **College enrollment:** 100% of the school's 1999 graduates enrolled in 4-year colleges and universities. Over the past five years, the largest numbers of students have enrolled in: UC Berkeley (69), Stanford (25), UC Santa Cruz (22), UC San Diego (21), UCLA (20), UC Riverside (20), Harvard (19), NYU (18), Yale (16), Cornell (14), UC Davis (14), Brown (13), Dartmouth (12), Oberlin (12), Vassar (11), Wellesley (11), and Columbia (11). (N/P re this year's grads)

## OTHER INDICATORS THE SCHOOL IS ACCOMPLISHING ITS GOALS

SAT II Tests: Mean Scores (+ number takers) (Class of 1999): American Hist 634 (61); Biology 619 (41); Chemistry 617 (35); French 681 (12); Literature 627 (24); Math 1 w/calc 595 (62); Math 2 w/calc 668 (53); Physics 714 (9); Spanish 665 (12); Writing 674 (84).

## CAMPUS/CAMPUS LIFE

**Campus description:** The campus is located in the Pacific Heights/Presidio Heights neighborhood of San Francisco, in the northern part of the city. The refurbished and newly constructed campus spans two city blocks. The original 1917 Italianate building was designed by architect Julia Morgan. The campus includes three science labs, student lounges, music and drama facilities, a 500-seat auditorium, outdoor tennis and basketball courts, gymnasium, language lab, three art studios, darkroom, dance studio, and a climbing wall. **Library:** 7,500 sq. ft. (N/P re # volumes, computers, hours, etc) **Open/closed campus:** Open. **Classroom space per student:** N/P. **Lunches:** Full service cafeteria. **Bus service:** Public only. **Uniform/dress code:** "Casual." **Co-curricular activities/clubs:** Amnesty International, Cards Club, *Devil's Advocate* (school paper), Drama Club, Environmental Club, Garden Club, Gay Straight Alliance, Junior Statesmen of America Club, Klafter's Gallery, M.O.R.E. (Moving on Racial Equality), Outdoor Education Club, Quantum Club (physics), *Retrospect* (school yearbook), Student Affairs Club, *Vox* (school literary magazine). **Foreign exchange program:** Founding member of School Year Abroad; participates in Main Coast

Semester and CityTerm. **Opportunities for community service:** Edgewood Family Center, Florence Crittendon Services, Golden Gate National Recreation Area, J.D. Randall Museum, John Swett Alternative Elementary School, Martin de Porres, The Names Project, Newcomer High School, Pets Unlimited, Project Open Hand, Russian American Community Services, Ruth Anne Rosenberg Adult Day Health Center, St. Anthony's Foundation, Sutro Elementary School. **Typical freshman schedule:** N/P.

## STUDENT SUPPORT SERVICES

**Counselor/student ratio (not including college counselors):** 1:389. **Counseling:** The school has a licensed counselor who meets with students or parents on their request and who holds evening meetings for parents on developmental issues. The director of college counseling meets individually with students and their parents beginning junior year and also works with the class as a whole. **Learning disabilities/differences:** "If a student is admitted, University seeks to accommodate the needs of that student. We offer extended time for tests and extra tutorials in subjects that students with learning differences might need." **Career apprenticeship programs:** "University aids students in helping and identifying summer work and volunteer opportunities. The community service learning program and school academic departments announce opportunities throughout the year. Faculty members also are available for advice and counseling."

## STUDENT CONDUCT AND HEALTH

N/P.

## SUMMER PROGRAMS

For six weeks in the summer, the school hosts Summerbridge, a tuition-free academic enrichment program for talented seventh and eighth graders from the local public and parochial schools.

## PARENT INVOLVEMENT

**Parent participation:** All families are asked to donate their time to the Parent Association and to contribute to the school's fundraising efforts. **Parent/teacher communication:** N/P. **Parent education:** "The Parent Association works with the office of the Dean of Students and the Health office to offer programs and seminars for the parent body. These seminars include topics ranging from health, college counseling, and intellectual/academic development." **Donations:** (See above.)

## SPORTS

Boys' cross-country, golf, basketball, badminton (coed), baseball, lacrosse, swimming, tennis, and volleyball. Girls' cross-country, field hockey, tennis, volleyball, basketball, badminton (coed), soccer, swimming, and softball. Boys' and girls' track.

## WHAT SETS SCHOOL APART FROM OTHERS

N/P.

## HOW PARENTS/STUDENTS CHARACTERIZE SCHOOL

N/P.

# SAN FRANCISCO WALDORF HIGH SCHOOL

at Fort Mason Center
Mailing Address:
2938 Washington Street
San Francisco, CA 94115

(415) 931-2736 *fax (415) 440-9405*

Joan Caldarera, High School Chair
Barbara Allen, Director of Admissions

## GENERAL

**Coed** day high school based on the Waldorf method. Founded in 1997, lower school founded in 1979. **Nonprofit. Enrollment:** Approximately 70 in G9-11. **Average class size:** 12-15. **Accreditation:** Currently seeking accreditation through WASC. **School year:** 9.5-month calendar (180 instructional days). **School day:** 8 a.m. to 3:30 p.m. **Location:** Fort Mason, at the north end of San Francisco, accessible from MUNI lines 22, 30, 45, and others.

## STUDENT BODY

**Geographical breakdown (counties):** 70% from San Francisco; 10% from Marin; 10% from the East Bay; and 10% from the South Bay. **Ethnicity:** 65% Caucasian (non-Latino); 10% Asian; 10% African-American; 5% Latino; 10% other. **Foreign students (I-20 status):** 3. **Single parent/two f/t working parent families:** 90%. **Middle schools:** 80% of most recent entering class came from all Bay Area Waldorf grade schools; 5% from public middle schools; and 15% from 3 private, non-parochial schools. (N/P # other schools)

## ADMISSION

**Applications due:** Approximately January 21 (call for date). **Application fee:** $50. **Application process:** In addition to responses regarding interests and musical instrument study, applicants are asked to submit a self-portrait using any media or art-form and a piece of academic work. Parents write a biography of the child. The BAIHS recommendation forms are used (the school follows the BAIHS timetable). Prospective students are required to attend a half-day of school and an open house. Call for admissions calendar. Interviews of parents and students by the admissions committee are "the most important part of your application ...." **No. of applications:** "75-100." **Admission cut-off:** None. **Preferences:** Siblings and Waldorf lower school students. **"We are looking for** ninth and tenth grade students who have a special pioneering spirit and unique personal talents, skills, and goals [as well as] qualities of openness and good will and enthusiasm for all kinds of work." **What sort of student do you best serve?** "We serve Bay Area students of diverse backgrounds who demonstrate the desire and ability to challenge themselves and to serve others."

## COSTS

**Latest tuition:** $11,500 payable in full or monthly. **Sibling discount:** 10%. **Tuition increases:** Approximately 5-8% annually expected. **Other costs:** Books, field trips, sports programs. **Financial aid:** Waldorf High School devotes 12-14% of its budget to financial assistance. **Percentage of students receiving financial aid:** 38%. **Average grant:** $3,000. **No. of full-tuition grants:** One. **No. of half-tuition grants:** 6-10. **Grants of half-tuition or more:** 37%.

## SCHOOL'S MISSION STATEMENT/GOALS

"Imaginative thinking, social conscience, cultural awareness, and environmental stewardship are the guiding ideals of San Francisco Waldorf High School. ... The inspiring dedication and leadership of the faculty will meet the practical and intellectual needs of today's adolescent through the school's academic, co-curricular, athletic, and extensive internship programs. Within a framework of the traditional liberal arts and sciences, we emphasize the quality and nature of work—from hand crafts to the professions, from technology to entrepreneurship—to develop in each individual student self-reliance, responsibility to community, and a sense of life purpose. Our students will be prepared to meet a multicultural, multifaceted world with enthusiasm, and [will have] the capacity to make a positive impact in their chosen fields of endeavor, at university and workplace."

# ACADEMIC PROGRAM

The school "will accomplish its mission through a program that provides exposure to a very broad range of ideas in the arts and sciences along with practical experience. The Waldorf High School curriculum incorporates both college preparatory and vocational education to provide young people with the satisfaction of acquiring both intellectual and practical life skills. The integration of the fine, performing, and applied arts throughout the academic curriculum meets the adolescent's need for positive soul experiences and develops imaginative thinking." Each year's curriculum is designed around a theme: Polarities, Process, Identity, and World Consciousness, respectively, for G9-12. **Courses offered (AP=Advanced Placement, H=Honors, (AP)=AP option, (H)=Honors option):** (Topics in parentheses show progression of the area of study over four years). Biology (Human Anatomy, Mineralogy, Embryology, Botany, Cell Biology, Zoology, Evolution), Chemistry (Organic Chemistry, Acids, Bases, Salts, The Periodic Table, Chemical Technology), Physics (Acoustics, Energy, Mechanics, Electricity & Magnetism, Optics), Geology (Land Masses, Water Systems, Astronomy, Environmental Sciences), Math (Pre-Algebra or Algebra I, Computer Keyboarding, Geometry, Trigonometry, Computer Construction and Repair, Algebra II, Projective Geometry, Computer Programming and Applications, Calculus, Economics, Senior Computer Project), History (Modern World History, Revolutions, US Revolution to Civil War, Ancient History, Middle Ages, Growth of Law, Indigenous America, Renaissance, Reformation, Enlightenment, Cultural Identities in America, Symptomatology, Emerging Nations, Current Issues in America), Cultural Studies (Indigenous People of the Pacific Rim, Africa & West Asia, Cultural Anthropology, History of Ideas, History of Religion), Language Arts (Dramatic Expression in Literature, Spanish or German, Origins of Language, Ancient Epics, Romanticism & The Quest, Creative Writing, Modern World Literature), Aesthetics (Art History, Poetics, History of Music, Architecture), Music (Choir, Orchestra, Musical Ensembles, Solo Work), Eurythmy (Contemporary & Original Poetry & Music, Students' Choreography, Dramatic Tales & Orchestral Music, Solo Work), Physical Education/Movement (Bothmer Gymnastics, Dance, Outdoor Education (crew, sailing, rock climbing, ice skating), Athletics, First Aid, Health), Theater (Storytelling, Stagecraft, Building a Character, Play Production), Drawing (Black & White, East Asian Calligraphy, Forms of Calligraphy, Perspective Life Drawing, Senior Project in Painting and Drawing, Elective Media), Painting (Watercolor, Media Exploration), Sculpture (Free-form, Vessels and Containers, Human Figure, Carving), World of Work

(History of Labor, History of Crafts, History of Technology & Science, History of Commerce), Practical Arts (including basketry, gardening, car repair, weaving, furniture making, bookbinding, graphic design, internship, and student-run business). **Computer lab/training:** "The school has a small computer lab for progressive instruction, though use of the computer for word processing is not expected until after 10th grade." (N/P re #, etc.) **Grading:** Letter grades as well as detailed written evaluations. **Graduation requirements:** Students completing the 4-year program will have to fulfill all UC requirements plus work in the arts. Each senior will be required to do an extensive Senior Project. **Average nightly homework:** G9: 1.5-2 hours; G10-12: 2 hours; G11: 2.5-3 hours. **Faculty:** Of the 20 faculty members, 9 are male, 11 female. Five hold bachelor's degrees as highest degree; 10 hold master's (or other advanced) degrees; and 5 hold doctorates. **Faculty ethnicity:** 80% Caucasian (non-Latino); 10% Latino; 5% African-American; 5% other. **Faculty selection/training:** "Our teachers are Waldorf-trained or in the process of completing their training, with at least a bachelor's degree (though in most cases higher) in their field of specialization. We attend the annual West Coast Waldorf Teachers' Conference, send representatives to the annual national conference, and spend 1-3 weeks each summer at curriculum and education workshops. 2-3 master teachers visit to work with the faculty each year." **Teacher/student ratio:** 1:8. **Teacher's daily student load in required academic subject:** N/P. **AP courses/exams:** Not yet available. **Senior class profile (mean):** The school has not yet had its first senior class. **National Merit Scholarship Program:** Not yet available. **College enrollment:** Not yet available.

## CAMPUS/CAMPUS LIFE

**Campus description:** The campus is located in Fort Mason Center next to the Marina Green. There are currently 8 classrooms located in the Herbst and Festival Pavilions and in Landmark Building C. Additional classroom space is rented as needed. The Young Performers Theater is used for drama classes and the Cowell Theater for Performances. The campus will relocate in the summer of 2000 to a new site that will accommodate the 4-year program. **Library:** There is currently a small library that shares space with the computer science labs. **Open/closed campus:** N/P. **Classroom space per student:** N/P. **Lunches:** Students bring their own lunches or purchase them at Green's Restaurant or Cooks and Company in Fort Mason Center. **Bus service:** N/P. **Uniform/dress code:** The dress code prohibits clothing with symbols pertaining to alcohol, drugs, sex, or violence as well as sweat pants and short shorts. "Students should be prepared for all kinds of school-related activities." **Co-curricular activities/clubs:** Yearbook, literary magazine, student council, drama club, forensic team, service club, photography club, and others as student interest dictates. **Foreign exchange program:** A foreign exchange program began in the 1998-99 year with 3 exchanges to and from Germany. The school will work with the more than 600 Waldorf schools worldwide to arrange further exchanges in G10 and 11. **Opportunities for community service:** "Students perform community service as part of the regular curriculum." **Typical freshman schedule:** The main lesson is 2 hours every morning; its subject rotates through 3- to 6-week blocks. After a 20-minute break, skills classes are held. These are 50-minute classes meeting 3-4 times a week (math, English, music, and foreign language). Students have a 40-minute lunch break followed by art classes (2 hours) 2 times a week. P.E. is held for 1-2 hours, 2 times a week after lunch. Sports and after-school activities take place from 3:30 to 6 p.m. Students have 4 hours of music instruction—vocal and instrumental—each week.

## STUDENT SUPPORT SERVICES

**Counselor/student ratio (not including college counselors):** Consultants only. **Counseling:** Each grade level works as a group with two faculty sponsors over the four years. Additionally, the students choose an academic mentor who assists in academic and **college planning**. No **personal counselors** as of yet, but three consultants. **Learning disabilities/differences:** "The school has a resource person on staff, currently working in a tutorial capacity with students with special needs as she develops what we are calling a 'parallel curriculum' to be used in the future." **Career apprenticeship programs:** "The school's internship program begins in the 11th grade when students will spend one week working in a field of their choice. They will be expected to maintain an ongoing working relationship with this internship through the 11th grade year and then complete the internship with a deeper involvement and time commitment during the 12th grade year."

## STUDENT CONDUCT AND HEALTH

**Code of conduct:** Violations of school rules result in disciplinary action and may result in suspension or dismissal. **How school handles drugs/alcohol usage:** "No cigarette, drug, or alcohol use is tolerated on campus. Students with substance abuse problems are referred to counseling. Drug use is viewed as being incompatible with the work of the Waldorf curriculum, and both students and parents must sign off on an understanding of the school's policy as stipulated in the Student handbook." **Drug/alcohol abuse prevention/AIDS awareness program:** Part of the overall health curriculum over four years.

## SUMMER PROGRAMS

The school offers a two-week Summer Seminar designed for students entering the high school from non-Waldorf schools.

# Parent Involvement

**Parent participation:** "Purely voluntary. As a pioneering venture, we hope for enthusiastic hard-working parents to assist with the Winter Fair, fundraising, car pooling, and other activities." **Parent/teacher communication:** Yearly conferences, quarterly grades, and report cards. Evening meetings 2-3 times a year. **Parent education:** The school holds 3 class parent evenings each year devoted to developmental issues as well as guest lectures 2-3 times per year. It plans to host parent workshops on specific issues such as drugs, technology, and risk-taking. **Donations:** "Parents are asked to contribute to the school through volunteerism and the annual giving campaign."

# Sports

Junior varsity and/or varsity competition in the Bay Counties League in: girls' and boys' cross-country, basketball, and track and field; girls' volleyball; and boys' baseball. Intramural golf and tennis competition are offered through clubs; rowing with the Marina Rowing Association.

# What Sets School Apart From Others

"Integration of arts and academics. Education of the full person: the mind, the heart, and the ability to do and achieve. A curriculum based upon time-tested indications put to use in Waldorf schools since 1919. An articulated philosophy of life as well as of education out of which the faculty works."

# How Parents/Students Characterize School

**Parent response(s):** "The school has an adventuresome and exciting spirit that fosters independent and creative thinking."
**Student response(s):**
"Learning is fun. I enjoy all my classes. I like the broad curriculum—especially the integration of the arts. Classes are exciting—classroom activities are diverse."

*Illustration by Serra student Alexander Lo*

# JUNIPERO SERRA HIGH SCHOOL

451 W. 20th Ave.
San Mateo, CA 94403

(650) 345-8207 *fax (650) 573-6638*

www.serrahs.com
padres@serrahs.com

C. Michael Peterson, Principal
Randy Vogel, Admissions Director

## GENERAL

**Boys'** day school. **Catholic** (78% Catholic). Operated by the Archdiocese of San Francisco. Founded in 1944. **Nonprofit. Enrollment:** 950. **Average class size:** 25-26. **Accreditation:** WASC (6-year term: 1997-03). **School year:** 11-month calendar (approx. 183 instructional days). **School day:** 8:10 a.m. to 2:50 p.m. **Location:** In residential San Mateo, 22 miles south of San Francisco, 9 miles north of Palo Alto. The school is just off Highway 92, which intersects with Highways 280 and 101.

# STUDENT BODY

**Geographical breakdown:** 98% from the Peninsula (from San Francisco through Palo Alto, including the coastal areas of Half Moon Bay and Pacifica). **Ethnicity:** 64% Caucasian (non-Latino); 14% Latino; 10% Filipino; 10% Asian/Pacific Islander; 2% African-American. **Foreign students (I-20 status):** Less than 1%. **Single parent families:** Approx. 20%. **Two f/t working parent families:** Approx. 70%. **Middle schools:** 23 Catholic feeder schools in the county including St. Gregory (San Mateo), St. Matthew (San Mateo) and Our Lady of Angels (Burlingame) and more than 35 public feeder schools including Central (San Carlos), Ralston (Belmont), and Crocker (Hillsborough). (N/P re # students/ schools)

# ADMISSION

**Applications due:** Mid-January (call for exact date). **Application fee:** $50. **Application process:** Applications are available in late October. The school hosts an open house in early January for boys in grades 6-8 and their families. Full day shadow visits may be scheduled for Tuesdays-Thursdays October-February. (Appointments need to be made a week in advance of the visit.) Transcripts and recommendation forms (from a middle school counselor or principal) are needed by early February. Clergy recommendation forms are optional, though most applicants submit them. (The form seeks a recommendation from any clergy member who knows the child, or alternatively, asks for information on the applicant's spirituality.) Applicants are interviewed in February, and decision letters are sent mid-March. Students take the HSPT exam at the school in April. **No. of applications:** More than 500 applications were received for 255 places. Eight new students were admitted to G10, 5 to G11. **Admission cut-off:** "We generally look for students who are at or above grade level in their testing with better than average grades." **Preferences:** Catholic. **"We are looking for** students seeking a college preparatory education and who wish to participate in the school community." **What sort of student do you best serve?** "We are designed to meet the needs of Catholic boys in San Mateo County; students who are average to above average academically are usually successful at Serra."

# COSTS

**Latest tuition:** $7,045. Payments can be made monthly (by Direct Debit), once each semester (July 20th and December 20th), or once for the entire year (due July 20th). **Sibling discount:** None. **Tuition increases:** Approx. 5%. **Percentage of students receiving financial aid:** 20%. **Average grant:** $2,015. **No. of full-tuition grants:** "Few." **No. of half-tuition grants:** 5% (5). **Grants of half-tuition or more:** 3% (3).

## SCHOOL'S MISSION STATEMENT/GOALS

"Junipero Serra High School is the Archdiocesan Catholic school educating the young men of San Mateo County. We are an academic high school, reflecting the cultural richness of San Mateo County with a strong college preparatory curriculum. Our mission is to develop the gifts and talents of each student and to foster Gospel values in an environment of academic excellence and mutual respect.

"Our Philosophy .... Empowered by parents, the primary educators of their children, and the Archdiocese of San Francisco, Junipero Serra High School is a Catholic school participating in the educational ministry of the Church. Junipero Serra has the responsibility to provide an integrated ministry through the celebration of Word and Sacrament, the building of community and the promotion of service to the world in which we live. At Junipero Serra High School the educational process, grounded in the Catholic tradition, affirms the dignity of the human person. The unique gifts and talents of each Junipero Serra student are developed in two complementary ways: first, through the fostering of intellectual capabilities, artistic creativity, and physical skills and secondly, through the nurturing of spiritual, moral, psychological, and social growth. Through an integration of faith, life and culture, each student is encouraged to look critically at the diversity and challenges of our society and to make responsible choices based on the Gospel values of justice and compassion. The purpose of Junipero Serra High School is to develop mature Christians who live lives of faith and service and who, like Blessed Junipero Serra, find Christ in and bring Christ to the people with whom they live, work and serve."

## ACADEMIC PROGRAM

**Courses offered (AP=Advanced Placement, H=Honors, (AP)=AP option, (H)=Honors option): English:** English 1-2-3-4 (H), Study Skills, Junior English, AP English Language and Composition, Journalism, Senior Literature and Composition, Non-Fiction, Humanities, The Age of Shakespeare, Senior Writing, Creative Writing, Publications 1-2, AP English Literature and Composition, Diagnostic Reading; **History:** World History 1-2 (H), US History (AP), American Political Systems, American Government and Politics (AP), Economics, California History; **Math:** Introduction to Integrated Mathematics, Integrated Algebra 1-2 (H), Business Accounting, Integrated Geometry (H), Integrated Algebra and Trigonometry, Trigonometry (H), Pre-Calculus (H), Calculus (AP), Business Finance; **P.E.:** P.E.-Health, P.E.2-3, Physical Education Athletics; **Science:** Discovering Science (H), Chemistry (H), Biology (H), Earth Space Science, Earth Science, Physics, Advanced Biology (AP), Anatomy and Physiology, Introductory Astronomy; **Foreign Language:** French 1-4, 51-52, 53-54 (H), AP French Language, Spanish 1-4, 41-52, 53, 54, 60 (H), Advanced Spanish, AP Spanish Language, German 1-4, German 51-52, 53, 54 (H), Language TA, Sign Language; **Theology:** Religious Studies 1, 2, 3a, 3b, 4a, 4b, Bioethics; **Music/Art:** Advanced Band, Jazz Band, Beg/Inter Guitar, Percussion 1-2, Winds 1-2, Chorus, History of Rock Music, Dramatic Workshop, Musical Theater Workshop, Advanced Drama, Art, Basic Art, Ceramics, Architectural Design, AP Art History, Films, Photography; **Computers:** Computer Literacy, Computer Programming, Advanced Computer Literacy; **Other:** Speech, Psychology, Yearbook Publication. **Coed classes:** At Mercy High School in Burlingame, Art, Photography, Anatomy and Physiology; at Notre Dame High School in Belmont, Economics, Honors French IV, AP French, Basic Art, Drama, Bioethics, Ceramics, Speech, AP Art History, AP Spanish. **Computer lab/training:** The school has 2 computer labs, one for students to use on their own, the other for class instruction, one with 30 PCs, the other with 32 PCs. 18 PCs are in the science labs, 7 in the library, 8 in the history lab, and 1 in each classroom. The school computers are all networked and all students will have e-mail accounts. One semester Computer Literacy required. **Grading:** Letter grades are issued 6 times a year. **Graduation requirements:** (Designed to meet or exceed the minimum admission requirements for the UC system.) 4 years English, 3.5 years social studies, 3.5 years religion, 3 years math, 2.5 years science, 2 years of a foreign language, 1 year P.E., .5 year computer literacy and fine arts, 80 hours of Christian Service. **Average nightly homework (Mon-Th):** G9-10: 3-4 hours; G11: 4 hours; G12: 2-4 hours. **Faculty:** 82% male; 18% female. 49% of faculty hold bachelor's degrees as highest degrees; 51% hold master's degrees. **Faculty ethnicity:** 98% Caucasian (non-Latino); 1% Latino. **Faculty selection/training:** "Faculty have teaching credentials and higher degrees. Periodic in-services are held throughout the school year and continuing education and workshops are encouraged." **Teacher/student ratio:** 1:26. **Teacher's daily student load in required academic subject:** Fewer than 145 students. **AP courses/exams:** 32% of juniors and seniors are currently taking AP courses. (N/P re exams) **Senior class profile (mean):** N/P. **GPA:** 3.0. **National Merit Scholarship Program:** N/P. **College enrollment:** 68% of last year's graduating class enrolled in 4-year colleges, 30.5% in 2-year colleges. Acceptances include: American, Amherst, Ariz. State, Boston U, Boston C, Chaminade U, Claremont-McKenna, C of Notre Dame, Creighton, Cal State campuses (all), Duke, Georgetown, George Washington, Gonzaga, Harvard, Indiana U, Linfield C, Loyola Marymount, Menlo, New Mexico Tech, NYU, Northern Arizona U, Northwestern, Occidental, Pepperdine, Princeton, Regis, Rensselaer Polytech, Rice, Rutgers, St. Mary's, Santa Clara, Seattle, Southern Methodist, Stanford, UC (all campuses), US Naval Academy, U of Arizona, U of Colorado-Boulder, U of Dallas, U of Nebraska, U of Nevada-Reno, U of Notre Dame, U of Oregon, UOP, U of Puget Sound, U of the Redlands, U of San Diego, USF, USC, U of Texas-Austin, U of Utah, Washington U, Willamette, and Yale.

# OTHER INDICATORS THE SCHOOL IS ACCOMPLISHING ITS GOALS

"The success of our graduates in a wide variety of areas upon graduation from school."

# CAMPUS/CAMPUS LIFE

**Campus description:** The school has a 13-acre campus with a building complex that includes two stories of classrooms, science labs and offices, a chapel, an 800-seat auditorium, cafeteria, gym, locker room, weight room, architectural design studio, music room, pool, and shop. At the back of the campus are basketball courts, a football field and track, a baseball field, soccer field, and an art building with drawing and painting studios. **Library:** 16,000 volumes; 40 periodical subscriptions; Infotrak; 7 networked computers; on-line catalog; study space for 80 students; open from 7:30 a.m. to 5 p.m.; full-time librarian with 2 part-time assistants. **Open/closed campus:** Closed. **Classroom space per student:** N/P. **Lunches:** Students may purchase hot lunch daily. **Bus service:** SamTrans (public). **Uniforms/dress code:** Jeans in good condition are permitted; sweats, overalls, military pants, surgical pants and work pants are not. Walking shorts are allowed in fall and spring. Shirts must have collars or a full turtleneck and sleeves. No drug, alcohol, etc. messages allowed. No professional team jackets, no hats. No facial hair, hair longer than collar, dyed hair, piercings, or tattoos allowed. (Certain dress-up days require buttoned collared dress shirt, tie, non-denim slacks and dress shoes.) **Co-curricular activities/clubs:** More than 25 clubs including yearbook, a monthly newspaper, and an annual literary magazine. On each publication, students have the opportunity to contribute writing, photography, or aid in design. **Foreign exchange program:** No formal program. **Opportunities for community service:** All students are required to complete 80 hours of volunteer service with a non-profit agency before graduation. Students participate in two blood drives and an annual Holiday Food Drive. Students are also "strongly encouraged" to participate in activities of their parishes. **Typical freshman schedule:** English, Integral Algebra, World History, Religion, foreign language (French, Spanish or German), and Introduction to Science/Computers.

# STUDENT SUPPORT SERVICES

**Counselor-student ratio (not including college counselors):** 1:240. **Counseling:** The school has four full-time counselors who engage in personal, academic and college counseling, as well as a staff member for the College and Career Center. College counseling begins freshman year. **Learning disabilities/differences:** "A learning resource specialist assists teachers and counselors of students with learning differences to make the necessary accommodations to [help students achieve] success in the classroom." **Career apprenticeship programs:** N/P.

## STUDENT CONDUCT AND HEALTH

**Code of conduct:** Besides prohibiting violations of the law, cheating and other honor code provisions, the code prohibits beepers, cell phones, and walkmen, skateboards and roller skates. **How school handles drug/alcohol usage:** On first offense the student is subject to expulsion, though a student who has a clean record may be placed on probation if the violation did not involve drug or alcohol sales. On second offense, he is dismissed. **Drug/alcohol abuse prevention/ AIDS awareness:** "Program for Student Assistance."

## SUMMER PROGRAMS

The school offers a coed summer recreational camp for ages 5-12; a coed summer swim school; a coed summer school program with enrichment for junior high students; enrichment and review for incoming students; and high school courses.

## PARENT INVOLVEMENT

**Parent participation:** No requirement, though parents are invited to participate in the Board of Education, Mothers' Auxiliary, Fathers' Club and Boosters' Club. **Parent/teacher communication:** Parent-teacher conferences. **Parent education:** The school hosts various orientation programs, college night programs, discussion of teenage issues, back-to-school night, report card conference nights, and beginning introduction to computers nights. **Donations:** "Each family is asked to make a yearly gift or pledge based on whatever is a comfortable amount for them to Junipero Serra's Parent Pledge Program. The amount donated by our families varies greatly."

## SPORTS

Junipero Serra has teams in 13 sports competing in the West Catholic Athletic League in football, water polo, cross-country, basketball, wrestling, soccer, baseball, track, golf, swimming, tennis, volleyball, and crew. (Most all sports offer three teams: freshman level, junior varsity, and varsity competition.)

## WHAT SETS SCHOOL APART FROM OTHERS

"Junipero Serra offers the best of both worlds. We allow our students to be themselves in an all-male environment where camaraderie and school spirit are much more commonplace than competition and fashion. We also enjoy a relationship with two sister schools: Mercy in Burlingame and Notre Dame in Belmont. This allows for healthy interaction and includes coed classes, retreats, performing arts and dances. Junipero Serra has something for everyone. With an enrollment of nearly 950 students, we are small enough that you won't get lost in the shuffle, but big enough to offer the same activities and course offerings of much larger schools. Junipero Serra places its students at various levels in our college preparatory program according to their needs and abilities. Outside of the classroom, our students are involved in a host of activities including music and drama productions, team sports, student publications, student government and other numerous clubs." The school offers "a good atmosphere for learning; a dedicated faculty (with a dozen or so alumni who have come back to teach), and a true sense of community including teachers, staff, students and their families."

## How Parents/Students Characterize School

"A quality education in a caring environment." "Students can thrive in a variety of areas." "Strong academics, athletics and extra curricular." "Good atmosphere and feeling of community." "Great spirit."

# Spraings Academy

1963 Tice Valley Blvd.
Walnut Creek, CA 94595
Office:
89 Moraga Way
Orinda, CA 94563

(510) 253-1906 *fax (510) 253-1595*

Violet Spraings, Ph.D., Director
Diane Emberlin, Assistant Director

## General

**Coed** day high school with elementary and middle school. **Nonsectarian.** Founded in 1967. (N/P re nonprofit or proprietary). **Enrollment:** Approximately 70. **Average class size:** 8-10. **Accreditation:** The school is a candidate for WASC accreditation and is certified by the California State Dept. of Education to teach the learning handicapped. **School year:** 10-month calendar (195 instructional days). **School day:** 8:30 a.m. to 2:30 p.m. **Location:** In Walnut Creek, accessible from the Walnut Creek BART stop by a bus that stops in front of the school.

# Student Body

**Geographical breakdown (counties):** 50% from Solano; 46% from Contra Costa; 2% from San Francisco; 2% from Alameda. **Ethnicity:** Approximately 65% Caucasian (non-Latino); 25% African-American; 6% Asian; 3% Latino. **Foreign students (I-20 status):** 20%. **Single parent/two f/t working parent families:** N/P. **Middle schools:** 45% of the most recent entering freshman class came from 50 public middle schools; 50% from 6 private, non-parochial schools; 5% from parochial schools.

# Admission

**Applications due:** Accepted throughout the year. **Application fee:** N/P. **Application process:** Interested families should contact the school to arrange for the student to be interviewed with the Director and the Assistant Director. At the time of the interview, a screening examination will be scheduled. **No. of applications:** 50 applications were received for 25 places in prior year's class. Fifteen new students were admitted to G10, 10 to G11 and 1 to G12. **Admission cut-off:** N/P. **Preferences:** N/P. **"We are looking for** students who show a discrepancy between their ability levels and their achievement levels as well as students needing a general college preparatory program." **What sort of students do you best serve?** "The student who evidences a discrepancy between his ability and achievement. The school is dedicated to resolving learning disabilities."

# Costs

**Latest tuition:** $16,216 payable in 12 payments (payment plans available). **Sibling discount:** Yes. **Tuition increases:** 2-3% annually. **Financial aid:** In 1998-99, 50% of the students received funding under a federal program for learning disabilities. **Percentage of students receiving financial aid:** See above. **Average grant:** N/P. **No. of full tuition/half-tuition grants:** N/P.

# School's Mission Statement/Goals

"We will challenge each student through strong academics, character building, and on-going improvements to develop the abilities and character needed to contribute maximally to his or her community and to the world."

# Academic Program

"Spraings Academy offers a full academic program. The courses needed for university entrance are offered as well as the academic intensity needed to resolve learning disabilities." Each student is screened through the diagnostic center and an appropriate program is set up. **Courses offered (AP=Advanced Placement,**

**H=Honors, (AP)=AP option, (H)=Honors option):** English 9-12 Literature and Composition, Writing Workshop, German 1-4, General Math, Consumer Math, Algebra I-II, Geometry I-II, Trigonometry, World Cultures, US History, Economics, World History, California History, Geography & Civics, General Science, Biology I & II (includes lab), Physiology (includes lab), Physics (includes lab), Chemistry & Earth Science, Keyboarding, Word Processing, Art I-III, Photography I-II, Drama I-III. **Computer lab/training:** Spraings has one computer lab with 10 computers; in addition, there are computers in every classroom. IBM and Macs. (N/P re training) **Grading:** Letter grades. **Graduation requirements:** 4 years English, 4 years math, 1 year biological science, 1 year physical science, 1 year world history, geography & culture, 1 year US history, 1 year US government/economics, 2 years foreign language (German) or fine arts, 3 years P.E., 1 semester drivers' ed/health, electives to equal 240 credits, passing score on Spraings Academy's reading, writing, and math tests. **Average nightly homework:** 2 hours. **Faculty:** 53% male, 47% female. 20% of faculty hold bachelor's degrees as highest degree; 50% hold master's degrees; and 30% hold doctorates. **Faculty ethnicity:** N/P. **Faculty selection/training:** N/P. **Teacher/student ratio:** 1:10 or fewer. **Teacher's daily student load in required academic subject:** 20-45. **AP courses/exams:** 1% of students are currently taking AP courses. (N/P re exams) **Senior class profile (mean):** N/P. **GPA:** 3.0. **National Merit Scholarship Program:** N/P. **College enrollment:** 30% of last year's graduating class enrolled in 4-year colleges, 30% in 2-year colleges, including: University of California, Diablo Valley C, CSU-SF, CSU-Somona, Linfield C (OR), LaVerne U (CT) and SCU-Hayward.

## Other Indicators the School is Accomplishing its Goals

"Each year, the number of students seeking enrollment in our school increases as well as the number of graduates applying for and entering higher education."

## Campus/Campus Life

**Campus description:.** The school is located in the facility formerly occupied by Del Valle High School—a one-story building with 15 classrooms. **Library:** The school uses a nearby public library. **Open/closed campus:** N/P. **Classroom space per student:** N/P. **Lunches:** Student-run store and snack bar. **Bus service:** N/P. **Uniforms/dress code:** N/P. **Co-curricular activities/clubs:** After-school sports program. **Foreign exchange program:** The German language class visits Germany each year. **Opportunities for community service:** In future years community service will be required. **Typical freshman schedule:** English Literature and Composition, math, social studies, foreign language, P.E., and elective.

# STUDENT SUPPORT SERVICES

**Counselor/student ratio (not including college counselors):** N/P. **Counseling:** Two psychologists and one MFCC are available for personal counseling. Academic counseling and college counseling/career guidance are also available. **Learning disabilities/differences:** The school is certified by the state of California to teach students with learning disabilities. 50-60% of students in the school have learning disabilities; approximately 1/3 of the students are both learning disabled and mentally gifted. The school is dedicated to resolving learning disabilities; the school believes that if a child is of average or above average ability, there is a good chance of resolving a learning disability. **Career apprenticeship programs:** N/P.

# STUDENT CONDUCT AND HEALTH

**Code of conduct:** Standard. **How school handles drugs/alcohol usage:** Students caught using drugs or alcohol are expelled. **Drug/alcohol abuse prevention/AIDS awareness programs:** Included in health education curriculum.

# SUMMER PROGRAMS

Academics, drama, and visual arts program.

# PARENT INVOLVEMENT

**Parent participation:** Parents are asked to participate in a parent group. **Parent/teacher communication:** Conferences between parents and teachers are held twice a year and report cards are issued quarterly. **Parent education:** N/P. **Donations:** Parents are requested to make contributions to the school.

# SPORTS

Interscholastic sports include softball, flag football, and basketball.

# WHAT SETS SCHOOL APART FROM OTHERS

"Conceptual Development Lab where students are taught to think and how to learn, and the remedial plus academic emphasis."

## How Parents/Students Characterize School

**Parent response(s):** "Parents feel that this is an ideal campus where students are taught in small groups and helped to 'be all they can be.'"
**Student response(s):** "Students feel this is a place where they can learn."

# Stuart Hall High School

1715 Octavia St. (at Pine)
San Francisco, CA 94115

(415) 563-2900 *fax (415) 292-3183*
www.sacred.sf.ca.us

Gordon Sharafinski, Head of School

[Ed. Note: the school is just being established as of the date of this publication—it will not open for students until fall, 2000. Information not yet available or applicable is designated as "N/A".]

## General

**Boys'** day high school (Stuart Hall for Boys, K-8, is located several blocks away at Broadway and Fillmore Streets). Founded 2000. (The lower school was founded in 1956.) **Independent Catholic.** (The lower/middle school is 50% non-Catholic.) **Nonprofit,** member CAIS, NAIS, BAIHS. **Enrollment:** Expected enrollment 225. **Average class size:** 14. **Accreditation:** WASC/CAIS (N/P term), Network of Sacred Heart Schools. **School year:** 9-month calendar (180 instructional days). **School day:** 8:15 a.m. to 3:15 p.m. **Location:** Pacific Heights residential area, two blocks from Japantown, accessible by the 1 California and 4 Sutter Muni lines, and all lines running on Van Ness Avenue.

## Student Body

**Geographical breakdown (counties):** The majority of students are expected to be from San Francisco and Marin, also from San Mateo County and the East Bay. **Ethnic breakdown:** N/A. **Foreign students (I-20 status):** N/A. **Single parent/two f/t working parent families:** N/P. **Middle schools:** Private independent, parochial, and public middle schools.

# ADMISSION

**Applications due:** Approximately January 9 (call for date). **Application fee:** $75.
**Application process:** Tours will be conducted September through February. Open
houses will be held in November for students and their families. **No. of applications:** N/A. **Admission cut-off:** None. **Preferences:** Siblings and legacies. "We
are looking for young men who want to be engaged in their education and are
willing to take on a strong academic program and leadership roles within the
school community." **What sort of student do you best serve?** N/P.

# COSTS

**Latest tuition:** (The school will not open until fall, 2000—tuition has not yet
been set. It will be payable in 1 or 2 payments or through a 10-month payment
plan.) **Sibling discount:** None. **Tuition increases:** Approximately 4-5% annually. **Other costs:** $300-$600 for books. **Financial aid:** Need-based. **Percentage
of students receiving financial aid:** N/A. **Average grant award:** N/A. **No. of
full-tuition grants:** N/A. **No. of half-tuition grants:** N/A. **Grants of half-tuition or more:** N/A.

# SCHOOL'S MISSION STATEMENT/GOALS

Philosophy: "The Schools of the Sacred Heart in the United States, members of
a world-wide network, offer an education that is marked by a distinctive spirit.
Sacred Heart schools are committed to the individual student's total development: spiritual, intellectual, emotional, and physical. Stuart Hall High School
will emphasize serious study, sportsmanship, artistic discovery, social responsibility, and faith development. All Schools of the Sacred Heart schools commit themselves to educate to: a personal and active faith in God; a deep respect for intellectual values; a social awareness which impels to action; the building of community
as a Christian value; and personal growth in an atmosphere of wise freedom."

# ACADEMIC PROGRAM

"Every student will be enrolled in a challenging and enriching academic program
and will be an active participant in his own education. The learning that will take
place, both in and out of the classroom, is intended to be collaborative between
faculty and students. The administration, faculty, and student body will be committed to intellectual honesty and leadership development and students will be
treated seriously as scholars and leaders. Each student will be required to take a
minimum of six courses for credit each semester. Every student will graduate
with a program which satisfies the University of California course requirements
for admission." **(Projected) Courses offerings (AP=Advanced Placement,
H=Honors, (AP)=AP option, (H)=Honors option):** Religious Studies I-IV,

Philosophy, English I (H), English II (H), American Literature (H), British Literature, English Literature and Composition (AP), Creative Writing, Writers Workshop, Controversial Literature, Contemporary Novel, Journalism, History I-II, US History (AP), American Politics & Policy, Asian Studies, American Government (AP), International Relations, Economics, Environmental Science (AP), Comparative Government and Politics (AP), European History (AP), Psychology (AP), French 1-2, French 3 (H), French 4 (H), French Language (AP), French Literature (AP), Japanese 1-4, Spanish 1-2, Spanish 3 (H), Spanish Language (AP), Spanish Literature (AP), Mandarin I, Advanced Mandarin, Asian Studies, Integrated Science, Biology (AP), Chemistry (H, AP), Physics, Physiology, Integrated Mathematics including Algebra/Geometry/Trigonometry I-III (H in II, III), Pre-Calculus, Pre-Calculus with Calculus (H), Calculus, Calculus AB (AP), Statistics, Introduction to Art for Freshmen, Humanities, Art Studio (AP), Art History (AP), Choir, Drama, Notables, Instrumental Music, Independent Study, Ceramics, Photography, Seminar in Art (Drawing, Painting, Printmaking, The Art of Crafts), Open Studio, P.E. I-II, Team Sports, Physical Education (Independent Study—high level studies outside school), Computer Studies I-II, Computer Science A (AP), Computer Science AB (AP). **Computer lab/training:** Each student will have an e-mail address and unlimited access to a computer on campus; all computers will be linked to the Internet. Technology is integrated throughout the curriculum. Students have access to equipment including scanners and digital cameras. One year computer science will be required. **Grading:** A-F. **Graduation requirements:** 4 years English, 4 years history, 4 years mathematics, 4 years theology, 3 years lab science, 3 years foreign language, 2 years P.E., 1 year fine arts, 1 year computer science, 100 hours community service. (Requirements are designed to satisfy UC admission standards.) **Average nightly homework:** 3-3.5 hours. **Faculty:** N/A. **Faculty ethnicity:** N/A. **Faculty selection/training:** "We look for teachers who are knowledgeable in their subject area, who have a strong commitment to education, who desire small classes for interactive learning, who want to support students outside of the classroom through athletics, service, or club activities, who will accept and embrace the goals of a Sacred Heart education, who understand the benefits of teaching in a single sex environment and who have the desire and ability to engage students in the classroom. Departments will take advantage of the school's full support for professional development by attending conferences and workshops together." **Teacher/student ratio:** N/A. **Teacher's daily student load in required academic subject:** N/A. **AP courses and exams:** N/A. **Senior class profile (mean):** N/A. **National Merit Scholarship Program:** N/A. **College enrollment:** N/A.

# OTHER INDICATORS THE SCHOOL IS ACCOMPLISHING ITS GOALS

N/A.

## Campus / Campus Life

**Campus description:** Located in a new and in renovated buildings, the school will include new classrooms, science and computer labs, art studios, library, and a full-court gymnasium. It will have total technological accessibility and an enclosed outdoor courtyard. **Library:** N/A. **Open/closed campus:** Closed. **Classroom space per student:** N/A. **Lunches:** N/A. **Bus service:** N/A. **Uniforms/ dress code:** Dress code. **Co-curricular activities/clubs:** Extensive co-curricular activities will be offered, including coed (with CSH High School) drama, orchestra, photography and clubs. **Foreign exchange program:** N/A. **Opportunities for community service:** Students will fulfill their required 100 hours of community service through a variety of activities relating to the elderly, the environment, the handicapped, the sick, the economically disadvantaged, and the newly immigrated. **Typical freshman schedule:** English I (honors option), Theology I, History I, French, Spanish, Japanese or Mandarin, Integrated Math I (honors option), Integrated Science or Biology, Computer Studies I (1 semester), Introduction to Art (1 semester), and Physical Education I.

## Student Support Services

**Counselor-student ratio:** N/A. **Counseling:** N/A. The Head of School and Dean of Studies will provide **academic counseling** and advising to students. During the freshman year, students will take the National Education Development Test. Freshman and sophomores will have one group presentation each year by the college counselor and will meet individually with a college counselor as well. Sophomores will also take the PSAT in the spring. During the junior year, students will take the PSAT in the fall, have weekly group meetings and individual sessions with a College Counselor, and take the ACT, SAT I, and SAT II in the spring. Seniors will continue to meet with the college counselor both individually and in group sessions, and take the ACT, SAT I, and SAT II again in the fall. **Learning disabilities/differences:** N/A. **Career apprenticeship programs:** N/A.

## Student Conduct and Health

**Code of conduct:** The Code of Ethics, discussed in the Student Handbook, will focus on respect for others, respect for others' property and school property, respect for education, and school spirit. **How school handles drugs/alcohol usage:** "Drug and alcohol usage or possession will not be tolerated and will result in serious punishment of either expulsion or suspension. This policy will be in effect whether a student is on campus, in uniform, or attending a school-sponsored function." **Drug/alcohol abuse prevention/AIDS awareness program:** N/A.

## SUMMER PROGRAMS

N/A.

## PARENT INVOLVEMENT

**Parent participation:** Parents will be invited to participate through the Parents' Association as Room Parents, and as volunteers for various events and activities. **Parent/teacher communication:** Formal reports will be sent to parents four times a year. Other evaluations will be given as needed. **Parent education:** Frequent seminars will be offered through the Parent Association. **Donations:** N/P.

## SPORTS

SHHS students will compete through the Bay Counties Athletic League in basketball, lacrosse, soccer, baseball and cross-country.

## WHAT SETS SCHOOL APART FROM OTHERS

"A strong academic program utilizing San Francisco and all the resources the city has to offer. Individualized instruction, leadership opportunities, a values-based education. Member of the Network of Sacred Heart Schools and partner with Convent of the Sacred Heart High School."

## HOW PARENTS/STUDENTS CHARACTERIZE SCHOOL

N/A.

# THE URBAN SCHOOL OF SAN FRANCISCO

1563 Page Street
San Francisco, CA 94117

(415) 626-2919 *fax (415) 626-1125*
www.urbanschool.org

Mark Salkind, Director
Jennifer Beams, Director of Admission, jbeam@urbanschool.org

## GENERAL

**Coed** day high school. **Nonsectarian.** Founded in 1966. **Nonprofit**, member CAIS, NAIS, BAIHS. **Enrollment:** Approximately 240. **Average class size:** 14. **Accreditation:** WASC/CAIS (6-year term: 1994-00). **School year:** 9.5-month calendar (N/P re instructional days). **School day:** 8:20 a.m. to 3 p.m. **Location:** One block south of Haight Street and two blocks from Golden Gate Park in the Haight-Ashbury neighborhood. The school is accessible by the 6, 7, 33, 43, 66, and 71 MUNI bus lines.

## STUDENT BODY

**Geographical breakdown (counties):** 73% from San Francisco; 10% from Marin; 6% from San Mateo (South San Francisco); 11% from the East Bay. **Ethnicity:** 72% Caucasian (non-Latino); 9% Asian-American; 8% African-American; 5% Latino; 5% other. **Foreign students (I-20 status):** N/P. **Single parent/two f/t working parent families:** N/P. **Middle schools:** 70% of the most recent entering freshman class came from private, non-parochial schools; 27% from public middle schools; 3% from parochial schools. (N/P # schools)

## ADMISSION

**Applications due:** Approximately January 20 (call for date) (BAIHS deadline). **Application fee:** $45. **Application process:** Open houses are held on weekends in the fall (October-December). Interested families should contact the admission office in the fall of the student's 8th grade year. All applicants are scheduled for a half-day visit which includes an interview with a member of the admissions staff. The current application form requests the student to write essays and several short answers to application questions. Parents are asked to share thoughts or concerns about their child that might further the school's understanding of him or her. The school uses the BAIHS recommendation forms and student's transcripts. Urban also requires the SSAT but will work with families if it is not possible for an applicant to take the test. SSAT waivers are also available. Decisions are mailed in the 3rd week of March. **No. of applications:** 461 applications were received for 60 places in prior year's class. One new student was admitted to G11. **Admission cut-off:** None. **Preferences:** N/P. "We are looking for students with an enthusiastic approach to learning and a clear capacity for success in a challenging academic environment. The school draws from public and private schools in San Francisco, the East Bay, and Marin and strives to reflect the ethnic, racial, and socioeconomic diversity of the Bay Area." **What sort of student do you best serve?** "As a small, progressive college preparatory school, Urban is able to serve a variety of students from those who are high achievers looking for challenge, individual attention, and greater freedom, to those who have difficulty with some college prep material but have a strong desire to achieve."

## COSTS

**Latest tuition:** $15,800 payable in 2 payments or 10 monthly installments. (Loans are available through outside companies.) **Sibling discount:** None. **Tuition increases:** Approximately 5% annually. **Other costs:** Books and fees cost $550. **Financial aid:** Need-based. **Percentage of students receiving financial aid:** 20% of students received a total of $395,400 in support the past year. **Average grant:** $8,400. **No. of full-tuition grants:** 0. **No. of half-tuition grants:** 42 partial awards ranging from $1,000 to $15,000. **Grants of half-tuition or more:** 50%.

## SCHOOL'S MISSION STATEMENT/GOALS

Urban's mission "is to ignite a passion for learning in its students and to inspire them to become self-motivated, enthusiastic participants in their education."

## ACADEMIC PROGRAM

Urban has a block schedule that divides the academic year into six 6-week blocks, with each course meeting 4 days a week for 6, 12, or 24 weeks. Three of the class sessions run 70 minutes, while the fourth lasts 2 hours and 15 minutes. The purpose is to promote in-depth study and thoughtful discussion, and to allow trips off campus to integrate the resources of the Bay Area into the curriculum.

Urban's pedagogical approach is based upon the following principles: "the expectation that students be active participants in their education; a commitment to cooperative learning and collaboration among students; an understanding and respect for the achievements, experiences, and perspectives of various peoples, cultures, and races, both Western and non-Western; and the use of the Bay Area's environmental, cultural, and intellectual resources to extend learning beyond the classroom. (Note: "Many Urban courses are designated Honors but not in a format that coincides with the format of this publication.") **Courses offered (AP=Advanced Placement):** Writing and Thinking, Composition:

American Voices and Greek Literature, Shakespeare, Classicism, Romanticism, and Modernism, Latin American Literature, Modern Japanese Literature, Biblical Literature, Advanced Composition, British Literature: Monsters and Morality, Russian Literature, 20th Century American Literature, Shakespeare's History Plays, Creative Writing, AP English (in alternate years: Faulkner, The Literature of Existentialism, Native American Literature, African American Literature, French Novels from the Romantic Period, Charles Dickens, Women Writers), 20th Century History, World History: Ancient Worlds, World History: Middle East, World History: Asia, World History: Latin America, Revolutionary Europe, African History, Peacemakers, The Middle Ages, History of Women in America, The American Revolution and the Constitution, The Civil War, Recent America, Constitutional Law, Comparative Religion, Historical Research (alternate years: Modern Japan, Russian and Eastern Europe, America Transformed, Modern China), Spanish I-V, French I-V, Acting I, Acting II: Comedy, Acting III, Peer Education Theatre Ensemble, Playwriting: One-Acts, Circus Techniques, Theater Productions, Music Theory, Urban Chorus, Jazz Ensemble, Drawing, Watercolor, Painting, Advanced Painting: Oil, Printmaking, Ceramics, Photography, Video Production and Film History, AP Art, Museum, (alternate years: Renaissance Art History), Math 1-3, Trigonometry, MMAPS, Advanced Math, Mathematics of Motion, Calculus (AP), Advanced Topics in Computing, Fractals, Biology A: Fundamentals, Biology B: Human Biology, Field Biology and Natural History, Introductory Physics: Motion, Introductory Physics: Matter, Ornithology, Marine Biology, Chemistry, Neurobiology, Genetics, Advanced Physics A: Electricity & Magnetism, Advanced Physics B: Modern Physics, Health, Lab Assistant Projects, Independent Science Experiments, Freshman Groups Project, 10th Grade Urban Workshop, 11th and 12th Grade Project, Senior Exhibition, Independent Study, Teaching Assistants/Teachers, Senior Theater Production Project, California Studies. **Computer lab/training:** All students are required to learn programming as part of the math curriculum. All classrooms and the library are linked to the Internet. The school's new building has three computer labs with 38 Macintosh Quadras, PowerPC 5400s, six Apple G3s, and laptop labs with Mac 1400s, and 35 new Apple I-Books. The library has seven new I-Macs and three PCs running Windows. **Grading:** Every six weeks, teachers provide students a full written evaluation with specific goals for improvement. At the end of the course, each student submits a self-evaluation of his or her work in the class, to which teachers respond. Teachers assign grades reflective of the students' work for college application only. These grades are not revealed to the students unless the student applies to a college (such as a UC university) that requires students to provide grades on the application (rather than the school providing a transcript). **Graduation requirements:** 4 years English, 3 years math, 2 years science, 2 years history (including 1 year US history), 3 years foreign language, 2 years art, 2 years Project, 4 years advanced course work. **Average nightly homework:** G9: 1.5-3; G10-12: 2-4. **Faculty:** Of 39 full and part-time faculty members, 54% are female, 46% are male. 19 hold master's degrees. **Faculty ethnicity:** 82% Caucasian; 8% Asian; 5% African-American; 5%

multicultural. **Faculty selection/training:** "Faculty are carefully selected based on experience. Qualified candidates must sample teach as well. School in-services, professional development experiences (conferences, classes, opportunities) are examples of continuing faculty education which is supported and encouraged." **Teacher/student ratio:** 1:9. **Teacher's daily student load in required academic subject:** N/P. **AP courses/exams:** "AP classes are offered in Calculus, English, French, Spanish and Studio Art." (N/P re exams, etc.) **Senior class profile (mean):** (Scores are recentered) SAT Math 620, SAT Verbal 620. **GPA:** Median GPA for class of 1998 was 3.35. **National Merit Scholarship Program:** N/P. **College enrollment:** 98% of last year's graduating class enrolled in 4-year colleges, 1% in 2-year colleges, and 1% other (San Francisco Ballet), including: American C of Paris, Berklee C of Music, Boston U, Brown, Haverford, Howard, Lewis & Clark, Macalester, NYU, Oberlin, Occidental, Pitzer, Pomona, Reed, SF Art Institute, CSU-San Francisco, Sarah Lawrence, Scripps, Smith, Tufts, U of Arizona, U of California (Berkeley, Irvine, LA, Santa Barbara, Santa Cruz and San Diego), U of Chicago, U of Colorado, U of Oregon, U of Michigan, U of Washington, Vassar, Washington U, Wesleyan, and Whitman.

# OTHER INDICATORS THE SCHOOL IS ACCOMPLISHING ITS GOALS

N/P.

# CAMPUS/CAMPUS LIFE

**Campus description:** The school owns three side-by-side buildings in a residential neighborhood and uses the St. Agnes gym just across the street for sports practices and games. The buildings house classrooms, biology, physics, and chemistry labs, two Macintosh computer labs, one art computer lab, library, theater, and art, printmaking, and ceramics studios. There is also a student-run snack bar. **Library:** 11 computer work stations including 6 Power Macs; 2 AST Pentiums; on-line catalog; 9,000 print volumes; 100 periodical subscriptions; study space for 30. Open to students from 7 a.m. to 5 p.m. (N/P sq. ft.) **Open/closed campus:** Open. **Classroom space per student:** N/P. **Lunches:** Students bring their own lunches daily. **Bus service:** City buses only. **Uniform/dress code:** Students "are expected to use good judgment and dress appropriately." They may not wear clothes showing emblems or slogans that are profane or that represent rap, drugs, alcohol, or tobacco products. **Co-curricular activities/clubs:** Admissions Hosts, Amnesty International, Community Outreach Club, Computer Club, Dance Committee, Diversity Forum, Friday Night Live, Improv Theater, Junior Statesmen of America, Math Club, Model UN, NOW, Poetry Club, Peer Resources, Student Committee, MAD (Multi-cultural Alliance for Diversity), Blue Notes (singing group), Urban Chorus, Jazz Ensemble, Chamber Music, mno, UFO's (Juggling Club), *Urban Journal* (Literary Magazine), Environmental Club, Yearbook, *Urban Tribune* (newspaper), Gay/Straight Alliance, Chess Club, Yoga,

Interschool Council, Outdoor Trips (backpacking, kayaking, river rafting, skiing, biking). **Foreign exchange program:** Arranged on an individual basis according to student's interest. **Opportunities for community service:** All students are required to take a course called "Project" that instills a sense of connection and responsibility to the larger community. Over the four years, students learn about the neighborhood, local government, health issues, service organizations, and community involvement. In 11th and 12th grades, students go into the community as interns and/or apprentices or engage in a service activity. **Typical freshman schedule:** Monday, Tuesday, and Friday: 20th Century History (8:20-9:30), advising (9:35-10:05), break (10:05-10:20), Math I (10:20-11:30), lunch (11:30-12:25), Biology A (12:25-1:35), break (1:35-1:50), Freshman Project (1:50-3 p.m.). Wednesday and Thursday: 20th Century History (8:20-10:50), Reading Activity Period (10:55-11:40) (co-curricular activities), lunch (11:40-12:30), Biology A (12:30-3 p.m.).

## STUDENT SUPPORT SERVICES

**Counselor/student ratio (not including college counselors):** 1:10. **Counseling:** Upon entering Urban, students are assigned a faculty advisor with whom they meet weekly in groups and individually. The advisor assists in academic and non-academic areas. Each freshman is assigned a senior as a "junior mentor." The school has one full-time and one part-time college counselor. Formal college counseling begins junior year with group and individual discussions about college choice and applications. During senior year, college counselors hold weekly meetings with the seniors and individual conferences upon request. The school also has a school psychological counselor for students and families. For Peer Resources, students in G10-12 are trained by the school counselor to assist in recognizing peers in need of help. **Learning disabilities/differences:** "Reasonable accommodations can be made on an individual basis." **Career apprenticeship programs:** None.

## STUDENT CONDUCT AND HEALTH

**Code of conduct:** Standard. **How school handles drugs/alcohol usage:** Sale or distribution of illegal drugs or alcohol will result in immediate expulsion. Students found using, in possession of, or under the influence of illegal drugs or alcohol will be suspended and will be required to undergo a substance abuse assessment. Second violations will result in immediate expulsion. Students who seek help with substance abuse problems will not be subject to disciplinary consequences. Smoking is prohibited on campus and in the surrounding off-campus neighborhood and at all school sponsored events. **Drug/alcohol abuse prevention/AIDS awareness program:** N/P.

## SUMMER PROGRAMS

Urban hosts "Aim High," a tuition-free summer enrichment program for middle school students from low-income families.

## PARENT INVOLVEMENT

**Parent participation:** "Not required, but over 80% of parents volunteer or are involved in everything from admissions open houses to auction fundraisers to the board of trustees." **Parent/teacher communication:** The student's faculty advisor calls parents during the school year to keep them informed of the student's progress. Evaluations are sent to parents every six weeks. **Parent education:** The school holds parent networking evenings. All 9th and 10th grade parents are required to attend a peer resource/education theater performance. **Donations:** Parents are solicited for the Annual Fund and capital drives.

## SPORTS

Students participate through the Bay Counties League in baseball, basketball, golf, cross-country, soccer, tennis, and volleyball in jv- and varsity-level teams. No "cuts" are made on the jv level—everyone gets to play.

## OTHER

Students, faculty, and administration are all on a first-name basis. Classroom focus is usually on cooperative learning and group discussion rather than lecturing. (Classroom desks and tables are normally configured in a U-shape.)

## WHAT SETS SCHOOL APART FROM OTHERS

"Urban is an innovative, coeducational day school which seeks to ignite a passion for learning and to inspire its students to become self-motivated enthusiastic participants in their education. Through field work, community service, and internships, students also explore and contribute to the larger community. The focus at Urban is on the here and now of learning—whether in the classroom or using the city as a resource."

## HOW PARENTS/STUDENTS CHARACTERIZE SCHOOL

N/P.

# WOODSIDE INTERNATIONAL SCHOOL

1555 Irving St.
San Francisco, CA 94122
(415) 564-1063

John Edwards, Headmaster

## GENERAL

**Coed** day high school with middle school. **Nonsectarian.** Founded in 1976. **Proprietary. Enrollment:** Approximately 100. **Average class size:** 14. **Accreditation:** WASC (6-year term: 1996-04). **School year:** 10-month calendar (167 instructional days). **School day:** 8 a.m. to 4 p.m. **Location:** Located in the Sunset District one block south of Golden Gate Park and two blocks east of 19th Avenue, the school is accessible by the N Judah streetcar and the 28 MUNI bus line.

## STUDENT BODY

**Geographical breakdown (counties):** 85% from San Francisco; 11% from San Mateo; 1% from Marin; 1% from Alameda; 1% from Contra Costa. **Ethnicity:** 49% Caucasian (non-Latino); 33% Asian; 3% African-American; 3% Latino; 12% other. **Foreign students (I-20 status):** 33-50%. **Single parent/two f/t working parent families:** N/P. **Middle schools:** N/P.

## ADMISSION

**Applications due:** Enrollment occurs year-round; most applications are due in March (call for date). **Application fee:** $40. **Application process:** Interested students are encouraged to spend a day at the school touring the school with a current student. Students applying must submit the completed application, test scores, copies of transcripts, and at least one letter of recommendation. A visit and an interview are then scheduled. **No. of applications:** N/P. **Admission cutoff:** None. **Preferences:** N/P. **"We are looking for** students who are motivated to improve themselves, to develop and share their individual talents in a small community designed to help prepare for college and life." **What students do you best serve?** "Woodside International School's programs and small size allow for individual attention and enable students of a wide ability range to succeed."

# COSTS

**Latest tuition:** $9,672 if paid in 12 monthly payments; $9,068 if paid in 1 payment. **Sibling discount:** 15%. **Tuition increases:** 3-5% annually. **Other costs:** Registration: $175 (including Parents' Assn. dues); Foundation contribution of $210; other fees of approximately $100. **Financial aid:** Need-based financial aid is available. Students with a strong financial need can apply for scholarships of 10%-30%/year discounts. These are awarded on the basis of academic and citizenship performance and are renewable every year provided conditions are met. **Percentage of students receiving financial aid:** 12%. **Average grant:** $1,400. **No. of full/half-tuition grants:** 0. **Grants of half-tuition or more:** 0.

# SCHOOL'S MISSION STATEMENT/GOALS

"As educators our goal is to ensure that each one of our students progresses academically, socially, and personally. We realize that for real learning to take place, students require individual attention and personal freedom. We have purposefully maintained Woodside as a small school with a low student-teacher ratio (the average is 14:1) so that students have the support and space to develop their strengths. Teachers provide students with the guidance and skills that enable them to take personal responsibility for their education and for a healthful lifestyle; we encourage these in every possible way. By practicing a variety of skills, such as organization, communication, research, problem-solving, decision-making, and other study skills, our students learn how to achieve in the academic world while also preparing themselves for the outside world."

# ACADEMIC PROGRAM

"Woodside provides a solid college preparatory curriculum with courses that are UC- and NCAA-approved. The curriculum is government-approved for foreign students. Our carefully planned sequence of study consists of core classes in English (ESL/EFS for foreign students), math, science, social studies, languages, and physical education. In addition, students take a number of personal development courses and can participate in creative arts courses, additional language courses, and/or student government for course credit. The flexibility of the schedule usually enables students to take as many electives as they wish." **Courses offered (AP=Advanced Placement, H=Honors, (AP)=AP option, (H)=Honors option):** General English Literature, US Literature I-II, World Literature, English Language I-IV, English as a Second Language (ESL I-IV), English for Foreign Students (EFS I-III), Elementary Math, Pre-Algebra, College Prep Math I-III, Advanced Math & Calculus, General Science, Chemistry (AP), Biology, Physics (AP), World Geography, US History, World History, Civics, Economics, California History, Philosophy, Spanish I-III, French I-III, Russian I-III, Mandarin

I-III, Japanese I-III, Latin I-III, P.E., Basketball, Volleyball, Extracurricular P.E., Word Processing, Computer Lab, Typing, Career-College Prep., Current Events, Health, Parenting, Study Skills, Driver's Ed, Student Government, Intro to Art, General Art, Yearbook, Drama, Music, Film, Songwriting, Creative Writing, independent study, and work credit. **Computer lab/training:** The school has a lab with 4 Macs networked together with Internet access, printers, scanners, and CD-ROMS. One year typing/computers required. **Grading:** Letter grades and comments. Parents or students can request weekly updates in addition to the eight regular monthly progress and two semester reports. **Graduation requirements:** Students can earn a regular diploma or an honors diploma. 4 years English language, 4 years English literature, 4 years lab science, 1 year US history, 2.5 years foreign language, 1 year geography, 3 years physical education, 1 year civics/economics/Cal. history, 2 years art/music/drama, 4 years current events and study skills, 3 years mathematics, 1 year health, 1 semester driver's ed and parenting, 1 year typing/computer, 5 workshops in college prep, 75 hours community service, 75 hours work experience at a paying job, and electives to equal 225 credits for the regular diploma and 265 for the honors diploma. The program for foreign students includes ESL, EFS, American history, general science, and current events, all taught in classes specifically for the school's foreign students. **Average nightly homework:** 2 hours. **Faculty:** 45% male, 55% female. 60% of faculty hold bachelor's degrees as highest degree; 40% hold master's degrees. **Faculty ethnicity:** 60% Caucasian (non-Latino); 30% Asian; 10% Latino. **Faculty selection/training:** "Teachers are selected based on the college they attended, their performance in college, their level of expertise in their field, their ability to work as part of a team, their ability to work with teenagers, and their commitment to the educational process. Teacher credentials are not required as they have not proven to be a reliable indication of teaching ability. All teachers are encouraged to take classes at local colleges and universities to further develop their skills. Costs for these are covered by the school. Frequent and regular faculty meetings insure good communications amongst faculty." **Teacher/student ratio:** 1:14. **Teacher's daily student load in required academic subject:** N/P. **AP courses/exams:** 8% of students are currently taking AP courses. In 1998, 7 students took 4 AP examinations in one subject. 66% received scores of 3 or above. **Senior class profile (mean):** N/P. (Some students take ACT.) **GPA:** "Average of students' GPA is not figured." **National Merit Scholarship Program:** One student in 1996 was a finalist. **College enrollment:** 30% of last year's graduates enrolled in 4-year colleges, 70% in 2-year colleges, including: CSU-San Diego, CSU-San Francisco, Stanford, CSU-Humboldt, St. Mary's, California Culinary Academy, SF City C, Pace U, C of Marin, and Auburn U.

# OTHER INDICATORS THE SCHOOL IS ACCOMPLISHING ITS GOALS

"Students are progressing—all of them—(at their own pace). Our American and foreign-born students are becoming more united. Almost half of the student body is involved in the school-student government. Parents are enthusiastic about how the school benefits their children. The Parents' Association enjoys supporting the school in numerous ways including preparing a weekly lunch for the faculty."

# CAMPUS/CAMPUS LIFE

**Campus description:** Woodside occupies two buildings in the Sunset district of San Francisco (a neighborhood of residences and small businesses). The main building, a storefront on Irving Street, has eight classrooms, a library, and a recreation room; a building across the street has four classrooms. The school has an open campus; students can visit the many cafes and delis in the neighborhood, and visit the public library and Golden Gate Park nearby. **Library:** 500 sq. ft.; study space for 16 students; 4 computers; on-line catalog; 10 periodical subscriptions; Internet access; open to students 8 a.m.-4 p.m. (N/P re # volumes) **Open/closed campus:** Open. **Classroom space per student:** 90 sq. ft. **Lunches:** No. **Bus service:** None. **Uniform/dress code:** No dress code. **Co-curricular activities/clubs:** Many students are involved in student government. In addition, the school has monthly school field trips, dances, community service projects, class field trips, cultural activities, Sports Day, guest speaker presentations, a snow boarding trip, and a summer Yosemite camping trip. **Foreign exchange program:** No formal programs. **Opportunities for community service:** The school organizes community service field trips including to Glide Memorial Church, soup kitchens, Point Reyes (clean up trails, food drives, etc.). **Typical freshman schedule:** 6-8 periods of 45 minutes each, such as: Algebra I, Freshman English, Geography, General Science or Biology, foreign language, P.E., study hall, and extracurricular class such as art, music, drama, or film.

# STUDENT SUPPORT SERVICES

**Counselor/student ratio (not including college counselors):** (See below.) **Counseling:** The headmaster and all of the teachers engage in counseling students. Parents are kept informed as needed. The headmaster also meets with students and families as needed, and teachers meet with a student as difficulties or schedule changes are needed. The school has regularly-scheduled career/college prep workshops open to all students. Often they are led by community members. One-on-one counseling is always available by appointment. **Learning disabilities/differences:** "No special programs. However, the school's program is designed to accommodate learning differences without there being any teacher trained in special education. This has allowed the enrollment of students who have diagnosed learning disabilities." **Career apprenticeship programs:** None.

## Student Conduct and Health

**Code of conduct:** Standard. **How school handles drugs/alcohol usage:** "We prohibit the use of drugs/alcohol at or around the school and we educate students on the effects of drug/alcohol use and on self-esteem and prevention." **Drug/alcohol abuse prevention/AIDS awareness program:** The school has annual and semi-annual prevention programs and separate workshops on tobacco, drugs, and alcohol. Community teen AIDS prevention programs are offered with guest speakers who are HIV-positive. The school also holds workshops on self-esteem, abstinence, and safe sex.

## Summer Programs

The school offers a morning summer school program during the month of July to all students to work individually with teachers, make up a class, work ahead, and/or improve skills in specific areas. Students earn a semester's credit through intensive work in specific areas. (ESL students can take an intensive 4-week program in all aspects of English.) Cost: $950 for full-load (2 courses) and $975 for the ESL program.

## Parent Involvement

**Parent participation:** No required hours. The Parents' Association fee is waived for active parents. Meetings are once every six weeks. Five or six committees sit annually. **Parent/teacher communication:** Progress reports every four weeks keep parents informed. The dates of these reports are on the calendar with reminders in the monthly newsletter. Conferences can be arranged at any time. **Parent education:** "None. However, we encourage parent teacher conferences whenever issues arise and provide advice and recommendations. We also can refer parents to professional counselors outside the school." **Donations:** Currently an annual contribution of $210 to the Wildshaw Foundation is requested; an annual $70 contribution to the Parents' Association is required unless waived by parent participation.

## Sports

The school offers a basketball and a volleyball program. Students may also earn credit by enrolling in outside programs that can confirm attendance and participation.

## WHAT SETS SCHOOL APART FROM OTHERS

"Its special qualities include: its willingness to accommodate the individual needs of its students, its smallness, its open lines of communication with parents and students, its diverse student body, and the flexibility of its programs."

## HOW PARENTS/STUDENTS CHARACTERIZE SCHOOL

**Parent response(s):** "Finally I've found a school where my child feels wanted and accepted, and where I know how my child is doing." "Students are able to work at their appropriate level and speed in a challenging environment."
**Student response(s):** [From student-written student handbook.] "What students like about W.I.S.: One-on-one attention, teachers' availability, off-campus privileges, pool table, foose-ball, ping-pong, couches, vending machines, pay phone receiving incoming calls, no dress code, close to Golden Gate park, field trips, freedom, being treated with respect, extra privileges as you prove yourself, can work independently, can wear a Walkman, can get a lot of work done during study hall."

# WOODSIDE PRIORY SCHOOL

302 Portola Road
Portola Valley, CA 94028-7897

(650) 851-8221 *fax (650) 851-2839*
www.woodsidepriory.com

Tim Molak, MA, Headmaster
Al Zappelli, Director of Admissions, azappelli@woodsidepriory.com

## GENERAL

**Coed** day high school with boarding for boys in G9-12. The school also has a coed day middle school. **Catholic** (N/P %). Founded in 1957, the school is run by the Order of St. Benedict. **Nonprofit**, member CAIS, NAIS. **Enrollment:** Approximately 250. **Average class size:** 15-18. **Accreditation:** WASC/CAIS (6-year term: 1994-00). **School year:** (180 instructional days) (N/P re #month calendar). **School day:** 8 a.m. to 3:15 p.m. **Location:** In Portola Valley, a rural suburban community near Stanford U, 32 miles south of San Francisco and 30 miles north of San Jose. The school provides a shuttle bus to and from the Menlo Park CalTrain Station to accommodate students commuting from communities between San Francisco and San Jose.

# Student Body

**Geographical breakdown (counties):** N/P. **Ethnicity:** 77% Caucasian (non-Latino); 14% Asian; 8% Latino; 1% African-American. **Foreign students (I-20 status):** 8%. **Single parent/two f/t working parent families:** N/P. **Middle schools:** 58% of the most recent entering freshman class came from the school's own middle school; 22% from private, non-parochial schools; 11% from public middle schools; and 9% from parochial schools. (N/P # schools)

# Admission

**Applications due:** Approximately January 20 (call for date). **Application fee:** $40. **Application process:** The school hosts two open houses on Saturday mornings in the fall (November) and early winter (January) for families. Students interested in the school are encouraged to spend a day "shadowing" a current student; students interested in boarding are invited to spend a night. Applicants must submit a Student Interest and Writing Sample, transcripts, teacher/principal recommendation, and take the HSPT or the SSAT. Applicants are interviewed. Responses are mailed mid-March. **No. of applications:** N/P. **Admission cut-off:** "We do not have any specific cut-off score that would automatically rule out a candidate. Each student is evaluated individually and in the context of his/her own background. Standardized test scores are most useful in looking at patterns of strength and weakness, and in making predictions about how students will handle the WSP reading load, but they are never more than one component of an admissions evaluation." **Preferences:** N/P. **"We are looking for"** N/P. **What sort of student do you best serve?** "Intellectually curious and college bound; they will exhibit a broad spectrum of capabilities, show evidence of creativity and generosity, and be ready to learn [as well as ready] to participate in extra-curricular activities, sports and/or service."

# Costs

**Latest tuition:** $14,960 for day and approximately $28,860 for boarding payable in 1, 2, or monthly payments. **Sibling discount:** None. **Tuition increases:** Approximately 4% annually. **Financial aid:** Need-based. **Percentage of students receiving financial aid:** Approximately 28% of students receive a portion of the $503,000 in available financial aid. **Average grant:** $6,500. **No. of full-tuition grants:** None. **Grants of half-tuition or more:** N/P.

# School's Mission Statement/Goals

"The Woodside Priory School is a Catholic coeducational, college preparatory school conducted by Benedictine monks who are assisted by religious and lay men and women. The educational program and the school's sense of community take their character from the Saint Benedict's Rule for Monasteries and from the tradition of Benedictine education spanning fifteen centuries. That tradition embodies a love of learning and an intellectual and spiritual quest which supports and promotes individual and societal freedom. It encourages students to be creative, generous, and to mature emotionally which leads to higher standard of personal and societal responsibility. We hope to communicate to our students a love of God and a vision of life, of the universe, of society, and of themselves which is stable in its foundations, adaptive in its applications, forward-looking in its goals and satisfying in its fulfillment. Students, faculty and staff—supported by parents, alumni, and benefactors—are dedicated to this dynamic process of education which regards learning and personal growth as a lifelong endeavor."

## Academic Program

"The basic curriculum prepares students for University of California requirements and those of most highly regarded four-year colleges. It particularly stresses strong writing and math-science skills. The curriculum is traditional and highly structured; it offers students an interdisciplinary approach to learning and the ability to reach across academic boundaries in their thinking and achievement."
**Courses offered (H=Honors, AP=Advanced Placement, (H)=Honors option, (AP)=AP option, E=Elective):** Computer Applications, Computer Graphics (E), Computer Technology (E), Computer Graphics and Advanced Computer Graphics, Algebra I-II, Geometry, Pre-Calculus, AP Calculus AB and BC, Physics (AP), Biology (AP), Chemistry (AP), Literary Genres, Writing Lab, Transitional English, Speech, Overview of British Literature, American Literature, World Literature, AP English, Literature in Film (E), Fiction and Fiction Writing, French I-IV, German (independent study), Latin (independent study), Japanese I-IV, Spanish I-IV, Art I, Studio Drawing, Integrated Fine Arts (music, drama, studio art integrated with humanities, world religion, and literature—10-20% history, 80-90% projects in the arts), Photography (E), Drama, Music, World History, Global Issues, US History (AP), Environmental Science (AP), Economics, American Government, Humanities, AP European History (E), Psychology (E), War and Revolution (E), Introduction to Philosophy (E), Hebrew Scriptures, Christian Scriptures, Church History, Christian Morality, Justice and Peace, The World's Religions, The Process: Life, Death (E), P.E./Health Education, Conditioning, Chorus/Orchestra. **Computer lab/training:** The school has 120 PCs in classrooms, writing labs, library, dormitories, and computer labs. Students are required to take a semester of computer science. **Grading:** A-F grades. Parents are sent report cards quarterly and academic progress reports mid-quarter. **Graduation requirements:** 4 years English plus an additional intensive semester or writing techniques and a semester of speech, 3 years Spanish, French, German or Japanese, 3 years math, 4 years science, 1 semester computer science, 3.5 years social studies, 1 year humanities, 4 years electives, 3 years theology, 1 year fine and performing arts, 1 year health/physical education, 100 hours community service. **Average nightly homework:** 3-3.5 hours. **Faculty:** Of the 50 faculty

members, 28 are men, 22 women. 17 hold bachelor's degrees as their highest degree; 29 hold master's degrees; and 4 hold doctorates. Four are Benedictine monks. **Faculty ethnicity:** N/P. **Faculty selection/training:** N/P. **Teacher/student ratio:** 1:10. **Teacher's daily student load in required academic subject:** N/P. **AP courses/exams:** N/P. **Senior class profile (mean):** SAT Math 570, SAT Verbal 580. **National Merit Scholarship Program:** In class of 1998, 2 finalists, 2 commended. **College enrollment:** 96% of last year's graduating class enrolled in 4-year colleges, 4% in 2-year colleges. "Priory graduates continue their education at colleges and universities throughout the world including Boston C, Claremont McKenna, Cal Poly, Cornell, Dartmouth, Duke, Georgetown, Johns Hopkins, Notre Dame, NYU, Northwestern, Reed, Santa Clara, Stanford, Syracuse, Wellesley, Williams, U of Chicago, U of Wisconsin, USF, USC, UC Berkeley, UC Davis, UC Irvine, UCLA, UC Santa Barbara, UC Riverside, UC San Diego and UC Santa Cruz." (N/P re last year)

## Other Indicators the School is Accomplishing its Goals

"WASC clear accreditation in 1995 (for 6 years); one-half of all students on objective standard grading system are on the honor roll."

## Campus/Campus Life

**Campus description:** The school has a 60-acre campus in Portola Valley, a rural suburban setting. The campus includes a faculty office building, chapel, fine arts studio, Campus Ministry Center, the Briggs Science Center, Assembly Hall and Theater with seating for 300, two dormitories, Founders Hall, three language labs, and 23 classrooms. Sports facilities include a 10,000 sq. ft. gym, 25-meter heated pool, three soccer fields, two baseball diamonds, four tennis courts, and two basketball courts. **Library:** 18,000 print volumes; 30 periodical subscriptions; 18 computers (with Internet access); and an on-line catalog. (N/P re sq. ft., hours, etc.) **Open/closed campus:** Closed. **Classroom space per student:** N/P. **Lunches:** Hot lunches are included in tuition. **Bus service:** Van service from Menlo Park CalTrain station (a.m. and p.m. shuttle). **Uniform/dress code:** "College prep dress code." **Co-curricular activities/clubs:** Yearbook, student newspaper, and literary magazine, Photography Club, Politics and Current Events Club, Amnesty International, student government, athletics adventures (biking, rock climbing, annual ski trip), International Languages and Cultures Club, Student Ambassadors, Science and Astronomy Club, National Honor Society, Chess Club, Youth Leadership. Clubs and activities change every year—students are encouraged to start new ones. In addition the school has a 20-piece orchestra, a string quartet, guitar and jazz ensembles, as well as the Priory Singers, and Choral Ensemble. **Foreign exchange program:** None. **Opportunities for community service:** Students fulfill their 100 hours of required community service by serving the infirm and elderly in the freshman year, children and youth in the sophomore year, homeless and hungry in the junior year, and the handicapped and institutionalized in the senior year. **Typical freshman schedule:** (Classes are 50 minutes long) English I, Algebra I or Geometry, World History, Conceptual Physics, foreign language I or II, Health/P.E., Theology, Computer Science, Writing Structures Lab.

## STUDENT SUPPORT SERVICES

**Counselor/student ratio (not including college counselors):** 1:7. Each teacher is an advisor under a program coordinated by the Director of Academic Service. College and career counseling is provided by two counselors. **Learning disabilities/differences:** "Assessed by Director of Academic Services." **Career apprenticeship programs:** N/P.

## STUDENT CONDUCT AND HEALTH

**Code of conduct:** Standard. **How the school handles drugs/alcohol usage:** Suspension at a minimum. **Drug/alcohol abuse prevention/AIDS awareness program:** Part of the health curriculum.

## SUMMER PROGRAMS

The school hosts a summer camp—Camp Unique—for grades 3-7.

## PARENT INVOLVEMENT

**Parent participation:** No requirements, though parents are active in the school's parents' association which has bimonthly meetings with speakers on topics of interest to families. Many parents come to campus as speakers or helpers for various projects. They also serve on committees in areas of interest or expertise. **Parent/teacher communication:** Quarterly progress reports; semester grades twice a year. Weekly progress reports at parents' request. **Parent education:** See above. In addition, the Campus Ministry Director holds monthly Parent Enrichment programs with issues relating to teenagers. **Donations:** "Operating expenses for 1998/99 are more than $4 million, with more than $800,000 in Annual Giving. A network of more than 800 alumni work for the School in the areas of volunteerism, public relations, admissions, and fundraising."

## SPORTS

High school students compete in the Peninsula Private Schools Athletic League in soccer, volleyball, basketball, tennis, cross-country/track, baseball, and softball. Eighty percent of all students participate in team sports.

## WHAT SETS SCHOOL APART FROM OTHERS

"Values and spiritual aspect; boarding and international program; safe and secure campus environment. A family atmosphere."

## HOW PARENTS/STUDENTS CHARACTERIZE SCHOOL

**Parent response(s):** "The Priory meets all aspects of students' lives and celebrates their individuality."—Parent, Portola Valley, CA
"Students get individual encouragement in a real-world centered community."—Parent, Palo Alto, CA
**Student response(s):** "I love it here, it's a great place to be yourself and to be challenged."—Student, Menlo Park, CA
"It's great to be able to move ahead academically."—Student, Palo Alto, CA

# ADDITIONAL SCHOOLS

(These school have chosen not to provide profiles or have have failed to respond to requests to update information from the last edition of this book. The following information is based upon past profiles and/or publicly available information.)

## BISHOP O'DOWD HIGH SCHOOL

9500 Stearns Avenue
Oakland, CA 94605
(510) 577-9100
www.odowd.pvt.k12.ca.us

**Coed** day high school. Founded in 1951. **Catholic. Accreditation:** WASC. Latest tuition: $5,875 + $250 fees (1989-99). **Enrollment:** 1,050. **Location:** 7-acre campus off Highway 580 (98th Ave. exit) between Oakland and San Leandro. **Senior Class Profile (1998):** SAT Verbal 588, SAT Math 588. **National Merit Scholarship Program:** 5 finalists; 1 semi-finalist; 18 commended. **AP courses/exams:** In 1998, students took 491 exams; 73% received scores of 3 or above. **College enrollment:** 93% of 1997 grads enrolled in college.

## CARONDELET HIGH SCHOOL

1333 Winton Drive
Concord, CA 94518
(925) 686-5353

**Girls'** day high school. **Catholic.**

## DE LA SALLE HIGH SCHOOL

1130 Winton Drive
Concord, CA 94518
(925) 686-3310 *fax (925) 686-3474*
www.delasalle.org/1.2.1.6.4.html

Br. Robert Wickman, FSC, Principal

**Boys'** day high school. **Catholic** (75% Catholic). **Nonprofit**, member BAIHS. **Enrollment:** Approx. 925. **Ethnicity:** 74% Caucasian; 10% Asian; 8% Latino; 3% African-American. **Faculty:** 4 Brothers, 41 lay men, 41 lay women.

# Drew College Preparatory School
2901 California Street
San Francisco, CA 94115
(415) 346-4831 *fax (415) 346-0720*

**Coed** day high school. **Nonsectarian.** Founded in 1908. **Nonprofit**, member CAIS, NAIS, BAIHS. **Enrollment:** Approximately 165. **Average class size:** N/P. **Accreditation:** WASC/CAIS. **School year:** Approximately Sept. 2-June 4. **School day:** 8:15 a.m. to 2:45 p.m. Monday-Wednesday, to 3 p.m. Thursday, and to 1:30 p.m. Friday. **Location:** Drew is located in a residential neighborhood between Pacific Heights and Presidio Heights in San Francisco, accessible by the 1 California and 24 Divisidero MUNI bus lines. **Applications due:** Mid-January (call for date). **Application fee:** $35. **"We are looking for** students who demonstrate talents and academic abilities consistent with those necessary for future success in college and beyond. We attract students who have a positive attitude and the commitment and motivation to achieve academic success. Drew students also have an interest in participation in a wide range of co-curricular programs including athletics, art, music, and community service." **Campus description:** The campus includes the original Victorian building used since 1911 and two adjacent building built in the 1960's. The campus has a small theater/art gallery, photography darkrooms, two science labs, an art studio, two computer labs (PC and Mac), and a courtyard for gatherings. The school uses nearby facilities for auditorium, theater, and athletic spaces.

# Hebrew Academy of San Francisco
645 14th Avenue (at Balboa)
San Francisco, CA 94118

(415) 752-7333 *fax (415) 752-5851*

**Coed** day high school (with lower schools grades nursery through 8). **Jewish** (100% Jewish). Founded in 1969. **Nonprofit. Enrollment:** Approximately 96 in high school. **Accreditation:** National Association of Hebrew Day Schools. **Location:** In a residential neighborhood one block from Golden Gate Park. Accessible by the 31, 38, 5, and 15 MUNI bus lines. **Ethnicity:** 97% Caucasian (non-Latino); 2% Asian; 1% African-American. Note: Although the majority of students are not from traditional Jewish homes, the school expects all families to support the school in maintaining a traditional Jewish environment at school. **Applications due:** Rolling admission (call for dates). **Preferences:** Siblings. **"We are looking for** students who will be happy in a small school, who value and respect the intellectual and spiritual life we offer. We want students who want to be active in and contribute to a learning community which has high intellectual and moral standards. We value a positive attitude towards learning, personal creativity, kindness, and moral strength. We value students who want to contribute to their families, their community, and the Jewish people." **Latest tuition:** $9,500 payable in 12 monthly installments. **Sibling discount:** None. **Tuition increases:** Approximately 5% annually. **Uniforms/dress code:** The school's dress code requires modest dress. Girls must wear skirts covering the knee; boys, button-down shirts and pants without tears (jeans are allowed). No dyed hair, extreme haircuts, tattoos, nose rings, etc. **Other costs:** Book use fee; contribution to school's building fund. **Mission statement:** To give Jewish students a Jewish education integrating demanding academic courses with courses of Hebrew language and Judaic studies. **Campus description:** The Hebrew Academy High School shares a 30,000 sq. ft. campus with its lower schools. Constructed in 1986, the facility includes a large gym, a library, computer labs, and science labs.

# IMMACULATE CONCEPTION ACADEMY
3625 24th Street (at Guerrero)
San Francisco, CA 94110
(415) 824-2052 *fax (415) 821-4677*

**Girls'** day high school. **Catholic.** Founded in 1883 by the Dominican Sisters of Mission San Jose. **Enrollment:** Approximately 270. **Average class size:** 25. **Accreditation:** WASC (6-year term: 1994-00). **Location:** Between Guerrero and Dolores on 24th Street, between San Francisco's Mission District and Noe Valley. Accessible from the 24th Street BART station, MUNI bus lines 48, 14, 26, and 49; the MUNI J streetcar, and SamTrans 22D and 5M buses. **Applications due:** On-going. **Application fee:** $40. **"We are looking for ..."** "Admission to ICA is based upon the following criteria: (1) Desire to receive a Catholic education; (2) Admission interview; (3) Performance on ICA's placement test; (4) Academic and personal recommendations from teachers/principals; (5) Satisfactory conduct, effort, and attendance." **Latest tuition:** $5,000 payable in 1, 2, or 10 payments + $300 registration. **Campus description:** The school consists of three buildings and a chapel enclosing a private garden. The school has two computer labs, a gym, and several new classrooms. **Faculty-student ratio:** 1:13. **Colleges:** 98% enroll in college. **Parent participation:** Each family is required to give 10 hours of service to the school each academic year or pay $100 or $10 for each uncompleted hour. **Donations:** The school asks that each family contribute $250/year to the school's Building Maintenance Endowment Fund.

# St. Mary's College High School

1294 Albina Avenue
Berkeley, CA 94706
(510) 559-6240 *fax (510) 559-6277*
www.delasalle.org/1.2.1.6.5.html

Dr. John Collins, Principal
Mr. Lawrence Puck, Director of Admissions, (510) 559-6240

**Coed** day high school. Founded in 1863. **Catholic** (54% Catholic). **Enrollment:** Approx. 556. **Average class size:** 27. **Accreditation:** WASC. **Location:** A residential neighborhood in North Berkeley, a short walk from the North Berkeley BART station. **Ethnicity:** 39% Caucasian (non-Latino); 25% African-American; 15% Asian; 10% Latino. **Admission:** The admission process includes an application, HSPT, recommendation form from principal or counselor, math and English teachers, and a personal interview. **Latest tuition:** $6,630 (1989-99). **Financial aid:** Need-based. More than 35% of students receive financial aid; most for 25% of tuition, a few for 40%. **Mission statement:** "Saint Mary's seeks to educate the whole person, promoting the intellectual, spiritual, and physical development of each student in a caring and moral environment." **Faculty:** 4 Brothers, 18 lay men, 18 lay women. **Graduation requirements:** 4 years English, 3 years math, 3 years history, 2 years foreign language, 1 year fine arts, 2 years science, 4 years religious studies, 1 year PE and health, 4 years community service. **AP courses/exams:** "84% of students who took AP exams in May, [1998] passed." **Colleges:** 95% enroll in college; 75% in 4-year colleges and universities.

# APPENDIX

At parents' request (in response to the first edition of this book), certain statistics from the schools' profiles are compiled below.

## CLASS SIZE

| | |
|---|---|
| North Bay Marin | 8 |
| North Bay Orinda | 9 |
| Bentley | 10 |
| Spraings | 10 |
| Arrowsmith | 12 |
| Maybeck | 12 |
| San Domenico | 12 |
| Lick | 13.5 |
| SF Waldorf | 12-15 |
| Branson | 14 |
| Castilleja | 14 |
| College Prep | 14 |
| Convent | 14 |
| Stuart Hall | 14 |
| Urban | 14 |
| Woodside Int'l | 14 |
| Athenian | 15 |
| Beacon | 15 |
| Bridgemont | 15 |
| Crystal Springs | 15 |
| Harker | 15 |
| Head-Royce | 15 |
| Marin Academy | 15 |
| Sacred Heart Prep | 15 |
| IHS | 15-17 |
| Menlo | 14-18 |
| Woodside Priory | 15-18 |
| Pinewood | 15-20 |
| Lycee | 18-20 |
| King's Academy | 22 |
| Notre Dame-Belmont | 24 |
| Marin Catholic | 24 |
| Holy Names | 25 |
| St. Lawrence | 25 |
| Mercy-SF | 25 |
| Mercy-Burlingame | 25 |
| Serra | 25-26 |

| Bellarmine | 26 |
| Riordan | 26 |
| Salesian | 26 |
| Mitty | 27 |
| Notre Dame-SJ | 27 |
| Presentation | 28 |
| Sacred Heart Cathedral | 28 |
| St. Ignatius | 28 |
| St. Joseph | 28 |
| Moreau | 30 |
| St. Francis | 30 |

N/P: SF University

# SCHOOL SIZE

| St. Francis | 1,455 |
| Mitty | 1,430 |
| St. Ignatius | 1,415 |
| Bellarmine | 1,350 |
| Sacred Heart Cathedral | 1,216 |
| Moreau | 1,200 |
| Serra | 950 |
| Notre Dame-Belmont | 740 |
| Marin Catholic | 740 |
| Presentation | 712 |
| Riordan | 700 |
| King's Academy | 580 |
| St. Joseph | 560 |
| Mercy-SF | 550 |
| Menlo | 532 |
| NotreDame-SJ | 525 |
| Salesian | 500 |
| Mercy-Burlingame | 445 |
| Sacred Heart Prep | 430 |
| SF University | 389 |
| Castilleja | 385 |
| Marin Academy | 375 |
| Lick | 360 |
| College Prep | 327 |
| Branson | 320 |
| St. Lawrence | 310 |
| Head-Royce | 300 |
| Holy Names | 300 |

| | |
|---|---|
| Athenian | 262 |
| IHS | 250 |
| Woodside Priory | 250 |
| Crystal Springs | 240 |
| Urban | 240 |
| Harker | 215 |
| Pinewood | 200 |
| Convent | 198 |
| San Domenico | 130 |
| Maybeck | 105 |
| Arrowsmith | 100 |
| Bridgemont | 100 |
| North Bay Orinda | 100 |
| Woodside Int'l | 100 |
| North Bay Marin | 93 |
| Lycee | 86 |
| Bentley | 80 |
| Spraings | 70 |
| SF Waldorf | 70 |
| Beacon | 48 |

## TEACHER'S DAILY STUDENT LOAD

| | |
|---|---|
| Spraings | 20-45 |
| Beacon | 36 |
| Bentley | 45 |
| North Bay Marin | 45 |
| Maybeck | 48 |
| Arrowsmith | 50 |
| Castilleja | 52-66 |
| Lick | 56-70 |
| College Prep | 60 |
| Crystal Springs | 63 |
| Head-Royce | 60-75 |
| Convent | 70 |
| Sacred Heart Prep | 70 |
| Harker | 75 |
| Pinewood | 70-80 |
| Notre Dame-SJ | 125 |
| Salesian | 125 |
| Mercy-SF | 130-150 |
| St. Ignatius | 140 |
| Riordan | 143 |
| Serra | less than 145 |

# TOTAL COSTS/TUITION/OTHER COSTS

| | |
|---|---|
| Branson | $16,500/$15,500/$1,000 |
| Urban | $16,350/$15,800/$550 |
| San Domenico | $16,282/$16,132/$150 |
| Spraings | $16,216/$16,216/0 |
| Marin Academy | $16,190/$15,990/$200* |
| SF University | $16,175/$16,175/0 |
| Castilleja | $16,200/$15,200/$1,000 |
| IHS | $16,000/$15,250/$750 |
| Menlo | $15,975/$15,625/$350 |
| Harker | $15,575/$15,200/$375 |
| Lick | $15,570/$15,170/$400 |
| College Prep | $15,250/$14,750/$500 |
| Head-Royce | $15,150/$14,450/$700 |
| Woodside Priory | $14,960/$14,960/$0 |
| Crystal Springs | $14,900/$14,300/$600 |
| Convent | $14,900/$14,260/$650 |
| Athenian | $14,650/$14,650/$0 |
| Bentley | $14,180/$13,780/$400 |
| Sacred Heart Prep | $13,965/$13,965/$0 |
| North Bay Marin | $13,000/$12,800/$200* |
| SF Waldorf | $11,700/$11,500/$200* |
| North Bay Orinda | $11,350/$11,000/$350 |
| Pinewood | $11,600/$10,900/$700 |
| Beacon | $10,700/$10,200/$500 |
| Lycee | $10,440/$9,440/$1,000 |
| Woodside Int'l | $10,157/$9,672/$485 |
| Arrowsmith | $9,650/$9,650/0 |
| Maybeck | $9,130/$8,800/$330 |
| Notre Dame-Belmont | $8,087/$7,437/$650 |
| St. Ignatius | $7,815/$7,245/$570 |
| Marin Catholic | $7,550/$7,250/$300 |
| Riordan | $7,575/$6,750/$825 |
| Serra | $7,045/$7,045/0 |
| Mercy-Burlingame | $7,650/$6,700/$950 |
| Sacred Heart Cathedral | $7,375/$6,650/$725 |
| Bellarmine | $6,365/$6,165/200* |
| Mercy-SF | $6,875/$6,150/725 |
| St. Lawrence | $6,350/$6,150/$200* |
| Moreau | $6,347/$6,072/$275 |
| Mitty | $6,370/$5,970/$400 |
| Presentation | $5,920/$5,920/0 |
| St. Francis | $5,875/$5,875/0 |
| Notre Dame-SJ | $6,600/$6,200/$400 |

| Holy Names | $6,250/$5,750/$500 |
| Bridgemont | $6,659/$5,559/$1,100 |
| St. Joseph | $6,350/$5,400 (approx)/$950 |
| King's Academy | $6,200/$5,700/$500 |
| Salesian | $5,200/$4,750/$450 |

* Other costs not specified are presumed $200

# % Students on Financial Aid

| | |
|---|---|
| Spraings | 50% |
| Convent | 40% |
| IHS | 40% |
| Lick | 38% |
| SF Waldorf | 38% |
| Sacred Heart Prep | 35% |
| Maybeck | 31% |
| Arrowsmith | 30% |
| Mercy-SF | 30% |
| Woodside Priory | 28% |
| Holy Names | 27% |
| Notre Dame-Belmont | 25% |
| Lycee | 25% |
| Salesian | 25% |
| Riordan | 22% |
| Marin Academy | 21% |
| St. Joseph | 21% |
| Athenian | 20% |
| Bridgemont | 20% |
| Marin Catholic | 20% |
| Mercy-Burlingame | 20% |
| Moreau | 20% |
| SF University | 20% |
| Serra | 20% |
| Urban | 20% |
| Crystal Springs | 18% |
| St. Ignatius | 18% |
| Bellarmine | 17% |
| College Prep | 17% |
| Bentley | 16% |
| Beacon | 15% |
| Branson | 15% |
| Harker | 15% |
| Menlo | 15% |

| | |
|---|---|
| Sacred Heart Cathedral | 14% |
| Castilleja | 13% |
| Head-Royce | 13% |
| Presentation | 13% |
| Woodside Int'l | 12% |
| King's Academy | 10% |
| North Bay Marin | 10% |
| Notre Dame-SJ | 10% |
| North Bay Orinda | 8% |
| St. Francis | 8% |
| St. Lawrence | 7% |

N/P: Pinewood, Mitty, San Domenico

# % AWARDS OF 1/2 TUITION OR MORE

| | |
|---|---|
| Crystal Springs | 86% |
| Athenian | 85% |
| Branson | 81% |
| College Prep | 75% |
| Lick | 75% |
| North Bay Orinda | 75% |
| Harker | 70% |
| Marin Academy | 70% |
| North Bay Marin | 66% |
| Castilleja | 61% |
| Lycee | 60% |
| Bentley | 55% |
| Arrowsmith | 50% |
| Head-Royce | 50% |
| Urban | 50% |
| Bellarmine | 42% |
| St. Francis | 42% |
| SF Waldorf | 37% |
| Notre Dame-Belmont | 16% |
| Menlo | 15% |
| Sacred Heart Prep | 15% |
| Salesian | 13% |
| St. Joseph | 12-15% |
| Maybeck | 5-10% |
| Bridgemont | 5% |
| Serra | 3% |
| St. Lawrence | .5% |

| | |
|---|---|
| Mercy-SF | 0 |
| Notre Dame-SJ | 0 |
| Riordan | 0 |
| Sacred Heart Cathedral | 0 |
| Woodside Int'l | 0 |

N/P: Beacon, Mitty, Moreau, Pinewood, Presentation, San Domenico, SF University, Spraings, Woodside Priory, Holy Names, IHS, King's Academy, Marin Catholic, Mercy-Burlingame, St. Ignatius, Convent

# SAT VERBAL SCORES (MEAN)

| | |
|---|---|
| College Prep | 695 |
| Head-Royce | 687 |
| Lick | 680 |
| Castilleja | 663 |
| Marin Academy | 657 |
| SF University | 647 |
| North Bay Orinda | 630 |
| Lycee | 627 |
| Sacred Heart Prep | 627 |
| Urban | 620 |
| Menlo | 619 |
| Bellarmine | 611 |
| Pinewood | 603 |
| Arrowsmith | 602 |
| St. Ignatius | 598 |
| King's Academy | 591 |
| Mercy-Burlingame | 590 |
| Athenian | 585 |
| Beacon | 580 |
| Convent | 580 |
| Notre Dame-Belmont | 580 |
| Woodside Priory | 580 |
| St. Francis | 564 |
| North Bay Marin | 560 |
| Presentation | 560 |
| IHS | 550 |
| San Domenico | 530 |
| Notre Dame-SJ | 530 |
| Moreau | 528 |
| Sacred Heart Cathedral | 509 |
| Salesian | 500 |

| | |
|---|---|
| Bridgemont | 473 |
| Riordan | 471 |

N/P: Mitty, Branson, Crystal Springs, Holy Names, Marin Catholic, Maybeck, Mercy-SF, St. Joseph, Serra, Spraings, Woodside Int'l

# SAT MATH (MEAN)

| | |
|---|---|
| College Prep | 699 |
| Head-Royce | 688 |
| Castilleja | 672 |
| SF University | 666 |
| Lick | 660 |
| Menlo | 640 |
| Marin Academy | 639 |
| Lycee | 638 |
| Pinewood | 626 |
| Bellarmine | 623 |
| IHS | 620 |
| Urban | 620 |
| Sacred Heart Prep | 610 |
| Athenian | 605 |
| North Bay Orinda | 602 |
| King's Academy | 595 |
| St. Ignatius | 586 |
| San Domenico | 572 |
| Notre Dame-Belmont | 570 |
| Woodside Priory | 570 |
| St. Francis | 563 |
| Convent | 562 |
| Beacon | 560 |
| Arrowsmith | 557 |
| Presentation | 541 |
| North Bay Marin | 534 |
| Sacred Heart Cathedral | 526 |
| Mercy-Burlingame | 524 |
| Moreau | 523 |
| Notre Dame-SJ | 520 |
| Salesian | 500 |
| Bridgemont | 483 |
| Riordan | 478 |

N/P: Mitty, Branson, Crystal Springs, Holy Names, Maybeck, Marin Catholic, Mercy-SF, St. Joseph, Serra, Spraings, Woodside Int'l

# SAT Combined Verbal/Math

| | |
|---|---|
| College Prep | 1394 |
| Lick | 1340 |
| Castilleja | 1335 |
| Head-Royce | 1315 |
| SF University | 1313 |
| Marin Academy | 1296 |
| Lycee | 1265 |
| Menlo | 1259 |
| Urban | 1240 |
| Sacred Heart Prep | 1237 |
| Bellarmine | 1234 |
| North Bay Orinda | 1232 |
| Pinewood | 1229 |
| Athenian | 1190 |
| IHS | 1190 |
| King's Academy | 1186 |
| St. Ignatius | 1184 |
| Arrowsmith | 1159 |
| Notre Dame-Belmont | 1150 |
| Woodside Priory | 1150 |
| Convent | 1142 |
| Beacon | 1140 |
| St. Francis | 1127 |
| Marin Catholic | 1123 |
| Mercy-Burlingame | 1114 |
| San Domenico | 1102 |
| Presentation | 1101 |
| North Bay Marin | 1094 |
| Moreau | 1051 |
| Notre Dame-SJ | 1050 |
| Sacred Heart Cathedral | 1035 |
| Salesian | 1000 |
| Bridgemont | 956 |
| Riordan | 949 |

N/P: Mitty, Branson, Crystal Springs, Holy Names, Maybeck, Marin Catholic, Mercy-SF, St. Joseph, Serra, Spraings, Woodside Int'l

# Percentage enrolling in college upon graduation

| | |
|---|---|
| Branson | 100% |
| College Prep | 100% |
| Convent | 100% |
| Crystal Springs | 100% |
| Head-Royce | 100% |
| IHS | 100% |
| Lycee | 100% |
| Marin Academy | 100% |
| Marin Catholic | 100% |
| Mercy-SF | 100% |
| North Bay Marin | 100% |
| North Bay Orinda | 100% |
| Notre Dame-Belmont | 100% |
| Notre Dame-SJ | 100% |
| Pinewood | 100% |
| Presentation | 100% |
| Sacred Heart Cathedral | 100% |
| Sacred Heart Prep | 100% |
| St. Francis | 100% |
| St. Ignatius | 100% |
| San Domenico | 100% |
| SF University | 100% |
| Woodside Int'l | 100% |
| Woodside Priory | 100% |
| Bellarmine | 99.5% |
| Castilleja | 99% |
| Mercy-Burlingame | 99% |
| Mitty | 99% |
| Riordan | 99% |
| Salesian | 99% |
| Urban | 99% |
| Athenian | 98% |
| Lick | 98% |
| Moreau | 98% |
| St. Joseph | 98% |
| Serra | 98% |
| Holy Names | 96% |
| Arrowsmith | 90% |
| Bridgemont | 90% |
| Beacon | 87% |
| Maybeck | 70% |
| Spraings | 60% |

N/P: King's Academy, Menlo

# % ENROLLING IN 4-YEAR/2-YEAR COLLEGES

| | | |
|---|---|---|
| Branson | 100% | 0 |
| College Prep | 100% | 0 |
| Crystal Springs | 100% | 0 |
| Head-Royce | 100% | 0 |
| IHS | 100% | 0 |
| San Domenico | 100% | 0 |
| SF University | 100% | 0 |
| Castilleja | 99% | 0 |
| Marin Academy | 98% | 2% |
| Urban | 98% | 1% |
| Athenian | 98% | 0 |
| Lick | 98% | 0 |
| Pinewood | 96% | 4% |
| Woodside Priory | 96% | 4% |
| Convent | 95% | 5% |
| Sacred Heart Prep | 95% | 5% |
| St. Ignatius | 94% | 6% |
| Holy Names | 94% | 2% |
| Bellarmine | 93.5% | 6% |
| Presentation | 88% | 12% |
| Notre Dame-Belmont | 87% | 13% |
| St. Francis | 86% | 14% |
| Marin Catholic | 85% | 15% |
| Beacon | 85% | 2% |
| St. Joseph | 83% | 15% |
| Lycee | 80% | 20% |
| North Bay Marin | 80% | 20% |
| Sacred Heart Cathedral | 80% | 20% |
| Notre Dame-SJ | 78% | 22% |
| Mitty | 77% | 22% |
| Salesian | 75% | 24% |
| Moreau | 71% | 27% |
| Mercy-SF | 70% | 30% |
| Arrowsmith | 70% | 20% |
| Bridgemont | 70% | 20% |
| Mercy-Burlingame | 69% | 30% |
| Serra | 68% | 30% |
| Riordan | 63% | 36% |
| Maybeck | 60% | 10% |
| North Bay Orinda | 47% | 53% |
| Woodside Int'l | 30% | 70% |
| Spraings | 30% | 30% |

N/P: Menlo, King's Academy

# FREE MAP

For a free map showing school locations, send a self-addressed, stamped envelope to:

Pince-Nez Press/Map
1459 18th St.
PMB No. 175
San Francisco, CA 94107

# UPDATES

Free tuition updates will be available by mail at one- to two-year intervals while this book is in print. (We'd love to put out a new edition of this book every year but the cost is prohibitive—not to mention the difficulty of making sure bookstores have the current edition on their shelves.) For information on how to obtain updates for this edition, please check the Pince-Nez Press web site at: www.pince-nez.com or call 415-267-5978.

# OTHER BOOKS AVAILABLE FROM PINCE-NEZ PRESS

### San Francisco Private Schools K-8

By Susan Vogel. In its third edition, this book contains extensive information on more than 70 San Francisco private and parochial K-8 schools and advice from admission directors on how to apply. Published in 1997 (with tuition update and map included in book), 102 pages. ISBN 0-9648757-0-5 $16.95

### Finding a Preschool for Your Child in San Francisco

By Vera Obermeyer, Lori Rifkin, and Irene Byrne. A new edition of this popular book is due out in early 2000. It contains in-depth information on different types of preschools; how to know which preschool is right for your child; and how to help your child become ready for kindergarten. ISBN 0-9648757-2-1

### Private Schools of the San Francisco Peninsula/Silicon Valley

By Ellen Lussier. This book provides Peninsula families extensive profiles of elementary and middle schools from Burlingame through San Jose and valuable information on the admission process. Expected publication date is late 1999. ISBN 0-9648757-6-4.

If you cannot find these books in your local bookstore or on-line book supplier, please call (415) 267-5978 for ordering information.

See the Pince-Nez Press web site for the latest information on new titles: www.pince-nez.com

# NOTES

# NOTES

# NOTES

# NOTES

# NOTES

# NOTES

315
- 9167